JOHN WESLEY IN AMERICA

John Wesley, *c*.1742 by J. M. Williams. Photograph of an early copy, courtesy of The Oxford Centre for Methodism and Church History, Oxford Brookes University.

John Wesley in America

Restoring Primitive Christianity

GEORDAN HAMMOND

OXFORD
UNIVERSITY PRESS

OXFORD
UNIVERSITY PRESS

Great Clarendon Street, Oxford, OX2 6DP,
United Kingdom

Oxford University Press is a department of the University of Oxford.
It furthers the University's objective of excellence in research, scholarship,
and education by publishing worldwide. Oxford is a registered trade mark of
Oxford University Press in the UK and in certain other countries

Published in the United States of America by Oxford University Press
198 Madison Avenue, New York, NY 10016, United States of America

British Library Cataloguing in Publication Data
Data available

Library of Congress Control Number: 2013955005

ISBN 978-0-19-870160-6

Printed and bound by
CPI Group (UK) Ltd, Croydon, CR0 4YY

Links to third party websites are provided by Oxford in good faith and
for information only. Oxford disclaims any responsibility for the materials
contained in any third party website referenced in this work.

To Iulia
With love and gratitude

Preface

This book is a study of John Wesley in Georgia. While Wesley's biographers have all discussed his Georgia sojourn, no one has yet produced a book-length investigation of his experience in America. The central argument of this study is that the Georgia mission, for Wesley, was a laboratory for implementing his views of primitive Christianity. The ideal of restoring the doctrine, discipline, and practice of the early church in the pristine Georgia wilderness was the prime motivating factor in Wesley's decision to embark for Georgia and in his clerical practice in the colony. Understanding the centrality of primitive Christianity to Wesley's thinking and pastoral methods is essential to comprehending his experience in the New World.

Traditionally Wesley's biographers have not seen his ministry in Georgia as crucially important except insofar as it was perceived to have contributed to a crisis in his Christian faith. This has been partly due to the central role his post-Georgia evangelical 'conversion' at Aldersgate has played in the Wesleyan tradition. Along with this, his Methodist successors on both sides of the Atlantic tended to disparage the Georgia period as a misguided High Church phase. Therefore, it is not surprising that many biographers have seen little of value in the Georgia mission and have labelled it a failure. As a result, Wesley's passion for restoring primitive Christianity has been underappreciated. In order to re-evaluate this period of his life, a careful consideration of the documents written by him and his contemporaries is essential.

The sources of Wesley's understanding of primitive Christianity were rooted in the revival of patristic scholarship in the Church of England in the seventeenth and early eighteenth centuries. Knowledge of the early church was conveyed to Wesley by his parents in the Epworth rectory and in the halls of academia at Oxford. However, his interest in the primitive church took a new and more intense direction following the beginning of his friendship with John Clayton and the Manchester Nonjurors in 1732. It was the pervasive influence of Clayton and his mentor, Thomas Deacon, that propelled Wesley to investigate the doctrine, discipline, and practice of the early church. Wesley began a rigorous course of studying primarily the Apostolic Fathers (including the *Apostolic Constitutions* and *Canons*), secondarily the ante-Nicene Fathers, and thirdly select holy men of the fourth century such as Ephraem Syrus. His study was enabled by utilizing editions of the Fathers by recent Anglican patristic scholars and was supplemented by influential works on the primitive church by William Cave, Claude Fleury, and Anthony Horneck amongst others.

This book critically analyses Wesley's application of his vision of primitive Christianity on the *Simmonds* and in his parish ministry in Georgia. It emerges that Wesley's ecclesiology was that of the Usager Nonjurors, which was in many respects identical to that of other contemporary High Churchmen. In common with the Nonjuring/High Church movement, Wesley's ecclesial practice stressed the centrality of the sacraments in worship. On the *Simmonds*, the views of Wesley and his colleagues on the early church were manifested in their devotional discipline, sacramental doctrine and practice, and conduct in leading public worship. In Georgia, his endeavour to imitate the practices of the primitive church manifested itself variously through interest in prayer book revision, precise sacramental observance, confession, penance, ascetical discipline, deaconesses, religious societies, and mission to the Indians. Also on the *Simmonds* and in Georgia it is demonstrated that the subject of primitive Christianity dominated Wesley's interactions with the leaders of the Moravians and Lutheran Salzburgers, particularly on the subjects of discipline, episcopacy, the sacraments, hymns, and in his tensions with them.

The final chapter of the book examines opposition to Wesley's ministry in Georgia. Colonists who did not embrace his views of primitive Christianity variously accused him of being an enthusiast, a Roman Catholic, and a divisive clergyman. Opposition also came in the form of male disgust with the manner of Wesley's ministry to women and the magistrates' reaction to his advocacy for poor colonists whom he believed were being oppressed. These sources of hostility combined with the 'Sophia Williamson controversy' brought his Georgia sojourn to a swift conclusion.

Despite the sudden end to the Georgia mission, a close analysis of Wesley's ministry calls for a carefully nuanced view on the vexed question of his success or failure. An evaluation of his ministry in context necessitates an interpretation that does not simply compare it with his subsequent leadership in the Evangelical Revival.

This study also demonstrates that Wesley's interest in primitive Christianity did not end when he left the shores of America. As one might expect, his view of the early church was not static; areas of continuity and discontinuity can be observed in over fifty years of ministry after Georgia. Wesley maintained his belief in the primitive church as a normative model for Christian faith and practice. With this conviction in mind, he worked tirelessly towards the goal of seeing primitive Christianity restored in the Methodist movement.

Through providing a critical evaluation of Wesley's conception and practice of primitive Christianity in Georgia, this book can contribute to debates about the significance of one of the formative periods of his life.

Acknowledgements

This book is a revised version of a doctoral thesis completed at The University of Manchester. Throughout the project I have been supported by many individuals and institutions. Particular thanks are due to Professor Jeremy Gregory, who provided insightful supervision of the thesis. The initial research was made possible by a studentship granted by the John Rylands Research Institute. The university also generously provided several bursaries to support conference presentations and research trips. I am grateful to colleagues for awarding the thesis with the 2009 Wesleyan Theological Society Outstanding Dissertation Award and the 2011 Jesse Lee Prize in American Methodist History given by The General Commission on Archives and History of The United Methodist Church. Post-doctoral work on this book was greatly aided by sabbatical leave granted by Nazarene Theological College, part of which was happily spent as a Sugden Fellow at Queen's College, University of Melbourne, along with a productive week as a Farmington Fellow at Harris Manchester College, Oxford.

This study has benefited from the expert advice of Dr Gareth Lloyd, Dr Peter Nockles, and the staff of the Methodist Archives and Research Centre at The John Rylands Library. Excellent support was also given by the librarians and archivists of the Bodleian Library, the British Library, Cambridge University Library, The Dalton McCaughey Library at the United Faculty of Theology, the Evangelical Library, Lambeth Place Library, Manchester Wesley Research Centre and library at Nazarene Theological College, Moravian Archives, the Oxford Centre for Methodism and Church History at Oxford Brookes University, and the Sugden Collection at Queen's College, University of Melbourne.

Portions of several chapters have appeared in the following publications under my authorship and are used by permission here: 'High Church Anglican Influences on John Wesley's Conception of Primitive Christianity, 1732–1735', *Anglican and Episcopal History*, 78 (2009), 174–207 (chapter 1); 'The Wesleys' Sacramental Theology and Practice in Georgia', *Proceedings of The Charles Wesley Society*, 13 (2009), 53–73 (chapters 2 and 4); 'Versions of Primitive Christianity: John Wesley's Relations with the Moravians in Georgia, 1735–1737', *Journal of Moravian History*, 6 (2009), 31–60 (chapter 3); 'John Wesley's Relations with the Lutheran Pietist Clergy in Georgia', in Christian T. Collins Winn et al. (eds), *The Pietist Impulse in Christianity* (Eugene, OR, 2011), 135–45 (chapter 3); 'John Wesley in Georgia: Success or Failure?', *PWHS* 56 (October 2008), 297–305 (introduction and conclusion).

This research has profited from engagement with scholars (including students) though my work as Director of the Manchester Wesley Research Centre and Senior Lecturer in Church History and Wesley Studies at Nazarene Theological College. Knowing that it would require a very long list to acknowledge all to whom thanks is due, I would like to express my gratitude as a whole to the many family, friends, and colleagues who encouraged and challenged me along the way. Without the generous support of my parents this research would not have begun, and apart from the consistent support of my wife, Iulia, it would not have been completed.

Contents

Abbreviations

BCP	Book of Common Prayer (1662 version unless otherwise noted)
BIJ	Benjamin Ingham's Journal in L[uke] Tyerman, *The Oxford Methodists* (London: Hodder and Stoughton, 1873), 63–80
BJRL	*Bulletin of the John Rylands University Library of Manchester*
Boltzius, Letters	*The Letters of Johann Martin Boltzius, Lutheran Pastor in Ebenezer, Georgia: German Pietism in Colonial America, 1733–1765*, ed. and trans. Russell C. Kleckley, 2 vols (Lewiston, NY: Edward Mellen Press, 2009)
Bowmer	John C. Bowmer, *The Sacrament of the Lord's Supper in Early Methodism* (London: Dacre Press, 1951)
Campbell	Ted A. Campbell, *John Wesley and Christian Antiquity: Religious Vision and Cultural Change* (Nashville: Kingswood Books, 1991)
Collier	Jeremy Collier, *Reasons for Restoring some Prayers and Directions: as they Stand in the Communion-Service of the First English Reform'd Liturgy*, 2nd edn (London: John Morphew, 1717)
CRG	*The Colonial Records of the State of Georgia*, 32 vols (1904–89)
CWJ	*The Manuscript Journal of the Reverend Charles Wesley, M.A.*, vol. 1, ed. S T Kimbrough, Jr and Kenneth G. C. Newport (Nashville: Kingswood Books, 2008)
Detailed Reports	George Fenwick Jones (ed.), *Detailed Reports of the Salzburger Emigrants Who Settled in America...Edited by Samuel Urlsperger*, vols 3–5 (Athens: University of Georgia Press, 1972–80)
Egmont, Diary	*Manuscripts of the Earl of Egmont. Diary of Viscount Percival afterwards First Earl of Egmont*, ed. R. A. Roberts, 3 vols, Historical Manuscripts Commission (London: His Majesty's Stationary Office, 1920–3)
Fleury	Claude Fleury, *The Manners of the Antient Christians*, ed. John Wesley, 5th edn (London: G. Paramore, 1791)
Fries	Adelaide L. Fries, *The Moravians in Georgia 1735–1740* (Raleigh, NC: Edwards and Broughton, 1905)

GHQ	*Georgia Historical Quarterly*
Grisbrooke	W. Jardine Grisbrooke, *Anglican Liturgies of the Seventeenth and Eighteenth Centuries*, Alcuin Club Collections (London: SPCK, 1958)
Hammond	Geordan Hammond, 'Restoring Primitive Christianity: John Wesley and Georgia, 1735–1737', Ph.D. thesis (University of Manchester, 2008)
Letters (Telford)	*The Letters of the Rev. John Wesley, A.M.*, ed. John Telford, 8 vols (London: Epworth Press, 1931)
Hunter	Frederick Hunter, *John Wesley and the Coming Comprehensive Church* (London: Epworth Press, 1968)
Johnson	John Johnson, *The Unbloody Sacrifice, and Altar, Unvail'd and Supported*, 2 vols (London: Robert Knaplock, 1714, 1718)
JW	John Wesley
JWD	John Wesley's Diary in *Works*, 18:312–571 [unless otherwise indicated JWD, JWJ, and JWMSJ references are to the date given vol. 18 *Journal and Diaries I (1735–38)*]
JWJ	John Wesley's published *Journal* in *Works*
JWJ (Curnock)	*The Journal of the Rev. John Wesley, A.M.*, ed. Nehemiah Curnock, 8 vols (repr. London: Epworth Press, 1938)
JWMSJ	John Wesley's Manuscript Journal in *Works*, 18:312–571
LES	E. Merton Coulter and Albert B. Saye (eds), *A List of Early Settlers of Georgia* (Athens: University of Georgia Press, 1949)
MARC	Methodist Archives and Research Centre, The John Rylands Library
MH	*Methodist History*
Nelson	James Nelson, 'John Wesley and the Georgia Moravians', *Transactions of the Moravian Historical Society*, 23 (1984), 17–46
NS	New Style (Gregorian calendar)
ODNB	H. C. G. Matthew and Brian Harrison (eds), *Oxford Dictionary of National Biography*, 60 vols (Oxford: Oxford University Press, 2004) [online edn]
PWHS	*Proceedings of the Wesley Historical Society*
Rack	Henry D. Rack, *Reasonable Enthusiast: John Wesley and the Rise of Methodism*, 3rd edn (London: Epworth Press, 2002)
SPCK	Society for Promoting Christian Knowledge and SPCK Archives, Cambridge University Library
SPG	Society for the Propagation of the Gospel in Foreign Parts and SPG Archives, Rhodes House Library, Oxford

Tailfer   Tailfer, Pat[rick], Hugh Anderson, Da[vid] Douglas, and
                   others, *A True and Historical Narrative of the Colony of
                   Georgia in America* (Charles-Town: P. Timothy, 1741)
Wheatly   Charles Wheatly, *A Rational Illustration of the Book
                   of Common Prayer of the Church of England*, 3rd edn
                   (London: A. Bettesworth, 1720)
Works   *The Works of John Wesley* (Bicentennial Edition),
                   general ed. Frank Baker and Richard P. Heitzenrater
                   (Oxford: Clarendon Press, 1975–83 and
                   Nashville: Abingdon Press, 1984–)
Works (Jackson) *The Works of the Rev. John Wesley*, ed. Thomas Jackson,
                   3rd edn, 14 vols (London: Mason, 1829–31)

Note to the Reader

Unless otherwise indicated, all dates are given in Old Style, the calendar in use in Britain and Colonial America before 1752 when the New Style or Gregorian calendar was adopted. The Old Style or Julian calendar was eleven days behind New Style and the year began on 25 March; however, in this book the year is taken to begin on 1 January.

The term 'Methodist' is employed in this study, since it was currently in use (often derogatorily) as a description of John Wesley and his friends at Oxford. However, to use the word in the contemporary sense as referring to the Methodist Church would be anachronistic for the period covered in this book. In this study, the term 'Methodist' is utilized primarily in reference to the immediate context of Wesley's Georgia mission without reading subsequent developments in the Evangelical Revival back into the period. The word 'Methodist', as used in this book, refers to the methodological approach to spirituality of Wesley and his friends.[1] The label 'Holy Club' is avoided as it was only in use for a few months from the autumn of 1730, Wesley disparaged the term, and it was popularized by Luke Tyerman and other biographers, who mistakenly believed the Oxford Methodists were pursuing 'works-righteousness'.[2] Another contemporary term of derision, 'supererogation men', sheds light on how the Oxford Methodists were viewed by their fellow students and tutors. This designation, denoting their tendency to go beyond what was deemed to be required of pious Anglicans, can usefully be recalled when the word Methodist is used.

[1] On the possible origins of the term as it was applied to the Oxford Methodists, see Richard P. Heitzenrater, *Mirror and Memory: Reflections on Early Methodism* (Nashville, 1989), 13–32.
[2] See Richard P. Heitzenrater, 'The Founding Brothers', in William J. Abraham and James E. Kirby (eds), *The Oxford Handbook of Methodist Studies* (Oxford, 2009), 33.

Introduction

Ever since John Wesley's first biographer, John Hampson, called Wesley's churchmanship in Georgia 'absolute and despotic', the theme of Wesley as an intolerant High Churchman during his Georgia sojourn has featured prominently in many biographies.[1] To the Anglican poet Robert Southey and Reginald Heber, bishop of Calcutta and reviewer of Southey's biography of Wesley, Wesley in Georgia was a High Church enthusiast bordering on the edge of fanaticism.[2] Predictably, amongst British biographers, interest in Wesley's churchmanship increased in the nineteenth and early twentieth centuries in the aftermath of the Oxford Movement, accompanied by the growth of Anglo-Catholicism in the Church of England. In evaluating Wesley's churchmanship, his Georgia ministry was uniformly considered to be of especial importance. The influential Methodist historian, Luke Tyerman, who generally treated Wesley as a venerable hero, was a strident critic of what he saw as Wesley's 'high church nonsense'. Tyerman's comment that Wesley displayed 'high church bigotry and intolerance' in Georgia teaches us more about his disdain for 'half papistical priests and ritualists' of his day than about Wesley himself.[3] American Methodists have likewise traditionally read Wesley 'with a low-church anti-intellectualist bias'; in other words, they evaluated Wesley in the light of what the Methodist Church had become.[4] Nineteenth-century Anglican and Methodist biographers tended to agree that Wesley's High

---

[1] *Memoirs of the Late Rev. John Wesley, A.M.* (Sunderland, 1791), 1:176. For a useful study on portraits of Wesley by his biographers, see Richard P. Heitzenrater, *The Elusive Mr. Wesley*, 2nd edn (Nashville, 2003), 341–94. On his early biographers from 1791 to 1831, see Henry D. Rack, 'Wesley Portrayed: Character and Criticism in Some Early Biographies', *MH* 43 (2005), 90–114. Rack has accurately noted that Wesley's early biographers found it difficult 'to understand the significance and possible value of Wesley's early high church phase' (p. 111).

[2] Southey, *The Life of Wesley and the Rise and Progress of Methodism* (London, 1820); [Heber] 'The Life of Wesley; and the Rise and Progress of Methodism', *The Quarterly Review*, 24 (Oct. 1820). On the identification of the author, see Hill Shine and Helen Chadwick Shine, *The Quarterly Review under Gifford: Identification of Contributors 1809–1824* (Chapel Hill, NC, 1949), 71. The view of Southey and Heber mirrored the criticism of Bishops Gibson, Lavington, and Warburton in the eighteenth century.

[3] Tyerman, *The Life and Times of the Rev. John Wesley, M.A.* (London, 1870), 1:151, 168; cf. Henry Bett's comment that Wesley's conduct was 'deplorably bigoted and tactless': *The Spirit of Methodism* (London, 1937), 18.

[4] Albert C. Outler, 'Towards a Re-Appraisal of John Wesley as a Theologian', in Thomas C. Oden and Leicester R. Longden (eds), *The Wesleyan Theological Heritage: Essays of Albert C. Outler* (Grand Rapids, 1991), 53.

Church principles were overly rigid.[5] However, the Wesleyan Methodist minister James Rigg, despite his general intention of playing down Wesley's High Churchmanship, saw parallels between Wesley's ministry in Georgia and nineteenth-century High Church practices such as establishing a service of early morning prayer and a separate service for communion; encouraging fasting, confession, and weekly communion; refusing the sacrament to those who had not been baptised by an episcopally ordained clergyman; requiring baptism by immersion; rebaptizing Dissenters; and refusing to bury those who had not received episcopal baptism.[6] Even more recent biographers such as Frank Baker have seen Georgia as 'an experiment in legalistic churchmanship'.[7] Once again, this comment reveals at least as much about Baker as it does about Wesley. Wesley did not anticipate a future revival of High Churchmanship; he was motivated by renewing the liturgical, doctrinal, disciplinary, and moral life of the primitive church.

Negative assessments of Wesley's churchmanship have been a factor in some influential Methodist writers questioning whether Wesley was a 'true Christian', or at least whether he understood the true evangelical gospel during the Georgia period. Biographers who have taken this position have generally focused on Wesley's comment that he went to Georgia to save his soul, his supposed spiritual depression in Georgia, and his failure to convert the Indians. This strand of interpretation can be found from Thomas Coke and Henry Moore (1792) to A. Skevington Wood (1967), although recent biographers have shied away from this stark conclusion.[8] The reason Wesley was said to have not been a true Christian is simple: he was, according to these writers, not then acquainted with the fullness of the gospel and he was seeking salvation by works in a state of emotional and spiritual confusion.

The related vexed question of the 'success' or 'failure' of the Georgia mission has drawn the attention of nearly all of his biographers, as well as many other

---

[5] See Julia Wedgwood, *John Wesley and the Evangelical Reaction of the Eighteenth Century* (London, 1870) and R. Denny Urlin, *The Churchman's Life of Wesley* (London, 1880).

[6] *The Churchmanship of John Wesley: And the Relations of Wesleyan Methodism to the Church of England* (London, 1878), 28–9.

[7] *John Wesley and the Church of England* (London, 1970; repr. 2000), 43.

[8] Coke and Moore, *The Life of the Rev. John Wesley, A.M.* (London, 1792), 97; Whitehead, *The Life of the Rev. John Wesley, M.A.* (London, 1796), 2:1; Henry Moore, *The Life of the Rev. John Wesley, A.M.* (London, 1824), 1:233, 257; Tyerman, *Life and Times*, 1:166; Matthew Lelièvre, *John Wesley: His Life and Work* (London, n.d. [1871]), 20, 21; Frederick E. Maser, 'Preface to Victory: An Analysis of John Wesley's Mission to Georgia', *Religion in Life*, 25 (1956), 280, 285, 288, 292; V. H. H. Green, *The Young Mr. Wesley* (London, 1961), 278 and *John Wesley* (London, 1964), 46; William Cannon, 'John Wesley's Years in Georgia', *MH* 1 (1963), 2–4; A. Skevington Wood, *The Burning Heart: John Wesley, Evangelist* (London, 1967), 53. See the examples given from Joseph Benson, Thomas Jackson, George Croft Cell, J. H. Rigg, and William Cannon in Charles Allen Rogers, 'The Concept of Prevenient Grace in the Theology of John Wesley', Ph.D. diss. (Duke University, 1967), 93–5.

writers who have considered the subject.[9] This issue has divided them into five interpretative camps, each represented by several writers. Some have not hesitated to call the Georgia mission a failure;[10] others have declined to declare it either a failure or a success;[11] while a third option has been to conclude that it was not a failure, although these interpreters have generally also declined to call it an unmitigated success.[12] An alternative approach has been to see Georgia as a 'preface to victory' and to emphasize what Wesley learned by the experience that prepared him for his Aldersgate 'conversion' and the revival;[13] a nuanced version of the first and fourth interpretations has been to label the venture a failure that involved positive developments in Wesley's life.[14]

These arguments have tended to detract from evaluating the Georgia mission in its historical context. Generations of biographers overlooked Wesley's interest in the primitive church during his time in Georgia until Nehemiah Curnock's edition of the Georgia journals and diary (1909) uncovered evidence, particularly from the diaries, that gave a fuller picture of Wesley's reading and practice. Martin Schmidt (1953) and V. H. H. Green (1961) were the first biographers to argue that this was a major theme of the Georgia mission.[15]

[9] See Geordan Hammond, 'John Wesley in Georgia: Success or Failure?', *PWHS* 56 (2008), 297–305.
[10] Richard Watson, *The Life of the Rev. John Wesley, A.M.* (New York, 1831), 35; George Smith, *History of Wesleyan Methodism*, 5th edn (London, 1866), 1:122–8; Wedgwood, *John Wesley*, 104, 113, 114; Lelièvre, *John Wesley*, 25; Cannon, 'John Wesley's Years', 2–4; Green, *John Wesley*, 44; Wood, *Burning Heart*, 53; John Pritchard, *Methodists and their Missionary Societies 1760-1900*, Ashgate Methodist Studies Series (Farnham, 2013), 3–4; the Calvinist C. H. Spurgeon, *The Two Wesleys: A Lecture Delivered in the Metropolitan Tabernacle Lecture Hall, on 6th December 1861* (London, 1894); and the historians of colonial Georgia, E. Merton Coulter: 'When John Wesley Preached in Georgia', *GHQ* 9 (1925), 344; David T. Morgan: 'John Wesley's Sojourn in Georgia Revisited', *GHQ* 64 (1980), 253–62; and in a more guarded sense Harold E. Davis: *The Fledgling Province: Social and Cultural Life in Colonial Georgia* (Chapel Hill, NC, 1976), 193, 214–16.
[11] Hampson, *Memoirs*, 186; Tyerman, *Life and Times*, 1:170; Umphrey Lee, *John Wesley and Modern Religion* (Nashville, 1936), 77; Baker, *John Wesley* and *From Wesley to Asbury: Studies in Early American Methodism* (Durham, NC, 1976), 21–3; Rack, 135 and the early historians of colonial Georgia William Bacon Stevens: *A History of Georgia* (New York, 1847) and Charles C. Jones, *The History of Georgia* (Boston, 1883).
[12] John Telford, *The Life of John Wesley*, rev. edn (London, 1924 [1886]), 87; John H. Overton, *John Wesley* (London, 1891), 51; John S. Simon, *John Wesley and the Religious Societies* (London, 1921), 145–6; Richard Green, *The Conversion of John Wesley* (London, 1937), 24; Warren Thomas Smith, 'The Wesleys in Georgia: An Evaluation', *Journal of the Interdenominational Theological Center*, 7 (1979), 1–11; Richard P. Heitzenrater, *Wesley and the People Called Methodists*, 2nd edn (Nashville, 2013), 66, 75 and 'Wesley in America', *PWHS* 54 (2003), 89.
[13] Whitehead, *Life of the Rev. John Wesley*, 2:31; Coke and Moore, *Life of the Rev. John Wesley*, 94; Haygood S. Bowden, *History of Savannah Methodism from John Wesley to Silas Johnson* (Macon, GA, 1929), 25; Leslie F. Church, *Oglethorpe: A Study in Philanthropy in England and Georgia* (London, 1932), 191, 211, 218; Lee, *John Wesley*, 73; Maser, 'Preface to Victory', 280–93; Baker, *John Wesley*, 51–2 and *From Wesley to Asbury*, 13.
[14] Thomas Jackson, *The Centenary of Wesleyan Methodism* (London, 1839), 47; Albert C. Outler (ed.), *John Wesley* (Oxford, 1964), 11–14; Luke L. Keefer, Jr 'John Wesley: Disciple of Early Christianity', Ph.D. diss. (Temple University, 1982), 81–6.
[15] *John Wesley: A Theological Biography*, vol. 1 (English translation, 1962) and *The Young Mr. Wesley*.

In his study of prevenient grace in Wesley's theology, Charles Rogers (1967) emphasized the Georgia period as being crucial for Wesley's theological development.[16] Frank Baker (1970) and Henry Rack (1989) noted the importance of primitive Christianity as a motivating factor for the Georgia mission, but neither of them expounded on this influence in great detail.[17] In the 1980s, three doctoral dissertations were published dealing with the theme of Wesley's primitivism and in a 2003 doctoral thesis Deborah Madden effectively utilized the concept of primitive Christianity to examine his *Primitive Physic* (1747), but, as with Baker and Rack, all of these studies were able to give only a limited treatment of the Georgia period, since their focus was on the whole of Wesley's life.[18] Roughly half of a recent doctoral dissertation on 'John Wesley's America' (2008) is devoted to a largely narrative account of Wesley in Georgia and pays minimal attention to Wesley's theology and the theme of primitive Christianity.[19]

If Wesley saw Georgia as a laboratory to implement his views on the primitive church, what were the sources of his inspiration? As one might expect, the sources ranged from the general context of his life (e.g. his family and the patristic revival in the Church of England) to the more direct influence of John Clayton and the Manchester Nonjurors. The centrality of the Nonjurors in Wesley's thought and practice in Georgia was hardly noticed prior to John Simon's *John Wesley and the Religious Societies* (1921), which was the first major biography to benefit from Curnock. Subsequently, their influence has been referenced in some detail by Frederick Hunter (1947, 1968).[20] In *Wesleyan and Tractarian Worship* (1966) Trevor Dearing argued that the Nonjurors and the appeal to the early church link Wesley to the leaders of the Oxford Movement.[21] However, this book is the first full-length study of the Nonjuror influence on the young John Wesley.

---

[16] Rogers, 'Prevenient Grace'. This study does not support his conclusion that Wesley's 'arrival in Georgia marked the end of the doctrinal confidence of the early Wesley, and the beginning of a period of theological uncertainty and change' (p. 70); cf. Albert C. Outler, 'John Wesley as Theologian—Then and Now', in Oden and Longden (eds), *Wesleyan Theological Heritage*, 58.

[17] *John Wesley and the Church of England* and *Reasonable Enthusiast.*

[18] Keefer, 'John Wesley'; Ted A. Campbell, 'John Wesley's Conceptions and Uses of Christian Antiquity', Ph.D. diss. (Southern Methodist University, 1984); Arthur C. Meyers, 'John Wesley and the Church Fathers', Ph.D. diss. (St Louis University, 1985); Deborah Madden, 'Pristine Purity: Primitivism and Practical Piety in John Wesley's Art of Physic', D.Phil. thesis (University of Oxford, 2003). A summary of Keefer's conclusions can be found in his essay 'John Wesley: Disciple of Early Christianity', *Wesleyan Theological Journal*, 19 (1984), 23–32. Campbell's dissertation was revised and published as *John Wesley and Christian Antiquity* (Nashville, 1991). Meyers's work is little more than a catalogue of Wesley's references to the Church Fathers. Madden's work has been published as *'A Cheap, Safe and Natural Medicine': Religion, Medicine and Culture in John Wesley's Primitive Physic* (Amsterdam, 2007).

[19] Adam Scott Zele, 'John Wesley's America', Ph.D. diss. (Duke University, 2008).

[20] 'The Manchester Nonjurors and Wesley's High Churchism', *London Quarterly and Holborn Review*, 172 (1947), 56–61 and Hunter, 9–53.

[21] Prior to the Liturgical Movement and related Parish Communion movement in the twentieth-century Church of England, most Methodist scholars either wrote off any connection

Though they do not focus on the Georgia mission, several studies have made significant contributions to a key concern of this book: Wesley's churchmanship. For example, in contrast to some previous studies, A. B. Lawson (1963) demonstrated substantial continuity before and after Georgia in Wesley's view of ministry and churchmanship.[22]

Recently, a substantial number of Wesley scholars have argued that polarities propagated by Methodist biographers between the pre- and post-Aldersgate Wesley have been overstated, contributing to caricatures of Wesley that stress the discontinuity between a supposed pre- and post-evangelical Wesley to the detriment of recognizing areas of continuity in his life.[23] Themes of life-long intellectual and spiritual unity in Wesley's thought and practice are not difficult to pinpoint. His enduring interest in the Church Fathers as reliable sources of scriptural interpretation and Christian doctrine and his ideal of reviving the primitive church was one of Wesley's consistent beliefs and visions. Even after he began to gradually revise his High Church vision of a near-infallible primitive church (a process which began in Georgia) he did not discard his belief that the early church was a community that embodied the kind of dynamic holiness of heart and life that he believed the Methodists were providentially raised up to reconstitute throughout the British Isles.

In sum, the Georgia mission, while treated by all biographers of Wesley, can arguably be considered the most neglected period of Wesley's much-studied life. Henry Rack has accurately stated that for Wesley's biographers his Georgia 'ministry has generally been judged to be fruitless and...significant chiefly for its role in bringing him to spiritual bankruptcy'.[24] This anachronistic approach, although avoided by Rack, has often served to devalue a significant period of Wesley's life that deserves to be evaluated in context without reading later developments back into the Georgia mission. When Wesley left England, the Methodists were a tiny loose grouping of like-minded Anglicans, which underscores the need to understand Wesley in his Anglican context. This study, therefore, can serve as a challenge to numerous biographies of Wesley— especially those written by nineteenth-century Methodists—that have 'de-anglicanized' him.[25] In terms of the field of Wesley Studies, this book may be seen as a contribution to what Albert Outler labelled 'Phase III' of Wesley

---

between Wesley and the Oxford Movement as due to the High Church bigotry of the young Wesley that ended with his evangelical conversion, and/or concluded that the commonality between them was insubstantial. J. Ernest Rattenbury was a pioneer in challenging the traditional interpretation in *The Eucharistic Hymns of John and Charles Wesley* (1948).

[22] A. B. Lawson, *John Wesley and the Christian Ministry: The Sources and Development of His Opinions and Practice* (London, 1963).

[23] See Randy L. Maddox (ed.), *Aldersgate Reconsidered* (Nashville, 1990).

[24] Rack, 133.

[25] Randy L. Maddox, 'Reclaiming an Inheritance: Wesley as a Theologian in the History of Methodist Theology', in Randy L. Maddox (ed.), *Rethinking Wesley's Theology for Contemporary Methodism* (Nashville, 1998), 215.

Studies: evaluating Wesley in his own historical context, which includes seeking to understand Wesley in the light of the sources that shaped him.[26]

For the fruitfulness of devoting research to a particular period of Wesley's life Richard Heitzenrater's influential study 'John Wesley and the Oxford Methodists, 1725–35' might be cited.[27] Additionally, at least four other Ph.D. theses have focused on the early Wesley from 1703–38.[28] Along with the overwhelming majority of theses dealing with Wesley, these studies are primarily theological in nature; therefore, there is a need for historical investigations of the early Wesley. An analysis of a short episode in Wesley's life (i.e. the Georgia mission) might be seen as a welcome addition to the numerous in-depth studies on particular aspects of Wesley's theology. In comparison to the large body of research on Wesley's theology there is a dearth of critical historical investigations of Wesley—one aim of this study is to contribute to our historical and theological knowledge of the early Wesley. Heitzenrater's examination of Wesley in Oxford has furthered our understanding of a significant period in Wesley's life; the Georgia mission also deserves a meticulous study.

A number of secondary themes follow on from the central argument that the ideal of restoring primitive Christianity was at the forefront of Wesley's thinking and is crucial to interpreting the Georgia mission. The first is to analyse Wesley in context as an Anglican clergyman rather than interpreting his Georgia sojourn as a 'preface to victory'. Second, when possible, the connection between Wesley's reading and practice of primitive Christianity is illustrated. Third, a fresh perspective on his interaction with the colonists, Moravians, Lutheran Pietists, and Sophia Williamson née, Hopkey is given by interpreting these relationships within the context of Wesley's goal of renewing primitive Christianity in the Georgia wilderness. In order to demonstrate adequately the primary and secondary arguments and themes, a thorough consideration of the primary documents written by Wesley and his contemporaries is essential. Therefore, a fourth secondary theme is an evaluation of Wesley's sources (i.e. his journals, diary, letters) and the way these documents have been used and sometimes misused by his biographers. Fifth, sources seldom utilized by

---

[26] Albert C. Outler, 'A New Future for Wesley Studies: An Agenda for Phase III', in Oden and Longden (eds), *Wesleyan Theological Heritage*, 125–42; 'The Place of Wesley in the Christian Tradition', in Ogden and Longden (eds), *Wesleyan Theological Heritage*, 82; cf. Kenneth E. Rowe, 'Editor's Introduction: The Search for the Historical Wesley', in Kenneth E. Rowe (ed.), *The Place of Wesley in the Christian Tradition* (Metuchen, NJ, 1976), 1–10.

[27] Ph.D. diss. (Duke University, 1972).

[28] Elizabeth Kristine Nottingham, 'The Making of an Evangelist: A Study of John Wesley's Early Years', (Columbia University, 1938); Lawrence McIntosh, 'The Nature and Design of Christianity in John Wesley's Early Theology', (Drew University, 1966); Thorvald Källstad, *John Wesley and the Bible: A Psychological Study* (University of Uppsala, 1974); Steve Harper, 'The Devotional Life of John Wesley, 1703–1738', (Duke University, 1981). V. H. H. Green's *The Young Mr. Wesley* also focused on the early Wesley up to 1735.

Wesley's biographers relating to the history of colonial Georgia are incorporated into the study in an effort to give a fuller picture of the Georgia mission than is possible through relying solely on Wesley's writings.

Wesley's journals and diary are key sources for this task, but they must be read critically and be compared to other contemporary accounts of Wesley and of colonial Georgia in general. Although all of Wesley's biographers have discussed the Georgia period, with only a few recent notable exceptions their studies have been deficient due to their reliance largely on an uncritical reading of Wesley's published *Journal*. Generally speaking, Wesley's biographers have usually consulted the journals of Charles Wesley and Benjamin Ingham, but they have rarely combined the evidence of these accounts with that of other lesser-known contemporary documents. The journals of the Moravians August Gottlieb Spangenberg, Bishop David Nitschmann, Johann Töltschig, and Johann Andrew Dober are essential sources for studying Wesley's mission in Georgia.[29] A wealth of primary documents relating to the Lutheran Pietists Johann Martin Boltzius and Israel Christian Gronau, their ministry to the Salzburgers, and relations with Wesley are also available.[30] Important comments about Wesley are made by his chief antagonist Thomas Causton in his journal, covering the period from 25 May to 24 July 1737.[31] The little-known *Memoirs* of Philip Thicknesse (1790) also provide valuable reflections on this young colonist's interaction with Wesley in Georgia. The most significant comments of opposition to Wesley's ministry in Georgia (apart from Wesley's journals) can be found in *A True and Historical Narrative of the Colony of Georgia in America* (1741) written by a group of discontented colonists.[32]

Wesley's biographers have also paid little attention to the extensive number of primary sources relating to the history of colonial Georgia. In over thirty volumes, *The Colonial Records of the State of Georgia* is the premier collection of primary documents relating to the history of colonial Georgia, but the records have seldom been used by scholars to shed light on Wesley's experience in Georgia. The diary and journals of John Perceval, first Earl of Egmont, a prominent member of the Trustees for Establishing the Colony of Georgia in

---

[29] Portions of these journals have been published in Adelaide Fries, *The Moravians in Georgia 1735–1740* (1905) and James Nelson's article 'John Wesley and the Georgia Moravians' (1984).

[30] See *Henry Newman's Salzburger Letterbooks*, ed. George Fenwick Jones (Athens, 1966) and the third to fifth volumes of the eighteen-volume *Detailed Reports*; Boltzius, *Letters*. Extracts of letters relating to Wesley have been published in Karl Zehrer, 'The Relationship between Pietism in Halle and Early Methodism', trans. James A. Dwyer, *MH* 17 (1979), 211–17. Of less importance are the journals of Philipp Georg Friedrich von Reck, the leader of two groups of Salzburger emigrants to Georgia: *An Extract of the Journals of Mr. Commissary von Reck...and of the Reverend Mr. Bolzius* (London, 1734) and *Von Reck's Voyage*, ed. Kristian Hvidt (Savannah, 1980).

[31] Published in Trevor Reese (ed.), *Our First Visit in America* (Savannah, 1974).

[32] On the genesis of this book, see Clarence L. Ver Stegg's introduction in the edition of the work he edited, which includes the counterpoints made by the Earl of Egmont (Athens, 1960), ix–xxxiv.

America, provides another underused yet invaluable source on the founding of Georgia through the eyes of the Trustees who were responsible for establishing and maintaining the colony for its first twenty-one years. The *Journal* of William Stephens (1742), who served as the Trustees' Secretary in Georgia during Wesley's last few turbulent months in the colony provides an informative source on this period. As with primary documents written by Wesley, it should be noted that some of these sources were edited and written in retrospect and, therefore, the possibility that they give interpretations of past events should be kept in mind.

In the context of this study, evaluating the nature of Wesley's journals and diary is crucial.[33] Following the suggestion of Jeremy Taylor's *Rules and Exercises of Holy Living*, Wesley first started keeping a diary at Oxford during the Lenten season of 1725.[34] Maintaining a diary, for Wesley, was a means of keeping himself accountable in disciplined living and a means to measure his spiritual growth. During his time in Georgia Wesley continued the practice of writing daily in his diary, recording his activities with some occasional reflections, often amounting to no more than a few words. W. R. Ward has found no evidence that he wrote a daily journal along with the diary. According to Ward, 'What seems to have happened, and what happened in Georgia on a larger scale and in a more complicated way, was that Wesley faithfully kept his brief daily diary and from time to time wrote up portions of it on a much larger scale with a view to use in the journal later.'[35] Ward believes these write-ups were done on loose paper, which was normally probably burned once a journal was in print.[36] Wesley called his published *Journals* 'extracts', indicating that the *Journals* were written using portions of the papers on which they were based.

Frank Baker has a somewhat different theory about the construction of Wesley's journals; in his view, Wesley composed his journal on a more regular basis. Baker thinks he wrote a 'continuous manuscript journal which he began to keep in Georgia, if not earlier, and apparently maintained throughout the major part of his life'.[37] In Baker's opinion, the manuscript journals were designed to be 'missionary letters' that described Wesley's actions in order to inform and encourage his friends and followers. During the time he was resident in Georgia and afterwards, Wesley sent selections of his journal to key people such as James Hutton and his brother Charles. These journal-letters

---

[33] In this book, Wesley's journals refer to both his published and manuscript journal; his published journal(s) is identified in italics as *Journal* and is distinguished from his manuscript journal which neither is italicized nor capitalized. In the sense that he wrote his diary in several notebooks, Wesley wrote diaries in Georgia. His diary, therefore, can appropriately be referred to in the singular or the plural.

[34] Wesley made this statement in the preface to his *Journal*: JWJ, 121.

[35] JWJ, 90.

[36] It was common practice to discard manuscripts once the work was set in type for publication.

[37] Frank Baker, 'John Wesley and Bishop Joseph Butler', *PWHS* 42 (1980), 93.

were then circulated and read by Wesley's friends individually and in religious societies and later Methodist societies.

Both of these theories have some merit. My purpose here is not to enter into this debate, but to cite the conclusions of Ward and Baker as a means of illustrating that the construction of Wesley's journals and diary was much more complex than many biographers have admitted. From this introduction it should already be evident that telling the story of Wesley's Georgia sojourn through a series of quotes from his *Journal* is inadequate, and, in fact, misleading. In studying Wesley's Georgia mission we have three layers of his journals and diary to consider: his diary; his manuscript journal; and his published *Journal*.

Wesley's diaries provide an important source for studying the Georgia mission. His private diaries are significantly different from the journals since they were written on a daily basis and were not intended to be published or read by others. Therefore, the diaries are a key source of unrevised data on Wesley's daily activities containing no hindsight. The diaries proved to be a useful tool for Wesley when on occasion he used them as a basic source to write his journal accounts.[38]

Wesley's published *Journal* reveals the aspects of his Georgia mission that he intended to make public. Fortunately, we can also study some of the background documents to Wesley's first *Journal*, which supply us with additional information he decided not to publish, as well as minor and significant variants from the published *Journal*. Three manuscript copies of the voyage journal exist, although none of them are in Wesley's handwriting. Also extant are five manuscript documents in Wesley's handwriting covering different periods of his ministry in Georgia from 7 March 1736 to 16 December 1737.[39] The available evidence leads to the conclusion that Wesley's *Journal* was composed as an edited version of his manuscript documents, giving account of his voyage to and from Georgia and his ministry in Georgia. Although these manuscripts show obvious signs of retrospective reflection and were, therefore, certainly not written as a daily running commentary, far less time elapsed between the moment they were composed and the events they describe than when they were extracted and revised for the published *Journal*. The manuscript journals form a more immediate and more 'objective' source for examining the Georgia

---

[38] For further discussion of Wesley's Georgia diary see Heitzenrater's comments in JWJ, 302–10.

[39] The three manuscript voyage journals are located in the Egmont Papers in the Special Collections of the University of Georgia Libraries, Athens, Georgia, the Bodleian Library, Oxford, and John Wesley's New Room in Bristol. All five of the Georgia manuscripts can be found in the MARC. These documents contain only minor variants from one another, the most important of which are included in brackets in the *Works*. For a discussion of these documents see Richard Heitzenrater's comments in JWJ, 299–302.

mission than the *Journal*, which was carefully extracted and revised for public consumption.

In sum, a study of any period of Wesley's life should proceed with the critical recognition that the published *Journals* were 'carefully edited accounts written up at a later date'.[40] In other words, Wesley substantially wrote and/or revised his journals in preparation for their publication, the significance of this being that the extracts were published 'in the light of his knowledge of subsequent events'.[41] Unfortunately, many Wesley scholars have treated the journals as objective records, when in fact as Henry Rack has noted, 'the *Journal* was essentially a vehicle for apologetic and propaganda, a selective and slanted account'.[42]

In the preface to his Georgia *Journal*, Wesley revealed that he may never have published it if he had not needed to defend himself from Captain Robert Williams's affidavit.[43] Once he determined to respond to Williams's action, he chose to do so by giving an account of his ministry in Georgia. The reader of the *Journal* must keep in mind that it was not published until around June 1740, nearly five years after his voyage to Georgia. It has been pointed out by Ward that 'we have no way of gauging how far the selection of material for the *Journal* was influenced in a general way by the things which were uppermost in Wesley's mind at the time when each part was prepared for publication'.[44] However, one should read Wesley's Georgia *Journal* with the assumption that it was shaped, to some degree, by the accusations brought against him.

The polemical purpose of Wesley's Georgia *Journal* does not necessarily take away from the accuracy of his account when read in conjunction with other contemporary records. Its narrative of the *Simmonds* voyage largely corroborates with the journals of Benjamin Ingham, Francis Moore, and two Moravians: David Nitschmann and Johann Andrew Dober.[45] The general accuracy of Wesley's account of his ministry in Georgia is supported by the combined evidence from the journals of Charles Wesley, Benjamin Ingham, Thomas Causton, Johann Boltzius and Israel Gronau, Philipp Georg Friedrich

---

[40] Frank Baker, 'The Birth of John Wesley's Journal', *MH* 8 (1970), 25.

[41] Baker, 'John Wesley's Journal', 25.

[42] Rack, 113.

[43] Williams had served on the Savannah Grand Jury that investigated Wesley's conduct in 1737. On 14 March 1740 he swore an affidavit before the mayor of Bristol accusing Wesley of unlawfully fleeing the colony while under bail awaiting trial on bills charged against him by the Grand Jury in Savannah. The text of the affidavit can be found as an appendix to *The Progress of Methodism in Bristol: Or, the Methodist Unmask'd* (Bristol, 1743), 43–8 or *The Life and Conversation of that Holy Man Mr. John Wesley, during his Abode at Georgia*, Bodleian Library, Oxford, Rawlinson MS J. fo. 5, which is almost identical to *The Progress of Methodism*, 43–56. The controversy was reported in the evangelical newspaper, *The Weekly History* on 7 and 14 August 1742.

[44] JWJ, 85.

[45] For example, these independent accounts give similar reports of the great storm of 25 January 1736. See JWJ and JWMSJ; BIJ, 74; Nitschmann and Dober in Fries, 16–17.

von Reck, and the *Memoirs* of Philip Thicknesse.[46] Read critically, Wesley's diary, manuscript journals, and published *Journal* provide an accurate and reliable picture of his experience as a missionary in Georgia.

This book is divided into five chapters. The first chapter investigates the influence of the concept of primitive Christianity on Wesley's theology and practice prior to the Georgia mission. The revival of patristic studies in the Church of England, promoted in particular by High Churchmen and Nonjurors, was an important aspect of the historical context that encouraged Wesley to embark for the New World.

Chapter 2 examines the theme of primitive Christianity on the voyage to Georgia. On the *Simmonds*, Wesley and his fellow missionaries resumed the ascetical and devotional practices characteristic of the Oxford Methodists. Wesley spent considerable time investigating the sacramental doctrine and practice of the primitive church with the aim of restoring the ecclesiology of the primitive church in Georgia. At sea he began to implement his clerical practices, which emphasized the centrality of the sacraments in worship inspired by the example of the early church and Nonjurors.

In chapter 3, Wesley's relations with the Moravians and Lutheran Pietists are analysed through the lens of his devotion to his High Church Anglican view of primitive Christianity, which dominated his interactions with them. He discussed the nature of the primitive church with them, including episcopacy and observance of Holy Communion. While the leaders of both Pietist groups respected Wesley's pastoral diligence, the Moravians critiqued his conceptions of the early church as being overly prescriptive, and the Lutherans believed they were too legalistic.

Wesley's application of his view of primitive Christianity in Georgia is the focus of chapter 4. The centrality of his vision of restoring primitive Christianity is most clearly seen in the manner in which he conducted his ministry in Georgia. His endeavours to imitate the practices of Christ and the early church manifested themselves variously through interest in prayer book revision, precise sacramental observance, confession, penance, ascetical discipline, deaconesses, religious societies, and mission to the Indians. By the end of his time in Georgia, his confidence in the early church councils and canons was diminished, but his pursuance of the form and spirit of the primitive church was maintained.

The final chapter is an exploration and analysis of the opposition to Wesley's ministry. He was variously accused by some colonists who rejected his conception of primitive Christianity as being an enthusiast, a Roman Catholic, and

---

[46] For example, all nine of the deaths reported in Thomas Causton's journal covering the period from 25 May to 24 July 1737 are also reported by John Wesley, who conducted the funeral services. See JWD, 13 June to 1 July 1737 and 'Journal of Thomas Causton Esq. 1st Bailif [sic] of Savannah', 24 June 1737, ed. Trevor R. Reese, in *Our First Visit in America: Early Reports from the Colony of Georgia, 1732–1740* (Savannah, 1974), 253–64.

a divisive clergyman. The argument is made that the Sophia Williamson controversy is best understood within the context of opposition by male colonists to Wesley's ministry to women. The Williamson affair, combined with opposition to Wesley's High Churchmanship, ministry to women, and advocacy for poor colonists he believed were being oppressed joined together to bring his Georgia sojourn to a swift conclusion.

The book concludes with an evaluation of Wesley's ministry in Georgia that suggests substantial revision of the claim made by numerous scholars that it was a failure. When assessed in context many positive aspects of his missionary work are evident. Consideration is also given to what became of Wesley's view of primitive Christianity after Georgia. Areas of continuity and discontinuity are explored by investigating topics such as his view of the ordained Christian ministry and his ordinations for the American Methodists, his attitude toward the Book of Common Prayer as seen in his publication of *The Sunday Service of the Methodists in North America*, his theology and practice of the sacraments, his continuing interest in the Church Fathers and the primitive church as a normative model for doctrine and practice, and his conviction that Methodism was the restoration of primitive Christianity.

1

John Wesley's Conception and Practice of Primitive Christianity

The appeal of primitivism was a significant cultural phenomenon in eighteenth-century Britain whether in architecture, art, economics, landscape gardening, literature, music, or religion.[1] It was the religious ideal of primitive Christianity that exerted a profound influence on John Wesley during the last few years he spent at Oxford before making the bold decision to become a missionary in the recently established colony of Georgia (chartered in 1732). This impulse to restore the purity of the early church was an established tradition within Anglicanism that was mediated to Wesley through his High Church predecessors including his parents, and the Nonjurors, Anglicans who declined to take the Oaths of Allegiance and Supremacy to William and Mary (r. 1689–1702 and 1689–94). For Wesley, primitive Christianity—especially as mediated to him through certain aspects of the High Church movement—was much more than a romantic ideal, it was a living tradition to be engaged both in the realms of academic study and Christian practice. His focus was particularly on the primitive standard for liturgical purity and holy living. Wesley approached the Georgia mission (14 October 1735 to 2 December 1737)[2] as a laboratory for implementing his vision of primitive Christianity.[3] Sophia Williamson, who knew him well, testified that he 'endeavoured to imitate the Primitive Fathers, who were the strict imitators of the life of Christ'.[4] Wesley saw his mission as one geared predominately towards reviving the apostolic faith and the primitive community of goods amongst the Indians.[5] The appeal

[1] Jeremy Black, *A Subject for Taste: Culture in Eighteenth-Century England* (London, 2005). This affected the early development of Georgia not only in religion but also through the Georgia Trustees' commitment to economic primitivism (on the latter, see Hammond, appendix 2).

[2] In this study, the Georgia mission is dated from the day Wesley left London to the date of his departure from Georgia.

[3] Ben Marsh has noted that Georgia, like other colonial frontiers, was a 'laboratory in which practical and theoretical experiments were conducted': *Georgia's Frontier Women: Female Fortunes in a Southern Colony* (Athens, 2007), 1.

[4] JWMSJ, 22 August 1737.

[5] See JW to John Burton (10 October 1735), *Works*, 25:439–42; and Geordan Hammond, 'John Wesley's Mindset at the Commencement of his Georgia Sojourn: Suffering and the Introduction

of primitive Christianity as an ideal was a central yet integrated part of the overall series of influences that culminated in Wesley's decision to leave his native land.

High Churchmen and Nonjurors placed a strong emphasis on apostolic succession, episcopacy, divine right monarchy, church discipline, liturgy, the sacraments, and the authority of the Church Fathers.[6] In this study, Nonjurors are considered together with other High Churchmen who influenced Wesley due to the high level of doctrinal agreement they held in common with their conforming brethren.[7] What initially separated them from conforming High Churchmen was political conviction, but by the time *A Communion Office* (1718) was published with the four Eucharistic 'usages' restored there was a level of theological differentiation among the Nonjurors due to the rigid stance on the usages adopted by some Nonjurors. Various viewpoints on the usages, which included the mixing of water with wine in the sacrament, the offering or oblation of the elements as a representation of Christ's sacrifice, a prayer for the invocation of the Holy Spirit on the elements, and prayers for the dead, internally divided the Nonjurors.

This chapter explores Wesley's conception and practice of the primitive ideal as mediated through High Church Anglicanism and most especially the Usager Nonjurors.

THE WESLEY FAMILY REVERENCE FOR THE PRIMITIVE CHURCH

John Wesley's introduction to High Church Anglican conceptions of the primitive church began at an early age. His parents, Samuel (1662–1735) and Susanna (1669–1742) Wesley, like many seventeenth- and eighteenth-century Anglicans, were fascinated by the ideal of primitive Christianity. Reflecting on his upbringing Wesley stated: 'From a child I was taught to love and reverence the Scripture, the oracles of God; and, next to these, to esteem the primitive Fathers, the writers of the first three centuries. Next after the primitive church I esteemed our own,

---

of Primitive Christianity to the Indians', *MH* 47 (2008), 16–25. For additional discussion on why Wesley went to Georgia, see Hammond, 54–6.

[6] For further definition of High Churchmanship, see F. L. Cross and E. A. Livingstone (eds), *The Oxford Dictionary of the Christian Church*, 3rd edn (Oxford, 1997), 767 and Peter Nockles, 'Church Parties in the Pre-Tractarian Church of England 1750–1833: The "Orthodox"—Some Problems of Definition and Identity', in John Walsh, Colin Haydon, and Stephen Taylor (eds), *The Church of England c. 1689–c. 1833: From Toleration to Tractarianism* (Cambridge, 1993), 335–6. One should not assume that the designation High Church or, to a lesser extent, Nonjuror, connotes a rigid category.

[7] Robert D. Cornwall, *Visible and Apostolic: The Constitution of the Church in High Church Anglican and Non-Juror Thought* (Newark, NJ, 1993).

the Church of England, as the most Scriptural national Church in the world.'[8] Samuel Wesley had no doubt that 'the best and purest Ages of the Church' were the earliest ages of the church.[9] His obituary in *The Gentleman's Magazine* accurately memorialized him as 'a most zealous Asserter of the Doctrine and Discipline of the Church of England.'[10] He was keen to defend the liturgical and episcopal constitution of the Church as being 'agreeable to the Primitive Pattern', and he was equally passionate about restoring 'the ancient church discipline.'[11] Wesley consistently implemented the Church statutes against ante-nuptial fornication by enforcing public penance on offenders in his parish.[12] He also hoped to revive the office of catechist; an office he believed had been integral to the early church's method of grounding Christians in the knowledge of the faith.[13]

In the year of his father's death John Wesley published Samuel's seventy-one page pamphlet, *Advice to a Young Clergyman*, written for his father's curate at Epworth, Nathaniel Hoole. This pamphlet should be seen as a (High Church) manual on pastoral care, part of a genre that included Bishop Gilbert Burnet's popular *Discourse of the Pastoral Care* that recommended reading a specific series of books in preparation for ordination in the Church of England.[14] Though it was not published until 1735, Samuel had sent a copy of the manuscript to John at Oxford during the winter of 1724/25 as John was preparing for ordination.[15] Approximately half the pages are devoted to advice on what a prospective clergyman should study. Unlike Burnet, who did not see the study of church history and the Church Fathers as something necessary for ordinands,[16] a significant portion of these pages recommend study of the Church Fathers, including the epistles of Clement, Ignatius, and Polycarp and the Greek Fathers: Irenaeus, Athanasius, Basil, and Chrysostom. In light of John Wesley's high regard for them, it is significant that due to 'Arian interpolations'

---

[8] 'Farther Thoughts on Separation from the Church' (1789), *Works*, 9:538; cf. Sermons 'Upon our Lord's Sermon on the Mount: Discourse the Thirteenth' (1750), *Works*, 1:694 and 'On Sin in Believers' (1763), *Works*, 1:317.

[9] Samuel Wesley, 'A Letter Concerning the Religious Societies', in *The Pious Communicant Rightly Prepar'd* (London, 1700), no pagination.

[10] *Gentleman's Magazine* 5 (April 1735).

[11] *The Athenian Oracle…* 2nd edn, corrected (London, 1706), 1:165, 302.

[12] Samuel Wesley, *Advice to a Young Clergyman* (London, 1735), 70–1; R. E. G. Cole (ed.), 'Speculum Dioceseos Lincolniensis Sub Episcopis Gul: Wake Et Edm: Gibson A.D. 1705–1723', *Publications of the Lincoln Record Society*, 4 (1913), 182; L[uke] Tyerman, *The Life and Times of the Rev. Samuel Wesley, M.A.* (London, 1866), 412–16.

[13] Wesley, *Advice to a Young Clergyman*, 62–5.

[14] John Wesley read Burnet's work at Oxford in October 1729; see Heitzenrater, 'John Wesley', appendix IV. All references to Wesley's reading at Oxford (1725–35) cited in this book are catalogued in the fourth appendix of Richard P. Heitzenrater, 'John Wesley and the Oxford Methodists', Ph.D. diss. (Duke University, 1972).

[15] Samuel Wesley to JW (26 January 1724/5), *Works*, 25:158. The work is mentioned in Wesley's diary in January 1725.

[16] Burnet, *A Discourse of the Pastoral Care* (London, 1692), 170.

Samuel questioned the usefulness of the *Apostolic Constitutions*.[17] Regarding the English divines, Wesley cited several of the principal promoters of the patristic revival in the Church of England, including John Pearson, George Bull, William Beveridge, William Cave, and Anthony Horneck. Noteworthy is his passing critical comment about the Nonjurors 'some of whom have writ well against the Deists; and I wish they had never worse employed their labour.'[18] While at Oxford, John Wesley read the epistles of Clement, Ignatius, and Polycarp and all of the Anglican divines mentioned earlier. While his Oxford colleagues played a considerable role in stimulating his study of primitive Christianity, the influence of his father's advice should not be discounted.[19]

That Susanna Wesley influenced the theological and spiritual development of her son, John, is abundantly clear, although the theme of primitive Christianity appears to have played a less prominent role in her thinking. However, her Jacobite political leanings are significant in the context of this study. The roots of the famous Wesley family quarrel during the first six months of 1702 date back to the Revolution of 1688 and the coming of William and Mary to the throne. Samuel appears to have had no doubts about the providential nature of the Revolution. John Wesley, in fact, later reported that his father viewed James II as a tyrant following the king's expulsion of the fellows of Magdalen College (16 November 1687) during Samuel's time at Oxford.[20] His conscience may have been eased, in terms of the continuance of hereditary monarchy, by the fact that Queen Mary was a daughter of James. However, Susanna's belief in divine hereditary monarchy led her to oppose the removal of a ruling monarch and sympathize with the Nonjuring clergy who were dismissed from their cures. We do not know whether Susanna made her views known prior to the 1702 conflict, or whether she did not arrive at a settled opinion until sometime after the Revolution. In any case, it was not the death of Mary in 1694 that caused the dispute, but the death of the exiled James II on 6 September 1701.

We have Susanna's account of the conflict from her letter to Lady Yarborough of Snaith Hall (fourteen miles northwest of Epworth). Samuel had called her into his study after she had refused to say 'Amen' at family prayers following his prayer for King William and declared he would have no physical relations with her until she asked God's pardon for this offence. The rift was not healed

---

[17] Wesley, *Advice to a Young Clergyman*, in Thomas Jackson, *The Life of the Rev. Charles Wesley, M.A.* (London, 1841), 2:514.

[18] Wesley, *Advice to a Young Clergyman*, in Jackson, 2:523.

[19] Samuel's *Advice*, however, shows a more critical assessment of the Fathers than the view adopted by John Wesley. See also *The Young Students Library*, sometimes attributed to Samuel Wesley as secretary of the Athenian Society where 'All the Fathers, as St. Ambrose etc', *The History of the General Councils*, Beveridge's *Synodikon*, and Cotelerius' *Ecclesaie Grecae Monumenta* ('Documents of the Greek Church') are recommended (London, 1692), iv.

[20] Adam Clarke, *Memoirs of the Wesley Family; Collected Principally from Original Documents*, 4th edn (London, 1860), 1:240–3; Henry D. Rack, 'Wesley, Samuel (*bap.* 1662, *d.* 1735)', *ODNB*.

until July 1702 when Samuel reneged on his vow after the rectory nearly burnt to the ground.

Susanna's four surviving letters describing the painful estrangement reveal the extent of her identification with the Nonjuring community. In her first letter to Lady Yarborough, Susanna requested that her dilemma be communicated to 'one of our Divines.' Her letters were forwarded to George Hickes, the deprived dean of Worcester and suffragan Nonjuror bishop of Thetford, who urged her to obey the dictates of her conscience. Her respect for the eminent Nonjuring divine is reflected by her comment that she was now 'much better satisfied' that she should not surrender her convictions. Following two letters to Lady Yarborough, she twice addressed Hickes, who condemned Samuel's vow as perjury against his wedding vows.[21]

The precise beginning and whether Susanna's attachment to the Nonjuring cause ever ended is unknown, but in 1709 she still upheld the doctrine of divine hereditary monarchy.[22] From the little we know about Susanna's Nonjuring principles, it appears that she considered herself a part of their communion at a time when the theological and political concerns surrounding divine right monarchy were paramount. While it is unclear whether Susanna advocated a forced restoration of James II and/or his male heirs, she would only pray for a monarch *de jure* (by right or law). Being further removed from the Revolution, John Wesley maintained the principles of passive obedience and non-resistance, but was content to apply them to a *de facto* government.[23] Whether she embraced (or was aware of) John's and Charles's participation in the later Nonjurors' attempt to revive the primitive liturgy of the early church is unknown.

THE PATRISTIC TRADITION IN THE CHURCH OF ENGLAND

During the Protestant Reformation Luther, Zwingli, Calvin, and the Anabaptists all looked to the New Testament for a model to restore the primitive Christian faith.[24] This impulse was fuelled by Erasmus's goal 'to restore the pristine purity

[21] Susanna's four letters and portions of Hickes's reply have been published by Robert Walmsley, 'John Wesley's Parents: Quarrel and Reconciliation', *PWHS* 29 (1953), 50–7.

[22] John A. Newton, *Susanna Wesley and the Puritan Tradition in Methodism*, 2nd edn (London, 2002), 87.

[23] J. C. D. Clark, *English Society 1660–1832: Religion, Ideology and Politics during the Ancien Regime*, 2nd edn (Cambridge, 2000), 286–7. At Oxford, in April 1732, Wesley read George Berkeley's *Passive Obedience: or, the Christian Doctrine of not Resisting the Supreme Power, Proved and Vindicated upon the Principles of the Law of Nature* (Dublin, 1712). For more on John Wesley's early political views, see Hammond, appendix six.

[24] Paul D. L. Avis, ' "The True Church" in Reformation Theology', *Scottish Journal of Theology*, 30 (1977), 319–45.

of the Christian faith by means of a return to its purified sources.'[25] The ideals of Christian Humanism made their way to England, which became a centre for patristic studies in the sixteenth and seventeenth centuries.[26]

Partristic scholarship was used by Church of England apologists to defend the Church's doctrine and practice. Primitivism enabled them to 'conceive of a past church that was true and pure, and which could be re-formed, temporally and spiritually, in their present.'[27]

Church of England apologists regularly asserted that the appeal to the primitive church was itself primitive. Tertullian's maxim 'This is a prejudice against all the heresies: that that thinge is true, whatsoever was first: that is corrupt, whatsoever came after' was often cited as evidence.[28] David Manning has argued that the restoration of primitive Christianity was so central to the Reformation Church of England that the Church staked its credibility on the ideology of primitivism.[29]

Whereas many restoration movements of the Reformation era sought to restore the characteristics of the New Testament church as described in its various settings in scripture, sixteenth-century Anglicans tended to define the primitive church as extending for five or six hundred years after Christ.[30] In contrast to the sixteenth century, the seventeenth and eighteenth centuries saw a propensity on the part of Anglican divines to limit the primitive period to the pre-Nicene church (325), but sometimes extending to the mid-fifth century so as to include Augustine (d. 430) and the Council of Chalcedon (451).[31] Wesley came to adopt the majority position amongst eighteenth-century Anglicans in defining the primitive church as the pre-Nicene and pre-Constantinian church of the first three centuries.[32] For Wesley, primitive practice was his primary

[25] Abraham Friesen, 'The Impulse Toward Restitutionist Thought in Christian Humanism', *Journal of the American Academy of Religion*, 44 (1976), 29.

[26] William P. Haaugaard, 'Renaissance Patristic Scholarship and Theology in Sixteenth-Century England', *Sixteenth Century Journal*, 10 (1979), 37–60.

[27] David Manning, '"That is Best, Which Was First"': Christian Primitivism and the Reformation Church of England, 1548–1722', *Reformation & Renaissance Review*, 13 (2011), 156–7.

[28] Manning, '"That is Best, Which Was First"', 167–9. Tertullian's saying is cited from John Jewel's *The True Copies of the Letters betwene the reuerend father in God Iohn Bisshop of Sarum and D. Cole vpon occasion of a Sermon that the said Bishop preached before the Quenes Maiestie* (London, 1560), 118.

[29] Manning, '"That is Best, Which Was First"', 153–93, at 156–7.

[30] This limitation was partially insisted upon as a critique of the Catholic Church subsequent to the fifth century. From the Reformation the term 'primitive church' had been in continuous use in the Church of England.

[31] Jean-Louis Quantin, *The Church of England and Christian Antiquity: The Construction of a Confessional Identity in the Seventeenth Century* (Oxford, 2009), 9, 73, 79; E. Gordon Rupp, *Religion in England 1688–1791* (Oxford, 1986), 17.

[32] John C. English, 'The Duration of the Primitive Church: An Issue for Seventeenth and Eighteenth Century Anglicans', *Anglican and Episcopal History*, 73 (2004), 35–52; Campbell, 5, 47, 49–51, 74, 85.

concern, therefore his reading of the Fathers focused on liturgy and their devotional lives.

Key sources for Anglican doctrine (the Thirty-nine Articles, the Book of Common Prayer, the Canons, and Homilies) hold scripture to be the pre-eminent authority for doctrine and practice.[33] Nonetheless, early church tradition played a role in the development of these formularies. In writing the Book of Common Prayer, Thomas Cranmer's (1489–1556) particular concern was to restore the purity of primitive liturgical life.[34] Anglicans such as Cranmer, John Jewel, Richard Hooker, and Lancelot Andrewes wanted to revive the purity of the primitive church freed from what they saw as the corruptions of medieval Catholicism. They shared a common suspicion of doctrinal and liturgical innovation and looked to the Fathers for an authority that, although not binding, was believed to be reliable.[35] From the Anglican reformers to the Caroline divines and beyond, the consensus of the Fathers was sought to support the teaching of the Church of England.[36] Sixteenth- and seventeenth-century appeals to antiquity were frequently designed to pass judgement on Catholic teaching;[37] however, while anti-Catholic uses of primitivism continued, there was an increasing tendency to see the primitive church as a model for the Church of England.

The seventeenth- and early eighteenth-century Anglican revival of patristic scholarship has been widely recognized by scholars. Wesley benefited much from this work, though it had reached its peak by the time he arrived in Oxford.[38] Many clergy and laity shared a common admiration for the primitive church, and the conviction that in terms of continuity the Church of England was the most apostolic Church on earth. Numerous Anglican divines looked to the history of the early church and interpreted it as a 'chain of testimony'

[33] See, for example, Article VI of the Thirty-nine Articles.

[34] Henry Chadwick, 'Tradition, Fathers and Councils', in Stephen Sykes, John Booty, and Jonathan Knight (eds), *The Study of Anglicanism*, rev. edn (London, 1998), 105.

[35] Andrewes argued that new opinions 'are not ours. We appeal to antiquity, and to the most extreme antiquity'; 'we do not innovate; it may be that we renovate what was customary among the ancients'. This was famously echoed in John Pearson's statement in the dedication of his *Exposition of the Creed* (1659): 'in Christianity there can be no concerning truth which is not ancient; and whatsoever is truly new, is certainly false'. These quotes can be found in H. R. McAdoo, *The Spirit of Anglicanism: A Survey of Anglican Theological Method in the Seventeenth Century* (London, 1965), 334, 387.

[36] Stanley L. Greenslade, 'The Authority of the Tradition of the Early Church in Early Anglican Thought', in G. Gassmann and V. Vajta (eds), *Oecumenica: Jahrbuch für ökumenische Forschung 1971–72* (Gütersloh, Germany, 1972), 9–33.

[37] The classic statement was John Jewel's *Apologia pro Ecclesia Anglicana* (1562), in which he challenged Catholics to prove that their doctrines were consonant with the church of the first six centuries.

[38] Leslie W. Barnard, 'The Use of the Patristic Tradition in the Late Seventeenth and Early Eighteenth Centuries', in Richard Bauckham and Benjamin Drewery (eds), *Scripture Tradition and Reason, A Study in the Criteria of Christian Doctrine: Essays in Honour of Richard P. C. Hanson* (Edinburgh, 1988), 174–203.

that could be applied to present concerns.[39] Orthodoxy commonly became synonymous with the primitive church and 'the appeal to antiquity became the criterion of orthodoxy.'[40] Whether or not one accepts H. R. McAdoo's contention that there was a loosely defined classic Anglican theological method consisting of scripture, appeal to antiquity, and reason, Jean-Louis Quantin has demonstrated that there was no single consensus on what constituted primitive Christianity.[41] Competing conceptions in the Church of England included with varying degrees of overlap, Reformed, Arminian, High Church, Low Church, orthodox, heterodox, and Nonjuring views. Broadly speaking, John Wesley's participation in the Anglican patristic tradition fits within High Church models of primitive Christianity. However, more specifically, his conception and practice of primitive Christianity in Georgia was that of the extreme High Church group of Nonjurors. To be even more precise, Wesley's theology and practice was aligned largely with that of the radical group of Usager Nonjurors.

While the earliest Church of England position of Richard Hooker (1554–1600) and other early reformers did not hold that a particular church polity was prescribed in scripture, a tradition developed which argued that episcopacy (and bishops as a superior to presbyters) was both scriptural and of apostolic origin and fundamental to the Church.[42] This emphasis in Anglican patristic scholarship was exemplified by Lancelot Andrewes (1555–1626), James Ussher (1581–1656), and Henry Hammond (1605–60), who focused on the Ignatian epistles and the works of St Cyprian ('the patron saint' of High Churchmen) in polemics against Catholic and presbyterian doctrines of the priesthood. Archbishop William Laud (1573–1645) and his supporters began to argue for the observance of church practices inherited though the succession of apostolic tradition. As an innovation from earlier Anglican tradition, the height of Laudianism was the claim of apostolic succession of bishops going back to the early church.[43] Succeeding generations of Anglican divines typified by Jeremy Taylor (1613–67) and William Cave (1637–1713) were primarily concerned with the primitive church as a model for Christian devotion. Put together, these emphases highlighted the Fathers as exemplars of orthodox doctrine and practice. The martyrdom many of them faced increased their prestige.[44]

---

[39] John Spurr, ' "A Special Kindness for Dead Bishops": The Church, History, and Testimony in Seventeenth-Century Protestantism', *Huntington Library Quarterly*, 68 (2005), 313–15.

[40] Eamon Duffy, 'Primitive Christianity Revived; Religious Renewal in Augustan England', in Derek Baker (ed.), *Renaissance and Renewal in Christian History*, Studies in Church History, 14 (Oxford, 1977), 287.

[41] McAdoo, *Spirit of Anglicanism*; Quantin, *Church of England and Christian Antiquity*.

[42] Quantin, *Church of England and Christian Antiquity*, 88–105, 267; Norman Sykes, *Old Priest and New Presbyter: Episcopacy and Presbyterianism since the Reformation with Especial Relation to the Churches of England and Scotland* (Cambridge, 1956), 17.

[43] Quantin, *Church of England and Christian Antiquity*, 298, 71, 199–202.

[44] Spurr, ' "Special Kindness for Dead Bishops" ', 319–23; Gareth Vaughan Bennett, 'Patristic Tradition in Anglican Thought, 1660–1900', in G. Gassmann and V. Vajta (eds), *Oecumenica*, 64–9.

Anglican patristic scholarship flourished following the Restoration of Charles II in 1660 and was aided by the state support of Anglicanism enshrined in the Act of Uniformity (1662). It had come to be seen as a badge of loyalty to the Established Church, and a sign of anti-Puritanism. The trauma of the Civil War helped propel Anglicans to champion patristic authority in opposition to Puritan ambivalence towards the Fathers.[45] The blossoming of patristic scholarship was embraced by many in the Church, but particularly thrived in parallel with the burgeoning High Church movement.[46] Post-Restoration patristic interpreters retained the earlier uses of the Fathers as pre-eminent interpreters of scripture and arbiters of doctrinal disputes, while stressing the unique continuity of the Church of England with the primitive church and the Fathers and early church as models of piety and discipline. Emphasis on piety and church discipline fuelled numerous works on the sacraments, liturgy, and episcopacy.[47]

Anglican theologians, in their new-found Post-Restoration security, gradually began to feel less need to use the Fathers as a means to defend Church doctrine. Following the Restoration, it became clear that the restoration of the Church was not in itself sufficient to inspire an increase in religious piety amongst the nation as a whole. In response to the perceived corruption of society, Anglican divines increasingly appealed to the primitive church as a model to be restored in the Church of England.[48] Bishop William Beveridge (1637–1708)[49] and William Cave, fellow students at St John's College, Cambridge, became two of the leading patristic scholars of the late seventeenth century. Both men became influential High Church-oriented clergymen. In his parish ministry, Beveridge modelled the restoration of primitive Christianity through daily services, weekly communion, the formation of religious societies, and the exercise of firm clerical discipline—all of which were features of Wesley's ministry in Georgia.[50]

---

[45] Quantin, *Church of England and Christian Antiquity*, 113, 203, 252–67. The Puritans resembled Elizabethan Anglicans in their stress on *sola Scriptura* and their admiration for Continental reformers.

[46] Bennett, 'Patristic Tradition', 74–6; Duffy, 'Primitive Christianity Revived', 287–300; Robert D. Cornwall, 'The Search for the Primitive Church: The Use of Early Church Fathers in the High Church Anglican Tradition, 1680–1745', *Anglican and Episcopal History*, 59 (1990), 303–29; Quantin, *Church of England and Christian Antiquity*, 407.

[47] Cornwall, 'Search for the Primitive Church', 303–29.

[48] On the practice of primitive Christianity as an antidote to corruption, see Geordan Hammond, 'The Revival of Practical Christianity: The Society for Promoting Christian Knowledge, Samuel Wesley, and the Clerical Society Movement', in Kate Cooper and Jeremy Gregory (eds), *Revival and Resurgence in Christian History*, Studies in Church History, 44 (Woodbridge, 2008), 116–27, at 119–20.

[49] Although Beveridge took the oath of loyalty to King William and Queen Mary, he showed himself to be a sympathizer with the Nonjurors by his refusal to accept his 1691 appointment to the see of Bath and Wells, which had been vacated by the Nonjuror Thomas Ken.

[50] Peter Doll, 'The Architectural Expression of Primitive Christianity: William Beveridge and the Temple of Solomon', *Reformation & Renaissance Review*, 13 (2011), 278–9.

Beveridge wrote two works that Wesley read in Georgia.[51] In 1672, he published a two-volume study entitled *Synodikon, sive Pandectae Canonum SS. Apostolorum et Conciliorum Ecclesia Graeca Receptorum* ('Synodikon, or, Summaries of the Apostolic Canons and Councils Received in the Greek Church'), in which he translated into Latin the Greek and Syriac texts of the general councils accepted by the Eastern Church. The *Apostolic Canons* were given prominence of position at the beginning of Beveridge's work. The *Canons* are made up of eighty-five teachings attributed to the Apostles, which deal with the ordination, responsibilities, and moral conduct of the clergy. Beveridge further pursued his interest in the *Canons* in his *Codex Canonum Ecclesiae Primitivae Vindicatus ac Illustratus* (1678) ('The Book of Canons of the Primitive Church Vindicated and Illustrated'), which in opposition to the 'arch-enemy' of Anglican patristic scholars, the French Protestant Jean Daillé (1594–1670), argued for the orthodoxy of the canons and dated them to the second or third century.[52] Wesley first read this work at Oxford, which contended that since the *Canons* represent genuine apostolic practice, they should be adopted by the Church of England.[53]

William Cave's patristic research led him to emphasize slightly different elements in his analysis. Instead of following Beveridge in stressing the doctrinal and liturgical purity of the early church, Cave was interested in the early church as a model of practical piety. Cave stated this aim at the outset of his *Primitive Christianity* (1673): 'I studiously avoided controversies, it being no part of my design to enquire, what was the judgment of the Fathers in disputable cases, especially the more abstruse and intricate speculations of theology, but what was their practice, and by what rules and measures they did govern and conduct their lives.'[54] This, no doubt, appealed to Wesley's well-known hatred of doctrinal disputes, which he shared in common with many eighteenth-century Anglicans.[55] Cave attempted to inspire his readers to emulate the primitive Christians with his concluding exhortation 'to *admire* and *imitate* their piety and integrity, their infinite hatred of sin, their care and zeal to keep up that strictness and purity of manners that had rendered their

---

[51] JWJ and JWMSJ, 13 and 20 September 1736. Wesley's Oxford diaries record that he read eight of Beveridge's works, making Beveridge his second most widely read author during this formative period of his intellectual and spiritual development.

[52] Quantin, *Church of England and Christian Antiquity*, 349–52, 398.

[53] Campbell, 28, citing Wesley's Oxford diaries for 8 and 25 August 1732; also read February 1735.

[54] William Cave, *Primitive Christianity: or, the Religion of the Antient Christians, in the First Ages of the Gospel*, 7th edn (London, 1714), preface, no pagination.

[55] Jeremy Gregory, '*Homo Religiosus*: Masculinity and Religion in the Long Eighteenth Century', in Tim Hitchcock and Michèle Cohen (eds), *English Masculinities 1660–1800* (London, 1999), 104. For this theme early in Wesley's life, see JW to Susanna Wesley [24 January 1726/7], *Works*, 25:208, in reference to the dispute between Francis Atterbury and Benjamin Hoadly on the interpretation of 1 Corinthians 15:19.

Religion so renowned and triumphant in the world.'[56] Cave drew upon the appeal of the *imitatio Christi* ideal by representing the primitive Christians as a worthy model to be imitated. For Anglican patristic scholars, in the same way that the Fathers were the pre-eminent authority for scriptural interpretation, the primitive Church as a whole was the highest authority for unblemished devotional practice. For Anglicans, Cave's inspirational book was one of a number of popular accounts of primitive Christianity that 'offered an ideal standard of Christian living. It was to be experienced personally in the present, revived as practical holiness, the secret to genuine happiness and serenity.'[57]

High Church Anglicans developed a hermeneutic of the early church that differed markedly from Richard Hooker's view that special reverence was not due to a particular age of the church. With their Elizabethan forebears they maintained that the Church of England was in doctrinal succession with the early church, while also asserting that its clergy were in apostolic succession.[58] Theirs was a hermeneutical narrowing to ante-Nicene Christianity; this they believed was the only way to solve modern controversies and restore the Church to its primitive unity. While it was a contested issue, many High Churchmen were convinced that there was a consensus of the primitive church that could be determined and restored. They were confident that through their patristic scholarship they could elucidate the doctrine, discipline, and practice of the primitive church in a way that would allow it to be restored in the Church. Determining what primitive Christianity was had become a task of historical study to be investigated by scholars. The Church Fathers were seen as the pre-eminent interpreters of scripture. For matters that could not be resolved by scripture, the widely held rule became the Vincentian Canon (what has been believed everywhere, always, and by all) applied to ante-Nicene Christianity. Wesley followed many High Churchmen in advocating the Vincentian Canon as a method for interpreting scripture and guidance for liturgical and devotional practices.

THE NONJUROR VISION OF PRIMITIVE CHRISTIANITY

The most immediate influence that propelled John Wesley to view Georgia as a laboratory for restoring primitive Christianity was the Nonjurors. Several

---

[56] Cave, *Primitive Christianity*, 467.

[57] Sarah Apetrei, '"The Life of Angels": Celibacy and Asceticism in Anglicanism, 1660–c.1700', *Reformation & Renaissance Review*, 13 (2011), 259.

[58] Quantin, *Church of England and Christian Antiquity*, 396, 397; Sykes, *Old Priest and New Presbyter*, 16, 108.

decades ago Frederick Hunter noted that 'the influence of this High Church group on the Wesleys was wider, deeper, and more lasting than even yet has been recognized.'[59] Nonetheless, no scholar has followed up on Hunter's short study with a detailed account of the links between Wesley and the Nonjurors, although their impact has been acknowledged in many recent studies of the young Wesley. In more specific terms, it was through an extreme sect known as Usagers that the Nonjuring reverence for the primitive church was mediated to Wesley. Before we examine Wesley's relations with the Usagers, it is necessary to contextualize the Nonjuring appeal to the ancient church.

Nonjurors—Anglicans who refused to take the Oaths of Allegiance and Supremacy to William and Mary (1689–90) on the ground that this would violate their previous oaths to the Stuarts (James II and his heirs)—originated as a movement of political protest.[60] Wesley was informed of the Nonjurors' political convictions through John Kettlewell's 'Declaration and Profession' setting out his defence of his refusal to take the oaths and his accusation that those who had taken them were responsible for causing schism in the Church.[61] By their refusal to take the oaths, over four hundred Nonjuring clergy, including eight bishops, were expelled from the Church of England. Many accomplished scholars, including Henry Dodwell (1641–1711), George Hickes (1642–1715), and Thomas Deacon (1697–1753), were among their number. In their late seventeenth-century context, the political views of the Nonjurors should not be separated from their theological concerns.[62] The doctrine of divine hereditary monarchy with its corollaries, the doctrines of passive obedience and non-resistance, were not merely political stances; they presupposed the providence of God over political affairs. As Wesley later put it, from 'God, and not the people' comes 'the origin of all civil power'; these doctrines were thought to be essential to a stable society.[63] The interlinking of their political ideals in theological language indicates that the Nonjurors cannot be understood in political terms alone; they increasingly distinguished themselves from conforming clergy by a High Church theology, which came to be characterized

---

[59] Hunter, 10; cf. Trevor Dearing, *Wesleyan and Tractarian Worship: An Ecumenical Study* (London, 1966).

[60] The word 'Nonjuror' is derived from the Latin *juro*, which means 'swear'. There was a range of belief amongst the Nonjurors regarding the propriety of restoring the Stuart monarchy to the throne. Not all Nonjurors were part of the Jacobite movement.

[61] *The Practical Believer: Or, the Articles of the Apostles Creed*, 3rd edn (London, 1713), 357–61. Read August 1733.

[62] Robert D. Cornwall, 'The Theologies of the Nonjurors: A Historiographical Essay', in M. Caricchio and G. Tarantino (eds), *Cromohs Virtual Seminars. Recent Historiographical Trends of the British Studies (17th-18th Centuries)* [online journal] (2006-7), 1–7, <http://www.cromohs.unifi.it/seminari/cornwall_nonjuror.html>, accessed 16 August 2012; Richard Sharp, 'New Perspectives on the High Church Tradition: Historical Background 1730–1780', in Geoffrey Rowell (ed.), *Tradition Renewed: The Oxford Movement Conference Papers* (London, 1986), 4.

[63] JW to the editor of the *Gentleman's Magazine* (24 December 1785), *Letters* (Telford), 7:305–6.

by their burning reverence for the primitive church. Theirs was not simply an antiquarian admiration, but a practical vision for using history as 'a chain of testimony' to support their goal of renewing the Church along primitive lines.[64] It was this theological imperative that would captivate Wesley.

It is the 'later Nonjurors', those who remained Nonjurors following the death of the last of the original Nonjuring bishops in 1710, who are of primary concern in this study. With the accession of George I to the throne in 1714, the Nonjuring community was in crisis. Most of the early Nonjurors had either died or returned to the Established Church, although the succession of the monarchy to the House of Hanover, which led to the proclamation of a new Abjuration Oath (1716), strengthened the Nonjurors' cause by bringing additional High Churchmen into their camp. The second generation of Nonjuring leaders increasingly saw themselves as a community independent of the state.[65] This emphasis left them to focus primarily on their internal theological development rather than on the political and theological doctrines associated with the divine right of monarchs. Their separation from the Church granted them the freedom to develop their theological concerns apart from political considerations.[66] However, their inward turn and separation made them appear to be a nonconformist sect and led to the marginalization of their influence within the Established Church.[67]

The first generation of Nonjuring clergy who served in Anglican or separated churches officiated in their congregations using the standard 1662 Book of Common Prayer.[68] This was in line with a developed tradition amongst Anglican patristic scholars that the prayer book resembled and was in continuity with ancient Christian liturgies. Most Nonjurors, however, regarded (or came to regard) the communion office of the first prayer book of Edward VI (1549), reprinted by George Hickes in 1707, as a more accurate expression of primitive Eucharistic practice than the revised prayer book of 1662.[69]

Despite this general agreement, the Nonjurors were divided over the propriety of pursuing liturgical reform. The majority opposed altering the

---

[64] Hence, they continued and adapted to their own purposes the work of the seventeenth-century Anglican revival of patristic scholarship: Spurr, '"Special Kindness for Dead Bishops"', 313–15; Cornwall, 'Theologies of the Nonjurors', no pagination.

[65] Cornwall, *Visible and Apostolic*, 73–93.

[66] Cornwall, 'Theologies of the Nonjurors', no pagination.

[67] Conforming High Churchmen such as John Johnson and Nathaniel Marshall that influenced the Nonjurors and shared similar theological convictions to them did not receive preferment in their clerical careers: Cornwall, *Visible and Apostolic*, 106.

[68] For example, Thomas Brett was a committed Nonjuror but remained in the Established Church until 1715, while other clergy set up Nonjuring communities severed from the Church of England.

[69] See the appendix in volume two of Hickes's, *Two Treatises, One of the Christian Priesthood, the Other of the Dignity of the Episcopal Order*. Wesley read this work in Georgia (JWD, 8 November 1736). The same view was held by other High Churchmen that Wesley read—for example, John Johnson and Charles Wheatly.

established liturgy, while a vocal minority held that 'four usages' (i.e. practices) contained in the 1549 book ought to be restored.[70] Wesley was familiar with the usages through his June 1733 reading of Thomas Deacon's *The Doctrine of the Church of Rome Concerning Purgatory* (1718) in the company of the Oxford Methodists.[71] In Deacon's words, the four usages of the Nonjurors included: '(1) The mixture of water and wine in the sacramental cup; (2) The oblation of the Eucharistick elements as the representative sacrifice of Christ's body and blood; (3) The Blessing of them or the Invocation of the Holy Ghost upon them; and (4) The recommending of the faithful departed to God's mercy at the Celebration of the Christian Sacrifice'.[72] The prayer of oblation was said before the congregation received the elements in order to 'emphasize the sacrificial aspect of the Eucharist'; the prayer of invocation or *epiclesis* intended as a petition for the descent of the Holy Spirit on the elements was conducted during the consecration of the elements and formed one prayer with the prayer of oblation;[73] the mixture was done in public view after the oblation and invocation and was placed on the altar, and the words 'militant in earth' were removed or omitted from the prayer book liturgy 'so that the prayer for the whole estate of the Church might include the living and the dead'.[74] As we see in the latter part of this chapter, Wesley's writings and reading from 1732 provide abundant evidence that he favoured these usages.

Nonjurors who ascribed to the four usages have been variously labelled 'Essentialist' or 'Usager' Nonjurors—Jeremy Collier (1650–1726) and Thomas Brett (1667–1744) being two of the most prominent among them—as distinct from most Nonjurors, who even if convinced that the usages were preferable, continued to adhere to the established 1662 prayer book liturgy.[75] Some High Churchmen believed that the usages (or some of the usages) could be implemented in the liturgy for Holy Communion, either by appeal to the precedent of the 1549 prayer book or by asserting that they are not forbidden or that they are implied in the 1662 book.[76] However, uncompromising adherence to the

---

[70] Robert D. Cornwall, 'The Later Nonjurors and the Theological Basis of the Usages Controversy', *Anglican Theological Review*, 75 (1993), 170.

[71] On Deacon see Henry Broxap, *A Biography of Thomas Deacon: The Manchester Non-Juror* (Manchester, 1911) and Robert D. Cornwall, 'Deacon, Thomas (1697–1753)', *ODNB*.

[72] Thomas Deacon, *The Doctrine of the Church of Rome Concerning Purgatory* (London, 1718), xx.

[73] Richard Sharp, '100 Years of a Lost Cause: Nonjuring Principles in Newcastle from the Revolution to the Death of Prince Edward Stuart', *Archaeologia Aeliana*, 5th series, 8 (1980), 40. In this study, Sharp (p. 44) notes that it was the issue of oblation that was the main point of contention between the two groups of Nonjurors: 'the non-Usager party not being prepared to dispense with the BCP order, which obstructed notions of a material sacrifice in the Eucharist by placing this prayer *after* communion.'

[74] Rupp, *Religion in England*, 18.

[75] On the differences between Usager and non-Usager Nonjurors, see Cornwall, 'Later Nonjurors', and James David Smith, *The Eucharistic Doctrine of the Later Nonjurors: A Revisionist View of the Eighteenth-Century Usages Controversy*, Joint Liturgical Studies, 46 (Cambridge, 2000).

[76] Wheatly, chapter 6.

usages, and particularly use of unauthorized liturgies for Holy Communion, could be seen as evidence of separation from the Church of England.[77]

A split between the two groups of Nonjurors was precipitated by the publication of *A Communion Office* in 1718 by the Bishops Brett and Collier with assistance from Thomas Deacon.[78] The aim of the new liturgy was initially to restore the primitive practices of the early church, which they believed had been largely maintained in the 1549 prayer book of Edward VI, but in the process of revision the authors became convinced that the first Edwardian book was deficient and needed to be supplemented by primitive liturgies, especially the *Apostolic Constitutions*, a compilation of ecclesiastical law, liturgical material, and prayers. They believed that the work, though not of apostolic authorship, represented true apostolic tradition and was the purest and most primitive liturgy in existence.[79] Their intention was for the liturgy to be used by Nonjuring clergy in place of the Book of Common Prayer. While many High Churchmen would have agreed with most modern scholars of the early church that there was no universal apostolic liturgy, they believed that the Apostles handed down liturgical instructions to the churches, and careful historical scholarship could recover the most apostolic liturgies of the primitive church.[80] They were confident that through the combined evidence of such scholarship a Eucharistic liturgy could be reconstructed containing all essential elements of apostolic tradition on the topic. Brett followed up the *Communion Office* with *A Collection of the Principal Liturgies, Used by the Christian Church in the Celebration of the Holy Eucharist* (1720), containing the Eucharistic liturgy in the *Apostolic Constitutions* as the first item in the book.[81]

Following the publication of the *Communion Office* of 1718, a pamphlet war comprising over forty tracts and lasting until 1725 erupted between the Usagers and non-Usagers regarding the appropriateness of restoring the

---

[77] Canon 36 (1604) required use of the BCP in 'the form in the said book prescribed, and none other'. All references in this book to the *Canons and Constitutions Ecclesiastical* (1604) can be found in Gerald Bray (ed.), *The Anglican Canons, 1529–1947*, Church of England Record Society, 6 (Woodbridge, 1998).

[78] Many elements of this liturgy, including assertion of the superiority of the 1549 prayer book and use of the *Apostolic Constitutions*, were prefigured in Edward Stephens's *The Liturgy of the Ancients Represented, as Near as Well may be, in English Forms* (London, 1696) and William Whiston's *The Liturgy of the Church of England, Reduc'd nearer to the Primitive Standard* (London, 1713).

[79] Grisbrooke, 94–7, 103–4, 108–10; see also Leonel L. Mitchell, 'The Influence of the Rediscovery of the Liturgy of the Apostolic Constitutions on the Nonjurors', *Ecclesia Orans*, 13 (1996), 207–21. The revisions made are clearly stated in the book's preface: see *A Communion Office, Taken Partly from Primitive Liturgies, and Partly from the First English Reformed Common-Prayer-Book* (London, 1718), no pagination. On authorship see Collier, 6; Thomas Brett, *A Collection of the Principal Liturgies, Used by the Christian Church in the Celebration of the Holy Eucharist* (London, 1720), 426.

[80] Henry Chadwick, *The Early Church*, rev. edn (London, 1993), 271.

[81] Brett concluded that it was the standard by which other liturgies should be judged: *Collection of the Principal Liturgies*, 30–1, 428.

usages.[82] The crux of the conflict primarily focused on the issue of authority. As Wesley accurately remarked on his return voyage from Georgia, the Usagers made 'antiquity a co-ordinate (rather than a subordinate) rule with Scriptures', a theological claim that he had entirely accepted.[83] Although the Usagers were willing to admit that the usages were not scriptural commands, they asserted that they were still necessary because of the strength of patristic testimony regarding them.[84] For the non-Usagers, as with the majority of Anglicans (supported by Article VI), tradition could never be accepted as essential to salvation or as a rule of faith.[85] However, for Wesley and the Usagers primitive tradition was an avenue through which they could critique contemporary Anglican practice. Usagers therefore used ancient tradition as a justification to restore primitive practices they believed were binding on all Christians, while most Anglicans saw this type of restoration as an unwarranted innovation that violated Article VI.

The schism between some of the Nonjurors ended in 1732 with the signing of the *Instrument of Union* by Thomas Brett on behalf of the Usagers. In actual fact however, the *Instrument* was an ill-conceived and unsatisfactory compromise that caused further schism.[86] Former Usagers and non-Usagers who abided by the *Instrument* formed the Unionist party, while substantial numbers of non-Usagers and Usagers stayed true to their convictions and maintained their separate identities. The Usager party hence became known as Usagers or Essentialist Nonjurors due to their separation from the vast majority of Nonjurors.[87] They were now left free to pursue their goal of utilizing the surviving primitive liturgies and testimonies of the Fathers to restore a purer and more ancient catholic liturgy than they believed the Book of Common Prayer provided. One of their number, Thomas Deacon, heavily influenced Wesley through his disciple John Clayton and his own personal interaction during Wesley's May 1733 and subsequent visits to Manchester.[88]

Thomas Deacon, one of the leaders of the Manchester sect of Usagers, consecrated bishop in 1733, took a more radical step than the Nonjuror *Communion Office* by publishing *A Compleat Collection of Devotions* (1734), a heavily

---

[82] Smith, *Eucharistic Doctrine of the Later Nonjurors*, 3.

[83] JWJ, 25 January 1738. Wesley's manuscript fragment 'Of the Weekly Fasts of the Church' proves this point. The surviving section of this essay argues 'that every Particular Church, is obliged to conform to Every Custom, which is injoined [*sic*] by the Church Universal': MARC, MS Colman Collection 12; Campbell, 123.

[84] Collier, 10, 19.

[85] Smith, *Eucharistic Doctrine of the Later Nonjurors*, 6–12; Cornwall, 'Later Nonjurors', 186.

[86] The *Instrument* called for liturgical uniformity with the allowance for some usages to be maintained. Several scholars have concluded that the formation of the Unionist party was largely a triumph for the non-Usagers: Grisbrooke, 113–15; Cornwall, 'Later Nonjurors', 185.

[87] James David Smith uses the term 'Extreme Usagers': *Eucharistic Doctrine of the Later Nonjurors*, 4.

[88] On Wesley's four visits to Manchester before going to Georgia, see Henry Derman Rack, 'The Wesleys and Manchester', *Proceedings of The Charles Wesley Society*, 8 (2002), 6–11.

revised version of the Book of Common Prayer, which advocated the reintroduction of neglected aspects of the *Apostolic Constitutions* and a return to the
four usages based on the *Constitutions* and the 1549 prayer book.[89] Most of
Deacon's revisions were derived from the Eucharistic teaching of the so-called
Clementine Liturgy, which forms the eighth book of the *Constitutions*.[90] In his
preface, Deacon laid out the two principles upon which his work was founded:

> 1st. That the best method for all churches and Christians to follow, is to lay aside
> all modern hypotheses, customs, and private opinions, and submit to all the doc-
> trines, practices, worship, and discipline, not of any Particular, but of the Ancient
> and Universal church of Christ, from the beginning to the end of the fourth cen-
> tury … 2dly. That the Liturgy in the Apostolical Constitutions is the most Ancient
> Christian Liturgy extant; that it is perfectly pure and free from interpolation; and
> that the book itself, called the Apostolical Constitutions, contains at large the doc-
> trines, laws, and settlements, which the first and purest ages of the gospel did with
> one consent believe, obey, and submit to … That therefore the said book … ought
> to be received, submitted to, and allowed it's [*sic*] due authority.[91]

Deacon was not alone in his view of the apostolic origins of the *Constitutions*.
Other churchmen also believed they had been derived from oral traditions
faithfully passed on by the Apostles. Some thought St Clement of Rome or
St Clement of Alexandria[92] had a role in compiling them. Modern scholars,
however, believe they are of Syrian origin and have dated them to *c*.380.[93] The
Apostolic Canons, which form the final chapter of the *Apostolic Constitutions*,
were also an important part of the Usagers' restoration programme.

As Deacon's second principle illustrates, he believed the *Constitutions*'' pure
and ancient liturgical practices should be universally reinstated in the Church
to promote catholic unity. His liturgy was probably not used regularly until
1748, when, as senior bishop of the dwindling Usager communion, he decreed
that it be adopted.[94]

---

[89] Wesley first read this work in May 1734.

[90] The eighth book is often referred to as the Clementine Liturgy because the *Constitutions*
claim that Clement of Rome was their author: see the title page, title page of book one, and
Constitutions VIII.46 in the second volume of William Whiston's *Primitive Christianity Reviv'd*
entitled *The Constitutions of the Holy Apostles, by Clement; in English and in Greek; with the
Various Readings from all of the Manuscripts* (London, 1711).

[91] Thomas Deacon, *A Compleat Collection of Devotions, both Publick and Private: Taken from
the Apostolical Constitutions, the Ancient Liturgies, and the Common Prayer Book of the Church of
England* (London, 1734), iii–iv. Frank Baker accurately noted that 'Throughout his life, however,
he [Wesley] remained loyal to the first, as well as to Deacon's overall catholic purpose': Baker,
John Wesley, 33.

[92] This was William Beveridge's view: Alexander Roberts, James Donaldson, and A. Cleveland
Coxe (eds), *Ante-Nicene Fathers* (Peabody, MA, 1994), 7:388.

[93] For a concise overview of the *Constitutions*, see W. Jardine Grisbrooke (trans. and ed.), *The
Liturgical Portions of the Apostolic Constitutions: A Text for Students*, Alcuin/GROW Liturgical
Study, 13–4 (Bramcote, 1990).

[94] Grisbrooke, 115. Although the Nonjuring movement died out, their legacy has lived on in
Anglican liturgy: Grisbrooke, 136–59; Hunter, 14–15.

WESLEY AND PRIMITIVE CHRISTIANITY

John Wesley's Oxford diaries from 1725 to 1731 show that the Church Fathers accounted for only a small proportion of his readings. However, he read many of the Anglican divines recommended by his father. His father's advice coupled with his early Oxford reading put him in touch with many respected Anglican theologians, most of whom drew on the Fathers and were enamoured with the early church. Wesley's interest in the early church was so well known that in 1730 his friend Mary Pendarves nicknamed him '*Primitive Christianity*'.[95] Though his father's influence was not the immediate impetus, from 1732 he embarked on an intensive study of the Apostolic Fathers and High Church interpreters of primitive Christianity.[96] In a January 1738 theological reflection penned on his return voyage from Georgia, Wesley recalled, 'Providence brought me to those who showed me a sure rule for interpreting Scripture, viz., *consensus veterum*—'quod ab omnibus, quod ubique, quod simper creditum' ('The consensus of antiquity: what has been believed everywhere, always, and by all'). The providential opening that brought Wesley to adopt St Vincent of Lérins's (d. *c*.450) threefold test for determining catholic tradition (commonly known as the Vincentian Canon) was almost certainly John Clayton (1709–73), a tutor at Brasenose College, who provided the inspiration and companionship that set Wesley on this course.[97] In his reflection Wesley referred to those whom he labelled 'the Essentialist Nonjurors', hence, he consciously linked himself with the Usagers, whose vision for the restoration of primitive Christianity he adopted and sought to bring to fruition during the period from 1732 to 1737. He also noted that they 'insisted upon a due regard to the One Church at all times and in all places', an emphasis he felt was lacking in the works of many Anglican divines.[98] Although Wesley did not explicitly state it here, his other writings during this period make it clear that he was attracted to the notion of the universal uniformity to true Christianity, which he believed was best realized in the primitive church.[99]

[95] Mary Pendarves (née Granville) to Ann Granville (4 April 1730), in Mary Delany, *The Autobiography and Correspondence of Mary Granville, Mrs. Delany*, ed. Lady Llanover (London, 1861–2), 1:250.

[96] This can be seen in his 1733 resolution to read the Fathers (MARC, MS Colman Collection 7; printed in full in Baker, *John Wesley*, 36).

[97] If he was not already aware of it, Wesley read about Lérins' threefold test in Beveridge's *Codex Canonum* in August 1732 and read Lérins' *Commonitorium* read in June 1733. Clayton was a Jacobite conforming High Churchman. Therefore, because he remained a clergyman within the Church, he was not a Nonjuror in the original strict definition of the term. Nonetheless his theology, along with Wesley's, was that of the Usager Nonjurors. A key difference between Clayton and Wesley was that Clayton was definitively a Jacobite. See Rack, 'The Wesleys and Manchester', 8.

[98] JWJ, 25 January 1738.

[99] See the discussion of Wesley's *A Collection of Forms of Prayer for Every Day in the Week* (1733) in 'The Unity of the "Holy Catholick Church"' in this chapter.

On 20 April 1732 Wesley first met Clayton, who immediately embraced the work of the Methodists. Clayton's presence reinforced their public ministry and frequent (at least weekly) celebration of communion, which was an unusual practice in eighteenth-century England,[100] though it was feasible for the Methodists given their residence near the collegiate churches of Oxford. Clayton contributed to the devotional practice of the Methodists by persuading Wesley to join with him in observing the stationary fasts, i.e. to imitate the ancient practice of Wednesday and Friday fasts (Wednesday because it was the day Christ was brought to trial and Friday because it was the day Christ was crucified) and observation of other days of fasting as specified by the prayer book.[101]

A catalogue of Clayton's library survives and it lists nearly every book that influenced Wesley during this period, providing strong evidence that he swayed Wesley's reading in a High Church/Nonjuring direction.[102] Clayton's father was a Manchester bookseller and he was in contact with Charles Rivington, a High Churchman and London-based printer who sympathized with the Nonjurors.[103] Therefore, he was closely connected to men who could supply him with the latest theological treatises. In all likelihood, Wesley drew upon Clayton's personal library for his reading before Clayton returned to Manchester to become curate of Sacred Trinity, Salford, in 1733.

---

[100] F. C. Mather, 'Georgian Churchmanship Reconsidered: Some Variations in Anglican Public Worship 1714–1830', *Journal of Ecclesiastical History*, 36 (1985), 255–83.

[101] JWJ, preface, 131–2 and 24 May 1738, p. 245; JW to Susanna Wesley (28 February 1731/32), *Works*, 25:328; cf. Luke 18:12. The word 'station' was adapted from the ancient military duty of being on watch. The Oxford Methodist scheme of self-examination for Wednesdays and Fridays focused on questions relating to the theme of mortification and self-denial: Richard P. Heitzenrater, 'The *Imitatio Christi* and the Great Commandment: Virtue and Obligation in Wesley's Ministry with the Poor', in M. Douglas Meeks (ed.), *Good News to the Poor in the Wesleyan Tradition* (Nashville, 1995), 57. On the rationale for Wednesday and Friday fasting, see the *Apostolic Constitutions* V.15; Fleury, 14; [Robert Nelson], *A Companion for the Festivals and Fasts of the Church of England*, 15th edn (London, 1732), 483–5. Later in life Wesley recalled that the Oxford Methodists explicitly fasted 'in imitation of the Primitive Church': Sermon 'Causes of the Inefficacy of Christianity' [1789], *Works*, 4:94.

[102] 'Catalogue of the Library of the Revd John Clayton M.A. Fellow of the Collegiate Church Manchester', Manchester Central Library, MS, BRG 109.2 CLI. The catalogue includes works published in the 1750s, but it may have originated long before this. It contains roughly 1,000 titles, some of which he probably had in Oxford during the 1730s. Many of the books discussed in this chapter are also mentioned in the Oxford Methodist Benjamin Ingham's diary: see the bibliography of his reading in *Diary of an Oxford Methodist Benjamin Ingham, 1733–1734*, ed. Richard P. Heitzenrater (Durham, NC, 1985), appendix 3.

[103] John Clayton to JW (1 August 1732), *Works*, 25:334; *The Diaries of Thomas Wilson, D.D. 1731–37 and 1750*, ed. C. L. S. Linnell (London, 1964), 9 September 1734, p. 119.

The Unity of the 'Holy Catholick Church'

Wesley's 1738 testimony written on his voyage back to England from Georgia is confirmed in his first publication, *A Collection of Forms of Prayer for Every Day in the Week* (1733).[104] The *Collection* follows a similar pattern to one of its sources—Archbishop William Laud's *A Summarie of Devotions* (1667)—with prayers for each day from various writers. Clayton assisted Wesley in preparing this prayer manual, which opens with a preface attesting to Wesley's commitment to interpret scripture 'by keeping close to that Sense of them which the Catholic Fathers and ancient Bishops have deliver'd to succeeding Generations.'[105] In keeping with his desire (shared by many Anglicans) to promote catholic interpretation of scripture, Wesley's prayers contain numerous references to the unity of the church universal. Appropriate to this concern, he refers to the 'Branch' of the 'Holy Catholick Church' 'which Thou hast planted in these Kingdoms.'[106] At the same time, in typical High Church fashion, he pleaded: 'Defend our Church from Schism, Heresy, and Sacrilege, and the King from all Treasons and Conspiracies.' Wesley expressed his ideal of a unified church through the petition, 'May the Church, the Catholick Seminary of divine Love, be protected from all the Powers of Darkness.'[107] The desire for Christian unity is seen in the following prayer extracted with slight modifications from William Laud: 'bless thy holy Catholick Church, and fill it with Truth and Grace; where it is corrupt, purge it; where it is in Error, rectify it; where it is right, confirm it; where it is divided and rent asunder, heal the Breaches thereof.'[108] In accordance with the High Church/Nonjuring tradition, Wesley called for unity through a return to the primitive church: 'Lord, let it be thy good Pleasure to restore to thy Church Catholick, primitive Peace and Purity'; endow the clergy with 'apostolical Graces'; and 'restore to her her ancient Discipline.'[109] However, while in Georgia, Wesley began to have some doubts about the extent of early church unity.[110]

---

[104] The first extant edition was printed in 1738; the manual went through a total of nine editions: Frank Baker, *A Union Catalogue of the Publications of John and Charles Wesley*, 2nd edn (Stone Mountain, GA, 1991); see Wesley's manuscript draft: 'Prayers', MARC, MS Colman Collection 8. In a 14 May 1765 letter, Wesley noted that this was his first publication: JWJ, 21:511; see also Ingham, *Diary*, 287.

[105] Under his name, Clayton's 'Catalogue' lists 'Prayers by him [Clayton] and J. Westley [*sic*] London 1733'.

[106] JW, *A Collection of Forms of Prayer for Every Day in the Week*, 5th edn (Bristol, 1755), iv, 43; cf. Kettlewell's *Practical Believer*, 358.

[107] JW, *Forms of Prayer*, 25 (cf. 62), 20.

[108] JW, *Forms of Prayer*, 33, from Laud, *A Summarie of Devotions* (1667) quoted in Marion J. Hatchett, *Commentary on the American Prayer Book* (New York, 1980), 557.

[109] JW, *Forms of Prayer*, 62, 71.

[110] See 'Wesley's Reflections on the Primitive Councils and Canons' in chapter four and his January 1738 reflection.

Fredrick Hunter has shown that Wesley was well informed of Anglican pro-posals for union with German Lutheranism, Gallican Catholicism, and the Nonjurors' discussions with the Eastern Orthodox Church.[111] Wesley shared the view of contemporary High Churchmen that four steps were required to revive catholic unity. Dissenters must conform to the Church of England; Rome must be reformed from her corruptions; the German Protestant Churches must revive episcopacy; and the Church of England must re-impose her authority and discipline.[112]

The Primitive Christians as a Model for Devotion

The influence of John Clayton on Wesley is clearly discernible, both through Wesley's documentation of his reading in his Oxford diaries and through the presence of the works that influenced him in Clayton's 'Catalogue'.[113] Almost immediately after meeting Clayton in 1732, Wesley began to show an intense interest in the early church in his choice of readings. In June 1732, he read William Cave's *Primitive Christianity*, a call for the revival of early Christianity, which Cave defined in terms of the practical piety embodied by the church of the first three to four centuries. This appears to have been a foundational text for Wesley's adoption of the primitive ideal that encouraged him to delve more deeply into patristic sources. Wesley's enthusiastic response to Cave placed him in a large group of clergy and laity who cited Cave's account as a model by which the Church could be revived. Later in life Wesley continued to draw on Cave for inspiration, as indicated by his publication of Cave's work in his fifty-volume *Christian Library* (1749–55).[114]

With other Oxford Methodists, Wesley subsequently read Anthony Horneck's (1641–97) *A Letter to a Person of Quality, Concerning the Holy Lives of the Primitive Christians* appended to *The Happy Ascetick* (1681).[115] This work

---

[111] Hunter, 21–4. In January 1734, Wesley read the *Confessio Fidei Ecclesiae Orientalis*. This was probably the catechisms of the Orthodox Church published in Greek and Latin in Leipzig (1695). According to Hunter, Wesley would have known of the Orthodox acceptance of the eighty-five *Apostolic Canons* through this reading (p. 32).

[112] Hunter, 29. See Clayton's report of Wesley's thoughts that the church must be preserved from error: Clayton to JW (2 August 1734), *Works*, 25:393.

[113] See the references to Cave, Horneck, and Fleury in Clayton's 'Catalogue' and to Cave and Horneck in Ingham, *Diary*, appendix 3.

[114] John S. Simon has argued that Wesley utilized Cave's work when later forming Methodist societies: *John Wesley and the Methodist Societies* (London, 1923), 105–13.

[115] He also read *The Exercise of Prayer: or, A Help to Devotion Being a Supplement to the Happy Ascetick* (1685) (read March 1733 and February 1735). According to Scott Thomas Kisker, Anthony Horneck's 'Anglican Pietism', influenced by his German Reformed roots, was 'a forerun-ner of Methodism': Scott Thomas Kisker, *Foundation for Revival: Anthony Horneck, the Religious Societies, and the Construction of an Anglican Pietism*, Pietist and Wesleyan Studies, 24 (Lanham, MD, 2008), xxvi.

carried on Cave's programme of upholding the early Christians as a pattern to be restored in the Church and was likewise published in Wesley's *Christian Library*. Another similar work read by Wesley in Georgia was *Les Moeurs des Israelites et des Chretiens* (1681–2), a work of the French Catholic ecclesiastical historian, Claude Fleury (1640–1723), which Wesley later published as *The Manners of the Antient Christians* (1749).[116]

The early and continued influence of these two works on Wesley's view of the primitive Christians makes them informative treatises for understanding the idealistic vision of primitive purity that Wesley imbibed and passed on to the early Methodists. Horneck and especially Fleury presented the primitive Christians as nearly, if not entirely, perfect. They praised the entirety of the primitive church without offering any critique. For Fleury, Christianity 'received its full perfection at the beginning of it.' 'The apostles...were living images of Jesus Christ' and the first Christians provided 'a pattern of the most perfect life.' Horneck was more guarded in his language for fear that some might accuse him of writing a 'Spiritual Romance'; nonetheless he claimed that devotion and holiness was characteristic of the primitive Christians.[117]

A second trait of the primitive church commended by Horneck and Fleury was its unity. According to Horneck, social distinctions were disregarded; they called one another brethren, lived together in intimate community, were entirely orthodox in doctrine, and worshipped together in song and prayer. Similarly, Fleury believed the early church acted in union as one body (an ideal shared by the Methodists), abhorred novelty, avoided disputation, and focused on communal worship and devotion.[118]

Thirdly, the primitive Christians distinguished themselves from the world around them by their unyielding acts of charity. Horneck particularly exalted the work of virgins who cared for unwanted infants, women who cared for the sick, and widows who became deaconesses and devoted their lives to serve the church. Fleury mentioned their care for the poor and the sick, as well as their hospitality.[119]

Lastly, the primitive Christians exuded an all-encompassing spirituality that manifested itself in certain devotional disciplines. Horneck stressed their obedience to their pastors and political rulers, their devaluation of wealth, avoidance of the theatre, and their celebration of sacramental 'Love-Feasts' as well as night vigils. Fleury viewed modesty, seriousness, and pacifism as key disciplines exhibited by the first Christians. Horneck and Fleury shared the

---

[116] Probably first read in April 1736, but certainly read in September of that year: JWD, 24, 25, 27 April 1736, 13 September 1736; see also 28 July 1737 and JWMSJ, 23 October 1737.

[117] Fleury, 2, 6; Horneck, *The Happy Ascetick* (London, 1681), 481, 450.

[118] Horneck, *Happy Ascetick*, 484; 485; 493; 524, 527–8; 500; Fleury, 17–18; 13.

[119] Horneck, *Happy Ascetick*, 485; 497; 499; Fleury, 21–3.

conviction that the earliest Christians lived ascetic lives, fasted on Wednesdays and Fridays, and accepted suffering and persecution with joy.[120]

The works of Horneck and Fleury represent a trans-confessional shared ideal of the primitive church embraced by Wesley. The characteristics of the primitive Christians outlined in their treatises were a model for Wesley's personal spirituality that he later promoted as a prototype for all Methodists.

The *Apostolic Constitutions* and *Canons* and the Apostolic Fathers

In the same month that Wesley read Cave's *Primitive Christianity* (June 1732), the Methodist group that met in Clayton's room began studying the *Apostolic Constitutions* in the second volume of William Whiston's (1667–1752) popular yet controversial *Primitive Christianity Reviv'd* (5 vols, 1711–12), subtitled *The Constitutions of the Holy Apostles, by Clement; in English and in Greek; with the Various Readings from all of the Manuscripts.*[121] Whiston, an anti-Trinitarian, adopted the semi-Arian Christology of the *Constitutions*, and was expelled from the University of Cambridge for heresy in 1710. He had become convinced that the *Apostolic Constitutions* were apostolic and Arian. For the last forty years of his life Whiston was convinced he had a divine calling to restore primitive Christianity. However, his extravagant claims for the *Constitutions* did not win him much support. He dated them to 67 AD and argued that they 'were delivered Personally by our Saviour to the Eleven Apostles, after the Resurrection and first Ascension, during the Forty Days of his continuance with them'. Whiston even claimed that they should be granted the highest authority in the canon of scripture.[122]

Though we do not know whether Wesley read volume three of *Primitive Christianity Reviv'd* with Whiston's detailed account of his views, or to what extent he was aware of the controversy around Whiston's claims, he likely

---

[120] Horneck, *Happy Ascetick*, 495, 526, 534–5; 517; 520–2, 531; Fleury, 13–16, 19–21, 24.

[121] This was the first translation of the *Constitutions* and *Canons* into English. The *Constitutions* had been first translated into Latin in 1563. Work on them by the Catholic scholars Bovius and Francisco Torres ('Turrianus') was partly aimed at using them to combat 'Protestant heresy'. They were known by earlier generations of Anglican scholars but they do not seem to have been widely discussed prior to Whiston and the Nonjurors.

According to Geoffrey Wainwright, the *Constitutions* and *Canons* are also mentioned in Wesley's diary in August 1732, June 1733, and March 1734 and Whiston's *Primitive Christianity Reviv'd* in February and December 1734: ' "Our Elder Brethren Join": The Wesleys' *Hymns on the Lord's Supper* and the Patristic Revival in England', *Proceedings of The Charles Wesley Society*, 1 (1994), 7 n. 9, 11. For rebuttals of Whiston's views, see Richard Smalbroke, *The Pretended Authority of the Clementine Constitutions Confuted* (London, 1714) and Robert Turner, *A Discourse of the Pretended Apostolical Constitutions* (London, 1715). Whilst Smalbroke's dismissal of them was an extreme view, Turner's conclusions align relatively well with those of modern scholars.

[122] Whiston, *Primitive Christianity Reviv'd* (London, 1711), 3:14, 33–4, 72–3.

learned something about this during his meeting with Whiston sometime prior to 1734.[123] While it does not appear that Wesley accepted the more eccentric views of Whiston, all of the core beliefs he adopted regarding primitive Christian faith and practice can be found in this volume.[124]

Wesley came to admire not only the liturgical practice recommended by the *Constitutions* but also the devotional prayers, some of which he included in a manuscript notebook of prayers he collected from various sources.[125] Given that the Methodists encountered the *Apostolic Canons*, which follow the eighth and final book of the *Constitutions* in Whiston's edition, they naturally turned to Beveridge's Latin defence of the *Canons*, which the 'Clayton group' read (perhaps from Clayton's copy of the book) in August 1732.[126] What made Wesley's hermeneutic of the early church different from most High Churchmen was the heavy authority he came to ascribe to the *Apostolic Constitutions* and *Canons*. Wesley's reading of *The Penitential Discipline of the Primitive Church* (1714) by the highly regarded authority on Christian antiquity, Nathaniel Marshall (*c*.1680–1730), reflected his desire to restore the disciplinary fervour of the early church. Marshall proposed the reintroduction of public penance into the Church of England, a practice Wesley may have encouraged in Georgia.[127]

Wesley's study of the Church Fathers focused primarily on the Apostolic Fathers (those who were thought to have been of the generation that had contact with the Apostles) and dated back to his reading and translation of Justin Martyr's *Apology* in November 1726.[128] At about the same time that he read the *Apostolic Constitutions* and Cave's *Primitive Christianity*, Wesley indicated in his diary a desire to translate the 'Patres Apost.' up to the year of 350 and to write on the 'Decreta Concilium'.[129] This task may have been abandoned due to the readily available English translations he subsequently read. His reading included (September 1733) Archbishop William Wake's (1657–1737) *The Genuine Epistles of the Apostolical Fathers, S. Barnabas, S. Ignatius, S. Clement, S. Polycarp, the Shepherd of Hermas, and the martyrdoms of St. Ignatius and St. Polycarp* (1693). Wake stated that this work would show the reader that the Church of England '*in all respects comes the nearest up to the Primitive*

---

[123] See *Memoirs of the Life and Writings of Mr. William Whiston*, 2nd edn (London, 1753), 1:121.
[124] For a summary of these, see Whiston's thirty-five propositions in *Primitive Christianity Reviv'd*, 3:705–18.
[125] 'Prayers', MARC; Heitzenrater, 'John Wesley', 164. This manuscript formed the basis for Wesley's *Forms of Prayer*.
[126] *Codex Canonum Ecclesiae Primitivae Vindicatus ac Illustratus* (London, 1678); Campbell, 28 citing Wesley's Oxford diaries for 8 and 25 August 1732. Wesley reread this work in February 1735.
[127] Read in July 1734; Campbell, 18. See 'Confession and Penance' in chapter four.
[128] See the twenty-five references to Justin in Wesley's Oxford diaries between 20 August and 7 October 1730 (Wainwright, '"Our Elder Brethren Join"', 6 n. 4).
[129] Heitzenrater, 'John Wesley', 161 and 161 n. 2. Wesley may here have been referring to Jean-Baptiste Cotelier's highly regarded *Patres Apostolici*, 2 vols (1672).

Pattern *of any* Christian Church *at this Day in the World*.'[130] The martyrdom of Ignatius and Polycarp, along with the epistles of St Clement, were studied by the Methodists, presumably from Wake's translation.[131] Wesley added to his study (September 1734) William Reeves's (1667–1726) *The Apologies of Justin Martyr, Tertullian, and Minutius Felix, in defence of the Christian Religion, with the Commonitory of Vincentius Lirinensis, Concerning the Primitive Rule of Faith...Together with a Prefatory Dissertation about the Right Use of the Fathers* (2 vols, 1709). The Nonjurors favoured Reeves's text in part due to his high regard for the prized Vincentian Canon, a principle adopted by Wesley as 'a sure rule for interpreting Scripture.'[132] Wesley, in common with his Anglican contemporaries, honoured the Apostolic Fathers for their willingness to die for their faith. On the theme of the primitive martyrs he read Lactantius's *De Mortibus Persecutorum* ('On the Deaths of the Persecutors').[133] Wesley also on occasion read individual works of the Fathers, including the eastern Syriac father Ephraem Syrus, whom he later emphasized 'above all' the Fathers as 'the man of the broken heart.'[134] Wesley read Ephraem's call to repentance and ascetical holy living in a newly published translation: *A Serious Exhortation to Repentance and Sorrow for Sin, and a Strict and Mortified Life* (1731).[135] His continued preference for the Apostolic Fathers was evident in his abridgement of them based on Wake's edition published in the first volume of his *Christian Library* (1749).[136]

The Influence of John Clayton and the Manchester Nonjurors

Wesley had read the works of at least six Nonjurors before he met Clayton.[137] However, the devotional nature of the books he chose reveals that these

---

[130] Wake, *The Genuine Epistles of the Apostolical Fathers...and the martyrdoms of St. Ignatius and St. Polycarp* (London, 1693), vi.

[131] Read March 1734.

[132] JWJ, 25 January 1738; see George Hickes, 'A Letter to the Author', in R[oger] Laurence's *Lay Baptism Invalid*, 2nd edn (London, 1709), no pagination.

[133] Perhaps *A Relation of the Death of the Primitive Persecutors*, ed. Gilbert Burnet, 2nd edn (1713).

[134] JW, *Address to the Clergy* (1756), *Works* (Jackson), 10:484.

[135] All of the works mentioned in this section can be found in Clayton's 'Catalogue' except for the Ephraem title, but Clayton had a copy of Ephraem's works in Greek. Of the books discussed in this section, Ingham read Cave, Beveridge, Reeves, and a work by Ephraem at Oxford: Ingham, *Diary*, appendix 3.

[136] Ted A. Campbell, 'Wesley's Use of the Church Fathers', *Asbury Theological Journal*, 50:2–51:1 (1995–6), 69 n. 15.

[137] Jeremy Collier, George Hickes, Thomas Ken, John Kettlewell, William Law, and Robert Nelson. He read works of other Nonjurors such as Ambrose Bonwicke (the elder), Thomas Deacon, and Charles Leslie after meeting Clayton.

Nonjurors were simply part of his general devotional reading which, on the whole, included a high proportion of High Churchmen. None of the works of the 1717 to 1725 'Pamphlet War' found their way into Wesley's known reading at Oxford.[138] The available evidence does not reveal how much Wesley might have known about the usages controversy and there is no indication of his knowledge of it prior to 1733. Nonetheless, Wesley was familiar with a positive view of the primitive nature of the usages through reading Charles Wheatly's *A Rational Illustration of the Book of Common Prayer of the Church of England* (3rd edn, 1720) in 1731, a book he reread in Georgia.[139] In June 1732, Wesley made a journey to Clayton's native Manchester, where he met Clayton's close friend Thomas Deacon, an Essentialist Nonjuror. In the same month, Wesley encountered Deacon's account of the usages in his *The Doctrine of the Church of Rome Concerning Purgatory*. The Eucharist as an offering or oblation to God of the elements as a commemoration or representation of Christ's sacrifice on the cross was implicitly present in Wesley's 1732 sermon 'The Duty of Constant Communion'.[140] A prayer of oblation and a commitment to praying for the dead appear in Wesley's 1733 *Collection of Forms of Prayer*.[141] His July 1733 letter to John Clayton also reveals that he was determined to communicate at a church that observed the mixture of water and wine in the sacramental cup.[142] As we shall observe in chapter two, these three usages and the invocation of the Holy Spirit on the sacramental elements were explicitly listed as 'a duty to observe' in Wesley's resolutions that were probably written to guide his clerical practice in Georgia.[143]

Three letters from Clayton to Wesley reveal Wesley's increasing zeal for the practices of the primitive church. In these letters Clayton responded to a number of questions Wesley had raised in his letters to Clayton.[144] Clayton's first reply to Wesley came soon after Wesley's June 1733 visit to Manchester, where he met the prominent Nonjurors, Thomas Deacon and John Byrom. It was probably during this visit that Deacon enlisted Wesley to write on the primitive practice of observing the stationary fasts for inclusion in his *Compleat Collection of Devotions*. In his appendix, Deacon published an extract of Wesley's 'Essay Upon the Stationary Fasts' in which Wesley attempted to show 'That the Stations were instituted by the Apostles.'[145] In writing the essay,

---

[138] However, many of these controversialist works are in Clayton's 'Catalogue'.

[139] JWD, 4, 12, 21 May 1737. See chapter six of Wheatly's work on the Lord's Supper.

[140] *Works*, 3:430.

[141] *Forms of Prayer*, 13, 76. The *Prayer*[s] arguably contain a prayer (usually two prayers) for the dead for each day of the week: E. Theodore Carrier, 'Wesley's Views on Prayers for the Dead', *PWHS* 1 (1898), 123–4.

[142] John Clayton to JW ([25] July 1733), *Works*, 25:352.

[143] *Apostolic Constitutions*, Wesley's Chapel, City Road, London, MS, LDWMM/1998/7129.

[144] Wesley's letters to Clayton have not survived.

[145] Deacon, *Devotions*, appendix, 72. The brief extract from Wesley's work can be found on pp. 72–4. An incomplete version of what was probably an earlier draft of this essay entitled 'Of the Weekly Fasts of the Church', can be found in the MARC. The surviving section argues that

Wesley had been assisted by William Whiston.[146] Wesley's studies on the apostolic practice of fasting were a natural outcome of his decision (under the influence of Clayton) in June 1732 to begin fasting on Wednesdays and Fridays until 3 p.m.[147] His 'Essay' also provides clear evidence that he had fully adopted the rule of St Augustine (*'That which is held by the Universal Church, and was not instituted by Councils, but always was, is delivered down from the Apostles'*) and the Vincentian Canon, which he used as his primary justification for the observance of the stations.[148] In the larger context of Wesley's theological interest in the unity of the church, the stations were one aspect of a growing number of devotional and liturgical practices that he believed (along with Deacon) would contribute to catholic unity if revived by the Church of England and all Christians seeking to live holy lives.

In July 1733, Clayton responded to Wesley's 'question about Saturday' by explaining his practice of treating Friday as a fast day in 'preparation for the celebration of both the Sabbath [Saturday] and the Lord's Day [Sunday].' Clayton's practice was to celebrate Saturday with 'festival prayers' at the 'three primitive hours' (9 a.m., noon, and 3 p.m.) and morning and evening prayer taken from the *Apostolic Constitutions*.[149] Wesley had already taken up the practice of praying at the 'three primitive hours' as indicated by one of his 'General Questions' of self-examination aimed at aiding his diary keeping: 'Have I used the Collects at 9, 12, 3?'[150] The *Apostolic Constitutions* (VIII.34; cf. V.14) recommended prayer six times daily, including the third hour (9 a.m.) 'because at that hour the Lord received the sentence of condemnation by Pilate; at the sixth [12], because at that hour He was crucified; at the ninth [3 p.m.], because all things were in commotion at the crucifixion of the Lord.'

In the same letter, Clayton informed Wesley that Deacon could not presently respond to his question about the moral doctrines of the primitive church as his studies had been focused strictly on the worship and discipline of the primitive church. Given Wesley's lifelong concern for social holiness, one wonders if he might have been troubled by Deacon's seeming lack of attention to early Christian ethics. Regarding religious society rules, Deacon and Clayton agreed that 'Observing the stations and weekly communion are duties which stand

---

it is 'Our Duty to obey the Antient Injunctions of the Catholic Church', which includes weekly Wednesday and Friday fasts. Wesley made this argument through his translation of William Beveridge's comment on I Corinthians 11:16 in his *Thesaurus Theologicus*: Campbell, 121; see Campbell's transcription of this document, 122–4.

[146] See Whiston, *Memoirs*, 1:121; cf. *Works*, 25:412 and 412 n.

[147] See JWJ, 123–4 n. 17 and Heitzenrater, 'John Wesley', 163; cf. Wheatly, 201.

[148] Augustine's rule from *De Baptism contra Donatist*, 4.15 was cited by Collier, 19; read by Wesley 16–17 November 1735: JWD.

[149] See Fleury, 8, on early church observance of prayers at the three primitive hours. Clayton may have used the thanksgiving prayers for morning and evening from the *Constitutions* VIII.37–8.

[150] Heitzenrater, *Elusive Mr. Wesley*, 59. He began developing these questions in 1730.

upon a much higher footing than a rule of a society.[151] It is important to note that Wesley was being advised (by respected friends) to place liturgical observance of the ancient church above contemporary Anglican practice. The clear implication of Clayton's letter was that he and Deacon valued ecclesiology over moral theology and communal piety based on religious society rules. Wesley's stress on ecclesiology in Georgia suggests that he took their counsel to heart. However, his continued interest in ethics and religious societies suggests that there were significant areas of differing emphasis between Wesley and Deacon, although these issues did not lead to a disruption of their friendship in the short term.

A few months later, Clayton addressed Wesley's query 'As to reading the ancients' by recommending works that were largely already familiar to him. Clayton recommended Jean-Baptiste Cotelier's edition of the Apostolic Fathers, which includes the *Apostolic Constitutions*, as a starting point and then Beveridge's defence of the *Apostolic Canons*, which also vindicates the Constitutions (*Codex Canonum Ecclesiae Primitivae Vindicatus as Illustratus*).[152] Wesley had already read the latter work (perhaps in Cotelier's appendix) with the Methodist group that met in Clayton's room at Oxford. Two years later Wesley took both of these works to Georgia.[153] Regarding his personal devotions Clayton commented that on Wednesday and Friday he used the devotions for Passion Week out of the Nonjuring Bishop Nathaniel Spinckes's (1654–1727) *Devotions* (1721).[154] The *Devotions* include prayers of the High Churchmen Lancelot Andrewes and William Laud as well as the Nonjurors Thomas Ken (1637–1711), George Hickes, John Kettlewell (1653–95), and Spinckes himself. Prior to this recommendation Wesley had been deeply moved by Spinckes's compilation of devotional prayers, which he had begun 'collecting' in a manuscript notebook that formed the basis of his *Collection of Forms of Prayer*.[155]

Nearly a year later, Wesley was still actively seeking the advice of Clayton and Deacon on matters relating to primitive Christianity and the spiritual

[151] Clayton to JW ([25] July 1733), *Works*, 25:352. See Kisker's *Foundation for Revival* on the religious society movement.
[152] See Jean-Baptiste Cotelier's SS. *Patrum qui temporibus Apostolicis floruerunt: Barnabae, Clementis, Hermae, Ignatii, Polycarpi opera, vera et suppositicia* also titled *Patres Apostolici*, 2 vols (Paris, 1672). Clayton's 'Catalogue' contains the note that Beveridge's tome was appended to Cotelier. The surviving evidence shows that Wesley read Cotelier in October 1736 and Beveridge in August 1732 and February 1735: JWD, 5 October 1736; Campbell, 28.
[153] Cotelier: JWD, 5 October 1736; Beveridge: JWJ and JWMSJ, 20 September 1736.
[154] Clayton to JW (10 September 1733), *Works*, 25:355–6. The devotions for the Passion Week were written by Lancelot Andrewes and can be found on pages 250–63 in the sixth edition of Spinckes's *Devotions* (London, 1731). The fuller title of the work is *The True Church of England-Man's Companion to the Closet: or, A Complete Manual of Private Devotions Fitted for Most Persons and Cases.*
[155] 'Prayers', MARC; October 1732.

life. Regarding the Church Fathers, Clayton recommended in general 'all the Fathers of the three first centuries' in order to avoid 'the monkish mysticism of the fourth century and lukewarm indifferency of the present age'.[156] On the question of how the merits of Christ are applied to the believer through the Eucharist, Clayton recommended a work Wesley had read two years earlier (probably under Clayton's direction): John Johnson's (1662–1725) *The Unbloody Sacrifice* (2 vols, 1714, 1718) 'in that ch[apter] which proves the Holy Eucharist to be a sacrifice both expiatory and propitiatory'.[157] In other words, the Eucharistic sacrifice atones for sin, appeases the wrath of God and restores one to right relationship with God. Clayton went on to reveal his unorthodox belief that by the Eucharist 'alone remission of sins is to be attained.' Wesley seems to have adopted the view that the Eucharist was 'the highest means of grace'; however, it is uncertain whether he believed it was the only means for 'remission of sins'.[158] The letter reveals that he was open to learning how the Nonjurors explained the application of 'the merits of Christ to the receiver' of the sacrament and how it could be justified as 'the only means' for the forgiveness of sins.[159]

In Wesley's correspondence with Clayton, his interest in the application of primitive Christianity was at the forefront of his thoughts. His prime concern with the practice of Christian antiquity was held in common with the Anglican tradition of Cave and Horneck as well as the more narrow tradition of the Nonjurors.[160] Wesley's interest in catholic unity, devotional practice, moral theology, and Eucharistic theology were all aimed at his overarching concern with first understanding and then applying the practices of the primitive church. Georgia became the laboratory where Wesley implemented his vision of primitive Christianity. His reverence for the early church was instilled in him by his parents and mediated to him at Oxford through his study of ancient Christianity inspired by John Clayton and aided by the contemporary revival of patristic scholarship. Wesley's conception of the character and importance of the primitive church reflected the influence of High Church Anglicanism, especially the Usager Nonjurors.

---

[156] Wesley had read the fourth-century monk Ephraem Syrus, whom he would reread in Georgia along with Macarius: August 1732; JWD, 422–49, 405–6. Combined with his later statements of reverence for Ephraem and Macarius as well as John Chrysostom and Basil the Great, this shows that at least in the long run he did not agree with Clayton on this point: Campbell, 'Wesley's Use of the Church Fathers', 61.

[157] June 1732; Clayton's 'Catalogue'; Johnson, 1:284–300. See 'The Influence of the Eucharistic Theology of John Johnson on the Nonjurors and Wesley' in chapter two.

[158] Wesley did connect sacramental observance with the forgiveness of sins: JW to Susanna Wesley [18 June 1725], *Works*, 25:170; 'The Duty of Constant Communion' (1732), *Works*, 3:429. This is supported by the *Apostolic Constitutions* VIII.14 and the 1662 BCP.

[159] Clayton to JW (2 August 1734), *Works*, 25:391–3.

[160] Campbell, 112–13.

2

Primitive Christianity on the *Simmonds*

The voyage of the Methodists to Georgia is significant to the overall study of Wesley's mission to Georgia for several reasons. His conduct on the *Simmonds* (also spelled *Symonds* by contemporaries) provides the first glimpse of how he intended to carry out his ministry in Georgia. At the same time, one can observe and analyse the books he read in order to prepare himself for the work ahead. On-board the *Simmonds*, he readied himself for the Methodist's agreed goal of reviving the discipline and practice of the primitive church in the primitive Georgia wilderness. His churchmanship at this point in his life was firmly rooted in his vision of the primitive church. This chapter continues to lay the foundation for Wesley's time on Georgian soil and examines his ministry on the *Simmonds* in more detail than has hitherto been attempted by his biographers, who have generally emphasized Wesley's introduction to the Moravians above all else.

A rich array of sources written by Wesley provides a substantial amount of evidence regarding his perspective on the Georgia mission. First of all, his diary, which consists largely of short phrases and names indicating how he spent his time and with whom he spent it, provides a key source covering the majority of the mission (17 October 1735 to 31 August 1737). The diary is useful for the amount of information it supplies (typically making it possible to know in a general sense what Wesley did each hour of the day) rather than the detail and depth of its account. The diary also supplies occasional insights into Wesley's thoughts. Fortunately, second, for the period of the Georgia mission Wesley's manuscript journal survives. Third, we have his published *Journal*, which is a revision of the manuscript designed for public consumption. Fourth, like the diaries, his letters, written to address immediate concerns, allow a window into Wesley's thoughts at the time they were written. While both the manuscript journal and published *Journal* contain some significant gaps during the period Wesley was in Georgia, they give a fairly complete account of the voyage, especially when considered together with his diary and letters.[1]

---

[1] The MS journal covers the period from 17 October 1735 to 16 February 1736, followed by a short summary of events between March and July of 1736, continuing with an entry for 26

A well-rounded picture of the voyage from the viewpoint of the Methodists can be gained by reading Benjamin Ingham's journal alongside Wesley's.[2] Although Ingham's account agrees with Wesley's on many details and displays a remarkably similar worldview, it also supplies some additional information and another man's perspective.

A third set of important sources are the diaries of two Moravian passengers, Bishop David Nitschmann and Johann Andrew Dober. These diaries affirm Wesley's keen interest in the Moravian community and his regular attendance at their evening services, as well as the details of significant storms the passengers endured. They also contain the majority of comments we have about the Methodists. Although they say very little save a few remarks about John Wesley, unfortunately we have even less from the English passengers. The only *Simmonds* voyage account by an Englishman apart from Wesley's and Ingham's journals is Francis Moore's, *A Voyage to Georgia* (1744), which adds no new information about the Methodists. Despite the lack of evidence from ordinary colonists, the *Simmonds* voyage was the most thoroughly documented of all journeys to Georgia during the Trustee period.

The departure of James Oglethorpe (1696–1785) and the three clergymen for Georgia was widely noted in the London press.[3] The Oxford Methodists went to the colony as a missionary team. In September 1735, expressly for the Georgia mission, Charles Wesley (1707–1788), twenty-seven years of age, had been successively ordained deacon by the bishop of Oxford, John Potter and priest a week later by the bishop of London, Edmund Gibson. He was officially named 'Secretary of Indian Affairs' to serve as a secretary for the *de facto* governor James Oglethorpe and minister to the colonists in the yet-to-be built town of Frederica, located eighty-five miles south of Savannah and designed to defend the colony against Spanish invasion. Charles's position entailed that he would write letters for Oglethorpe and issue licenses to Indian traders from

---

July and regular account of events between 13 August 1736 and 16 December 1737, with a fairly substantial gap between 23 September and 12 October 1737. The published *Journal* runs from 14 October 1735 to 1 February 1738 and has some significant gaps.

[2] A transcription of Ingham's journal can be found in the MARC Lamplough Collection, 657. This journal contains an undated narrative of the six weeks prior to his departure to Georgia and is loosely dated for the period from 10 October 1735 to 1 May 1736. Another copy of the journal is housed in the Lincoln Cathedral Library (MS 299) and has one entry unique to it. Overall, however, the absence of six entries and several other sentences, phrases, and words from the Lincoln Cathedral copy is the most significant difference between the two manuscripts. The journal has been published based on the Lamplough Collection text, with grammatical alterations and some small omissions of text by Tyerman (see BIJ, 63–80).

[3] See *The London Evening-Post*, 14–16 October 1735; *The Daily Gazetteer*, 15 October 1735; *The Daily Journal*, 15 October 1735; *The Weekly Miscellany*, 18 October 1735; *Read's Weekly Journal, Or, British-Gazetteer*, 18 October 1735; *The Gentleman's Magazine* 5 (October 1735), 617. John Wesley was first introduced to Oglethorpe by his elder brother, Samuel in August 1732: Heitzenrater, 'John Wesley', 174. On the links between Oglethorpe and the Wesley family, see Hammond, appendices 1, 4, and 5.

South Carolina that wanted to ply their trade in Georgia. Benjamin Ingham (1712–72), twenty-three years old, had been ordained deacon by bishop Potter in June 1735 and served as an assistant minister to the Wesley brothers and a teacher to the Yamacraw Indian children.[4] These were joined by a twenty-one-year-old of Huguenot descent, Charles Delamotte (1714–96), John Wesley's friend from London, whom Ingham believed 'had a mind to leave the world, and give himself up entirely to God.'[5] He spent most of his time assisting Wesley and teaching school children in Savannah. At thirty-two years of age, John Wesley went to Georgia as something of an elder brother figure and senior clergyman of the younger Methodists. The four men went to Georgia as 'Volunteer Missionaries' supported by the Trustees and Society for the Promotion of Christian Knowledge (SPCK).[6] John Wesley was appointed and given a license by the Trustees as minister of Savannah.[7] However, he had nearly arrived in Georgia by the time he was approved without consultation as a Society for the Propagation of the Gospel (SPG) missionary.[8] Wesley thought of himself as an independent volunteer missionary.[9] Therefore, it cannot be accurately said that he was an SPG missionary without considerably nuancing this statement.[10]

In accordance with their station, Oglethorpe granted the missionaries two cabins above deck in the forecastle of the ship. The Wesleys shared the larger cabin where the Methodists met, while Ingham and Delamotte occupied a smaller one. Both Wesley and Ingham commented that this arrangement provided them with sufficient privacy to continue their established pattern of ascetical discipline while en route to Georgia.[11] The manner in which the missionaries were accommodated above deck would have clearly demarcated their honoured social standing to the passengers.

The *London Merchant* containing 136 people and the *Simmonds* with 121 passengers set sail together on 21 October 1735. By 1 November the ships had reached the Isle of Wight, where Oglethorpe discovered that the HMS *Hawk*, the naval Man of War being prepared for the journey at Portsmouth, was not yet ready to escort them to Georgia.[12] The *Hawk* was finally ready

[4] On Ingham's experience in Georgia, see John Thomas Scott, ' "Next to Nothing?": Benjamin Ingham's Mission to Georgia', *GHQ* 92 (2008), 287–320.

[5] BIJ, 14 October 1735, p. 68.

[6] Henry Newman to Samuel Quincy (9 October 1735), *Henry Newman's Salzburger Letterbooks*, 178.

[7] *CRG*, 1:234–5.

[8] SPG Journal, 16 January 1736, vol. 6, fo. 305, SPG Archives, Rhodes House Library, Oxford; cf. Wilson, *Diaries*, 16 January 1736, p. 146.

[9] SPG Journal, 21 July 1738, vol. 7, fos 261–2; JW to the SPG [23–6 July 1737], *Works*, 25:516.

[10] For further details, see Hammond, appendix 5.

[11] JWMSJ, 14 October 1735; BIJ, 14 October 1735, p. 68.

[12] Extracts from correspondence of Captain Gascoigne of the *Hawk* have been published in JWJ (Curnock), 8:291–8.

on 19 November, but unfavourable winds did not allow them to sail until 10 December. As it turned out, the wait proved to be unnecessary as they parted from the slow-moving *Hawk* on 12 December.[13] This considerable delay added forty extra days on ship for all passengers and extended the length of voyage to nearly three-and-a-half months. The two months they spent at sea was typical of other journeys to Georgia. In this chapter, the 'voyage' is defined as the four-and-a-half months from Gravesend to permanent settlement in Savannah; therefore, the month between arrival in Georgia and residence in Savannah is included in the analysis. For our purposes, the lengthy journey allows a window from which to observe the Methodists in action.

THE METHODISTS' THEOLOGY AND PRACTICE OF PRIMITIVE CHRISTIANITY ON THE *SIMMONDS*

John Bowmer has accurately stated that 'the voyage to Georgia was simply the Holy Club on-board ship.'[14] Fundamentally, the Georgia mission was a transplantation of Oxford Methodism in the New World. This can be observed in the methodological approach to communal piety shared on the *Simmonds* by the Georgia-bound Methodists. Their decision to adopt a vegetarian diet was an extension of the rigorous fasting Wesley had been observing for several years. Wesley's liturgical doctrine and practice likewise was an expansion of his interest in reviving the primitive church under the influence of the Usager Nonjurors. His reading and preparation were particularly focused on the theology and practice of the sacraments of communion and baptism.[15]

The Devotional Discipline of the Methodists

On the *Simmonds* the missionaries formed a sort of monastic cell modelled upon a vision of imitating the piety of the primitive church. Even before the ship left its moorings, they spent concerted time 'exhorting and encouraging one another' and shared the Lord's Supper amongst themselves.[16] To enforce their togetherness, several common 'vows' were agreed to by all four men. As soon as the *Simmonds* set sail, the missionaries settled on a method of devoting

---

[13] Francis Moore, *A Voyage to Georgia* (London, 1744), 14.
[14] Bowmer, 31; cf. Simon, *John Wesley and the Religious Societies*, 118.
[15] For an overview of Wesley's reading on the *Simmonds*, see Hammond, 114–15.
[16] BIJ, 15–16 October 1735, p. 68. Though Bowmer (p. 31) thought that the Methodists continued the practice of sharing in the Lord's Supper amongst themselves, the evidence is unclear.

their time in common recorded by both Wesley and Ingham. They resolved to rise at 4 a.m. and spend the first hour of the morning in private prayer, the second in Bible study, and the third in reading 'something relating to the Primitive Church.'[17] At seven they breakfasted and at eight had public prayers. From nine to noon they each devoted themselves to different tasks: John Wesley usually studied German; Charles wrote sermons; Ingham instructed the children or continued his study of the primitive church;[18] and Delamotte studied Greek and sometimes navigation. At twelve they joined together for an hour of mutual accountability, prayer, edification, and exhortation. After the one o'clock dinner, they spent time ministering to the passengers, sometimes having religious conversation with them and at other times reading devotional treaties to interested parties. Evening prayer was held at four, where the children were often taught and catechized before the congregation. An hour of private prayer was observed from five to six. From six to seven, John often spent time reading books of devotional divinity to selected passengers. At seven, Ingham took over his role and read and instructed passengers while Wesley attended the Moravian public service of worship. At eight, the missionaries joined together to spend the last hour of their day holding one another accountable for what they had done that day; they discussed how to best minister to certain passengers, and exhorted each other to zealous performance of their religious duties.[19] In his journal, Francis Moore, who became the storekeeper in Frederica, concisely and accurately summed up the Methodists' activities on the *Simmonds* and Oglethorpe's tolerant attitude to religious matters: 'We had Prayers twice a day. The Missionaries expounded the Scriptures, catechized the Children, and administer'd the Sacrament on *Sundays*; but Mr. *Oglethorpe* shew'd no Discountenance to any for being of different Persuasions in Religion.'[20]

In his *Collection of Forms of Prayer*, Wesley urged his readers to adopt resolutions in keeping with their convictions.[21] This feature of Oxford Methodism was very much a part of the Georgia mission. During the layover on the Isle of Wight, the missionaries, after a long walk involving lengthy discussion, adopted the following written resolutions recorded by Ingham:

In the name of God, Amen.

We whose names are here underwritten, being fully convinced, that, it is impossible, either to promote the work of God among the heathen without an entire

[17] Ingham noted that he and John Wesley read the whole of the Old Testament during the journey: BIJ, 18 October 1735, p. 68.

[18] He noted there were about twelve children he instructed and catechized: BIJ, 20 October 1735, p. 69.

[19] BIJ, 21 October 1735, p. 69; JWJ and JWMSJ, 21 October 1735.

[20] Moore, *Voyage to Georgia*, 14–15.

[21] *Forms of Prayer*, v. The adoption of resolutions was a common feature stressed by some of Wesley's favourite authors. See William Beveridge, *Private Thoughts upon Religion, Digested into Twelve Articles, with Practical Resolutions form'd Thereupon* (1709), read November 1731.

union amongst ourselves; or, that, such an union should subsist unless each one will give up his single judgment to that of the majority, do agree, by the help of God:

First.   That none of us will undertake anything of importance without first proposing it to the other three.

Second. That, whenever our judgments or inclinations differ, any one shall give up his single judgment or inclination to the others.

Third.   That, in case of an equality, after begging God's direction, the matter shall be decided by Lot.[22]

Ingham also recorded the following resolution not mentioned in Wesley's journals or diary: 'If anyone upon being reproved, or upon any other occasion, shall feel any sort or degree of anger or resentment, he shall immediately, or at the next meeting, frankly and fully confess it.'[23] The obvious assumption with acting in common and discussing all important decisions together was that holiness could best be achieved in community rather than through lone individual endeavours. This, of course, represents an extension of the ideals of Oxford Methodism to the Georgia mission. Mutually binding accountability was the cornerstone of these resolutions and likely seen as a method to emulate the unity of the primitive church.[24] The latter resolution shows that differing opinions existed and that disagreements were to be confessed openly. The practice of resorting to sortilege (drawing lots) when there was disagreement was thought to leave the decision in the trust of God's providential care.[25]

While corporate holiness was central to Wesley's vision for embodying the spirit and practice of the primitive church, he also sought to cultivate holy living through personal resolutions designed to excite himself to strive after God more fervently. Throughout the voyage we find in his diary a series of resolutions: 'Resolved on more self-denial'; 'Resolved: To be more zealous and active'; 'Resolved: Not to please myself in eating or drinking'; 'Resolved not to praise myself'; 'Resolved: to follow Christ'.[26] None of these resolutions come as a surprise considering the influences that were weighing on Wesley's life at the time. He was reading William Law, who stressed self-denial and separation from the world as the foundation of the Christian faith. Likewise, he reread his recently published edition of Thomas à Kempis's *The Christian's Pattern; Or, a*

---

[22] BIJ, 3 November 1735, p. 70. Wesley's diary for this date records about four hours of 'very pleasant' religious conversation and under the heading of 'Providence' that he 'Agreed with Charles, etc.' For an example of this resolution in action, see JWJ, 7 October 1737.

[23] BIJ, 1 December 1735, p. 71.

[24] See the descriptions of Horneck (*Happy Ascetick*, 484–5) and Fleury (p. 17) on early church unity.

[25] Although Wesley's biographers have often claimed that the Moravians introduced him to the practice of casting lots, he had used this ritual at Oxford: Heitzenrater, *Wesley and the People Called Methodists*, 59–60. See 4 March 1737 in JWMSJ for his use of drawing lots in Georgia and JWJ, 221–2 n. 8 on his use of sortilege.

[26] 19 December 1735, 8, 17, 18 January, 8 February 1736.

Treatise on the Imitation of Christ (1735) that continued to inspire him to see the imitation of Christ as the goal of Christian spirituality.[27] 'Lively zeal' was a description Wesley used in his diary to express satisfaction with himself, but these resolutions show that he clearly felt he was often not zealous enough, as on 10 February 1736, which he characterized as 'A poor, careless, lukewarm day.' Occasional setbacks did not cause Wesley to waver from his determination to strive for Christian perfection.

Asceticism: Vegetarianism, Fasting, and Apostolic Poverty

Because of the prevalence of asceticism in the early church, Anglican advocates of primitive Christianity often stressed the restoration of ascetical spirituality—a controversial topic in the post-Restoration Church.[28] The asceticism of the Oxford Methodists was fully maintained during the Georgia mission. For several years Wesley's rule of acting had been to embrace Christian disciplines that did him good and reject any activities that did him harm.[29] In agreement with their resolution to share devotional practices in common, the Wesley brothers along with Ingham and Delamotte gave up the use of meat and wine and later gave up eating supper (the evening meal) while en route to Georgia.[30] Vegetarianism and fasting were two ascetical practices adopted by the Methodists and seen by them to complement their Nonjuror-inspired liturgical practice and rigorous discipline of study, prayer, worship, teaching, and preaching.[31] Such practices of denying bodily pleasures were seen by the Methodists (as in Orthodox and Catholic monastic traditions) as providing an avenue for opening one's inner self to God's direction. It may not have been a coincidence that Wesley's resolution to adopt a vegetarian diet was entered into his diary on a day when he read *The Life of Francis Xavier*, a Jesuit missionary known for his occasional vegetarianism and rigorous fasting.[32] It is also possible that Wesley deepened his desire to adopt a vegetarian diet and live a more rigorously ascetic life by giving up supper through reading the

---

[27] On the influence of à Kempis on Wesley, see Geordan Hammond, 'John Wesley and "Imitating" Christ', *Wesleyan Theological Journal*, 45 (2010), 197–212.

[28] Apetrei, '"The Life of Angels"'.

[29] JW to Samuel Wesley, Jr (17 November 1731), *Works*, 25:322.

[30] JWJ, JWMSJ, and JWD, 20 October 1735; JWJ, JWMSJ, JWD, 7 December 1735; BIJ, 7 December 1735, p. 71. For Wesley's views on diet and fasting within the context of eighteenth-century Methodism, see Charles Wallace, 'Eating and Drinking with John Wesley: The Logic of his Practice', in Jeremy Gregory (ed.), *John Wesley: Tercentenary Essays, BJRL* 85.2–3 (2003), 137–55.

[31] It appears that there was discussion in England during the Georgia mission that the 'Methodists' fasted and were vegetarians: JW to Lady Cox [7 March 1738], *Works*, 25:532 n. 2.

[32] JWD, JWJ, and JWMSJ, 20 October 1735.

Life of Gregory Lopez, which was first mentioned in his diary eight days after he read Xavier.[33] Undoubtedly, another (possibly subsequent) influence was Claude Fleury's *Manners of the Ancient Christians*, which he probably first read in April 1736. Fleury outlined an inspirational account of the 'plain and frugal' eating habits and the unified practice of Wednesday and Friday fasting in the early church that supported the steps already taken by the Oxford Methodists and the missionaries to Georgia.[34] While the importance of the Christian discipline of fasting as modelled by the primitive church was Wesley's key motivation for fasting, he had found modern support for eating a minimal amount of meat and, in general, simplicity in diet from Dr George Cheyne's *An Essay of Health and Long Life* (1724) over a decade earlier and this became a popular text amongst the Oxford Methodists.[35]

According to Claude Fleury, Jesus lived 'in great poverty' and Anthony Horneck claimed that the primitive Christians 'loved' poverty and saw it 'as a Companion, and a Friend.'[36] Wesley's letters to his friend John Burton (1696–1771), fellow of Corpus Christi, Oxford and member of the Georgia Trustees, and to the SPG make it perfectly clear that he was eager to abandon worldly goods and be content with nothing but 'food to eat and raiment to put on.'[37] Wesley initially determined to receive no salary for his clerical duties so that he would shun 'worldly desires and worldly cares.'[38] He expressed his opinion to Burton (by paraphrasing I Timothy 6:8–9) that if anyone even desired an overabundance of these basic necessities, 'the greatest blessing that could possibly befall him is to be cut off from all occasions of gratifying those desires, which, unless speedily rooted out, will drown his soul in everlasting perdition.'[39] Wesley's multifaceted asceticism included the desire to emulate the poverty of Christ and the early church. His determination in this regard can be seen in his note on the second lesson for the first Sunday he preached in Savannah. He interpreted Luke 18:29–30 in the tradition of St Francis of Assisi as Christ's 'gracious promise to those who are content *nudi nudum Christum sequi*' ('naked to follow a naked Christ').[40]

---

[33] It was said of López, 'He never tasted flesh; and when any happened to be given him, he received it with thanks, but touched it not': Francisco de Losa, *The Life of Gregory Lopez*, ed. JW, in *A Christian Library* (London, 1826), 27:392.

[34] Fleury, 14.

[35] JW to Susanna Wesley (1 November 1724), *Works*, 25:151; Clayton's 'Catalogue'; Ingham, *Diary*, appendix 3. Wesley later cited this work in the preface to his *Primitive Physic* (1747).

[36] Fleury, 4; Horneck, *Happy Ascetick*, 512.

[37] I Timothy 6:8; cf. Genesis 28:20, Matthew 6:25, Luke 12:23, John 6:27; *Forms of Prayer*, 22, 50, 57; William Law, *A Practical Treatise upon Christian Perfection* (London, 1726), 77, 129; William Law, *A Serious Call to a Devout and Holy Life* (London, 1729), 178. There were some reports circulating at about this time that the 'Methodists' required 'voluntary poverty in their members': JW to Lady Cox [7 March 1738], *Works*, 25:532.

[38] JW to the SPG [23–6 July 1737], *Works*, 25:516.

[39] JW to Burton (10 October 1735), *Works*, 25:442.

[40] JWJ, 7 March 1736. In his note on this passage, Ward pointed out that a similar phrase occurs in Wesley's edition of à Kempis (III.xxxvii.3). Ted A. Campbell has shown that John and Charles Wesley embodied the three strands of the medieval mendicant understanding of the poor

WESLEY'S EUCHARISTIC DOCTRINE AND
PRACTICE

Liturgical practice based on primitive church doctrine and liturgy was a central aspect of Wesley's programme to revive primitive Christianity in Georgia. Wesley's baptismal and Eucharistic practice was definitively shaped by his historical and theological views of the early church, which were primarily mediated to him by High Church and Nonjuring interpreters. The following sections examine Wesley's liturgical interests, including the Eucharist and baptism, before further considering his interest in devotional practice as a related and complementary aspect of his vision of primitive Christianity. Every work mentioned in the following sections that Wesley read on Holy Communion and baptism can be found in John Clayton's 'Catalogue', which strongly suggests that his influence continued to weigh heavily on Wesley.

The Influence of the Eucharistic Theology of John Johnson on the Nonjurors and Wesley

W. Jardine Grisbrooke has persuasively shown that Anglican Eucharistic liturgies of the seventeenth and eighteenth centuries were 'based upon that characteristic "appeal to the primitive Church" which was both the foundation, and dominant note of "high" Anglican faith and worship.'[41] As High Churchmen departed from the Anglican reformers on the doctrine of episcopacy and apostolic succession, they also developed 'a eucharistic theology which was at variance with, though not in absolute contradiction' to Cranmer's theology and the liturgy of the 1662 Book of Common Prayer.[42]

Wesley's reading, practice, and network of friends at Oxford from 1732 conclusively demonstrate his deep interest in Eucharistic liturgy and place him within this central stream of high Anglican piety. His thoughts on the Eucharist were fundamentally shaped during his latter years at Oxford by Clayton and the Nonjurors. The Eucharistic theology of the Nonjurors was profoundly influenced by John Johnson's *Unbloody Sacrifice* and differed little from that of mature high Anglicanism.[43] Like the Nonjurors, Johnson laid

in varying degrees: 'The Image of Christ in the Poor: On the Medieval Roots of the Wesleys' Ministry to the Poor', in Richard P. Heitzenrater (ed.), *The Poor and the People Called Methodists 1729–1999* (Nashville, 2002), 39–57.

[41] Grisbrooke, xiv.

[42] Byron D. Stuhlman, *Eucharistic Celebration 1789–1989* (New York, 1988), 11, quoted in Peter M. Doll, '"The Reverence of God's House": The Temple of Solomon and the Architectural Setting for the "Unbloody Sacrifice"', in Peter M. Doll (ed.), *Anglicanism and Orthodoxy 300 Years After the 'Greek College' in Oxford* (Oxford, 2006), 201.

[43] Grisbrooke, 71. Hymn VI in Charles Wesley's *Hymns for Our Lord's Resurrection* (1746) includes a reference to 'The great Unbloody Sacrifice'. He also referred to 'the unbloody

stress on the Clementine liturgy as being the most primitive Eucharistic liturgy in existence.[44] In 1732, Wesley read Johnson's earlier work, *The Propitiatory Oblation in the Holy Eucharist Truly Stated, and Defended, from Scripture, Antiquity, and the Communion-service of the Church of England* (1710) and *A Collection of Discourses, Dissertations, and Sermons* (2 vols, 1728), the first volume of which largely consists of Johnson's *The Primitive Communicant: In Three Discourses on the Sacrament of the Eucharist. In which the Sacrifice of Christ and of the Church are Fully Explain'd. With Devotions for the Altar.*[45] In the manuscript notebook containing his Georgia diary from 13 February to 31 August 1737, Wesley transcribed the first twenty sections (pages 3–29) of *The Primitive Communicant*, indicating the profound impression Johnson's view of the Eucharist as a sacrifice had on Wesley.[46] Wesley's reading of Johnson at Oxford was followed up by his study of Johnson's *magnum opus, The Unbloody Sacrifice*, on the *Simmonds*, to which he devoted a significant number of hours between 24 November and 24 December 1735, suggesting that he read the almost 1,000-page two-volume work thoroughly.

A short summary of Johnson's *Unbloody Sacrifice* will be given as essential context for Wesley's 'high' view of the Eucharist.[47] Johnson, who was vicar of Cranbrook in Kent, set out to show that the Eucharist properly understood is a sacrifice offered to God. To combat his concern that the Eucharist was commonly considered to be only a verbal, mental, or figurative sacrifice, he argued in contrast to over-spiritualizing tendencies that it was both spiritual and real.[48] He defined sacrifice as a material offering in continuity with sacrificial offerings of the nation of Israel as described in the Old Testament, which always contained a material element.[49] However, Johnson was careful to downplay the material aspect in the sense that 'Whatever Power or Efficacy is ascribed to the Eucharist, flows wholly from the Original Sacrifice' of Christ.[50]

Sacrifice' in an undated manuscript 'On a Weekly Sacrament' (Bowmer, 226). However, the Wesleys' *Hymns on the Lord's Supper* (1745) emphasize the 'bloody sacrifice' (hymns 52, 119). The *Apostolic Constitutions* (VIII.5) also use the term, which was commonly used in ancient Eastern Eucharistic liturgies from the late second century. Though rarely used in the Western Church, it appeared in the writings of some Anglican reformers and in the Eucharistic liturgies of Jeremy Taylor, Edward Stephens, and the Nonjuror *Communion Office*: Kenneth Stevenson, '"The Unbloody Sacrifice": The Origins and Development of a Description of the Eucharist', in Gerard Austin (ed.), *Fountain of Life: In Memory of Niels K. Rasmussen, O.P.* (Washington, D.C., 1991), 105–19; cf. Doll, '"Reverence of God's House"', 195, 207 n.32. Wesley read Jeremy Taylor's *The Worthy Communicant* (London, 1660) in September 1733, which refers to the sacrifice of Christ that 'bleeds no more' (p. 55).

[44] Johnson, 1:xlii–xliii, 40.
[45] *The Primitive Communicant* was later published separately in a second edition in Manchester in 1738.
[46] MARC, MS Colman Collection 12.
[47] I am indebted to Grisbrooke's concise and useful summary of Johnson (Grisbrooke, 72–87).
[48] Johnson, 1:lii; Stevenson '"The Unbloody Sacrifice"', 118.
[49] Johnson, 1:4.
[50] Johnson, 1:292.

Here he comes close to the doctrine of *instrumental causality*, which defines the elements not as the causes of the grace conferred, but as the instruments by which grace is imparted.[51] Johnson's emphasis differs somewhat from the prayer book stress on the communicants' 'sacrifice of praise and thanksgiving' and offering of him or her self to God.

Building on his Christ-centred interpretation of sacrifice, Johnson made it clear that while the bread and wine are not transformed into the body and blood in substance, they are Christ's *representative* body and blood 'in mystery and inward power' or in 'power and effect'.[52] Therefore, Johnson maintained a strong view of the presence of Christ in the Eucharistic celebration through the language of representation.[53] Theologians have labelled this as the doctrine of *transignification*, a concept which holds that while Christ is not locally present at the Eucharistic celebration, he is nonetheless personally present, which is sometimes explained as a 'pneumatic' presence. The meaning or significance of the bread and wine change so that while the actual substance of the elements remain, they express the presence of Christ.[54]

Johnson also upheld the presence of Christ through the language of *virtue*.[55] He often refers to Christ's presence in 'power and virtue' or 'virtue and effect'.[56] In theological terms this has come to be known as *virtualism*; a concept similar to instrumental causality and transignification, which defines the change in the elements as spiritual rather than in substance so that the faithful communicant receives the virtue of Christ's body and blood.

Johnson wrote of the Eucharist 'as the main Channel' for receiving the blessings of God's grace.[57] He followed the liturgy of the *Apostolic Constitutions* (VIII.12) in his assertion that the elements become an effective channel of God's grace by the agency of the Holy Spirit through a threefold process of consecration performed in the following order: '1. The Reciting the Words of Institution. 2. The Oblation [or offering] of the symbols. 3. The Prayer of Invocation.'[58] Johnson's emphasis was squarely on threefold consecration as the effective cause of Christ's presence, although the benefits of the Eucharist are received in proportion to the faith of the communicant.[59] Therefore,

---

[51] William Crockett, 'Holy Communion', in *The Study of Anglicanism*, 310.

[52] Johnson, 2:60; 1:141, 177.

[53] Johnson, 1:27, 31, 147, 151, 158, 159, 179, 239, 317, 355, 356, 2:xviii.

[54] Johnson, 1:lx, 158, 212, 257, 346, 355, 2:11.

[55] This technical term is also later found in the Wesleys' *Hymns on the Lord's Supper* (1745). See, for example, hymn 57.

[56] Johnson, 1:159, 184, 201, 223, 225, 351, 397, 2:29, 45, 171.

[57] Johnson, 2:150; cf. 1:183, 252, 2:28. Wesley later wrote that the Lord's Supper was the 'grand channel' for the conveyance of God's grace and the 'ordinary channels' were prayer, scripture, and the Lord's Supper: Sermons 'Upon our Lord's Sermon on the Mount: Discourse the Sixth' (1748) and 'The Means of Grace' (1746), *Works*, 1:585, 381.

[58] Johnson, 1:234; cf. Brett, *Collection of the Principal Liturgies*, 382–3.

[59] Johnson, 1:213, 348; see Johnson's emphasis on worthy reception, 2:225–48.

Johnson believed that consecration effected an objectively real presence of Christ, and, therefore, he did not teach a 'receptionist' doctrine since he maintained consecration was permanent.[60] Johnson specified that there were six essential liturgical components in celebrating the Eucharist; these include: the use of bread and wine; saying the words of institution; breaking the bread and pouring the wine; offering the bread and wine to God in 'Commemoration of Christ's Death, Resurrection, and Ascension'; the prayer of invocation of the Holy Spirit on the elements; and intercessory prayer for the whole church. The absence of any of these six rites makes the Eucharist 'defective and imperfect'. Johnson took the view derived from St Cyprian that schism and heresy invalidate the Eucharist. This led him to insist that Dissenters could not validly offer the Eucharist.[61]

In preparing the 1718 Nonjuror *Communion Office*, Thomas Brett noted that he and his colleagues came to the conviction that significant revisions to the 1549 prayer book were necessary. In the 1549 book the order is invocation, institution, and oblation; the Usagers determined that the ancient liturgies (with the exception of St Mark, the Ethiopian, and the Roman) including the Clementine were unanimous that the order should be institution, oblation, and invocation.[62] In their conception of a threefold process of consecration, the authors of the 1718 rite followed Johnson.[63] As far as Brett was concerned, matters were made much worse when the authors of the 1552 prayer book eliminated the prayer of invocation and moved the prayer of oblation to post-communion, changes maintained in the 1662 book.[64] The prayer book revisions suggested that consecration of the elements takes place during the recitation of the words of institution rather than by the invocation of the Holy Spirit. This matched the contemporary understanding of the Roman Catholic Church, whereas the Nonjurors' position came close to the Orthodox Church in their insistence that consecration was effected by the Holy Spirit through the prayer of invocation. As we shall see, it is probable that Wesley's comment that he 'Revised [the] Common Prayer book' in preparation for his ministry in Georgia indicates that he adopted the position that the primitive threefold order of consecration was essential.[65]

In sum, the majority of eighteenth-century Anglicans held closely to the theology of the 1662 prayer book, which they interpreted as promoting 'a

---

[60] Richard F. Buxton, *Eucharist and Institution Narrative: A Study in the Roman and Anglican Traditions of Consecration of the Eucharist from the Eighth to the Twentieth Centuries* (Great Wakering, 1976), 170. See the discussion of receptionism in 'Daniel Brevint's *Christian Sacrament and Sacrifice*' in this chapter.

[61] Johnson, 2:175–81; 2:175; 2:185–90.

[62] Grisbrooke, 96–7.

[63] Buxton, *Eucharist and Institution Narrative*, 180, 183. Their view of 'eucharistic presence' was also identical to Johnson's: Buxton, *Eucharist and Institution Narrative*, 187.

[64] Grisbrooke, 110.

[65] JWD, 5 March 1736.

memoralist doctrine of the eucharistic sacrifice, a real receptionist view of the presence, and a belief that the consecration of the elements was effected by prayer, a prayer that must include the institution narrative.[66] During his last few years at Oxford and in Georgia, Wesley held to the minority view in the Church of England that espoused:

> Firstly, a belief in the eucharistic sacrifice as a real, objective, and effectual Godward pleading of Christ's sacrificial offering of himself on Calvary (with which offering some would have wished to link the Last Supper). Secondly, a belief in a permanent and objective real presence, expressed by saying that by the action of the Holy Spirit, the bread and wine become in power, virtue, and effect the body and blood of Christ. Thirdly, a doctrine of consecration that was quite specific in regarding the Holy Spirit as the agent of consecration, combined with a belief that the institution narrative-oblation-epiclesis sequence was the necessary and essential liturgical material by which consecration was effected.[67]

Thomas Deacon's *Devotions* and Wesley's Resolutions

Given the pervasive influence of Thomas Deacon's thought on Wesley, it is no surprise that Deacon was the first author he read upon boarding the *Simmonds*. In fact, he (and Ingham) had already read Deacon's *Devotions* soon after it was published in the previous year.[68] And here he took up the same work again, which he read on each of the first nine days on the vessel 'with Delamotte, etc', presumably intending the etcetera to include his brother and Ingham.[69] On two of the days he mentioned reading 'Common Prayer' with Deacon, perhaps foreshadowing his revision of the prayer book upon his arrival in Georgia—a task that seems to have been intended to align the prayer book with Deacon's liturgy.[70]

On the day following his ninth consecutive day reading Deacon, Wesley noted that he 'thought' and then 'read resolutions'. This might be a reference to a document probably written on the voyage to Georgia in which he wrote out the liturgical practices he intended to observe in the colony.[71] These practices,

---

[66] Buxton, *Eucharist and Institution Narrative*, 192.

[67] Buxton, *Eucharist and Institution Narrative*, 193.

[68] May 1734; John Clayton to JW (2 August 1734), *Works*, 25:391–3. Wainwright also cites references to the *Devotions* in Wesley's diary for 7 September and 24 October 1734: ' "Our Elder Brethren Join" ', 7, n. 10; Ingham, *Diary*, appendix 3.

[69] JWD, 17–25 October 1735; cf. 8 November 1735; 'with Delamotte, etc': 17 October 1735.

[70] JWD, 24–5 October 1735; JWD, 5 March 1736. It is possible that Wesley intended to refer to Deacon's *The Order of the Divine Offices of the Orthodox British Church* (1734), an enlarged issue of his *Devotions*, which includes 'The Collects, Epistles and Gospels, to be used throughout the Year' and the Psalter from the BCP. However, two of the diary entries, which read 'Deacon and Common Prayer', seem to indicate two separate works and hence refer to Wesley's comparison of the two.

[71] JWD, 26 October 1735. The entry 'Read resolutions to Charles, etc.' could also be a reference to this document (JWD, 20 January 1736); Baker, *John Wesley*, 40.

which Wesley had given much thought to, represent what he believed to be genuine apostolic practice. It is probable that all four Methodists agreed together to follow the liturgical practices laid out in Wesley's manuscript.[72] Wesley's resolutions are here reproduced, followed by comments on them. (In the manuscript, a line is drawn through the words that are enclosed in brackets. The words in brackets that are italicized are my own additions for clarification.)[73]

I believe [myself] it a duty to observe, so far as I can [without breaking communion with my own church]:

1. To baptize by [*trine*] immersion.
2. To use Water [*mixed with wine*], Oblation of Elements [*i.e. present the elements as a sacrificial offering*], Alms, a Prothesis [*a table for preparation of the elements*], Invocation [*of the Holy Spirit on the elements*] in the Eucharist.
3. To pray for the Faithful Departed.
4. To pray standing on Sunday and in Pentecost.
5. To observe Saturday and Sunday Pentecost as festival.
6. To abstain from Blood, things strangled.

I think it prudent (our own Church not considered):

1. To observe the Stations [*i.e. stationary fasts*].
2. Lent, especially the Holy Week.
3. To turn to the East at the Creed.

As the following comments will show, these resolutions were drawn primarily from the *Apostolic Constitutions* and *Canons*, the Book of Common Prayer, and Deacon's *Devotions*. Support can also be found for most of them in Charles Wheatly's 'definitive liturgical commentary', *A Rational Illustration of the Book of Common Prayer*, showing they were broadly in line with common High Church concerns.[74] In addition to his reading of Deacon, Wesley

---

[72] This manuscript, catalogued LDWMM/1998/7129, is housed at Wesley's Chapel, City Road, London. It consists of a single sheet of paper folded in half to make four sheets. Pages one (in Latin) and two contain notes on the *Apostolic Canons*, which Hunter has shown were drawn from pages 9–55 and 58–99, respectively of William Beveridge's *Codex Canonum Ecclesiae Primitivae*: 'Wesley: Separatist or Searcher for Unity?' *PWHS* 38 (1972), 166. The third page contains the liturgical practices discussed later. On page four there is a list of names of members of a Methodist society(s). Based on the evidence provided by page four, R. Denny Urlin concluded that the manuscript was written just before or after 1741 and J. Ernest Rattenbury accepted this assessment: Urlin, *Churchman's Life of Wesley*, 67; Rattenbury, *The Conversion of the Wesleys: A Critical Study* (London, 1938), 223. Subsequently, Bowmer stated that it may date from 1736 or earlier; Heitzenrater agreed: 'John Wesley', 152 n.1; Outler, (*John Wesley*, 12–13 n. 42), concluded that its contents fit best with the Georgia period; Hunter dated it 1736 (p. 53); and Baker suggested it was penned sometime in the period 1735–6: *John Wesley*, 350 n. 10. It would seem that page three fits closely with Wesley's clerical preparation carried out on the *Simmonds*, while pages one and two almost certainly relate to his September 1736 re-evaluation of the *Canons*. Pages two and three have been reproduced by Bowmer (pp. 235–6), who also gives a useful history of the manuscript (pp. 233–5).

[73] A second related manuscript sheet containing notes on the *Apostolic Canons* is discussed in 'Wesley's Reflections on the Primitive Councils and Canons' in chapter 4.

[74] Doll, '"Reverence of God's House"', 198; cf. Doll, 'Architectural Expression', 287.

studied *Reasons for Restoring some Prayers and Directions: as they Stand in the Communion-Service of the First English Reform'd Liturgy* (1717), a work of the late Usager Bishop Jeremy Collier, the clergyman that had ordained Deacon in both deacon's and priest's orders.[75] Collier's treatise provides additional evidence for interpreting Wesley's liturgical thinking.

> 'I believe [myself] it a duty to observe, so far as I can [without breaking communion with my own church]':

> '**To baptize by [*trine*] immersion**' (Canon 50; 1549 BCP; Deacon, 111, 125).

See 'Wesley's Baptismal Doctrine and Practice' in this chapter and 'Resolutions Relating to Baptismal Practice' in chapter 4.

> '**To use Water [*mixed with wine*]**' (*Constitutions* VIII.12; 1549 BCP; Deacon, 85, 92, 318).

Wesley's reading of the Fathers would have made him aware of several streams of patristic interpretation of the mixed chalice; the first, used by Justin Martyr, Irenaeus, and Cyprian, links the mixture with the forgiveness of believers' sins through the redeeming blood of Christ.[76] Cyprian also saw it as symbolizing the unity of Christ and the Church.[77] Wesley's favoured interpretation employed by Ambrose seems to have been the symbolic reminder of the biblical testimony to the blood and water that flowed from the side of the wounded Christ.[78] Nonjurors commonly believed that the mixture was a Jewish custom and the *Constitutions* (VIII.12) claim that it was instituted by Christ himself at his Last Supper with his disciples. The use of the mixture was part of 'The Supper of the Lord and the Holy Communion Commonly Called the Mass' in the 1549 prayer book, but was omitted from the 1552 and 1662 books. In July 1733, Wesley had written to Clayton for advice on the 'mixture.' Clayton assured him that Jonathan Colley, chaplain of Christ Church, had agreed always to use the mixture at Christ Church. Clayton believed that while one should make an effort to communicate where the mixture was used, having no access to it was not a reason to neglect the sacrament.[79] Wesley probably continued this usage long after the Georgia mission if his 1749 defence of the mixture (citing Irenaeus, Cyprian, and Justin Martyr) in his *A Letter to the Reverend Dr. Conyers Middleton* is indicative of his own practice.[80]

[75] JWD, 16–17 November 1735. Since the diary entry simply cites 'Collier's *Reasons*', it is possible (but less likely) that he was referring to *A Defence of the Reasons for Restoring some Prayers and Directions of King Edward the Sixth's First Liturgy* (1717). Collier was ordained a bishop in the Nonjuror line in 1713 by George Hickes.

[76] Cave cites these three authors in support of the practice in his *Primitive Christianity: Christian Library*, ed. JW, 31:223 (Bristol, 1753).

[77] Wheatly, 279.

[78] Wainwright, '"Our Elder Brethren Join"', 9; Collier, 7; John 19:35; cf. I John 5:6–8.

[79] Clayton to Wesley ([25] July 1733), *Works*, 25:352. According to Bowmer this was a rare practice in the eighteenth century (p. 9).

[80] *Works* (Jackson), 10:8–9, 48.

'Oblation of Elements [*i.e. present the elements as a sacrificial offering*]'
(*Constitutions* II.52, VIII.13; 1549, 1552 and 1662 (post-communion) BCP;
Deacon, 97).

The *Constitutions* frequently call the Eucharist a sacrifice (e.g. II.57, VIII.12)
in the sense that the elements are an offering to God. Collier argued that the
offering of the wine and bread is implied in I Corinthians 10:21 and makes
the Eucharist 'a proper sacrifice.'[81] Deacon's Eucharistic rite instructs the priest
after having broken the bread placed on the altar '*to lift up his hands and eyes
to heaven,* [and say] we Offer to thee our King and our God, according to his
Institution, *And here to point with his right hand to all* this Bread and *here to
point with his left hand to the cup and every vessel on the Altar, in which there is
any wine and water*, this Cup . . .'[82] The fourth *Apostolic Canon* and Deacon also
term material offerings of congregants 'oblations.'[83]

'Alms' (*Constitutions* III.13, 14, IV.3, VII.12, VIII.10; BCP; Deacon, 84, cf. on alms
in general: xxxi, 18, 258, 304).

The *Constitutions* call on the faithful to willingly give alms to the poor and
widows and for the recipients of charity to repay their benefactors by praying
for them. According to the prayer book and Deacon's liturgy, the people are to
give 'free-will offerings' before receiving the Eucharist; this practice was maintained in early Methodism.[84]

'a Prothesis [*a table for preparation of the elements*]' (*Constitutions* VIII.12, BCP;
Deacon, 74, 85).

The use of a prothesis is characteristic of the Orthodox Church practice of
preparing the elements on a table set aside for that purpose before the Divine
Liturgy is celebrated. Deacon's liturgy calls for the deacon to prepare the elements in advance and to place them on a prothesis and cover them with a 'fair
white linen cloth' in preparation for the communion service.

'Invocation [*of the Holy Spirit on the elements*] in the Eucharist' (*Constitutions*
VIII.12; 1549 BCP; Deacon, 92–3).

The prayer of invocation or *epiclesis* characteristically contains a Trinitarian
prayer asking the Father to send the Holy Spirit upon the elements, which ena-
bles the recipients to receive the blessings of Christ in the Eucharist. This developed into a petition for the transformation of the bread and wine in Roman
Catholic tradition. It should be noted that Wesley here reverses the order of
the 1549 prayer book in favour of Deacon's liturgy, which places the oblation

---

[81] Collier, 27; cf. John and Charles Wesley, *Hymns on the Lord's Supper*, VI.1 ('real Sacrifice');
Johnson, vol. 1, chapter 1; Wheatly, 291.
[82] Deacon, *Devotions*, 92.
[83] Deacon, *Devotions*, 84, 211, 316, 330.
[84] Bowmer, 98–9.

before the invocation. Collier's view of the purpose of the prayer of invocation as 'transfusing the mystick Virtue upon the Elements, and giving them the Efficacy of the Institution' closely resembles the High Church Eucharistic theology of Johnson. Collier asserted that the need for such a prayer expressly ruled out the possibility of trans or consubstantiation because the descent of the Holy Spirit would be unnecessary if Christ was corporally present in the elements. From Collier's viewpoint, the problem was not that the *epiclesis* was wholly absent from the 1662 prayer book, but that it needed to be made explicit as in the 1549 version.[85]

'**To pray for the Faithful Departed**' (*Constitutions* VI.30, VIII.13, 41–4; 1549 BCP; Deacon, 17, 38, 69, 182, 194, 199, 257, 269, 276, 331, 339–40).

Collier pointed out that the words '*Remember not Lord our Offences, nor the Offenses of our Forefathers*' and the Burial Office in the 1662 prayer book seems to retain an implicit prayer for the faithful departed.[86] Nonetheless, the Nonjurors understandably felt that the 1662 pre-communion prayer 'for the whole state of Christ's Church militant here in earth' obscured the unambiguous prayer for the living and the dead found in the 1549 version. Collier explained the patristic understanding of prayers for the dead as being based on the 'Principle, That supreme Happiness is not to be expected till the Resurrection; and that the Interval between Death and the end of the World, is a State of imperfect Bliss: The Church might therefore believe her Prayers for good People might improve their Condition, and raise the Satisfaction of this *Period*.' If revived, he believed the benefit of prayers for the dead would include strengthening belief in the afterlife and immortality of the soul. Collier cited with approval St Augustine's contention that prayers could only assist those who had lived a tolerably godly life.[87] Wesley's *Collection of Forms of Prayer* of 1733 contains, amongst others, the following prayer for the faithful departed: '"O Lord Thou God of Spirits and of all Flesh, be mindful of thy Faithful from *Abel* the Just, even unto this Day." And for thy Son's Sake give to them and us, in thy due Time, a happy Resurrection, and a glorious Rest at thy Right-hand for evermore!'[88] A second related manuscript contains the following note taken directly from the *Constitutions* (VIII.42): 'Celebrate ye 3rd day of ye Departed, ye 9th & ye 40th.'[89] Whether he publicly carried out this practice is unknown, although later in life he continued to reprint his *Collection*

---

[85] Collier, 25, 23, 25.

[86] Collier, 20. Wesley's interpretation of the burial office agreed with Collier's assessment: *A Second Letter to the Author of The Enthusiasm of Methodists and Papists Compar'd* (London, 1751), 52.

[87] Collier, 18, 21, 17; cf. Wheatly, 279–80.

[88] *Forms of Prayer*, 76. Wesley took the first sentence from the liturgy of St Mark.

[89] Wesley's Chapel, City Road, London, MS, LDWMM/1994/2067.

of Forms of Prayer and defend prayers for the dead as a faithful usage of the prayer book, suggesting that he may have observed this ritual.[90]

'**To pray standing on Sunday and in Pentecost**' (*Constitutions* II.59, VII.44; Deacon, ix).

The *Apostolic Constitutions* (VII.44) speak of standing following baptism as a symbol of being risen with Christ. One of Deacon's 'General Rubricks' instructs that '*The posture for the Faithful in prayer, and at the reception of the Eucharist, is kneeling, on all days but the Lord's days and all days between Easter and Pentecost, on which it is Standing, in respect to and remembrance of our Saviour's resurrection: and therefore where-ever in this book the Faithful are ordered to kneel, those times are supposed to be excepted.*' For Wesley, 'in Pentecost' meant praying standing during the period between Easter and Pentecost, as Deacon recommended.

'**To observe Saturday and Sunday Pentecost as festival**' (*Constitutions* V.20, cf. II.59; BCP; Deacon, xxxi).

The *Constitutions* (V.20) stress the observance of Pentecost, which Deacon named as one of five 'Greater Festivals.' Whitsunday (Pentecost) was, of course, one of the festivals or feast days observed by the Church of England. True to this resolution, in Georgia, Wesley celebrated Holy Communion on Pentecost.[91] Amongst the category of 'Lesser Festivals', Deacon lists 'All the days between Easter and Pentecost, except Sundays' and 'All Sabbath-days or Saturdays, except the Saturday before Easter.' In Georgia, Wesley celebrated all of the greater festivals and a number of lesser feast days such as the Conversion of St Paul, the Annunciation, St Bartholomew's Day, and St Andrew's Day.[92]

Wesley had solicited John Clayton's advice on the primitive observance of Saturday. His response to Wesley's 'question about Saturday' was that his practice was to celebrate Saturday with 'festival prayers' at the 'three primitive hours' (9 a.m., noon, and 3 p.m.) and morning and evening prayer taken from the Apostolic *Constitutions*.[93] Clayton's observance was based on the *Constitutions* (VII.23), which stress the keeping of the Sabbath as a 'memorial of the creation' and the Lord's Day to remember 'the resurrection.' Wesley's *Collection of Psalms and Hymns* published in Charlestown in 1737 contains a series of 'Psalms and Hymns for Saturday.'[94]

[90] *A Letter to the Reverend Dr. Conyers Middleton, Works* (Jackson), 10:9–10; *A Second Letter to the Author of The Enthusiasm of Methodists and Papists Compar'd*, 52. Wesley later argued that the souls 'of the righteous' awaiting the resurrection of the dead 'are inexpressibly happy' and will become 'perpetually holier and happier': Sermon 'On Faith' (1791), *Works*, 4:189, 191.

[91] JWD, 13 June 1736 and 29 May 1737.

[92] See 'Holy Communion' in chapter 4.

[93] Clayton to JW ([25] July 1733), *Works*, 25:352. *Constitutions* VIII.37–8 may have been the source for Clayton's morning and evening prayer.

[94] See 'Hymns' in chapter 3.

'To abstain from Blood, things strangled' (*Constitutions* VI.12, cf. VII.21; *Apostolic Canon* 63).

Acts 15:29 reads, 'abstain from meats offered to idols, and from blood, and from things strangled' (cf. Acts 15:20). These prohibitions are referred to in the *Constitutions* and *Canons*. Wesley had engaged this issue at Oxford by reading [Thomas Sharp], *An Enquiry about the Lawfulness of Eating Blood* (1733) and [Patrick Delany], *The Doctrine of the Abstinence from Blood Defended* (1734).[95] Wesley clearly accepted Delany's argument that the prohibition was still in force over Sharp's assertion that it was temporary. In Georgia, Wesley asked August Spangenberg about the Moravian opinion on 'the Mosaic precepts concerning unclean meats' and received the reply that they are 'No further [binding] than is expressed, Acts 15.'[96] In his *Explanatory Notes upon the New Testament* (1755) Wesley argued that the prohibition against eating blood still applies and interpreted 'things strangled' as a law against eating anything that has been killed without first pouring out the blood.[97]

'I think it prudent (our own Church not considered)':

'To observe the Stations [*i.e. stationary fasts*]' (*Constitutions* V.15, 20; BCP [Friday]; Deacon, xxxi, appendix, 72–4).

The *Constitutions* state that Christians are 'to fast on the fourth and sixth days of the week; the former on account of His being betrayed, and the latter on account of His passion' (cf. VII.23; BCP; Deacon, xxxi). In mentioning the stations, Wesley was referring to observing Wednesday and Friday fasts in accordance with the practice of the early church (see his 'Essay Upon the Stationary Fasts' discussed in chapter 1). To Friday fasting as recommended by the prayer book, Wesley added Wednesday fasting under the influence of the Nonjurors, although he was not convinced it was 'strictly obligatory' and failed to convince some of his pupils that it was necessary.[98] Wednesdays and Fridays between Easter and Pentecost and Christmas were exceptions to the general rule of observing the stations.[99]

'Lent, especially the Holy Week' (*Constitutions* V.13, 15, 17–19, *Apostolic Canon* 69; BCP; Deacon, xxxi, 58)

The *Constitutions*, the prayer book, and Deacon agree that the faithful should fast during the forty days of Lent. The *Constitutions* and Deacon place special emphasis on fasting until at least three o'clock in the afternoon on the six days

[95] December 1733 and June 1734.
[96] JWMSJ, 31 July 1737.
[97] See his comments on Acts 15:20 and 15:29; cf. Samuel Wesley's contrary opinion: *Athenian Oracle*, 2:191–2.
[98] JW to Richard Morgan, Jr [30 September 1735]; cf. JW to Susanna Wesley [13 January 1735] and JW to Samuel Wesley, Sr (13 June 1733), *Works*, 25:438, 412, 350–1.
[99] See Clayton to JW (2 August 1734), *Works*, 25:393.

of the Holy Week preceding Easter. Wesley's devotional practice in Georgia shows that he followed the *Constitutions* and Deacon in observance of the Holy Week.[100]

'**To turn to the East at the Creed**' (*Constitutions* II.57, VII.44; Deacon, ix)

The *Constitutions* specify that churches should face eastward (II.57) and that baptized believers should 'Pray towards the east' (VII.44) because Christ ascended to heaven in the east and the Garden of Eden was in the east (II.57). Many eighteenth-century Anglican churches faced east towards Jerusalem, therefore when facing the altar the people would naturally be facing east.[101] F. C. Mather has found evidence that some churches observed turning to the east at the creed and *Gloria Patri* (ascription of praise to the Trinity) in the eighteenth century.[102]

The four usages observed by the Usager Nonjurors are stated in the second and third resolutions as 'a duty to observe'. It is significant that Wesley was committing to observe the practices of an extreme wing of the Nonjurors. Wesley's adoption of the principles of this group shows that he adhered to a somewhat different brand of High Churchmanship than his father, who had denied the efficacy of prayers for the dead.[103] Following his statement of duty, however, Wesley added the clause that he was bound to observe these resolutions as long as such observance does not lead to schism from the Church. This may indicate that Wesley, while attracted to the usages, was not fully aware of disputes that had arisen over them within the Nonjuring communion. Did he consider that the Usagers who were convinced of these practices developed their convictions in schism from the Established Church? Presumably Wesley knew that Deacon had recently declared the Usagers to be the Orthodox British Church (a name that is found on the title page of some versions of his *Devotions*), established in 1733 at the time of his ordination as bishop. Therefore, Wesley's clause, although crossed out in the manuscript, seems to indicate his loyalty to the usages coupled with his determination to avoid the separatist tendencies of the Usagers. It appears that the primary reason for Wesley's interest in the usages was the theological premise behind them, namely, the desirability of renewing the Church by reviving the practices of the primitive church; the resolutions cited are all clearly aimed at this goal. The sources Wesley used to arrive at the resolutions also support the thesis that they were designed to promote the restoration of primitive Christianity.

---

[100] It appears that Wesley ate primarily bread during Holy Week 1736: JWD, 19–24 April 1736; cf. JWJ and JWMSJ, 3 April 1737; BIJ, 18 April 1736, p. 79.

[101] Peter Doll, *After the Primitive Christians: The Eighteenth-Century Anglican Eucharist in its Architectural Setting*, Joint Liturgical Studies, 37 (Cambridge, 1997), 10–15. This was true of Wesley's City Road Chapel opened in 1778.

[102] Mather, 'Georgian Churchmanship Reconsidered', 260.

[103] *Athenian Oracle*, 2:484.

Wesley's Theology of the Eucharist in his Early Writings

Wesley's high regard for the Eucharist was a constant and unwavering aspect of his life and ministry. John Bowmer estimated that he received the Eucharist on average every five days during his lifetime.[104] According to his post-Georgia recollection, the observance of weekly communion, later recommended by his High Church friends, was adopted by Wesley in 1725.[105] In 1732, he wrote to his mother about communicating weekly at Oxford, which was a common ideal of High Churchmen, although attained by only a few clergymen such as William Beveridge.[106] Wesley's disciplined observance of the sacrament led to an exchange of letters with his mother in which they both affirmed the real presence (i.e. true presence) of Christ in the sacrament. They agreed that in the Eucharist Christ is united to the believer in a mysterious manner. Susanna wrote, 'surely the divine presence of our Lord, thus applying the virtue and merits of the great atonement to each true believer, makes the consecrated bread more than a bare sign of Christ's body, since by his so doing we receive, not only the sign, but with it the thing signified, all the benefits of his Incarnation and Passion!' Susanna's concise summary of the Eucharistic presence of Christ reveals she had adopted the High Church expression of this doctrine. Her use of the terms 'virtue' and 'merits' and 'consecrated bread' indicate her acceptance of the standard High Church view of the Eucharist. She quoted with approval the words of Wesley's friend that the presence of Christ is imparted 'by the operation of his Holy Spirit', perhaps hinting that she adhered to the Nonjurors' insistence that the prayer of invocation was an essential aspect of the communion service. Susanna's stress on the pneumatic presence of Christ firmly links her with doctrines of instrumental causality, transignification, and virtualism held by John Johnson and the Nonjurors.[107]

The two primary sources for Wesley's early views on the Lord's Supper are his sermon on 'Constant Communion' (1732; published in 1787) and his *Collection of Forms of Prayer* (1733). Clayton was influenced by the former text and helped compile the latter text and Ingham read both works; therefore, we can conclude with reasonable confidence that these writings were

---

[104] Bowmer, 17; cf. Dearing, *Wesleyan and Tractarian Worship*, 11.

[105] JWJ, 24 May 1738, p. 244. Charles Wesley's essay 'On a Weekly Sacrament', probably written prior to the Georgia mission, argued for apostolicity of at least weekly observance of the Eucharist. See Geordan Hammond 'The Wesleys' Sacramental Theology and Practice in Georgia', *Proceedings of The Charles Wesley Society*, 13 (2009), 62.

[106] JW to Susanna Wesley (28 February 1731/2), *Works*, 25:328; see also Clayton to JW ([25] July 1733), *Works*, 25:352; cf. George Whitefield to JW (April 1737), *Methodist Magazine* (1798), 170. Leonard W. Cowie, 'Beveridge, William', *ODNB*.

[107] Susanna Wesley to JW and JW to Susanna Wesley (21 and 28 February 1731/2), *Works*, 25:326, 328. This emphasis can also be easily ascertained in the Wesleys' *Hymns on the Lord's Supper*. See, for example, hymns 16 and 72.

representative of the Oxford Methodists.[108] In his prayer for Sunday morning there is a strong reference to the Eucharist as an oblation: 'Let the Prayers and Sacrifices of thy holy Church offered unto Thee this Day, be graciously accepted.' The Sunday evening prayer offers thanksgiving 'for so often feeding my Soul with thy most precious Body and Blood, those Pledges of Love, and sure Conveyances of Strength and Comfort.'[109] As expressed in Susanna Wesley's comments, there is a clear belief in Christ's presence in the Eucharist. In common with Johnson and Susanna Wesley, John Wesley's prayer sees the elements as conveyors or instruments of God's grace.

Wesley's sermon 'The Duty of Constant Communion' holds an important place in the corpus of his works due to its status as his 'fullest and most explicit statement' of his eucharistic doctrine and practice.'[110] Significantly it was first written as an extract of Robert Nelson's *The Great Duty of Frequenting the Christian Sacrifice* (1706), which was an expansion of the chapter on 'Vigils' from Nelson's *Companion for the Festivals and Fasts of the Church of England* (1704).[111] Wesley's utilization of Nelson to encourage his students at Oxford to disciplined observance of the sacrament is noteworthy because of Nelson's prominence as a High Church/Nonjuror liturgist.[112] During his ministry on the *Simmonds* and in Georgia, Wesley continued to read Nelson to willing parishioners.[113] Some of the authority traditionally ascribed to the sermon has been derived from Wesley's opening note 'To the reader' that, since the time it was written for his students, his 'sentiments' had not changed.

The thrust of the discourse is accurately reflected in its title, the benefits of which are 'the forgiveness of our past sins and the present strengthening and refreshing of our souls.' Wesley conceived of Eucharistic observance in terms of imitating 'the first Christians, with whom the Christian sacrifice was a constant part of the Lord's day's service. And for several centuries they received it almost every day.' Wesley identified himself with the High Church sacramental tradition by referring to the 'Christian sacrifice' indicating a belief in the

---

[108] See Clayton to JW (6 September 1732), in JWJ (Curnock), 8:280–1 on his pastoral use of Wesley's sermon; Ingham, *Diary*, appendix 3. Ingham also read the two Nelson works and Brevint discussed later in the chapter.

[109] *Forms of Prayer*, 13, 17.

[110] *Works*, 3:427. Wesley's sermon 'The Means of Grace' (1746) defines the ordinary means of obtaining God's grace as prayer, scripture, and the Lord's Supper: *Works*, 1:376–97. In the sermon, he insinuated that the ancient church had a higher regard for the Lord's Supper than his contemporaries (p. 378).

[111] *Works*, 3:427. The extract is in volume twenty of the MS Colman Collection, MARC. Wesley read *The Great Duty* in January 1732 and the *Companion* in September 1731. Nelson emphasized 'the Examples of the Primitive Saints' as models 'for our Imitation': *Companion*, xv.

[112] Buxton has commented that Nelson's doctrine of consecration is 'remarkably similar' to John Johnson's. This led Buxton to propose that Nelson's work may have influenced Johnson: *Eucharist and Institution Narrative*, 173.

[113] JWD, 24 December 1735 and 4 February 1737. Wesley frequently referred to colonists in Georgia as his parishioners: JWMSJ, 22 August, 8 September, 1736, 4 April 1737.

Eucharist as an offering or oblation to God of the elements as a commemoration or representation of Christ's sacrifice on the cross. To stress the centrality of the sacrament to the church, Wesley paraphrased the eighth and ninth *Apostolic Canons*: 'If any believer join in the prayers of the faithful, and go away without receiving the Lord's Supper, let him be excommunicated, as bringing confusion into the church of God.'[114] Because the manuscript of Wesley's text is no longer extant we cannot recover the aspects of the sermon he '*retrenched*' before printing it in the *Arminian Magazine*; however, his retention of terms such 'Christian sacrifice' and 'altar' identify the sermon with the High Church tradition.[115]

Daniel Brevint's *Christian Sacrament and Sacrifice*

Because John and Charles Wesley published *Hymns on the Lord's Supper: With a Preface Concerning the Christian Sacrament and Sacrifice. Extracted from Doctor Brevint* in 1745, Brevint deserves special attention in any study of the Wesleys' Eucharistic theology. Although the hymns were substantially influenced by Brevint, they also heavily draw on the Eucharistic theology of John Johnson and the Nonjurors.[116] Daniel Brevint (*c*.1616–95), dean of Lincoln, was descended from a Huguenot family in Jersey, where he was ordained as a Reformed pastor before being ordained in the Church of England during the Interregnum. His famous theological/devotional treatise *The Christian Sacrament and Sacrifice* (1673), influenced by the French Reformed tradition as well as the authoritative Anglican theologians Richard Hooker and Jeremy Taylor, inspired the Wesleys' hymns.[117] John Wesley first read Brevint's treatise in July 1732 at a time when he was being increasingly influenced by High Churchmen, including the Oxford Methodist John Clayton, who may have recommended this work to him. Wesley consulted this book again both on the *Simmonds* and in Georgia in his meetings with his Saturday evening religious society designed as a communion preparation class.[118]

The Wesleys' thirty-page abridgement of Brevint's treatise formed the preface of the *Hymns on the Lord's Supper*, which went through nine editions in

---

[114] *Works*, 3:428–30.

[115] *Works*, 3:428, 430, 434.

[116] This point was made by Paul Burnham in a paper delivered at a conference entitled 'An Eighteenth-Century Evangelical for Today: A Tercentenary Celebration of the Life and Ministry of Charles Wesley', Liverpool Hope University, 2007. In his essay 'The "Nonjuror" Influence on the Eucharistic Hymns of Charles Wesley and its Relevance for Today', Burnham also argued that this connection was hidden because of the Wesleys' desire to avoid any association with Jacobitism.

[117] Kenneth W. Stevenson, 'Brevint, Daniel (bap. 1616–95)', *ODNB*.

[118] JWD, 23 December 1735 and 30 April 1737; see 'Wesley's Religious Societies in Georgia' in chapter 4.

the Wesleys' lifetimes.[119] J. Ernest Rattenbury has stated that the *Hymns on the Lord's Supper* were the most widely used collection of Wesleyan hymns other than the General Collections.[120] The importance of the hymns shows that the Wesleys led a revival that was sacramental and evangelical.[121] A summary of the abridgement provides a reliable insight into the Wesleys' Eucharistic theology that continuously stretches from Oxford to the end of their lives. The paucity of their own writings on the Lord's Supper makes Brevint's treatise all the more important for understanding their theology of the Eucharist.

Brevint's epistolary dedication stated that his goal was 'to restore all back again both to the full meaning of and institution of Christ...and to the practice of the Holy Fathers'; an ideal shared by the Wesleys.[122] Because Brevint wrote in the generation prior to the Nonjuring schism his emphasis is not the threefold consecration; however, his treatise is representative of the High Church tradition the Nonjurors drew on; therefore, they share significant themes in common. As with the Nonjurors who came after him, Brevint saw the Eucharist as 'a kind of *Sacrifice*, whereby we present before God the Father that precious Oblation of His Son once offered.'[123] For Brevint, the sacramental event is a self-offering of both the communicant to God and of Christ (as the eternal high priest) to the believer.[124] Brevint's theology of Eucharistic sacrifice—and section IV of the *Hymns* on this theme—offers insight into what Wesley meant by referring to the 'Christian sacrifice' in his sermon on 'Constant Communion', since they approvingly published Brevint's words on the sacrament as 'a kind of *Sacrifice*'.[125] Brevint's emphasis is on Christ's heavenly intercession and continuous offering of himself on the 'heavenly altar' as the great high priest draws out his key theme of the meeting of heaven and earth in the Eucharistic event.[126] Although Brevint does not show the same concern as the Nonjurors for precise liturgical practice, they share a similar emphasis on the

---

[119] Baker, *Union Catalogue*.

[120] Rattenbury, *Eucharistic Hymns*, 11.

[121] Rattenbury, *Eucharistic Hymns*, 150; Bowmer, 205; Wainwright, '"Our Elder Brethren Join"', 6; William Crockett, 'Holy Communion', 313; cf. Ole E. Borgen, *John Wesley on the Sacraments: A Theological Study* (Nashville, 1972), 282 and the argument of David Rainey and Joseph Wood that John Wesley had an evangelical and sacramental ecclesiology: Rainey, 'The Established Church and Evangelical Theology: John Wesley's Ecclesiology', *International Journal of Systematic Theology*, 12 (2010), 420–34; Wood, 'Tensions Between Evangelical Theology and the Established Church: John Wesley's Ecclesiology', Ph.D. thesis (University of Manchester [Nazarene Theological College], 2012).

[122] Brevint, *The Christian Sacrament and Sacrifice* (Oxford, 1673), unpaginated.

[123] Brevint in John and Charles Wesley, *Hymns on the Lord's Supper*, VI.2; cf. Brevint, *Christian Sacrament and Sacrifice*, 78.

[124] Brevint in John and Charles Wesley, *Hymns on the Lord's Supper*, I.1, IV.7–8, VII.10.

[125] See *Works*, 3:430; see sections IV–V of the *Hymns* on the theme of sacrifice.

[126] Brevint in John and Charles Wesley, *Hymns on the Lord's Supper*, VI.2–3; section III of the *Hymns*; cf. the frontispiece of Wheatly's *Rational Illustration*.

Eucharist as a sacrifice and oblation.[127] Brevint saw Christ and the Church in unity as completing the sacrifice prefigured in Old Testament offerings.[128]

One of the persistent themes of Brevint's treatise is the envisioning of the past, present, and future aspects of the Eucharist; it looks back to Christ's sacrifice, conveys the graces of Christ's presence and the benefits of his Passion in the present, and provides hope for the future and an assurance of 'happiness in heaven'.[129] As already suggested, the real presence of Christ in the Eucharist is central to Brevint's thought.[130] When referring to the elements, he uses the language of representation and virtue to indicate the presence of Christ.[131] Fundamentally, Brevint was committed to the traditional Anglican stance that the manner by which Christ is present and God's blessings are conveyed is a mystery.[132] He frequently used the term 'virtue' when proposing that the consecrated bread and wine represent Christ's body and blood and are instruments for applying the merit and virtue of Christ's sacrifice to the soul of the believer. Hence, in Brevint, as with Johnson, we find the doctrines of instrumental causality, transignification, and virtualism. The primary difference between Brevint and the Nonjurors was the Nonjurors' concern for liturgical method as a means of invoking Christ's presence in the Eucharist. An important aspect of Brevint's theology (shared by the Wesleys) is that through celebrating the Eucharist, the faithful receive God's grace and are empowered for holy living.[133] Although Brevint's focus was more on devotional language and mystery than theological terminology and definition, his emphasis on conformity to Christ on the part of the believer approximates Thomas Cranmer's and Richard Hooker's doctrine of 'receptionism', which stresses that the union of God's grace and the recipients' faith makes the presence of Christ effective.[134] The need for 'worthy reception' is a major emphasis in the prayer book. The Wesleys' emphasis on communicating at all opportunities and their post-Georgia doctrine of the sacrament as a 'converting ordinance' downplayed a rigorous interpretation of

---

[127] Brevint in John and Charles Wesley, *Hymns on the Lord's Supper*, for example, I.1 and VI.2.

[128] Brevint in John and Charles Wesley, *Hymns on the Lord's Supper*, VII.8.

[129] Brevint in John and Charles Wesley, *Hymns on the Lord's Supper*, II, III, V,V.4, 5; cf. Johnson, 2:107.

[130] Brevint in John and Charles Wesley, *Hymns on the Lord's Supper*, IV.5; hymns 66, 89, 116.

[131] Brevint in John and Charles Wesley, *Hymns on the Lord's Supper*, representation: II.3, III.1, 6, VI.3; virtue: II.5, III.3, V.4.

[132] Brevint in John and Charles Wesley, *Hymns on the Lord's Supper*, I.1, IV.3; Crockett, 'Holy Communion', 311.

[133] Brevint in John and Charles Wesley, *Hymns on the Lord's Supper*, III.3, VII.12.

[134] R. T. Beckwith, 'The Anglican Eucharist: From the Reformation to the Restoration', in Cheslyn Jones et. al. (eds), *The Study of Liturgy*, rev. edn (London, 1992), 316; Crockett, 'Holy Communion', 309, 313. Similar to 'receptionism' is the 'personalist' view that grace is received through a grace–faith relationship rather than in a mechanical manner (p. 310). Wesley's stress was on God's promise of grace while he maintained the need for personal faith: Paul S. Sanders, 'Wesley's Eucharistic Faith and Practice', *Anglican Theological Review*, 48 (1966), 172.

worthy receptionism.[135] With the Nonjurors, they preferred to move beyond the Anglican reformers and link Christ's presence in the Eucharist to the *epiclesis*.[136]

WESLEY'S BAPTISMAL DOCTRINE AND PRACTICE

As with his Eucharistic theology and practice, Wesley's theology and practice of baptism was shaped by Anglican scholars who promoted the restoration of primitive Christianity. The central influence in this regard was William Wall (1647–1728), who served as vicar of Shoreham in Kent, and is almost solely remembered as the author of the diligently researched *History of Infant Baptism* (1705), which continued to be valued and reprinted into the nineteenth century.[137] The esteem Wesley had for Wall's *History of Infant Baptism* was handed down to the Methodist movement in his *Thoughts upon Infant-Baptism* (1751) consisting of twenty-one pages of extracts from Wall's two-volume work.[138]

Almost immediately after his book was published, Wall received an endorsement from the Lower House of Convocation led by the High Church dean of Carlisle, Francis Atterbury, later a friend of John Wesley's elder brother Samuel Wesley, Jr and exiled as a Jacobite conspirator. Although a leader of the Whig-dominated Upper House complained that there was no reason Wall's work should have been singled out for praise, the approval of the Lower House

---

[135] Worthy receptionism is stressed in Article XXVII and in the catechism of the BCP. In his sermon 'The Means of Grace', John Wesley recommended self-examination before communicating, but in 'The Duty of Constant Communion' he argued that this was 'not absolutely necessary': *Works*, 1:389, 3:430. On the occasions in which the Lord's Supper was offered in Methodist societies, communicants had to be society members in good standing, i.e. holders of a class-ticket: see 'Minutes of Conference' (1747) in *Works*, 10:204; John C. English, 'John Wesley and the Liturgical Ideals of Thomas Cranmer', *MH* 35 (1997), 232. Although John Johnson urged worthy receptionism, he was reluctant to declare that the sacrament did not benefit unworthy receivers: 1:213, 348. Later references by Wesley to communion as a converting ordinance include: Sermon 'The Means of Grace', *Works*, 1:381, 393; JWJ, 19:93, 121, 158, 20:42, 101, 21:233, 244; hymn 47 in *Hymns on the Lord's Supper*. The majority Anglican position was that Communion was a 'confirming ordinance' rather than a 'converting ordinance': John Spurr, *The Restoration Church of England, 1646–1689* (New Haven, 1991), 346; Colin Podmore, *The Moravian Church in England, 1728–1760* (Oxford, 1998), 64; Rack, 405–7.

[136] John R. Parris, *John Wesley's Doctrine of the Sacraments* (London, 1963), 9–10.

[137] Wheatly, chapter 7 contains similar views to Wall, whom Wheatly praises (p. 320).

[138] See also Wesley's 'A Treatise on Baptism', first published in *A Preservative against Unsettled Notions in Religion* (1758), *Works* (Jackson), 10:188–201. The 'Treatise' is an edited abridgement of his father's *The Pious Communicant Rightly Prepar'd* (1700), which contains an appendix on baptism.

gave the book an official recognition that would have appealed particularly to High Churchmen.[139]

Following the publication of the Nonjuror Roger Laurence's *Lay Baptism Invalid* (1708), the issue of the validity of lay baptism[140] was hotly debated at Convocation in 1712, at which Samuel Wesley, Sr served as a Proctor for the clergy of Lincolnshire. In response to Bishop William Wake's questionnaire for his episcopal visitation that same year Wesley uncharitably declared that his wife had received 'none but Presbyterian Baptism'—that is, lay baptism only.[141] While the Upper House of Convocation, echoing the declarations of the councils of Arles (314) and Nicaea (325), declared that no one baptized with water in the name of the Trinity should be rebaptized, the Lower House refused to concur. Wake responded to Samuel Wesley's request for a copy of his 1712 visitation sermon, which discussed lay baptism, by reiterating the position of the Upper House.[142]

Along with opposition to lay baptism, Nonjurors were concerned to promote trine, i.e. triple immersion. John Wesley had already sided with them against the Quakers on the necessity of water baptism in his December 1733 manuscript essay 'Water Baptism is the Baptism of Christ'.[143]

---

[139] Francis Atterbury, *Some Proceedings in the Convocation, A.D. 1705: Faithfully Represented* (London, 1708), 35; *An Account of the Proceedings in the Convocation...* (London, 1706), 58. The latter work has been variously attributed to either Edmund Gibson or White Kennett.

[140] Lay baptism referred to baptism by a dissenting minister—that is, anyone but a Church of England clergyman. Because they were not in communion with the Church of England, some High Churchmen believed that Dissenters could not validly perform the rite of baptism. This was accompanied by the conviction that dissenting baptisms were invalid because Dissenters had not been episcopally ordained in the apostolic succession. On the controversy, see Barnard, 'Use of the Patristic Tradition' and Robert D. Cornwall, 'Politics and the Lay Baptism Controversy in England, 1708-15', in William Gibson and Robert D. Cornwall (eds), *Religion, Politics and Dissent, 1660-1832: Essays in Honour of James E. Bradley* (Aldershot, 2010), 147-64. Compared to pre-Restoration Anglican tradition, the assertion of the invalidity of lay baptism was an innovation (Quantin, *Church of England and Christian Antiquity*, 106-8; cf. Spurr, *Restoration Church of England*, 159).

[141] *Bishop Wake's Summary of Visitation Returns from the Diocese of Lincoln 1706-1715*, ed. John Broad (Oxford, 2012), 1:18 n. 66.

[142] Wake to Wesley (12 August 1712), in Norman Sykes, *William Wake: Archbishop of Canterbury 1657-1737* (Cambridge, 1957), 1:180-1.

[143] 'Water Baptism is the Baptism of Christ', MS in 'Portraits and Letters of Presidents of the Wesleyan Methodist Conference', vol. 1, fo 14, MARC. In this five-page treatise, Wesley argued that the literal meaning of the Greek word *baptizo* is 'to wash', signifying the necessity of water baptism as a command of Christ. Insinuating that Dissenters had recently undermined the universal practice of the church, Wesley asserted that until the year 1650 no one from the age of the Apostles had spoken against water baptism. His argument for water baptism is summed up as follows: '1) Because Christ did practice Water Baptism, 2) Because the Apostles did it after him, and 3) Because the Catholic Churches have done it after Them.' Heitzenrater, 'John Wesley', 259 gives the date as December 1733. The essay has been transcribed in Bernard G. Holland, *Baptism in Early Methodism* (London, 1970), 158-62. In the same month he completed the essay Wesley had engaged with the issue of Quaker opposition to water baptism through reading the work of the Nonjuror Charles Leslie: *A Discourse Proving the Divine Institution of Water Baptism; wherein, the Quaker-Arguments against it are Collected and Refuted* (1697).

While there is evidence that Wesley may have read Roger Laurence's (1670–1736) work alongside William Wall's *History of Infant Baptism*, our discussion here is of the latter because of the strong evidence Wesley's diary provides for his reading of Wall.[144] Wesley had read *A Conference between Two Men that had Doubts about Infant Baptism* (1706) in 1732, an abridgement of Wall's larger work that focuses on his arguments from scripture and evidence from the primitive church. He 'began Wall on Baptism' less than two weeks after he had boarded the *Simmonds*, indicating that it was a high priority for him. It can be said with some confidence that Wesley read Wall's two-volume work due to the notes in his diary that he devoted approximately twenty-four hours to this task.[145] Nearly every day between 29 October and 25 November 1735, Wesley read Wall and prayed from six to seven o'clock in the morning (the missionaries' third hour of the day set aside for reading 'something relating to the Primitive Church'[146]).

In his preface, Wall admitted that the New Testament does not directly deal with the issue of infant baptism and that some would criticize his work because he was unable to prove his case from scripture. Nonetheless, he expressed unyielding confidence that the question can be validly and irrefutably solved by examining the practice of the primitive church as 'there is no Body that will doubt but that the Apostles knew what was to be done in this Case: and consequently, that the Christian Churches in their Time did as they should do in this Matter.'[147] Wall, therefore, staked his argument on the consensus position amongst High Churchmen that issues which cannot be resolved by scripture can and should be decided by appeal to Christian tradition. Wesley agreed and would have been particularly persuaded in this manner since his beloved *Apostolic Constitutions* (VI.15) called for the baptism of infants. Since the purity of the primitive church was widely upheld, Wall was convinced that he could persuade open-minded Baptists to accept the Church's teaching in favour of infant baptism by proving that this was the practice of the church in

---

[144] Wesley's diary indicates that he read 'Lawrence' from 12–15 November 1735. The circumstantial evidence of his theological affiliation with the Nonjurors, and the fact that he had already rebaptized Ambrose Tackner (discussed later in this section of the chapter), suggests that this was probably a reference to Laurence's work. That he read 'Lawrence' with Benjamin Ingham at least some of the time and Charles Wesley also read 'Lawrence' in Georgia and expressed his wish to read it 'over again with' him, lends slightly more weight to this probability: JWD, 12 November 1735; Charles Wesley to JW (1 May 1736), *The Letters of Charles Wesley: A Critical Edition, with Introduction and Notes, Volume I, 1728–1756*, ed. Kenneth G. C. Newport and Gareth Lloyd (Oxford, 2013), 55.

[145] Wall also published *A Defence of the History of Infant Baptism* (London, 1720), but it is unlikely that Wesley would have chosen this book over Wall's two-volume work or have devoted this much time to Wall's *Defence*.

[146] BIJ, 21 October 1735, p. 69.

[147] William Wall, *The History of Infant Baptism*, 3rd edn (London, 1720), 1:vii. The third edition is the final and most complete edition and almost certainly the version Wesley read.

its purest ages; at the least, he hoped to convince them not to separate from the Church over the issue of baptism.[148]

Part one of Wall's book consists of over five hundred pages of quotations from the Church Fathers and early councils comprising a compilation of witnesses to infant baptism in the primitive church, while part two deals with the historical practice and theological issues involved. In part two, Wall deals with three issues of historic baptismal practice that surface in Wesley's Georgia ministry: rebaptism, the mode of baptism, and private baptism.[149] As to rebaptism, Wall noted that the primitive church was divided over this question. On the one hand, St Cyprian stated the view held by the churches in Africa, Egypt, and Asia that any baptism received by the hands of those not in communion with the one true church is void; for the Western Church, converts from sects who baptized in the name of the Holy Trinity needed only to be confirmed by the church with the laying on of hands and anointing—this would procure the gift of the Holy Spirit, which could not be obtained outside the true church.[150] In his baptismal practice in Georgia, Wesley adopted the Cyprianic position, which was supported by one of his primary sources for theological guidance, the *Apostolic Canons*. Canon forty-seven declares that any bishop or presbyter who does not rebaptize 'him who is polluted by the ungodly'—in other words, any schismatic—shall be deprived of his clerical office.

Wall devoted a considerable number of pages to defending trine immersion as 'the general practice of all antiquity'.[151] For Deacon, 'The descending into the water represents his death, and denotes our mortification or dying to sin: the being under water represents his burial and denotes our being buried with Christ into his death: the ascending out of the water represents his resurrection, and denotes our rising again with him to newness of life.'[152] Charles Wheatly also noted the additional symbolism of the Trinity and the three days Christ was in the grave.[153] According to Wall, exceptions to the general rule of immersion include 'sickness, weakliness, haste, want of quantity of water, or such like extraordinary occasions'. In such circumstances, 'baptism by affusion of water on the face was...counted sufficient baptism'.[154] This general

---

[148] For the background of the Anglican–Baptist debate on infant baptism, see Oscar C. Burdick, 'Wall, William (1647–1728)', *ODNB*. The final chapter of Wall's work is 'A Dissuasive from Separation on Account of the Difference of Opinion about the Age or Time of receiving Baptism'.

[149] As to private baptism, Wall condemned 'indifferent' clergy who made no effort to persuade parents to bring their children to church to be baptized: *History of Infant Baptism*, 1:228.

[150] Wall, *History of Infant Baptism*, 2:133, 353–4, 394.

[151] In support, Wall cites Cave's *Primitive Christianity*: see *Christian Library*, ed. JW, 31:211, 214–15; cf. Fleury, 11.

[152] *A Full, True and Comprehensive View of Christianity* (London, 1747), 71; cf. *Apostolic Constitutions* III.17, VII.43–4.

[153] Wheatly, 340.

[154] Wall, *History of Infant Baptism*, 2:352, 381. This practice was acceptable based on the Church's Canon 30 (1604).

pattern was represented in the 1549 prayer book, which instructs the minister to immerse the child three times making the sign of the cross by dipping the child first to his right side, secondly to the left, and thirdly in front of him while saying, 'I baptize thee in the name of the father, and of the son, and of the holy ghost.' The act is to be 'discreetly and warily done…And if the child is weak, it shall suffice to pour water upon it.' The word 'thrice' was removed from the 1552 prayer book, while the 1662 book shifts the onus to godfathers and godmothers to tell the clergyman whether the child can 'endure' being immersed or 'certify' that the child is 'weak' and should receive baptism by pouring. Wall complained that the changes in the liturgy coupled with the discouragement of immersion during the Interregnum led to the demise of the primitive practice of trine immersion.[155]

Wesley's practice in Georgia shows that he agreed with Wall that the rubric was being abused both by godparents who rarely asserted that the child could endure immersion and clergymen who shirked their duty to ask if the child is weak. However, while Wall simply hoped to encourage immersion, Wesley wanted to restore the practice of trine immersion based upon the primitive standard reflected in the 1549 prayer book and the *Apostolic Constitutions*.[156] This was the consensus view of the Nonjurors and was reflected in Deacon's *Devotions* and Clayton's exhortation to Wesley at the time of his departure for Georgia.[157] The fiftieth *Apostolic Canon* probably reinforced Wesley's position with the radical demand that clergy who fail to perform trine immersion must be deprived.

Wesley also adopted the Nonjuror position that the only valid ordination was by an episcopally ordained bishop in the apostolic succession. This was deemed to be essential for the efficacious offering of the sacraments. Therefore, Wesley also believed that Dissenters should submit to rebaptism, since dissenting ministers were not ordained in either the episcopal manner or in the apostolic succession.[158] These issues were hotly debated by the Convocation of 1711–12 and left unresolved, although the majority of bishops came down firmly against rebaptism.

---

[155] Wall, *History of Infant Baptism*, 2:368–9.

[156] Wheatly believed that post-1549 the prayer book did not prohibit trine immersion (p. 341).

[157] Drawing on the *Constitutions*, Deacon advocated strict baptismal practices including: 1) trine immersion; 2) public baptism preformed only between Easter and Pentecost; 3) baptism only by a member of one's own sex (by a deaconess for women); and 4) exorcism of the baptismal candidate as part of the baptismal ceremony: *Devotions*, 102, 115, 117–18, 125. Regarding Wesley, we only have evidence for the first of Deacon's four practices. See [Clayton to JW], (written on a letter of 9 September 1735 from James Oglethorpe), *Works*, 25:433.

[158] Sermon 'On Laying the Foundation of the New Chapel' (1777), *Works*, 3:583. It seems that the Nonjuror (from 1691 to 1710) Henry Dodwell pioneered the view that only those episcopally ordained could validly administer the sacraments (Quantin, *Church of England and Christian Antiquity*, 381). See the question Wesley posed to the Moravians in Georgia: JWMSJ, 31 [July] 1737, question seventeen.

That Wesley intended to carry out his ministry in a High Church fashion was made evident by his first missionary act as the colonists were preparing to depart for Georgia. After conversing with a thirty-year-old German locksmith called Ambrose Tackner, who, as a Lutheran, had only received 'lay baptism', Wesley took an unorthodox step and baptized him 'at his desire' on the following day.[159] He believed that Lutheran clergy lacked episcopal apostolic succession and could not, therefore, offer efficacious sacraments. What Wesley meant by 'lay baptism' was baptism by a dissenting minister rather than baptism by someone who was not ordained. By taking this step, Wesley set himself in an extreme High Church camp opposed to the majority position within the Church.[160] Wesley's account leaves room for ambiguity by remaining silent about the level his own influence played in Tackner's decision to request baptism.

Substantial evidence exists that Wesley unsuccessfully attempted to rebaptize another *Simmonds* passenger, Michael Volmar, a German carpenter from Wittenberg who was recommended as a colonist by the Lutheran court chaplain in London, Friedrich Michael Ziegenhagen. Volmar, who travelled with the Moravians, deserted them and the Salzburgers after a short stay at New Ebenezer.[161] Because of his temporary association with the Salzburgers, we know from their pastor, Johann Boltzius, that Wesley failed to receive Volmar's permission to rebaptize him. Wesley's only mention of Volmar in his diary for 9 February 1736 seems to refer to this effort that would be indiscernible without the information provided by Boltzius.[162] Boltzius knew about the rebaptism of Ambrose Tackner, whom he notes was also a German born in Ulm.[163] Given that Volmar, like Tackner, was born in a Protestant town, we can assume that he had also received Lutheran baptism. This explains Boltzius's interest in their cases and his approval of Volmar's refusal.

A few weeks after the Tackner baptism, Wesley was pleased that after teaching the Hird family about the nature of Christian baptism, they requested to be baptized.[164] Members of the Hird family that were baptised included Thomas, a forty-two-year-old dyer, who later became constable at Frederica;

[159] JWMSJ, 18 October 1735; JWD, 17–18 October; BIJ, 18 October 1735, p. 68; Charles Wesley to Samuel Wesley, Jr (17 Nov[ember] 1735), *Letters of Charles Wesley*, 48. The professions of colonists are taken from Egmont's list of settlers published in *LES*.

[160] Sykes, *Old Priest and New Presbyter*, 94. Samuel Wesley, Sr, Samuel, Jr, and Edmund Gibson were amongst those opposed to this practice: *Athenian Oracle*, 2:131; Samuel Wesley, Jr to JW, [29 April 1736], *Works*, 25:458; Gibson to Samuel Myles [3 September 1724], Fulham Papers, Lambeth Palace Library, American Colonial Section, vol. IV, Massachusetts, 1698–1729.

[161] On Volmar, see *Detailed Reports*, 3:60, 88, 223, 255; Fries, 97, 102, 139.

[162] The diary entry reads: 'Religious talk with Volmar (gained no ground).'

[163] *Detailed Reports*, 16 May 1738, 5:110–11; *LES*, 53.

[164] JWJ and JWMSJ, 16 November 1735; Charles Wesley to Samuel Wesley, Jr (17 Nov[ember] 1735), *Letters of Charles Wesley*, 48.

his wife Grace, thirty-nine; Mark, their twenty-one-year-old son; and Phoebe, their seventeen-year-old daughter.[165] This was a gratifying event for a High Churchman, as the Hirds had been raised amongst the Quakers, a group that had rejected water baptism in favour of an inward experience of baptism wrought by the Holy Spirit. For Wesley, the ritual itself was divinely inspired and far from an empty ceremony, as some Quakers claimed. In winning over the Hirds to the Church, Wesley fulfilled one of his major goals by gaining four frequent communicants. The Hird family might be cited as one example of a positive impact Wesley had on a Georgian family who remained loyal to him.

During the time the passengers bound for either Frederica or Savannah were anchored at Pepper Island (now Cockspur) near Tybee Island before heading to their final destination, Wesley had an opportunity to observe the benefits of instituting the practice of the ancient Church when he baptized an eleven-day-old child, Mary Welch 'according to the custom of the first church and the rule of the Church of England, by immersion.' The results were dramatic: 'The child was ill then, but recovered from that hour.'[166] Two months earlier, the child's mother, Anne, had been near death as she prepared to deliver the baby. Wesley and Ingham witnessed her recovery from a serious illness after she had taken Holy Communion.[167] Surprisingly, Wesley had previously failed to record a baptismal healing when Ingham performed the rite on a child 'which was thought to be at the point of death; nay, some thought it was dead; but, from the moment it was baptized, it began to recover.'[168] There is no indication whether this was the child who had been privately baptized and was 'publicly received into the Church' during the height of a storm a few days later.[169] These cases represent Georgian examples of Wesley's life-long belief in providential supernaturalism and the efficacy of the sacraments as a transmitter of God's grace to bring healing into people's lives. He adhered to the Church's teaching on baptismal regeneration that original sin is washed away and the soul is spiritually reborn in baptism.[170] These two events were enthusiastically recorded in Wesley's diary and could only have strengthened his belief in the efficacy of renewing the practice of the primitive church.

---

[165] *LES*, 23.

[166] JWJ, 21 February 1736; JWD, 22 February 1736.

[167] JWJ and JWMSJ, 18 December 1735; cf. BIJ, 19 December 1735, p. 72. See also CWJ, 3 October 1736, p. 56.

[168] BIJ, 20 January 1736, pp. 73–4.

[169] JWJ and JWMSJ, 25 January 1736.

[170] See *Forms of Prayer*, 16.

THE MINISTRY OF WESLEY AND THE
METHODISTS

Evidence from Wesley's reading on the *Simmonds* suggests that he modelled
his missionary vision to an extent after the ascetical Roman Catholic models of
Francis Xavier (1506–52) and Gregorio López (1542–96).[171] We also know that
he patterned his liturgical practice after the Nonjurors' programme of primitive restoration. But does his reading reveal any models for his general pastoral
activity? While it is not clear that he consciously chose to read any pastoral
manuals on the *Simmonds* voyage, the description of the ideal pastor from
William Law's (1686–1761) *Serious Call to a Devout and Holy Life* (1729) cor-
responds with Wesley's pastoral approach at Oxford, which involved thought-
ful pastoral care of those within the realm of his influence.[172] Law describes
an archetypal 'holy priest' through the character of Ouranius. He is a man
of prayer whose 'prayers for others altered and amended the state of his own
heart.' He strives after Christian perfection, practising 'all the arts of holy living' including charity, humility, and fasting and mortification; but he is not
a reclusive mystic—he visits his parishioners from house to house, learns of
their spiritual state, advises and encourages them to holy living, and uses his
knowledge of them to 'intercede with God for them according to their particular necessities.'[173]

If, as seems to have been the case, Wesley, in part, went to Georgia to fulfil
his father's missionary dream,[174] his later comments on his father's pastoral
legacy can cautiously be cited as evidence of how Wesley believed he might
emulate his father. He recounted:

> My father's method was to visit all of his parishioners, sick or well, from house to
> house, to talk with each of them on the things of God, and observe severally the
> state of their souls. What he then observed, he minuted down in a book kept for
> that purpose. In this manner he went through his parish (which was near three
> miles long) three times. He was visiting it the fourth time round when he fell into
> his last sickness.[175]

As we shall observe, this sort of systematic care of souls was characteristic of
Wesley's Georgia ministry.[176]

---

[171] On this subject, see Hammond, 115–22.

[172] See *Forms of Prayer*, 15.

[173] Law, *Serious Call*, 264–7; cf. 'An Extract from *The Country Parson's Advice to his Parishioners*',
Christian Library, ed. JW (London, 1826), 26:516–20; cf. Burton's advice on visiting from house
to house: Burton to JW (28 September 1735), *Works*, 25:435.

[174] On his father's interest in foreign missions and Georgia, see Hammond, appendix 1.

[175] JW to a Gentleman [16 November 1742], *Works*, 26:90; cf. Wesley, *Advice to a Young
Clergyman*, 13–14.

[176] Ten years previously as he was preparing for ordination, Wesley read George Bull's *A
Companion for the Candidates of Holy Orders* (London, 1714), which contains some similar
emphases to Law in terms of the holiness required of clergy and fervent attention to the salvation

Public Worship

Wesley read David Humphreys's *An Historical Account* (1730) of the SPG in July 1737, which contains a summary of the 'instructions' for SPG missionaries.[177] We do not know whether he was acquainted with these guidelines prior to reading Humphreys, but it may nonetheless be informative to compare his conduct on the *Simmonds* with the Society's instructions. In addition to being advised generally to be a model of piety, missionaries were urged to hold daily morning and evening prayer and to preach and catechize on Sundays. Generally were requested to 'Instruct, Exhort, Admonish, and Reprove, as they have Occasion and Opportunity'.[178] In all of these particulars, Wesley was an exemplar of a faithful SPG missionary.

Wesley lost no time in developing a pattern of public worship on the *Simmonds*. Most days, morning and evening prayer, which was normally held in the great cabin, was observed at 8 a.m. and 4 p.m. until the southward course of the journey allowed morning prayer to be moved to 7 a.m. Wesley recorded in his diary his method for structuring prayers. His typical pattern was: scripture sentences or (in his terminology) ejaculations, prayer of confession, absolution, psalm, the Lord's Prayer, scripture (the first lesson), a hymn, scripture (the second lesson), exposition (on occasion), collects or creed, psalm, a prayer of thanksgiving, and blessing. Because of his desire to implement the Nonjurors' programme of reforming the 1662 prayer book liturgy along primitive lines, Wesley adopted the unusual practice, which he later noted was still observed in some English churches (i.e. by some High Churchmen and Nonjurors), of dividing Sunday prayers into three distinct services, as originally appointed by the 1549 book. Although morning prayer and communion were normally celebrated consecutively, Wesley separated them in order to recover what he was convinced was the more primitive practice of Matins, Communion, and Evensong.[179] Therefore, prayers with a short homily were generally held at 8 a.m., with the second prayer service beginning at 11 a.m. followed by a sermon and communion at midday, and evening prayer at 4 p.m., concluded with a short homily. Evidence from Ingham's journal seems to indicate that Wesley devoted his sermons to preaching on the Sermon on the Mount.[180] It is worth pointing out that although Wesley

---

of souls. George Herbert's *The Temple* (Cambridge, 1633), with its high view of the priesthood, should also be considered as an influence on Wesley's pastoral practice. Wesley read Herbert at Oxford (June 1730) and probably also in Georgia: JWD, 19 August 1736 and 13 May 1737.

[177] JWD, 12 July 1737.

[178] *A Collection of Papers Printed by Order of the Society for the Propagation of the Gospel in Foreign Parts* (London, 1715), 19.

[179] For details, see Wesley's voyage diary entries for Sundays; JWJ, 9 May 1736. Wesley's comment that he began this practice in Savannah is somewhat misleading, since his voyage diary shows he had had previously initiated it on the *Simmonds*: JWJ, 9 May 1736. Cf. Wheatly, 256–8.

[180] 19 October 1735, pp. 68–9.

valued the structure the daily prayers provided, he believed that repetition without 'Fervour' was insufficient.[181]

In his summary of the Methodists' activities on the *Simmonds*, Wesley claimed that between thirty and forty of the eighty British passengers on the ship attended morning prayer.[182] Unfortunately, he did not note attendance levels at individual services, as occasionally became his practice in Georgia. However, for thirteen of the twenty Sundays between Gravesend and settlement in Savannah, he recorded attendance at communion.[183] The total attendance at communion was 189 (it is unclear whether these numbers include the Methodist missionaries), while the highest number of communicants on a Sunday was twenty-three (18 January); the lowest attendance was three a few days before the *Simmonds* left Gravesend (19 October); and the average number of attendees was fourteen-and-a-half. Communion was also held on Christmas and New Year's Day/The Circumcision of Christ with nineteen and fifteen communicants as recorded by both Wesley and Ingham. Sunday 23 November was the sole occasion during the Georgia mission when Wesley named several of his communicants.[184] The evidence provided by Wesley shows that attendance increased over the course of the voyage to an average of twenty in January. While few firm conclusions can be drawn from these numbers, the fact that these statistics were kept shows the crucial importance of the sacrament of communion to Wesley, who, as a High Churchman, saw sacramental piety as central to spiritual life. The observance of weekly communion, which was atypical in the Church at the time, also illustrates the significance Wesley attached to the sacrament at a time when three communion services per year was required by the prayer book and four a year was common in country parishes. In light of what we know about attendance numbers at communion in English parishes, it seems that Wesley's efforts to persuade his parishioners to frequent the sacrament were fairly successful.[185]

From the outset of the voyage, Wesley began to experiment with his ecclesiastical practice. Regarding his first Sunday, he later recollected that he 'first preached extempore.'[186] Depending on whether he meant 'first' to refer to his

---

[181] See *Forms of Prayer*, 15.

[182] JWMSJ, 21 October 1735.

[183] Ingham recorded attendance at communion on five Sundays during the voyage. Both cited three communicants on 19 October and twenty on 25 January, while Wesley recorded fourteen on 7 December and Ingham fifteen. On 21 December, Wesley recorded fifteen communicants compared to twenty-one by Ingham. Ingham recorded eight communicants on 30 November, a Sunday that went unrecorded by Wesley.

[184] Eight of the twelve communicants were named; these included: Thomas, Grace, Mark, and Phoebe Hird, Ambrose Tackner, Betty Hassel, Thomas Burk, and one with the surname West: JWD.

[185] Mather, 'Georgian Churchmanship Reconsidered', 255–83.

[186] JWJ, 19 October 1735; cf. *Works* (Jackson), 10:447 and Wesley's later claim that he first preached extempore at Allhallows, London in 1735: JWJ, 28 January 1776, 23:3. The word 'first' does not appear in his manuscript journal. This was an experiment rather than a permanent practice. On the following day, he seems to have 'read [his] Se[rmon?]' at morning prayer.

earliest ever attempt or his initial endeavour to preach extempore during the Georgia mission, his claim may be misleading, since he had previously delivered a sermon in this manner at Epworth and at the Castle prison in Oxford.[187] This step to preach without notes was cited by Benjamin Ingham as a significant event justified 'according to the ancient usage.'[188] Although this justification was not specifically noted by Wesley, it is likely that this was a well thought-out act consciously intended as an imitation of primitive practice. Their praise of it illustrates that Wesley and Ingham were not entirely reliant on the Nonjurors in their interpretation of primitive Christianity. Extempore preaching was not a practice emphasized by High Churchmen and Nonjurors, who stressed set forms of prayer and orderliness in worship. Clayton would later criticize Wesley for this practice, which he believed was an act of self-will that was imprudent for anyone other than an Apostle.[189] This is the only specific mention of extempore preaching on the voyage, but he likely continued this practice in his frequent preaching or expounding after prayers, which he normally did once and sometimes twice a day.

Commenting on the prayers for the day was not a required part of the service and was probably a fairly atypical practice for an Anglican clergyman. While docked at Cowes in the Isle of Wight, Wesley confessed in his diary under the heading of 'Providence': 'All the people angry at my expounding so often.' For Wesley, receiving the disapproval of his parishioners was no reason to leave off preaching; if anything, this was the kind of 'persecution' he believed all true Christians were required to undergo. Clearly he exaggerated the extent of the opposition to some degree, since the people 'utterly protested against' the suggestion that the expounding be given up.[190]

Wesley was far from the opinion that in holding regular services he was fulfilling the whole of his duties. A week after the *Simmonds* set sail, Wesley buried an eight-month-old child, James Proctor.[191] As soon as the ship reached the open sea, widespread sickness struck the passengers for the first time, necessitating the deliverance gruel to them, an activity carried out by the Wesleys, Ingham, and Oglethorpe.[192] The danger of caring for the sick on-board ship should not be underestimated; with the knowledge that disease could spread, this was an activity that required great bravery. Wesley also regularly visited the passengers to enquire about their spiritual health. Although Ingham had

---

[187] Note by Albert Outler in *Works*, 4:347 and *Works*, 4:347 n. 3; JWJ, 23:3 n. 6.

[188] BIJ, 19 October 1735, p. 68.

[189] Clayton to JW (1 May 1738), *Works*, 25:539; cf. Wheatly, 17.

[190] JWMSJ, 16 November 1735; JWD 17 November 1735. On opposition to the Methodists' ministry on the *Simmonds*, see JWMSJ, 19, 22 November and 1 December 1735; BIJ, 2, 8, 30 November 1735 and 4 January 1736, pp. 70, 71, 73.

[191] JWD, 28 October 1735; Moore, *Voyage to Georgia*, 13.

[192] JWD, 19 December 1735; BIJ, 19 December 1735, p. 72. Canon 67 (1604) required ministers to visit sick parishioners. It is possible that Wesley may have used the liturgy in Deacon's 'Order for the Visitation of the Sick': *Devotions*, 159–71.

been involved in teaching the children, Wesley felt compelled to spend time catechizing them and took it upon himself to write a catechism, which he used publicly with six children after the second lesson at the evening service.[193] In Wesley's disciplined pastoral activity we see echoes of his wide-ranging labours at Oxford and his father's parish ministry, as well as a foreshadowing of his yet to be declared sentiment: 'I look upon *all the world* as *my parish*.'[194]

[193] Wesley's diary seems to indicate that he composed a catechism, but it is possible that he used extracts from Claude Fleury's, *An Historical Catechism*. Wesley's abridged version (with alterations of the text) of Fleury can be found in the MARC, MS Colman Collection 15, which later formed the basis for his *Instructions for Children* (1746). It is bound in a notebook identical to the Georgia diaries and appears to have been extracted for use in Georgia. His diary entry for 23 October 1737 may refer to his use of this abridgement. In the same notebook, Wesley abridged (again with his own alterations of the text) Fleury's *Les Moeurs des Israelites et des Chretiens*, which he translated and later published as *The Manners of the Antient Christians* (1749). This notebook also contains a list of books for the poor, which includes the titles of many SPCK books that the Society gave to Wesley for distribution to colonists, providing evidence that the abridgements of Fleury were written in Georgia. Wesley also read [Daniel Whiston], *A Primitive Catechism* (1718), which was recommended to him by Clayton: [John Clayton to JW] [9 September 1735], *Works*, 25:433; JWD, 18 October 1735. Given its focus on scripture and the *Apostolic Constitutions*, he may well have used this work in his catechizing. From 3 January 1736, Wesley's diary indicates that he catechised the children at around 2 p.m. on most days that month; cf. BIJ, 5 January 1736, p. 73.

[194] JW to [John Clayton?], [28 March 1739?], *Works*, 25:616; JWJ, 11 June 1739, 19:67.

3

Versions of Primitive Christianity

Wesley's Relations with the Moravians and Lutheran Pietists

Biographers of Wesley have generally been inclined to highlight his introduction to the Moravians as one of the (if not the most) significant results of the Georgia mission. Along with this there has been a tendency to describe his relations with the Moravians as one of mutual respect and harmony. Indeed, this is the picture painted in Wesley's *Journal*. However, his diary and manuscript journal, and especially sources from the Moravians, show that significant tensions existed between them. The first part of this chapter explores Wesley's associations with the Moravians on the *Simmonds* and in Savannah, investigating important issues that arose in the course of their interactions, such as the practice and discipline of the primitive church, episcopacy, and tensions that emerged. A close reading of Wesley's journals and diary alongside the journals and letters of the leaders of the Moravians demonstrates that their interactions were fundamentally shaped by the discussion of their views on the primitive church.[1] Wesley believed that the primitive church could be restored in Georgia through renewing the precise liturgical practice of the early Christians, while the Moravians' emphasis was on structuring their common life to recover the communal spirit of apostolic Christianity.

The second part of the chapter evaluates Wesley's contacts with the Lutheran pastors to the Salzburger emigrants; here a mixture of respect and tension present in their relationship can also be observed. The analysis focuses on what their discussions and writings reveal about Wesley's theology of baptism, episcopacy and communion, and his use of hymns in Georgia.[2] Various concerns regarding the restoration of primitive Christianity dominated Wesley's engagement with the Moravians and the Lutherans.

---

[1] This theme is neglected in Adelaide Fries' and John Nelson's studies of Wesley and the Moravians in Georgia.

[2] Boltzius's and Gronau's writings also shed light on the attempts of some of Wesley's parishioners to elude his ecclesiastical discipline through seeking to be married by the Lutheran

WESLEY AND THE MORAVIANS ON THE
SIMMONDS

Traditional emphasis in studies of Wesley on his experience at Aldersgate Street (24 May 1738) has tended to minimize his early relations with the Moravians to his interaction with Peter Böhler, who had a significant impact on him immediately prior to the Aldersgate event. Without downgrading the importance of Böhler, Wesley's encounters with the Moravians in the New World must be considered as essential context to his connections with them upon his return to England. While the story of the impression Wesley gained of the Moravians' spirituality during the great storm aboard the *Simmonds* is important, there is much more to be considered when evaluating their contacts in Georgia.[3] Although their interaction on-board ship was fairly cordial, hints of reservation regarding Wesley's spiritual state are present in the journals of two Moravian passengers, David Nitschmann and Johann Andrew Dober. Scholars have often overlooked the substantial tensions present from the beginning of Wesley's relationship with the Moravians and have rather highlighted the lessons Wesley learned from them.[4] At the same time, by stressing the knowledge Wesley gained from the Moravians, many scholars have neglected the fact that Wesley contributed to the communal life of the Savannah Brethren by persuading them to adopt some of his High Church practices, such as weekly communion. Their relations on the *Simmonds* are examined in this section, followed by a discussion of their interaction in Georgia.

Although Wesley had some acquaintance with the devotional and propagandist literature of German Pietism, there is no evidence regarding his knowledge of the Moravians, who had a deep and lasting impact on his quest for experiential holiness. Eighteenth-century Moravians saw themselves as direct descendants of John Hus's early fifteenth-century movement to purify the Bohemian Church and, in turn, the whole Catholic Church by restoring primitive Christianity. J. K. Zeman has placed the Unitas Fratrum in 'the restitutionist stream of late medieval dissent' and asserted that they 'represented "voluntary primitivism"' in the Franciscan tradition: individual Christians

---

clergy: see Hammond, 345–50. On their assessments of Wesley's ministry as being sincere but legalistic, see Geordan Hammond, 'John Wesley's Relations with the Lutheran Pietist Clergy in Georgia', in Christian T. Collins Winn et. al. (eds), *The Pietist Impulse in Christianity* (Eugene, OR, 2011), 143–5.

   [3] Nelson, 17.

   [4] While Heitzenrater neglected to discuss these tensions, Rack only made a passing comment on them: *Wesley and the People Called Methodists*; Rack, 122. Martin Schmidt noted that their friendship 'must have had its darker moments', but he thought 'all of this was nothing compared to the great amount he gained from them.' However, he appears to have derived this conclusion from the observation that nothing about disagreements between them can be found in Wesley's published *Journal*: *John Wesley: A Theological Biography*, trans. Norman P. Goldhawk (London, 1962), 1:169.

were called upon to choose poverty as one of the marks of Christian disci-
pleship.'[5] A small remnant of the Church that remained in Moravia survived
under periodic persecution and was revived on Count Nikolaus Ludwig von
Zinzendorf's (1700–60) estate at Berthelsdorf, Saxony, in 1722. These refugees
possessed a limited knowledge of the traditions of the Unitas Fratrum, which
were adapted and assimilated with Zinzendorf's Lutheran Pietism. The primitivist ideal lived on in the Moravian communion and was shared by Zinzendorf,
who instructed the Brethren in Georgia to 'lead godly lives, patterned after the
writings and customs of the apostles.'[6] Zinzendorf's instructions illustrate that
the Moravians tended to focus on the New Testament church as revealed in
scripture, which contrasted with Wesley's conception of primitive Christianity
as the ante-Nicene church. Through their respective Anglican and Moravian
traditions, Wesley and the Moravians shared a common interest in the primitive church.[7] Early Moravian congregations based their liturgical forms on
primitive practice, especially as promoted in Gottfried Arnold's (1666–1714)
Die erste Liebe, das ist Wahre Abbildung der ersten Christen (1696) ('The First
Love, that is True Portrayal of the First Christians');[8] nonetheless, a different
emphasis can be observed in the ecclesial practice of Wesley and the Georgia
Moravians. Whereas Wesley was focused on precisely restoring early church
liturgy, the Moravians sought to revive 'true Christianity' by restoring the piety
and general liturgical forms of primitive Christianity.

The twenty-six Moravians on-board the *Simmonds* sailed to join ten
others who had been in Georgia since April 1735. They were led by David
Nitschmann (1696–1772), who had previously spent a few months preaching
to African slaves on the island of St Thomas.[9] Nitschmann had been ordained
bishop a few months earlier by Daniel Ernst Jablonski (1660–1741), bishop of
the Polish branch of the Unitas Fratrum and a corresponding member of the
SPCK.[10] Jablonski was a grandson of Johann Amos Comenius (1592–1670),
who was also a bishop of the Unitas Fratrum. This ordination connected them
with the episcopal line of the old Unitas Fratrum and, in their view, constituted
the Herrnhut community as the renewed Church of the United Brethren. The
adherence to episcopacy, which Wesley considered to be an essential aspect of

---

[5] Zeman, 'Restitution and Dissent in Late Medieval Renewal Movements: The Waldensians,
the Hussites and the Bohemian Brethren', *Journal of the American Academy of Religion*, 44
(1976), 26.

[6] Fries, 46; Podmore, *Moravian Church*, 2.

[7] On the issue of Moravian identity, see W. R. Ward 'The Renewed Unity of the Brethren: Ancient
Church, New Sect, or Interconfessional Movement?', *BJRL* 70 (1988), 77–92.

[8] Paul Peucker, 'The Ideal of Primitive Christianity as a Source of Moravian Liturgical Practice',
Journal of Moravian History, 6 (2009), 7–29.

[9] *Periodical Accounts Relating to the Missions of the Church of the United Brethren* (London,
1831), 12:443.

[10] On the SPCK and Pietism, see Daniel L. Brunner, *Halle Pietists in England: Anthony William
Boehm and the Society for Promoting Christian Knowledge*, in K. Aland, E. Peschke, and G. Schäfer
(eds), Arbeiten zur Geschichte des Pietismus, 29 (Göttingen, 1993).

the true church, would prove to be an important aspect of his relationship with the Moravians in Georgia.

In the first daily entry of Wesley's Georgia diary we find the note that he 'Began [to study a] German Grammar' and spent about four hours on this task. Two days later he attended the Moravian evening worship service, where he 'Sang with [the] Germans.' The following day he 'Began English with Nitschmann and [Martin von] Hermsdorf';[11] these three activities—personal and mutual language learning and attendance at the Moravians' evening worship—continued for the duration of the voyage to Georgia. Wesley's diary records approximately 110 hours of studying the German language, forty-four hours of mutual language study, and attendance at the Germans' worship service on about 123 occasions. Wesley's presence at Moravian worship was the most consistent of these three activities, which was rarely omitted from his daily routine. Likewise, his personal study of German was a regular discipline, although there were periods of intensive study and times when this activity was neglected for a few days. Mutual language lessons with Nitschmann, von Hermsdorf, and Dober were conducted more sporadically. Since Nitschmann (and presumably the other Moravians) could not speak English or Latin, it was all the more incumbent on Wesley to learn German in order to converse with them.[12] Considering these activities together, Wesley spent about 275 hours learning German and observing their practice and conduct in worship. Wesley gained further knowledge of the Moravians through reading their newly published hymn book *Das Gesang-Buch der Gemeine in Herrn-Huth*, an 'Account of the Children in Herrnhut', and an 'Account of the Brethren.'[13]

Surprisingly, Wesley's journals and diary and Ingham's journal provide scant material on their interactions with the Moravians. Therefore, this must be reconstructed through combining Wesley's diary and both men's journals with the journals of Nitschmann and Dober, which are slightly more revealing. Wesley's first comment on the Moravians in his manuscript journal is unstinting in its praise of these Christians 'who have left all for their Master, and who have indeed learned of him, being meek and lowly, dead to the world, full of faith and of the Holy Ghost.'[14] Writing with a few months of retrospect, Ingham heaped praise on the Moravians in his first mention of them in his journal: they were 'a good, devout, peaceable, and heavenly-minded people', whose

---

[11] JWD, 17, 19, 20 October 1735.

[12] Fries, 93.

[13] JWD, 27 October 1735; 24 and 26 February 1736. The 'Account of the Brethren' may have been *Primitive Church Government, in the Practice of the Reformed in Bohemia: Or, an Account of the Ecclesiastick Order and Discipline among the Reformed; or, the Unity of the Brethren in Bohemia. With some Notes of John-Amos Comenius* (n.p., 1703).

[14] JWMSJ, 17 October 1735; cf. JWJ, 25 January 1736. The fact that this comment is omitted from the published *Journal* may hint at the tensions that arose between Wesley and the Moravians between 1738 and the publication of his *Journal* in 1740.

example was very edifying. They are more like the Primitive Christians than any other church now in the world; for they retain both the faith, practice, and discipline delivered by the Apostles. They have regularly ordained bishops, priests, and deacons. Baptism, confirmation, and the eucharist are duly administered. Discipline is strictly exercised without respect of persons. They all submit themselves to their pastors, being guided by them in everything. They live together in perfect love and peace, having, for the present, all things in common. They are more ready to serve their neighbours than themselves. In their business, they are diligent and industrious; in all their dealings, strictly just and conscientious. In everything, they behave themselves with great meekness, sweetness, and humility.[15]

The four Methodist missionaries found the Moravians' fervent spirituality attractive. Their humility, zealous devotion, strict sense of Christian discipline, mutual accountability, communitarian spirit, and skill at harmoniously singing hymns, were all traits they appreciated. These were characteristics they believed were present amongst the primitive Christians, but had been neglected by the contemporary church. In a sense, the Moravians seemed to be the embodiment of the spirituality after which the Oxford Methodists strove. It was significant to Ingham that the Moravians held all goods in common like the early church at Jerusalem. This was done on a somewhat larger scale than the Methodists at Oxford and in Georgia, who held some of their material goods and financial resources in common. The Methodists wanted a renewal of the doctrine, discipline, and practice of the primitive church, and the Moravians provided a model close to what they had envisioned, which was apparently the common practice of their entire Church. What the Methodists observed was more concrete than an imagined fulfilment of a preconceived notion, the Moravians held a similar belief in the desirability of modelling themselves after the primitive church. However, one wonders if, to a degree, they saw what they wanted to see in the Moravians and romanticized their spirituality. The mystery surrounding the Moravians because of the language barrier between them and the Methodists may have made the young missionaries somewhat prone to idealizing them. Some of the Georgia Trustees and colonists saw them in a less favourable light as fanatical enthusiasts or mysterious foreigners who segregated themselves from society.[16]

Nitschmann's diary provides us with the first clue regarding his conversations with Wesley during the time the *Simmonds* was docked at Gravesend

---

[15] BIJ, 17 October 1735, p. 68; cf. Oglethorpe's comments in 'Bringing Moravians to Georgia: Three Latin Letters from James Oglethorpe to Count Nicholas von Zinzendorf', ed. George Fenwick Jones, trans. David Noble, *GHQ* 80 (1996), 850, 858.

[16] Ver Stegg (ed.), *True and Historical Narrative*, 150; William Stephens, *Stephens' Journal 1737–1740*, 22 August 1739, *CRG*, 4:394.

with his note that he spoke to two English clergymen about 'our ordination and our faith.'[17] Wesley's immediate interest in their ordination was characteristic of the importance High Church clergy attached to episcopacy and apostolic succession. Wesley probably received an incomplete answer at this point because of the language barrier between himself and the Moravians; therefore, on the following day he began to study German. Wesley's enthusiasm for his new friends and his desire for Christian unity was expressed when mutual language lessons began three days later with the phrase, 'May God give us all not only to be of one tongue, but of one mind and one heart!'[18]

During the first Sunday on-board, the Moravians organized their worship services and respective ministries. Elders were installed, 'bands' were arranged, intercessory prayer was observed, and two daily services were begun: the *Frühbetstunde* (early prayer meeting) at five in the morning and the *Singstunde* (singing meeting) in the evening. The *Singstunde* did not consist of singing alone (as it did in subsequent Moravian practice); it was also a time for scriptural homilies and theological discourse. Hymns sung during the *Singstunde* were arranged thematically around the daily *Losung* (a short Bible text). The diaries of Nitschmann and Dober indicate that Wesley took part in the singing as well as the theological discussions.[19]

A little later in the voyage Wesley took up the subject of the Lord's Supper with Nitschmann 'saying he thought it a sacrifice which consecrated and improved the life.'[20] This reveals that Wesley effectively explained to Nitschmann the standard Anglican belief in the sacrament as a means of grace that provides empowerment for Christian living through the High Church language of terming the Eucharist a sacrifice. Unfortunately, Nitschmann did not report his response. From what we know of Wesley's existing theological persuasions and interests, his questions about the ministry and Eucharist are exactly what would be expected.

---

[17] Nitschmann Diary, 27 October 1735 (NS), in Fries, 102.

[18] JWMSJ, 20 October 1735; cf. JWJ, 20 October 1735.

[19] Dober remarked that Wesley 'loses no opportunity to be at our song service': 4 December 1735 (NS), in Fries, 108–9. The Moravian leader August Spangenberg noted that the group of Moravians that had sailed to Georgia the previous year discussed 'the words of the songs' and defined 'obscure words' contained therein: ' "We Have Come to Georgia With Pure Intentions": Moravian Bishop August Gottlieb Spangenberg's Letters from Savannah, 1735', ed. and trans. George Fenwick Jones and Paul Martin Peucker, *GHQ* 82 (1998), 99.

[20] Nitschmann Diary, 20 January 1736 (NS), in Fries, 112. Wesley was with the Germans from eleven to twelve in the morning and at their *Singstunde* during the evening of that day: JWD, 9 January 1736.

WESLEY'S RELATIONS WITH THE
MORAVIANS IN GEORGIA

Wesley continued to frequent Moravian worship services and study German in Georgia. While he was occasionally able to attend the *Frühbetstunde* and midday Bible study, he mainly concentrated on attending the Moravian *Singstunde*, as he did on the *Simmonds*. Wesley seems to have planned evening prayer at Savannah's parish church to either be held immediately before or after the evening singing meeting, which generally began between 6:30 p.m. and 7:30 p.m. Taken as a whole, Wesley was present at Moravian worship on about eighty per cent of the days he spent in Savannah. His study of German was also maintained in earnest.[21] He noted various activities such as reading, writing, and translating German, as well as compiling a German dictionary and transcribing a German grammar. Johann Boltzius reported that Wesley 'understands the German language rather well, although speaking is somewhat difficult.'[22]

The Practice and Discipline of the Primitive Church

Upon his arrival in Georgia in February 1736, Wesley's first conversations with August Spangenberg (1704–92), the leader of the nine Moravians that had been in the colony for nearly a year, focused on their conceptions of the practice and discipline of the primitive church.[23] Spangenberg's diary reveals that they discussed Nitschmann's ordination when they first met. Wesley's account of the conversation reads:

> He told me several particulars relating to their faith and practice and discipline, all of which were agreeable to the plan of the first ages, and seemed to show that it was their one care, without desire of pleasing or fear of displeasing any, to retain inviolate the whole deposition once delivered to the saints.[24]

On the following day, Wesley set out his dream for cooperative evangelism of the Indians, which he thought could best be carried out with the assistance of several Moravian women who would act as deaconesses to baptize Indian

---

[21] There are about one hundred diary references to studying German; these studies were tested on an almost daily basis in his participation in Moravian worship.

[22] Boltzius and Israel Christian Gronau to Gotthilf August Francke (29 July 1737), in Boltzius, *Letters*, 1:205.

[23] They probably spoke primarily in Latin, since Wesley was only beginning to learn German and Spangenberg could not speak English before he went to Georgia in 1735: Podmore, *Moravian Church*, 19. Wesley and Spangenberg also spent a considerable amount of time discussing mysticism: see Hammond, 223.

[24] JWMSJ, 7 February 1736.

women in the 'apostolic manner' by immersion.[25] The conversation progressed
to Wesley's assertion that the rule of faith should consist of 'Scripture and the
consensus of the fathers...of the first three centuries.'[26] Under the same date in
his *Journal* Wesley noted Spangenberg's claim that the Moravians 'hold fast the
discipline, as well as the faith and practice, of the apostolical church.'[27]

After spending the better part of a month on-board the *Simmonds*, Wesley
and Delamotte took up residence with the Moravians on 27 February. They
stayed until 15 March when Samuel Quincy, the previous missionary to
Savannah, moved out of the parsonage and returned to England.[28] During this
period, Wesley was able to observe the Moravian way of life first-hand and
confirmed his view of them as representing a model of the type of primitive
Christianity he hoped to cultivate in the colony.[29] Their practice of mutual
accountability was similar to that of Anglican religious societies, but this was
combined with rigorous communal discipline in which all Moravians played
a role. While the Methodists emphasized communal discipline, the Moravians
demonstrated that this could include the laity. The Moravians lived out their
conception of Christian discipline by the radical practice of living together.
Their observance of the primitive community of goods was a natural outcome of their commitment to communal discipline.[30] After observing the
ordination of Anton Seiffert, Wesley, in his excitement, wrote that although
he had feared leaving behind his friends in England, God 'hath opened me
a door into the whole Moravian church.'[31] In a letter to the Georgia Trustees,
Ingham echoed Wesley in lavishing extravagant praise on the Moravians, calling them 'the most pious and perfect Christians he ever saw or read of since
the Apostles' times.'[32] Wesley continued to embrace opportunities to participate in Moravian communal worship, such as a love feast that 'was begun and
ended with thanksgiving and prayer, and celebrated in so decent a manner as
a Christian of the apostolical age would have allowed to be worthy of Christ.'[33]

Moravian sources prove that Wesley's appeals to primitive practice were not
ignored by them. Following some preliminary discussions on episcopacy (discussed in 'Episcopacy' in this chapter) and the primitive church, Wesley took the
initiative to encourage Spangenberg to implement some of the primitive practices that were dear to him; these included, recitation of the Lord's Prayer at every

---

[25] The office of *diakonas* (deaconess) was introduced into the Moravian Church in 1745.

[26] Spangenberg's Diary, 19 February 1736 (NS), in Nelson, 27.

[27] JWJ and JWMSJ, 9 February 1736; cf. BIJ, 17 October 1735, p. 68.

[28] On Quincy, see Hammond, appendix 3.

[29] See JWJ, 25 February 1736.

[30] This practice had already been observed by the Moravians during their first year in Savannah
and was taken as the model for their community in Savannah: Fries, 135.

[31] JWJ, 29 February 1736.

[32] Egmont, *Diary*, 22 January 1737, 2:333.

[33] JWMSJ, 8 August 1737. On the love feast, see David B. Eller, 'The Recovery of the Love Feast
in German Pietism', in Fred van Lieburg (ed.), *Confessionalism and Pietism* (Mainz, 2006), 11–30.

public meeting,[34] the celebration of Saturday, the observance of fast days, and the administration of the Lord's Supper every Sunday. Wesley explicitly justified these practices by appeal to primitive custom and Spangenberg agreed to present the proposals to the elders and congregational officers. In his only words of direct response to Wesley's propositions, Spangenberg expressed scepticism over the propriety of introducing fast days into a Church where they did not already exist.[35] However, there is clear evidence that Wesley's petition was not entirely disregarded. While the Moravians had initially decided to observe the Lord's Supper every four weeks, they soon elected to draw lots on whether to increase the celebration of this rite. They drew 'The more the heart tastes the sweet Saviour the more it is awakened to holiness', and therefore resolved to make communion a fortnightly ritual.[36] Within a year the Moravians were celebrating the Eucharist weekly and every fourth Saturday.[37] Further evidence of the Moravians' adaptation of their liturgical life along lines suggested by Wesley can be ascertained in Töltschig's diary entry for 7 April 1737:

> in our conference we decided that the Lord's Supper should be observed in the evening, which is at once best for us and also closer to the practice of our Saviour, as it was in the evening that he observed it with his disciples...when the Our Father is prayed the Brethren shall speak the 'Amen' out loud, because it was so done by the earliest Christians.[38]

These modifications and additions to the communal practice of the Savannah Moravians demonstrate their desire to emulate the early church. They also reveal the respect they had for Wesley's opinions and show that, to a degree, he influenced their liturgical customs in a manner parallel to Anglican High Church primitivism.

Episcopacy

In 1737, drawing on his conversations with Wesley, Spangenberg sent a report to the Moravian community at Herrnhut.[39] This key document provides detailed insight into the subjects the two men discussed and Spangenberg's ambivalent attitude towards his English friend. The letter, which focuses on episcopacy, the Lord's Supper, and scriptural interpretation, exposes the

---

[34] Baron von Reck told Boltzius that he questioned the Moravians about their infrequent use of the Lord's Prayer and received an unsatisfactory answer: *Detailed Reports*, 1 March 1736, 3:60.

[35] Spangenberg's Diary, 9 March 1736 (NS), in Nelson, 30; cf. JWMSJ, 31 [July] 1737.

[36] Töltschig's Diary, 21 April 1736 (NS), in Nelson, 30.

[37] Extract Savannah Diary—1737, in Nelson, 31. The precise date that this practice began is unknown.

[38] Töltschig's Diary, 7 April 1737 (NS), in Nelson, 31.

[39] Nelson cites 11 November 1737 (NS) as the date of this letter. At this time, Spangenberg was sailing back to Pennsylvania following a short visit to Savannah.

differences between Moravian churchmanship and Wesley's High Church Anglicanism. (The second major topic of the report, Wesley's attempt to restrict Holy Communion to those he believed lived holy lives, is discussed in chapter 4.) Spangenberg reported:

> He has moreover several quite special principles, which he still holds strongly since he drank them in with his mother's milk. He thinks that an ordination not performed by a bishop in the apostolic succession is invalid.[40] Therefore he believes that neither Calvinists nor Lutherans have *legitimos doctores* and *pastores*. From this it follows that the sacraments administered by such teachers are not valid: this also he maintains. Therefore he thinks that anyone who has been baptized by a Calvinist or Lutheran pastor is not truly baptized: accordingly he baptizes all persons who come from other sects, although not those who have been baptized in Roman Catholicism. He considers Nitschmann's and Anton [Seiffert]'s baptism valid.[41] Reason: they have an episcopal order from the apostolic church…He will not therefore share the Lord's Supper with anyone who is not baptized by a minister who had been ordained by a true bishop. All these doctrines derive from the view of the episcopacy which is held in the Papist and English churches, and which rests upon the authority of the Fathers. Above all he believes that all Scripture of doubtful interpretation must be decided not by reason but from the writings of the first three centuries, e.g. infant baptism, foot-washing,[42] fast days, celibacy[43] and many others.[44]

This account gives a revealing portrait of Wesley's mindset during his ministry in Georgia and provides primary documentation linking his thought to what we know about his ecclesial practice. This material comes closer than any single document that we have from Wesley other than his notes on the *Apostolic Constitutions* and *Canons* to systematically laying out the theological principles upon which he based his Georgia ministry; therefore, it is invaluable as a succinct statement of his beliefs that can only be discovered elsewhere by a painstaking process of compiling evidence from other primary documents. Spangenberg's report is valuable as a second-hand reflection of Wesley's thinking that confirms the logic behind Wesley's ecclesiology.

Spangenberg's letter verifies the well-known fact that the foundation for Wesley's High Church ecclesiology was inherited from his parents. His

[40] See John Clayton's report of Wesley's reference to '[being] confined to the succession': Clayton to JW (2 August 1734), *Works*, 25:393.

[41] Wesley had been told that Seiffert was baptised as a Catholic: 'Töltschigs Diarium', 31 May 1736, in 'Berichte und Diaria von dem Etablessement der Brüder in Georgia, 1734–1744', MS, R.14.A.6.d.5, 7, 12a, Unitätsarchiv der Evangelischen Brüder-Unität, Herrnhut, Germany, trans. Achim Kopp, fo. 420.

[42] This practice was observed by the Moravians in Georgia: see Spangenberg, 'We Have Come to Georgia', 94.

[43] See Wesley's queries to Spangenberg about celibacy and fasting in JWMSJ, 31 [July] 1737.

[44] August Gottlieb Spangenberg, 'A Moravian's Report on John Wesley—1737', ed. Douglas L. Rights, *South Atlantic Quarterly*, 43 (1944), 408–9; cf. Schmidt, *John Wesley*, 138.

account shows that what he meant by referring to Wesley's 'special principles' was principally his High Church/Nonjuror view of 'episcopal exclusivity'.[45] We know from Wesley's diary note regarding their conversation held on 27 February 1736 that Spangenberg denied the apostolic succession. This appears to mean that he discounted it as an essential aspect of a true church. Given that Wesley's notes in his diary are generally extremely brief, any diary annotation of this nature is an indication of something important to him. These 'special principles' had already been applied on the *Simmonds* where he rebaptized Ambrose Tackner. Spangenberg's testimony corroborates with the irrefutable evidence that Wesley treasured the Fathers of the first three centuries and the consensus of their teaching as the means to determine matters on which scripture is either silent or unclear. The practices of infant baptism, fast days, and celibacy were all advocated by Wesley, in part due to the strong apostolic tradition attached to these practices. When he first met Wesley in February 1736, Spangenberg noted that Wesley 'asked immediately about Nitschmann's situation' and 'was pleased' with the answer he received.[46] Spangenberg summed up Wesley's view with the note, 'In the matter of episcopal succession, he is very precise in accord with the principles of the Anglican Church'.[47] A few months later Johann Töltschig (1703–64), the congregational warden or overseer of the Savannah Moravians, was able to convince Charles Wesley and Ingham that the Moravian episcopacy was apostolic in origin through historical links with the Unitas Fratrum and the Waldensian Bishop Stephen, who they believed consecrated as bishops the first three elders of the Unitas Fratrum.[48] Evidently, the three Oxford Methodists were easily persuaded that the Moravians maintained episcopal ordination.

A few weeks later, Wesley witnessed the ordination ceremony of Anton Seiffert (1712–85) by Nitschmann and commented:

> The great simplicity as well as solemnity of the whole almost made me forget the seventeen hundred years between, and imagine myself in one of those assemblies where form and state were not, but Paul the tent-maker or Peter the fisherman presided; yet with the demonstration of the Spirit and of power.[49]

---

[45] Cornwall, *Visible and Apostolic*, 106.

[46] Spangenberg's Diary, 17, 18 February 1736 (NS), in Nelson, 25–6.

[47] Spangenberg's Diary, 8 March 1736 (NS), in Nelson, 29.

[48] 'Töltschigs Diarium', 31 May 1736, fo. 419. As leader of the Lutheran Salzburgers in Georgia, Boltzius disputed the antiquity of the Moravians: Aaron Spencer Fogleman, 'Shadow Boxing in Georgia: The Beginnings of the Moravian–Lutheran Conflict in British North America', *GHQ* 83 (1999), 630. Colin Podmore has recently argued that the Moravians did not receive apostolic succession: ' "The Moravian Episcopate and the Episcopal Church": A Personal Response', *Anglican and Episcopal History*, 72 (2003), 351–84. Nonetheless, the Anglican bishops supported a 1749 bill passed in Parliament that recognized the validity of the Moravian episcopate: see Podmore, *Moravian Church*, 203–27.

[49] JWJ, 28 February 1736.

While Wesley's liturgical practice at this time involved precise ceremony, he also thought that the primitive church could be revived through simple, Spirit-filled assemblies. When pressed by Charles Wesley and Ingham, Töltschig later stated that Seiffert was a bishop; however, he was ordained a minister (*Prediger*).[50] Nonetheless, this was an important event, particularly since it may have been the first ordination by a Protestant bishop in America.[51] Hereafter, John Wesley referred to Seiffert as 'the Moravian bishop'.[52] The significance of this experience may lie in Wesley's willingness to allow his perception of the Holy Spirit's presence to overpower any possible scruples he had regarding the Moravians' liturgical practice.

What matters is that Wesley believed the Moravians upheld episcopacy and the dignity of the ministry; however, the reality is that his High Churchmanship was incompatible with the Moravians' democratization of the ministerial office flowing from their particular view of mutual priesthood within the Christian community. Their custom was to grant a type of ordination or consecration to community offices not normally deemed ministerial.[53] Spangenberg had been ordained in the Lutheran Church, which probably explains why we do not have any record of Wesley asking him about his clerical status, though it is not clear what Spangenberg told Wesley about his ordination.[54] While both being ministers of the gospel, their conceptions of the ordained ministry differed. An example of this divergence is provided by Spangenberg, who, en route to Georgia witnessed a dispute amongst Swiss colonists (who carried no ordained minister with them) over whether to baptize a newly born infant. Spangenberg's opinion that an ordained minister was not needed in order for the infant to be baptized illustrates the gulf between his churchmanship and Wesley's.[55] In the light of Wesley's opinion, it is ironic that one of the reasons Halle Pietists were suspicious of the Moravians was their opinion that the Moravians undermined the ordained ministry.[56]

Wesley's determination to believe that Seiffert was a lawful bishop probably shows a degree of naivety, as well as his hope that as an Anglican clergyman he could maintain a close communion and working relationship with another episcopal body that upheld the primitive order. However, in his absence, his brother and Benjamin Ingham asked whether the Moravians would rebaptize people baptized in churches (e.g. the Lutheran Church) lacking episcopal apostolic succession, and discovered that this was 'not of importance' to them.[57]

---

[50] Töltschig's Diary, 1 June 1736, in Nelson, 39.

[51] Fries, 134–5; JWJ, 151 n. 58.

[52] For example, JWMSJ, 5 February 1737.

[53] Fries, 129.

[54] Spangenberg had turned down an opportunity to take Anglican orders while in London: Spangenberg's Diary, 14–16 January 1735, in Nelson, 30.

[55] Spangenberg, 'We Have Come to Georgia With Pure Intentions', 98.

[56] For an example of this fear in Georgia, see Spangenberg, 'We Have Come to Georgia With Pure Intentions', 108.

[57] 'Töltschigs Diarium', 31 May 1736, fo. 420.

They also openly expressed some doubts about the function of the Moravian ministerial orders. Töltschig recorded:

> They asked me whether Brother Nitschmann had also given Anton full power and authority to ordain another person who could celebrate the Lord's Supper, to baptize and marry, etc., if he should be absent or perhaps become ill. They also asked whether one ordained to such functions would be called a Priest? I said, 'Yes,' 'Then, they said, 'Anton is a bishop.' I said, 'Yes, he is so regarded by our congregation also.' Then they went on to ask, why we were so quiet about it and why we didn't openly announce, here in Savannah, what we are. I gave them my same answer, that it was not our concern to flourish before the world, that we laid no value on having a swarm of unconverted people who confess themselves to us but who none the less remain in their old nature and in an unrepentant state. But as usual we were not able to talk properly with these English. But with our 'walk' we testified as to what we are and what our concern is and what our purpose is. They were very well pleased and approved of that. They bewailed and sighed over the decadence in their own church. They display an uncommon reverence and love for our Brother Anton.[58]

Töltschig's record of this conversation does little to clear up the ambiguity surrounding the Georgia Moravians' ministerial orders, and makes it appear that Wesley and Ingham were unsure of the viability, if not validity, of the orders. Töltschig himself was not ordained until 1742.[59] The account makes it appear as if Seiffert functioned as a chief minister in the Savannah congregation, but to please Wesley and Ingham, Töltschig was willing to call Seiffert a bishop. Töltschig did not record a clear answer as to whether Seiffert could ordain others. The guiding principle of the Moravians was clearly much more focused on holy living than carefully defined clerical offices; this was, and remained, a marked area of difference between the Moravians and the Anglican clergymen.

Tensions in Wesley's Relations with the Moravians

The three Oxford Methodists were convinced that the Moravians retained elements of apostolic Christianity. They admired the Moravians enough to inquire into being accepted into their community but were denied on the basis of them not knowing one another well enough.[60] Despite the fact that they had generally cordial relations, tensions emerged.

---

[58] Töltschig's Diary, 1 June 1736, in Nelson, 39. Nitschmann stayed in the colony for just over a month before travelling to Pennsylvania and back to Germany: Fries, 141.

[59] Colin Podmore, 'Töltschig, Johann', in Donald M. Lewis (ed.), *The Blackwell Dictionary of Evangelical Biography 1730–1860* (Oxford, 1995), 2:1112.

[60] 'Töltschigs Diarium', 20, 21 May, 1 June 1736, fos 418, 420–1; cf. Nelson, 34–8. Possibly due to their disappointment, the Methodists declined the offer to join the Moravians' celebration of communion.

What did the Moravians think of Wesley? Some evidence can be found in the *Simmonds* diary of Dober. Nitschmann's voyage diary is devoid of reflections on Wesley, seemingly indicating that he cautiously approached his contacts with Wesley. Dober observed that Wesley showed 'himself full of love for us.' He was also impressed that Wesley spared 'no pains to perform the duties of his office' and was 'very careful of the passengers welfare.' Dober noted his own desire that the Moravians 'could converse freely with him, so that we could carefully explain the way of God to him.'[61] Here, Dober hints at his reservation as to Wesley's knowledge of the way of salvation as understood by the Moravians—similar reservations are later found in the Georgia diaries of August Spangenberg and Johann Töltschig.

The journals of Nitschmann, Töltschig, and Spangenberg reveal a guarded respect for Wesley coupled with a lack of sympathy for his High Church scruples and the wish that he would focus more on 'the religion of the heart.'[62] (Their reluctance to praise Wesley may have been due in part to their knowledge that their accounts would be read in Herrnhut, which necessitated that they needed to remain faithful to the mother congregation in their trans-confessional dealings.) In his conversations with Wesley, Spangenberg did his utmost to avoid disputation and searched for areas of agreement.[63] This reluctance to discuss controversial subjects with Wesley reflected his desire to steer clear of the type of controversy that surrounded him in the aftermath of his dismissal from Halle (discussed in 'Wesley's Relations with the Lutheran Pietists in Georgia' in this chapter). A fairly negative view emerges from the diary of Johann Töltschig, who lived in Savannah with Wesley for nearly two years. After having been acquainted with Wesley for over a year, Töltschig made two critical assessments of Wesley: 'he is very unstable and flighty but is a very perceptive mind.' The second comment comes in a letter to Herrnhut: 'Mr. Wesley is an extremely unstable man and with that also sectarian. He has no inclination to go among the Indians and I believe it is a very good thing that he does not go...'[64] From Töltschig's point of view, Wesley's spiritual life was tumultuous and his clerical practice characterized by sectarianism. There is a degree of unintentional irony here since the Moravians were continually being condemned as separatists by the Lutherans.

Though Wesley regularly professed his affection for the Savannah Moravians, his dialogues with the Lutheran pastors indicate that he questioned some of

---

[61] Dober's Diary, 4 December 1735 and 27 January 1736 (NS), in Fries, 108–9, 113.

[62] See Ted A. Campbell, *The Religion of the Heart: A Study of European Religious Life in the Seventeenth and Eighteenth Centuries* (Columbia, SC, 1991), 91–8 on the place of the Moravians in this intra-European devotional movement.

[63] This can be observed in Spangenberg's answers to a series of questions Wesley asked him: JWMSJ, 31 [July] 1737; cf. Fries, 190.

[64] Töltschig's Diary, 21–22 June 1737 and letter dated October 1737, in Nelson, 37; cf. Töltschig's Diary, 28 May 1736 (NS), in Nelson, 36.

their beliefs and practices.[65] Wesley held numerous theological dialogues with Töltschig and Seiffert in which both the language barrier between them and Töltschig's and Seiffert's limited authority to speak for the Moravians played a role.[66]

In July 1737 Spangenberg arrived in Georgia from Pennsylvania after having received reports that the Moravians were considering abandoning their settlement in Georgia and moving to Pennsylvania. From that moment, sustained rounds of almost daily conversation resumed in the same manner as before Spangenberg left Georgia in March 1736. Discussion on those first few days was partly taken up by Wesley's questioning of Spangenberg about Moravian beliefs, which he still found mysterious after having been in almost daily contact with the Savannah Moravians for over eighteen months.

At Spangenberg's invitation, Wesley drew up a series of thirty-one queries, which he indicated were answered by Spangenberg in consultation with Töltschig and Seiffert.[67] Several of the issues discussed are particularly revealing of Wesley's focus on primitive Christianity and areas of theological difference between himself and the Moravians. Wesley first addressed the topic of conversion. This seems to reflect both the Moravian emphasis on conversion and Wesley's interest in the means by which conversion is wrought. Query three reads: 'Ought we so to expect the Holy Ghost to convert either our own or our neighbour's souls as to neglect any outward means?' In response 'Reading the scripture, hearing it, fasting, self-examination, the instructions of experienced persons, and fervent prayer' are named by Spangenberg as outward means not to be neglected. Unfortunately, Wesley neither answers his questions nor comments on Spangenberg's replies; however, one could confidently assume that he would have mentioned the sacraments of baptism and communion while not disagreeing with the methods mentioned by Spangenberg. As it is worded, Wesley's query hints that he was suspicious of Moravian quietism (or stillness) in Georgia—an issue that would later resurface in his dealings with the Moravians in London.[68]

---

[65] See 'Discussions of the Moravians' in this chapter.

[66] Presumably they conversed using a mixture of English and German. It is not clear whether either of the Moravians spoke Latin. Töltschig's command of English was limited as he still spoke broken English in the 1740s: see Podmore, 'Töltschig, Johann', *Dictionary of Evangelical Biography*, 2:1112.

[67] See Spangenberg, 'A Moravian's Report', 409 and JWD, 29 [July] 1737. These queries may have been discussed with Spangenberg while en route to New Ebenezer, where Wesley hoped to promote peace between the Moravian and Salzburger communities: on this episode see Fogleman, 'Shadow Boxing in Georgia', 652–3, 653 n. 30. Wesley seems to have sympathized with Boltzius's and Gronau's complaints about the Moravians and went away 'convinced' that Zinzendorf was 'but a man and not either wiser or better than the apostles': JWMSJ, 1 August 1737; cf. *Detailed Reports* MS, 28–29 June 1737, 4:119. Latin would have probably been the language of the written dialogue. Wesley later published critical *Queries Humbly Proposed to the Right Reverend and Right Honourable Count Zinzendorf* (London, 1755), which accused Zinzendorf and the Moravians of theological unorthodoxy and believing they were superior to the Apostles.

[68] Podmore, *Moravian Church*, 59–65.

The next question is: 'Ought we so to expect the Holy Ghost to interpret Scripture to us as to neglect any outward means? Particularly, inquiring into the sense of the Ancient Church?' Clearly, Wesley had surmised that the Moravians had adopted the Reformation slogan of *sola Scriptura* in a rather literal sense and stressed the role of the Spirit as interpreter of scripture. Spangenberg's response that 'Scripture is clear, in all things necessary to be known' was far more simplistic than the view of High Churchmen like Wesley, who believed that reason and tradition were God-ordained tools for interpreting scripture and defining doctrine. For Wesley, the most reliable guardians of tradition and the finest representatives of reasoned discourse (along with his Anglican forebears and contemporaries) were the Church Fathers.

As becomes clear from Wesley's following question ('What is the visible church?') the Moravian appeal to apostolicity was primarily geared towards 'apostolical order and discipline' in the Christian community. This perspective was undoubtedly incorporated by Wesley into his ideal of primitive Christianity, as illustrated by his emphasis on discipline in the early Methodist societies.

Other questions that pertain to Wesley's attraction to the primitive church include: '16. Is celibacy a state more advantageous for holiness than marriage? 17. Are ministrations of a man not episcopally ordained valid?' As a convinced celibate, Spangenberg answered, 'Yes, to them who are able to receive it' to the former question and declined to respond to the latter query.[69]

Public prayer was dealt with in several questions, which reveal that Spangenberg advocated hymns as 'forms of prayer' and extemporary prayer led by the Holy Spirit over 'set forms of prayer.' He curiously interpreted the Lord's Prayer 'As a command to avoid vain repetition in prayer.' These responses, showing a firm desire to avoid structured public prayers, set Spangenberg apart from Wesley's prayer book piety. They arise from his Lutheran Pietist and Moravian heritage and perhaps were vocalized to clearly draw distinctions between Moravian and Anglican public worship.[70]

It may not have been a coincidence that tensions in Wesley's relationship with the Moravians were most apparent during the latter part of his tenure in Georgia when the Sophia Williamson affair was at its height.[71] Töltschig may have had the thirty-one queries meeting in mind when he noted: 'We also had a conference with Wesley where he stated what he had to charge against us and we stated what we had against him, that we could not place confidence in him. He accepted everything very well.'[72] Martin Schmidt's conclusion that

---

[69] On the young Spangenberg's convictions about celibacy, see Craig D. Atwood, 'Spangenberg: A Radical Pietist in Colonial America', *Journal of Moravian History*, 4 (2008), 12.

[70] JWMSJ, 31 [July] 1737; cf. Böhler's Diary, 2 March 1738, in C. J. Podmore, 'The Fetter Lane Society, 1738', *PWHS* 46 (1988), 130.

[71] See 'The Sophia Williamson Controversy in Context: Opposition to Wesley's Ministry to Women' in chapter 5.

[72] Töltschig's Diary, 12 August 1737 (NS), in Nelson, 40.

between Wesley and Spangenberg 'the awareness of unanimity was stronger than that of difference' is certainly open to question, particularly in view of his relations with the Moravians as a whole, if the opinion of Töltschig is added to the equation.[73] Spangenberg's 1737 'report' written during this same period of time provides a clear account of what he saw as Wesley's misguided theological principles, which divided him from the Moravians.[74] Despite what seem to be indications of growing tensions, Wesley continued to associate with the Germans for daily services at noon and seven in the evening. The same is true for Spangenberg, who appears to have subsequently spoken at a religious society meeting of Wesley's parishioners.[75] Not long after these queries were written Wesley joyfully participated in a Moravian love feast.[76] Obviously, for the time being, differences in theology and differing theological emphases did not overpower the bonds of Christian friendship between Wesley and the Moravians. Their relationship was fairly cordial in Georgia, but the seeds of subsequent discord were planted. Wesley continued to share in fellowship with the Moravians, who provided something of a substitute for his missionary colleagues, especially after the departure of Charles Wesley (in July 1736) and Benjamin Ingham (in February 1737) from Georgia.[77]

Without discounting the discernible tension between Wesley and the Savannah Moravians, areas in which they influenced Wesley in a lasting manner may be detected. Reflecting upon his return to England, Wesley noted that his introduction to the Moravians was one of the several blessings that had resulted from his sojourn in Georgia.[78] Through their piety, communal discipline, and hymns, the Savannah Moravians had a long-term impact on Wesley. His interaction with the Moravians opened him up to an exciting new world of spirituality, since his study at Oxford had focused on High Church Anglican, Catholic, and patristic models of spirituality. He saw them as an incarnation of the primitive church in his day because they maintained three essential aspects of the early church: episcopacy, discipline, and holy living. Their stress on heart-felt faith in Christ and the transformative effects of the new birth was incorporated into his developed Anglican emphasis on purity of intention and pure love towards God. It might be said that through the influence of the Moravians, Wesley slowly began to assimilate an evangelical (in the sense of an

---

[73] Schmidt, *John Wesley*, 181.

[74] Spangenberg, 'A Moravian's Report'. Regarding this report, Nelson commented that 'With a dossier like his it should come as no surprise that he should be judged a *homo perturbatus* in Germany on 4 July 1738' (p. 42).

[75] JWD, 7 August 1737. On the religious societies, see 'Wesley's Religious Societies in Georgia' in chapter 4.

[76] JWMSJ, 8 August 1737.

[77] Källstad, *John Wesley*, 135.

[78] JWJ, 3 February 1738.

increasing focus on evangelical doctrines such as assurance of salvation) view of the primitive church into his existing vision of the early church.[79]

Moravian practices such as love feasts and watchnights were later adapted by Wesley for his Methodist societies. Moravian 'bands' also had an impact on the subsequent organization of Methodist societies, and they may have influenced the development of Wesley's religious societies in Georgia. The Moravians introduced Wesley to the joy of hymn-singing and its devotional and evangelistic usefulness. They also represented, on a much larger scale, the communal discipline Wesley sought to instil in the Oxford Methodist societies.

WESLEY'S RELATIONS WITH THE LUTHERAN PIETISTS IN GEORGIA

Wesley's conception of the Georgia mission as a laboratory to implement his views of the primitive church was a central factor in his relations with the German Lutheran ministers to the Salzburger emigrants. Pastors Johann Martin Boltzius (1703–65) and Israel Christian Gronau (d. 1745) had arrived in the colony in 1734 with a group of seventy-eight Salzburgers. These refugees were amongst the estimated 20,000 who had been expelled from the principality of Salzburg as a result of their refusal to conform to the Catholicism of the prince-bishop of Salzburg, Count Leopold von Firmian.[80]

From the time he became a member of the SPCK, in 1732, Wesley closely followed the plight of the Salzburger refugees, who were supported by the Society.[81] He was, therefore, aware of their presence in Georgia and was encouraged by the SPCK before his departure to 'supply the present wants' of the Lutheran ministers out of the stock of books he had been granted by the society.[82] He attended two SPCK meetings with Philipp Georg Friedrich von Reck, who led the third transport of Salzburgers to Georgia on the *London Merchant*.[83] He recorded conversations with von Reck on four occasions on the voyage to Georgia, when he was able to board the *London Merchant* for short stints. This provided him with an opportunity to be introduced to the

---

[79] Keefer, 'John Wesley: Disciple of Early Christianity' (1984), 24.

[80] On the Georgia Salzburgers, see George Fenwick Jones, *The Salzburger Saga: Religious Exiles and Other Germans along the Savannah* (Athens, 1984) and *The Georgia Dutch: From the Rhine and Danube to the Savannah, 1733–1783* (Athens, 1992).

[81] He read *An Account of the Sufferings of the Persecuted Protestants in the Archbishoprick of Saltzburg* (1732) in July 1732 and *A Further Account of the Sufferings of the Persecuted Protestants in the Archbishoprick of Saltzburg* (1733) in August 1733: see Hammond, appendix 5.

[82] Henry Newman to JW (13 October 1735), *Works*, 25:443.

[83] On the SPCK and the Salzburger emigration, see Leonard Cowie, *Henry Newman: An American in London 1708–43* (London, 1956), 223–49.

Salzburgers on-board.[84] While en route to Georgia he also read the journal of von Reck's previous journey to Georgia.[85]

Prior to the commencement of the Oxford Methodist sojourn to Georgia, the Halle Pietists were aware of events in Oxford. The first defence of the Oxford Methodists' activities, *The Oxford Methodists* (1733) was translated by the German community in London and dispatched to Germany.[86] W. R. Ward and Aaron Spencer Fogleman have shown that the arrival of Spangenberg with a group of nine Moravians in Georgia instigated an extension of the Halle–Herrnhut quarrel to North America. This intense rivalry was fuelling the emerging revival in Europe and their emigration to Georgia brought the incipient revival to the New World.[87] Once the Halle party failed to prevent the Moravians from embarking for Georgia, their tactic was to ensure minimal contact between the Salzburger and Moravian colonists and to commission Boltzius and Gronau to closely observe and send written reports on the behaviour of the Moravians.[88] Secondarily, Boltzius and Gronau were urged to become acquainted with Wesley to offset the potential Moravian influence on him. This concern arose in part because of the distribution of Wesley's manuscript journal in London, which was circulating by June 1736, and included accounts of his conversations with Spangenberg during his first ten days in Georgia. Interest was chiefly awakened by his short account of Spangenberg's life, which included an explanation of his controversial dismissal from the University of Halle.[89] Friedrich Michael Ziegenhagen, (1694–1776) preacher at the German court chapel in St James's, London, informed Gotthilf August Francke, the successor at Halle of his famous father, August Hermann Francke, about the esteem in which Wesley was held by many in London and the danger that 'this inaccurate passage would, thereby, be more widely known than is desirable.' Ziegenhagen took the opportunity to urge the unknown Anglican clergyman who had given him the journal 'to assure Mr. Wesley with our friendly greetings that Mr. Spangenberg's report of his own dismissal from Halle is, in any case, incorrect and false.'[90] Francke elected to export this news to Boltzius and Gronau, advising them that

---

[84] JWD, 20, 23, 24 October, 10 November 1735, 28 January 1736.

[85] *Extract of the Journals of Mr. Commissary von Reck…and of the Reverend Mr. Bolzius* (London, 1734). His journal was edited by the SPCK so that no negative light was shed on the Salzburger emigration: Cowie, *Henry Newman*, 234.

[86] W. R. Ward, *The Protestant Evangelical Awakening* (Cambridge, 1992), 4, 310.

[87] Ward, *Protestant Evangelical Awakening*, 3; Fogleman, 'Shadow Boxing', 631, 658–9. For a concise summary of Halle critiques of the Moravians, see Hammond, 145–6.

[88] Fries, 43–4; Podmore, *Moravian Church*, 10–23; Fogleman, 'Shadow Boxing', 641–2. Examples of some of these reports can be found in Boltzius, *Letters*. Spangenberg successfully convinced the Georgia Trustees and SPCK that the Moravians agreed entirely in doctrine with the Lutheran Church, only differing in discipline: Henry Newman to Samuel Urlsperger (21 January 1735), *Henry Newman's Salzburger Letterbooks*, 152.

[89] On this episode, see Ward, *Protestant Evangelical Awakening*, 139–41.

[90] Ziegenhagen to Francke (17 June 1736), in Zehrer, 'Relationship between Pietism', 212–13.

Unless it be said that the said Mr. Wesley did not properly appreciate the case of Mr. Spangenberg or has reported it poorly, we can certainly conclude with great exactitude from this report what Mr. Spangenberg's attitude is, and that he cannot have truthfully and uprightly reported that in which he was here involved, and that he must yet be ill-disposed, and taken in by Count Zinzendorf.[91]

In a subsequent letter, Francke encouraged them to become acquainted with the Anglican missionaries, keep him informed about their Indian mission, and the conflict between Wesley and Thomas Causton's niece, while Ziegenhagen advised them to 'maintain a good acquaintance and friendship'.[92]

While Wesley's journals contain numerous references to the Moravians, they make a single generalized comment on the industriousness of the Lutheran Salzburgers. Because of this, Wesley's biographers have often had very little to say about his contacts with Boltzius and Gronau, whose names do not appear in his published *Journal*. His diary includes several notations that he spent time in conversation with them (usually separately), primarily in the summer of 1737. From this it can be observed that a relationship was begun with the Lutheran ministers, but a study that relies on Wesley's writings can say nothing significant about his interaction with them. Older biographies generally display this limitation, since the journal and some letters of Boltzius and Gronau were not published in an English translation until the 1960s. Their jointly authored journal published under the title *Detailed Reports on the Salzburger Emigrants* contains almost daily accounts of life in Georgia, chiefly written by Boltzius. These *Reports* form an invaluable and underused source on the interaction of Wesley and the Lutheran ministers.[93] They should be read alongside the recently published selection of letters of Boltzius.[94] One aim of this chapter, therefore, is to raise awareness of the depth of the contacts between Wesley and Boltzius and Gronau, which should redress the historical imbalance found in many studies of Wesley's Georgia mission that focus on his relationship with the Moravians while neglecting his interaction with the Lutheran clergy. From the *Detailed Reports* and letters of Boltzius one can observe that the same tension,

---

[91] Francke to Boltzius and Gronau (22 October 1736), in Zehrer, 'Relationship between Pietism', 213.

[92] Francke to Boltzius and Gronau (10 December 1736), and Ziegenhagen to Boltzius and Gronau (1 March 1737), in Zehrer, 'Relationship between Pietism', 213, 214; summaries of Francke's letters of 8 February, 2 September, and 21 December 1737 in Thomas J. Müller-Bahlke and Jürgen Gröschl (eds), *Salzburg—Halle—North America: A Bilingual Catalog with Summaries of the Georgia Manuscripts in the Francke Foundations* (Tübingen, 1999), 273–4, 296–7, 320–1. Wesley later met Francke in Halle on 19 August 1738: see JWJ.

[93] Recent studies of Wesley by Henry Rack and Richard Heitzenrater contain no reference to this important source. Martin Schmidt made limited use of this journal, leaving room for a more detailed study and analysis: see Rack; Heitzenrater, *Wesley and the People Called Methodists*; Schmidt, *John Wesley*, 178–82.

[94] Boltzius, *Letters*.

coupled with mutual respect and friendship that was present in Wesley's relationship with the Moravians, was also evident in his interaction with the Lutherans. Through the eyes of Boltzius and Gronau we can observe key differences between their Lutheran Pietism and Wesley's High Church Anglican primitivism.

Although Wesley had some contacts with the Pietists von Reck and Gronau, his interaction was primarily with the head pastor of the Salzburgers, Johann Boltzius. Their conversations are recorded in *The Letters of Johann Martin Boltzius* and the *Detailed Reports* regularly forwarded to Halle and published and disseminated to uphold the emigration of the pious Salzburgers as a manifestation of God's providence designed to shame their Catholic persecutors, reinvigorate Lutheranism in Europe, and serve as an example to all Christians.[95] The contents of these reports were summarized in the Weimar Orthodox journal *Acta Historico-Ecclesiastica* and, therefore, would have been widely known in both Pietist and Orthodox Lutheran circles.[96] They reveal a number of significant topics of conversation and controversy between Wesley and Boltzius in particular. The most sensitive aspects of their discussions were omitted by Samuel Urlsperger, (1685–1772) patron of the Salzburgers (in tandem with Francke, Ziegenhagen, and the SPCK) and Senior Lutheran minister in Augsburg. Fortunately, the manuscripts have survived and the excised portions have been restored in the recently published English translation edited by George Fenwick Jones.

Not long after he was settled in Savannah, Wesley wrote in Latin to the Lutheran pastors seeking their 'friendship and the right hand of fellowship.' Boltzius and Gronau had served together, the former as a supervisor and the latter as a teacher, at the Latin School of the Orphanage at August Hermann Francke's Foundations at Halle, and had been selected and ordained in Germany as pastors to the Salzburger refugees. Gronau was appointed as catechist and assistant minister to Boltzius. They arrived in the colony in 1734 with the first group of seventy-eight Salzburgers and settled in Ebenezer (a Hebrew word meaning 'stone of help')[97] about twenty-five miles northwest of Savannah; in 1736, they moved six miles east to New Ebenezer on a bluff overlooking the Savannah River.[98] Through the letter Wesley offered his services to them, asked for their prayers, and exhorted them not to be troubled by the

---

[95] See 'The Secret Diary of Pastor Johann Martin Boltzius', ed. George F. Jones, *GHQ* 53 (1969), 7 February 1736, p. 85.

[96] W. R. Ward, 'Power and Piety: The Origins of Religious Revival in the Early Eighteenth Century', *BJRL* 63 (1980), 248; Ward, notes on the *Acta Historico-Ecclesiastica* loaned to the author.

[97] Behind this name are the biblical allusions to the place where the Israelites camped before they went into battle with the Philistines (1 Samuel 4:1) and the stone that Samuel set up after the Israelite victory (1 Samuel 7:12).

[98] For Wesley's description of Old and New Ebenezer, see JWJ, 2 December 1737.

sufferings they were called to.[99] He soon became involved in matters relating to the Salzburgers via Oglethorpe's request that he investigate the power struggles between John Vat, who had led the second transport of Salzburgers to Georgia, and von Reck.[100]

Baptism by Trine Immersion

When they began to be in regular contact with Wesley in 1737, Boltzius and Gronau became aware of growing conflicts between Wesley and his parishioners regarding his exercise of ecclesiastical discipline. Several of Wesley's parishioners approached the Lutheran ministers for their clerical services in attempts to escape from Wesley's authority and what they saw as his unwelcome imposition of church regulation. One of the issues that led to this was Wesley's insistence on baptism by trine immersion.[101] While in Savannah in January 1737 Gronau was asked to baptize a nine-month-old child of 'an old physician' and refused, since this fell within Wesley's jurisdiction.[102] The relation of this event is followed by the note that 'The people there are much displeased that Mr. N. [Wesley] does not wish to baptize children other than by immersing them in the water unless he can be convinced that the infants could not stand such treatment due to their feeble health.'[103] Nothing in this account is unexpected given Wesley's refusal to baptize Henry and Anne Parker's child because they would not submit to having the child immersed, nor would they 'certify' that the child was weak.[104] This episode reinforces the evidence from Wesley's journals and diary that a definite controversy surrounded Wesley's insistence on trine immersion of infants.

[99] JW to Boltzius and Gronau [13 March 1736], *Works*, 25:448–9.

[100] Oglethorpe to JW (16 March 1736), *Works*, 25:740–1; Oglethorpe to Trustees (16 March 1736), *CRG*, 21:105. Accordingly, Wesley wrote to von Reck and Boltzius about this issue and received a reply from Boltzius detailing Vat's transgressions: JWD, 24 March 1736, letter to von Reck; JWD, 31 March 1736, letters to von Reck and Boltzius; *Detailed Reports* MS, 30 March 1736, 3:96. Boltzius's 'Secret Diary' provides a detailed account of the tensions between Vat and von Reck, but he does not mention Wesley.

[101] Boltzius was aware that Wesley had rebaptized Ambrose Tackner on the voyage to Georgia and failed to convince another German, Michael Volmar, to submit to rebaptism. See 'Wesley's Baptismal Doctrine and Practice' in chapter 2.

[102] Dr Patrick Tailfer's profession, his dislike of Wesley, and Wesley's story about him having two children with the daughter of one of his distant relatives whom he had brought to Georgia makes it seemingly possible that he was the 'old physician': JWMSJ and JWD, 12 November 1736.

[103] *Detailed Reports*, 13 January 1737, 4:6.

[104] JWJ and JWD, 5 May 1736: see 'The Ministration of Publick Baptism of Infants' in the 1662 BCP.

Episcopacy, Apostolic Succession, and
Holy Communion

In June, July, and early August 1737, Wesley and Boltzius spent significant amounts of time together. Based on the records they have left, their conversations focused heavily on the contentious doctrine of episcopacy. Their interactions culminated with a summit Wesley organized between Spangenberg and the Lutheran ministers at New Ebenezer in August.[105] Overall, the two conscientious clergymen developed a significant level of respect and admiration for one another in spite of their theological differences.

The most extended round of discussions took place during Boltzius's visit to Savannah between 13 and 19 July. Wesley recorded spending over six hours of his day with Boltzius on 14 July, more than an hour on 15 July, and approximately three hours on Sunday 17 July. Upon his return to New Ebenezer, Boltzius wrote: 'I have become quite familiar with Mr. Wesley during this somewhat longer stay in Savannah, and we have joined our hearts in the Lord.' At the close of his reflections, Boltzius mildly hinted at an inconsequential disagreement that was nothing more than 'an unnecessary scruple' held by Wesley. Because the *Detailed Reports* were published in Halle, Boltzius evidently wanted to defer this issue for a private report 'at the proper place'. His cautious words suggest that he hoped to emphasize the unity between himself and Gronau with Wesley. Wesley's manuscript journal for Sunday 17 June contains the following sentence: 'I had occasion to make a very unusual trial of the temper of Mr. Boltzius, pastor of the Salzburgers, in which he behaved with such lowliness and meekness as became a disciple of Christ.' Thus far we have two cryptic statements; however, Wesley's diary sheds some light on this matter. Wesley and Boltzius spent several hours on Sunday morning in conversation that centred on the discussion of communion. The issue at hand stemmed from Wesley's insistence on episcopal ordination, as revealed by a letter from Boltzius and Gronau sent to Ziegenhagen two weeks after this event. The Lutheran pastors explained that Wesley declared

> He finds in Scripture and in the Fathers of the first 3 ages that episcopal ordination and the laying on of hands were required for the office of a minister, and since the ministers of our church do not have their ordination from a bishop, they can neither administer the Holy Sacraments in a salutary way according to the intention of Christ, nor can they verify that their own baptism, which they received in their youth, is proper.

They noted that 'He believes this with such certainty that no argument can be so powerful to dissuade him in the least from his opinion.' Though they opposed Wesley's belief and endeavoured to detail the Lutheran view on this

---

[105] Fogleman, 'Shadow Boxing'.

doctrine, from the perspective of Boltzius and Gronau, his position was made all the more problematic because they believed Spangenberg held that the Moravians maintained apostolic succession and was willing to consider the Anglican doctrine. Therefore, they reported that Wesley 'holds the Herrnhuter Brethren to be the true church because they understand a succession of bishops and continual ordination to derive from the apostles.'[106]

Although both Wesley and Boltzius avoided explicitly writing about the consequences of their disagreement over episcopacy, it led to Wesley declining to administer Holy Communion to Boltzius, since he was neither baptized nor ordained by a bishop who upheld apostolic succession. This contentious issue was reawakened when Wesley received a letter from Boltzius in 1749, which reminded him of his denial of communion to his friend. On this occasion, Wesley remarked, 'Can any one carry *High Church* zeal higher than this? And how well have I been since beaten with mine own staff!'[107] Wesley was right about Boltzius's genuine 'meakness [*sic*]' of spirit, since he maintained a friendship with Wesley despite undergoing this embarrassing affront to his clerical authority and Christian character.[108]

Discussions of the Moravians

While due allowance must be made for Boltzius's prejudice against the Moravians, Wesley did make some of his genuine concerns about the Moravians known to Boltzius at the time their friendship blossomed in June and July 1737. An extended conversation on this matter took place on 9 June during a day in which they spent all afternoon travelling together to and from Thomas Causton's plantation a few miles outside of Savannah. In the course of their discussion, Wesley confessed that he found the Moravians mysterious, since 'they hesitated making a full basic revelation of their belief', and regarding their teachings that 'they would only refer to the Bible, which,' Wesley noted, 'both old and new heretics are wont to do.' Although he expressed some doubts as to their 'honesty', he had not found any particular deceitfulness in their behaviour. Wesley recounted his reception of a letter from an unknown 'person close to the Herrnhuters in Germany' who 'argued that the time was approaching

---

[106] *Detailed Reports* MS, 19 July 1737, 4:135; JWMSJ, 17 July 1737; JWD, 14, 15, 17 July 1737; Boltzius and Gronau to Friedrich Michael Ziegenhagen (29 July 1737), in Boltzius, *Letters*, 215. Boltzius's and Gronau's opinion needs to be evaluated alongside Wesley's 27 February 1736 diary comment that Spangenberg denied the apostolic succession.

[107] JWJ, 30 September 1749, 20:305; cf. Sermon 'On Laying the Foundation of the New Chapel' (1777), *Works*, 3:583. Spangenberg recounted that Wesley 'will not therefore share the Lord's Supper with anyone who is not baptized by a minister who had been ordained by a true bishop': Spangenberg, 'A Moravian's Report', 409.

[108] Wesley's position was almost certainly inspired by the Nonjurors, since it was very rare before the Nonjuring schism: see Spurr, *Restoration Church of England*, 159.

when a greater holiness and purity of Christian dogma and life would be established'. According to Boltzius, Wesley saw this as arrogant enthusiasm, since 'truly holy dogma and truly holy life was that which is described and presented in the writings of the prophets, evangelists, and apostles of the Lord, and that no greater holiness and purity…could be expected in this life'.[109] Nonetheless, Boltzius consistently overestimated the hold the Moravians had on Wesley and still continued to fear that he would join the Moravians.[110]

It appears that at this time Boltzius extended an invitation for Wesley to visit New Ebenezer, which prompted him to reflect a few days later that Wesley 'finds it suspicious' that the Moravians 'have no creed'. Because he continued to be perplexed by their apparent unwillingness to be forthcoming about their beliefs, Wesley told Boltzius that he had 'resolved to read the New Testament with them', concentrating 'on important passages which contain the major tenets of Christian belief', so as to divine the basis of their creed'.[111] Boltzius's record of these conversations shows that Wesley had a very close relationship with the Moravians, but was nonetheless willing to critique them through the lens of the primitive church. Wesley's concerns point toward the conclusion that he held a broader definition of the primitive church by attaching greater importance to early church tradition and (perhaps) holiness than the Moravians. Although one could have speculated that the ambiguity of their beliefs as compared to those of the Church of England laid out in various formularies troubled Wesley, we do not have positive evidence that such concerns were voiced by him apart from Boltzius's and Gronau's reports.

HYMNS

Though Wesley knew well the ancient Christian hymns *Te Deum* and *Benedicite* used in morning prayer and had read Isaac Watts's *Hymns and Spiritual Songs*, his love of Pietist hymnody began in Georgia.[112] The *Detailed Reports* note Wesley's admiration of German hymns. Boltzius reported that he often attended the prayer meetings of the Moravians, where he 'learned to read a good amount of German' and sang hymns from the Moravian hymn book. During one of his visits to Savannah, Wesley praised the Lutheran Church above other bodies because of their 'treasure of songs'. Boltzius commented

---

[109] JWD, 9 June 1737; *Detailed Reports*, 10 June 1737, 4:92–3; cf. JW to Lady Cox (7 March 1738), *Works*, 25:534.
[110] Boltzius to Gotthilf August Francke (1 March 1737), Boltzius and Gronau to Friedrich Michael Ziegenhagen (29 July 1737) and Boltzius and Israel Christian Gronau to Heinrich Alard Butjenter (20 January 1738), in Boltzius, *Letters*, 1:193, 195, 225–6.
[111] *Detailed Reports*, 16 June 1737, 4:102.
[112] Wesley read *Hymns and Spiritual Songs* (1707) in September 1732.

with pleasure that Wesley was enthusiastic about German hymns to the point that he had learned their melodies, translated them along with some psalms set in English verse, and had them printed in Charlestown.[113]

Wesley consulted the Moravian hymn book on the *Simmonds* and began translating German psalms soon after his arrival in Georgia, later followed by translating German hymns.[114] In the early meetings of his religious societies in Savannah and Frederica, Wesley maintained the typical Anglican practice of singing psalms.[115] Wesley may have first regularly used hymns in public worship in the services he led for about a dozen Germans in Frederica.[116] In this case, Wesley sang hymns in German and did no more than adapt himself to the method of worship familiar to them. While psalms remained the norm for the initial meetings of his Georgia religious societies, he continued to be drawn to hymns, as indicated by notes in his diary, such as 'transcribed hymns' and 'Marked psalms and hymns.' In December 1736, he worked on a 'scheme for psalms' and a 'scheme for hymns' and in the following month he read Isaac Watts's 'hymns' and 'Psalms.'[117]

The Moravian *Singstunde* awakened in Wesley a love for hymns that was never quenched. Although Isaac Watts (1674–1748) had published hymns for the use of Dissenting congregations, there were no Anglican hymnals at this time designed for public worship.[118] Anglican churches sang metrical versions of the Psalms from either the Sternhold and Hopkins version or the newer Tate and Brady edition first published in 1696. It was probably the Tate and Brady book that Wesley 'Looked over' while preparing to commence his ministry in Savannah.[119] In any case, he was certainly not enamoured with either of the

[113] *Detailed Reports*, 16 (MS), 28–29 June, 19 July 1737 (MS), 4:102, 117–18, 135. In 1783, the name of the city was changed to Charleston.

[114] JWD, 27 October 1735, 23 February and 5, 7 May 1736; 'Töltschigs Diarium', 14 May 1736 and (NS), fo. 418.

[115] The Anglican-Methodist societies that met at James Hutton's home while Wesley was in Georgia continued the traditional custom of singing psalms: [Hutton] to JW (3 January 1737[/38]), *Works*, 25:526.

[116] JWMSJ, 18 October 1736.

[117] JWJ, 10 June 1736 and JWD, 18 December 1736; JWD 26, 28, 31 August 1736; JWJ, 18, 20 December 1736 and 15 January 1737. It is possible that the reference to having 'Marked psalms and hymns' referred to correcting proofs for an edition of the *Collection of Psalms and Hymns* published in 1736. According to Philip Thicknesse, Wesley's task in April 1737 was to have a second edition of his book printed: *The St. James's Chronicle*, 5 October 1780 in Rodney M. Baine, 'Philip Thicknesse's Reminiscences of Early Georgia', GHQ 74 (1990), 690. For a convenient catalogue of Wesley's activity in Georgia relating to psalms and hymns, see Carlton R. Young, *Music of the Heart: John & Charles Wesley on Music and Musicians: An Anthology* (Carol Stream, IL, 1995), 42–5.

[118] However, the SPCK had published *A Collection of Psalms and Divine Hymns, Suited to the great Festivals of the Church, for Morning and Evening and other Occasions* (London, 1727) for private, family, or devotional use with friends as a means of imitating the primitive Christians (see pp. 3–6, 10).

[119] JWD, 5 March 1736. Curnock's various conclusions that cipher in Wesley's diary referred to Tate and Brady does not seem to be credible based on Heitzenrater's interpretation of the cipher: JWJ (Curnock), 1:123, 175, 184, 302; Heitzenrater in JWJ, 308–10.

Anglican Psalters, since he used renderings of the psalms from Isaac Watts,[120] his father, and others for his Charlestown hymn book.

During his visit to Charlestown, which he claimed was primarily aimed at putting a stop to his parishioners being illegally married in South Carolina, Wesley had the manuscript of his psalms and hymns printed by Lewis Timothy, a Huguenot immigrant and prominent printer, who worked in partnership with Benjamin Franklin and published the *South Carolina Gazette*.[121] Wesley delivered his manuscript to Timothy on the morning he arrived in Charlestown (Thursday 14 April 1737). On the following Monday he read over the proof sheets, and returned them to Timothy the next morning before departing for Savannah on Saturday.

Wesley's *Collection of Psalms and Hymns* was first used in the summer of 1737.[122] He seems to have designed the book primarily for use in his religious societies, as they are separated into psalms and hymns for Sunday, Wednesday or Friday, and Saturday. This is significant because Sunday, Wednesday, and Saturday were the days his Savannah societies met on a weekly basis from March 1737.[123] Unfortunately, there is limited evidence about how the book was used. It is probable that when Wesley mentioned singing in his diary in reference to society meetings prior to the summer of 1737 he primarily meant the psalms, while this designation thereafter probably refers to his *Collection*. Thanks to the Grand Jury's August 1737 'Grievances' against Wesley, we know that his book was also introduced into public worship, including the communion service. They accused Wesley of deviating 'from the principles and regulations of the Established Church…*Prima*, by inverting the order and method of the Liturgy; Secondly, by changing and altering such passages as he thinks proper in the Version of Psalms publicly sung in the Church; 3. By introducing into the church and service at the altar, compositions of Psalms and Hymns not inspected or authorized to be sung in the Church.'[124] The second charge indicates that Wesley went further than merely looking over the psalmbook; at the same time as he revised the 1662 prayer book in accordance with the 1549 edition[125] he altered the version of psalms he used in public worship. It appears that Wesley was indeed guilty as accused of these charges.

The *Collection of Psalms and Hymns* should be considered one of the major accomplishments of the Georgia mission.[126] It consists of seventy items; forty

[120] Watts's *The Psalms of David* (1719). Wesley, did, however, include a number of Tate and Brady renderings of the psalms in his 1741 *Collection of Psalms and Hymns*.
[121] Robert Stevenson, 'John Wesley's First Hymn-book', in Frank Baker and George Walton Williams (eds), *John Wesley's First Hymn-book* (Charleston and London, 1964), xix.
[122] There are two known copies of the original edition of this hymn book; one can be found in the MARC and the other is housed in the New York City Public Library.
[123] Cf. Rack, 123. See 'Wesley's Religious Societies in Georgia' in chapter 4.
[124] JWMSJ, 22 August 1737.
[125] See 'Prayer Book Revision' in chapter 4.
[126] Indeed, this has been the consensus of Wesley scholars. For information on sources for Wesley's book discussed in this paragraph, see Randy L. Maddox (ed.), 'John Wesley's Poetry and

for Sunday, twenty for Wednesday or Friday, and ten for Saturday. This division fits exactly with Wesley's conception of significant days of the week observed by the primitive church. Saturday, of course, was the Sabbath, a day of preparation for the Lord's Day (Sunday), while Wednesday and Friday were fast days. The *Collection* is dominated by thirty-five psalms and hymns from Watts. The primitivist impulse to revive ancient liturgical practice that inspired George Hickes's *Devotions in the Ancient Way of Offices* encouraged Wesley to make frequent use of the psalms, hymns, collects, and scripture readings contained in this work. This collection was adapted for Anglican use by Susanna Hopton from the manual of the English Catholic, John Austin, and published by Hickes. The seven hymns from this book form the second most prominent source in Wesley's *Collection*.[127] Wesley's translations of five German hymns from the Herrnhut *Gesang-Buch* are found in the *Collection*; one was by Zinzendorf and the other four come from Pietists associated with Halle, including one from Johann Anastasius Freylinghausen.[128] As we might expect, these five hymns all contain references to devotion from the heart. Other important Anglican sources include six items from George Herbert's *The Temple* (1633), five from Samuel Wesley junior's *Poems on Several Occasions* (1736), four metrical psalms from his father's *The Pious Communicant Rightly Prepar'd* (1700), and two of his manuscript hymns.

The significance of Wesley's hymn book should not be underestimated. First, this was the earliest hymnal apparently designed in part for the use of an Anglican congregation, and perhaps the first hymn book printed in America. Second, the singing of hymns, which had already been a feature of revival in central Europe, became integral to the emerging evangelical revival in the English-speaking world. Some of these pioneering German hymns were introduced to English speakers through Wesley's translations. His promotion of hymn-singing, which began in Georgia, played no small role in its acceptance and use by early evangelicals. Third, though the selections of psalms and hymns in his 1738 *Collection of Psalms and Hymns* are different from the Charlestown hymnal, the two collections follow the same basic pattern in terms of numbers of psalms and hymns (seventy) and sections for Sunday, Wednesday or Friday, and Saturday. And while the earlier section headings were dropped from the 1741 *Collection of Psalms and Hymns*, Wesley included forty-four of the seventy hymns from the 1737 hymn book. Many of the hymns from the Charlestown book continued

Hymn Collections', *Duke Center for Studies in the Wesleyan Tradition* [website] <http://divinity. duke.edu/initiatives-centers/cswt/wesley-texts/poetry-hymn>, accessed 19 August 2012.

[127] Wesley included the doxology from the Nonjuror Thomas Ken in the tenth item in the *Collection*.

[128] John Nuelsen has maintained that Wesley translated thirty-three German hymns when those included in later editions of his hymns are counted: *John Wesley and the German Hymn*, trans. Theo Parry, Sydney H. Moore, and Arthur Holbrook (Calverley, 1972 [1938]), 27. See JWD, 27 October 1735 for his reading of the Moravian hymn book.

to be reprinted in later hymn books authored by John and Charles Wesley. The similarity of the Wesleys' final 1784 *Collection* proves John's 'loyalty even in old age to the religious insights of the Georgia days.'[129]

Journals and letters of the leaders of the Moravians and Salzburgers provide rewarding sources for evaluating Wesley's Georgia mission. In common with Wesley's diary and journals they demonstrate that Wesley's goal of renewing the primitive church in the primitive Georgia wilderness was at the forefront of his concerns. This ideal, however, was constricted by his Nonjuror-inspired High Churchmanship, which emphasized restoring the liturgy of the primitive church. While they shared some aspects of Wesley's vision of the primitive church (e.g. communal discipline and mission to the Indians), the Germans were primarily concerned with the spirit and communal form of the early church and showed (in the case of the Moravians) an openness and resistance to adopting Wesley's High Church principles. Their rejection of Wesley's belief in the centrality of apostolic succession to efficacious ministry formed a fundamental barrier. The end result of their relations was that Wesley's faithfulness to his High Church Anglican heritage coupled with the firm commitment of the Moravians and Lutherans to their respective traditions created division between him and his Pietist friends. Nonetheless, Moravian and Lutheran hymnody and theology exerted a lifelong influence on Wesley. Although, in the long-term, Wesley added greater emphasis on the spirit of primitive Christianity to his liturgical concerns, there is little evidence of an immediate and rapid refocusing of his beliefs due to his encounter with Continental Pietism. Likewise, the Moravians and Lutherans demonstrated to Wesley the value of a firm heartfelt faith and trust in God which, over time, he integrated into his quest for holy living.

---

[129] Stevenson in Baker and Williams, *John Wesley's First Hymn-book*, xxii. In a cursory comparison, I counted twenty-eight of the Charlestown hymns in the 1784 *Collection of Psalms and Hymns for the Lord's Day* (cf. Stevenson in Baker and Williams, *John Wesley's First Hymn-book*, viii). A substantial number are also found in the 1780 *A Collection of Hymns for the Use of the People Called Methodists* (i.e. hymns: 12, 22, 215–16, 231–2, 329, 343): see *Works*, vol. 7.

4

Creating Primitive Christianity Anew

Wesley's Ministry in Georgia

In 1789, Wesley recounted that he 'went to America, strongly attached to the Bible, the primitive Church, and the Church of England, from which I would not vary in one jot or title on any account whatever'. He also noted that at this time he 'observed all the rubric in the liturgy, and that with all possible exactness, even at the peril of my life'.[1] This chapter evaluates Wesley's theology and practice in Georgia, which will illuminate his application of primitive Christianity in the colony.[2] In the course of analysing Wesley's ministry in Georgia, the accuracy of his statements will be assessed. His imitation of primitive church practices will be examined as they manifested themselves through his work on prayer book revision, precise sacramental observance, confession and penance, ascetical discipline, deaconesses, religious societies, and mission to the Indians.

PRAYER BOOK REVISION

During the week Wesley was preparing to give his first sermon in Georgia, he noted in his diary that for roughly two hours on 5 March 1736 he 'Revised [the] Common Prayer book.' Fredrick Hunter is probably correct in concluding that Wesley worked on bringing the 1662 prayer book into line with the

---

[1] 'Farther Thoughts on Separation from the Church', *Works*, 9:538; cf. to Dr [John] Free (24 August 1758), *Works*, 9:325; JW to the Printer of the 'Dublin Chronicle' (2 June 1789), *Letters* (Telford), 8:140; Sermon 'On Laying the Foundation of the New Chapel' (1777), *Works*, 3:583. Historians have often concluded that his rubrical exactness was a prime source of Wesley's difficulties in Georgia: for example, see Samuel J. Rogal, 'William Stephens and John Wesley: "I cannot pretend to judge"', *GHQ* 90 (2006), 265.

[2] It can be shown in this regard that the Anglican missionaries acted in union: see Hammond, 160–1.

1549 prayer book;[3] however, as his clerical practice discussed in this chapter indicates, it is likely that he supplemented this revision by applying elements of the *Apostolic Constitutions* and Thomas Deacon's liturgy (such as his inversion of the 1549 order for Holy Communion by placing the oblation before the invocation) to his revised prayer book. Therefore, without the authorization of the Church, and in violation of Church law,[4] it appears that he reformed the liturgy to follow the usages. Even if Wesley did not physically mark up his prayer book, in this chapter we observe that in common with the 1549 book Wesley divided public prayers into three Sunday services, insisted on trine immersion, and mixed wine with water before administering the sacrament. He went beyond the 1549 book and followed the *Apostolic Constitutions* and Deacon by forcing non-communicants to depart before administering the sacrament, and he was possibly inspired by them to appoint deaconesses. Wesley offered communion to children, as supported by the *Constitutions* and possibly Deacon, while he went beyond them by administering the sacrament to the children before they were confirmed. He adhered to the forty-seventh *Apostolic Canon* in rebaptizing Dissenters. Finally, he moved beyond the *Constitutions* and *Canons* and Deacon by reducing the liturgy spoken before administering the sacrament and probably also by introducing confession.

The end result of these adaptations was a significantly altered prayer and Communion service, which would have been readily noticed by parishioners used to the 1662 order. In fact, one of the accusations later levelled against Wesley (along with those already mentioned) was 'inverting the order and method of the Liturgy.'[5] While some of the evidence for Wesley's liturgical revisions is difficult to interpret, there is substantial evidence that he officiated in Savannah parish church on the basis of having revised the prayer book. He undoubtedly believed that all of these changes made the prayer book more amenable to the liturgical practice of the primitive church. However, some parishioners were aware that Wesley's actions diverged significantly from the norms of Anglican liturgical practice.

WESLEY'S RESOLUTIONS ON CLERICAL PRACTICE

In addition to revising the prayer book, Wesley, in typical Oxford Methodist/ holy living tradition, prepared a series of resolutions on how he intended to

---

[3] Hunter, 'The Manchester Nonjurors', 58.
[4] See Canon 36 (1604).
[5] JWMSJ, 22 August 1737; cf. William Norris to Trustees (12 December 1738), *CRG*, 22.1:351.

carry out his duties.[6] On his first Sunday in Savannah he announced to his parishioners:

> (1) That I must admonish every one of them not only in public, but from house to house; (2) That I could admit none to Holy Communion without previous notice; (3) That I should divide the Morning Service on Sundays, in compliance with the first design of the church; (4) That I must obey the rubric by dipping all the children who were able to endure it; (5) That I could admit none who were not communicants to be sureties [i.e. godparents] in Baptism; (6) That in general, though I had all the ecclesiastical authority which was entrusted to any within this Province, yet I was only a servant of the Church of England, not a judge, and therefore obliged to keep her regulations in all things.

Although this event is not mentioned until the time of his legal trouble in September 1737, in his manuscript journal, Wesley noted that he had first read this statement to his congregation on the day he began his ministry in Georgia. This must have taken aback some of his parishioners who were used to irregular pastoral ministry before his arrival.[7] Wesley reread this resolution to his congregation following his discourse on Matthew 18:7 paraphrased as 'It must needs be that offenses will come.'[8] Wesley may have been thinking of this paper when in the introduction to his manuscript journal he stressed his 'resolution to speak once a week at least to every communicant apart from the congregation.'[9] The first three resolutions are discussed here, followed by the fourth and fifth resolutions in 'Resolutions Relating to Baptismal Practice', while the accuracy of the sixth resolution will be kept in mind throughout our analysis.

Pastoral visits from house to house were encouraged by the SPG and were a consistent feature of Wesley's ministerial conduct.[10] During the eighteen months of residency in Georgia covered by his diary, Wesley conversed with his parishioners on a daily basis. House visits were carried out on an average of approximately every other day and often took up several hours,

---

[6] In continuation with his practice at Oxford and on the *Simmonds*, religious resolutions were a significant aspect of Wesley's life in Georgia. His diary notes at least four written resolutions and sixteen occasions when he read his resolutions. In addition to this public resolution, he made other verbal resolutions of a more private kind, such as when he 'resolved not to touch Miss Sophy, [and] told her so' and read her resolutions (presumably regarding this matter) on the following day: JWD, 10, 11 November 1736.

[7] For example, 'in order to perform a marriage, a preaching frock was put on a man who was a soldier and was said to have lived an evil life': Johann Martin Boltzius to Georg Christoph von Burgsdorff (6 May 1734), in Boltzius, *Letters*, 1:78.

[8] JWMSJ, 11 September 1737. The first reading would have been on 7 March 1736, although there is no particular note of this in his diary. It appears that Wesley did publicly read resolutions to his congregation on 29 April 1736: see JWD.

[9] JWMSJ, 7 March 1736.

[10] *A Collection of Papers*, 24; cf. David Humphreys, *An Historical Account of the Incorporated Society for the Propagation of the Gospel in Foreign Parts* (London, 1730), 71.

generally in the late morning or early afternoon.[11] The frequency of these visits climaxed during May to August 1737, reaching a rate of nearly every day from Monday to Saturday that he was in Savannah. Unfortunately, we do not possess any accounts of conversations, although we know that they certainly focused on religious dialogue in an effort on Wesley's part to ascertain the state of his parishioners' souls, and on this basis offer words of exhortation. House visits were one important method by which Wesley sought to revive the community-focused spirit of the primitive church. The value of this was appreciated by Elizabeth Stanley, a midwife at Savannah, who commended 'Mr. John Wesley, our minister at Savannah, who goes from house to house exhorting the inhabitants to virtue and religion.'[12] However, his opponent, Hugh Anderson, one of the authors of *A True and Historical Narrative* (discussed later), alleged that he 'went from house to house to stir up the people to mutiny.'[13]

Wesley's second resolution was a succinct summary of the 1662 prayer book rubric, which states 'So many as intend to be partakers of the holy Communion shall signify their names to the Curate, at least some time the day before.' Little might he have known that uncompromising adherence to this rubric would directly lead to him being driven out of the colony. This was cited by Wesley and the jurors' minority report as the reason for repelling Sophia Williamson from Communion on 7 August 1737.[14] All available evidence supports the jurors' contention that Wesley 'had often in full congregation declared he did insist on a compliance with that rubric, and had before repelled divers persons for non-compliance therewith.'[15] Wesley's stress on communion preparation was best illustrated by his Saturday evening devotional group for his communicants.[16]

On 9 May 1736, Wesley instituted his third resolution by dividing prayers into three services following the layout of the 1549 prayer book. However, as already noted, this date merely represents the institution of this practice in Savannah, since Wesley had previously divided Sunday prayers on the *Simmonds*.[17] This move shows that Wesley expressly and intentionally went beyond the rubrics of the Church currently in force by returning to the 1549 prayer book order. He claimed this was 'the original appointment of the church',

[11] See JWJ, 10 May 1736; cf. JWMSJ, 10 September 1736 and JW to George Whitefield and the Oxford Methodists [10 September 1736], *Works*, 25:472 and JWMSJ, 30 July 1737.

[12] Egmont, *Diary*, 16 March 1737, 2:370.

[13] JWMSJ, 3 November 1737. This accusation is discussed in 'Wesley as a Divisive Clergyman' in chapter 5.

[14] JWMSJ, 12 September 1737.

[15] BCP, 'The Order for the Administration of the Lord's Supper or Holy Communion'; JWMSJ, 7 August and 12 September 1737; cf. Wesley, *Advice to a Young Clergyman*, 68–9 and Bull, *Companion for the Candidates of Holy Orders*, 48–50.

[16] See 'Wesley's Religious Societies in Georgia' in this chapter.

[17] See 'Public Worship' in chapter 2.

which seems to refer to the Church of England, but he may have been invoking the primitive church or both the Church of England and the early church.[18] As for many High Churchmen and Nonjurors, the Church of England at its best (which in terms of liturgy for Nonjurors and Wesley was the 1549 prayer book) closely resembled the purity of the primitive church.

Resolutions Relating to Baptismal Practice

Reflecting on clerical practice in Wiltshire, Donald Spaeth has argued that a flexible approach to the performance of baptisms (and funerals) could be essential for eighteenth-century Anglican clergymen to retain the support of their parishioners.[19] Wesley's High Church opinions on baptism were highly controversial in Georgia. His firm insistence on rebaptizing Dissenters and adhering to the method of trine immersion was maintained. Both of these practices characteristic of Nonjurors had been foreshadowed in Wesley's ministry on the *Simmonds* and were elements of his view of authentic primitive Christianity. In common with the Cyprianic tradition and *Apostolic Canon* forty-seven, and in opposition to the majority of Anglican bishops, he believed that Dissenters must be rebaptized because only clergy ordained within the apostolic succession could validly administer this rite. Wesley was convinced that trine immersion was the sole baptismal method of the primitive church, and this was also the rubric of the more 'primitive' 1549 Book of Common Prayer. Additionally, he adamantly opposed the practice of private baptism.

In total Wesley recorded administering twenty-five baptisms or christenings during his tenure in Georgia.[20] During the first week of his ministry in Savannah he baptized John Bradley, son of William and Elizabeth, by immersion at morning prayer.[21] In baptismal method, the Anglican missionary colleagues worked in tandem: Charles Wesley insisted on baptism by immersion

---

[18] JWJ and diary, 9 May 1736. In his diary for this date Wesley took special note that he and Benjamin Ingham 'agreed.' This was presumably a reference to agreeing on the division of prayers.

[19] Donald Spaeth, *The Church in An Age of Danger: Parson and Parishioners, 1660–1740* (Cambridge, 2000), 202. The SPG did not want its missionaries to take a flexible approach, but to 'duly consider the Qualifications' of baptismal candidates: *A Collection of Papers*, 24; cf. Humphreys, *Historical Account*, 70.

[20] JWD, 12 March, 8, 10, 16, 31 May, (two on) 3 June, 4 July, 23 September, 6, 7 October, 18, 29 November, 7 December 1736, 5 April, 5 June, 16 July, 18 August 1737; JWMSJ, 5 June and 30 November 1737. Almost certainly due to his controversial practise, Wesley's number is significantly lower than his predecessor Samuel Quincy's claim of thirty-four baptisms in seventeen months: Samuel Quincy to Harman Verelst (28 June 1735), *CRG*, 20:407.

[21] JWD, 12 March 1736. In British plantation colonies, baptism by immersion, while occasionally administered by Anglican clergy in South Carolina, seems to have been a rare practice that was associated with Baptist ritual: Nicholas M. Beasley, 'Domestic Rituals: Marriage and Baptism in the British Plantation Colonies, 1650–1780', *Anglican and Episcopal History*, 76 (2007), 345, 356.

in Frederica and while the Wesley brothers were in Frederica, Ingham 'baptized a child by trine immersion', which he called 'that good old way'.[22] Dissent soon arose on 5 May 1736, when Wesley was approached by Anne Parker, wife of Henry, the Second Bailiff of Savannah, with the request to baptize their child. True to his convictions Wesley followed the portion of the prayer book rubric that children should be immersed unless their godparents could 'certify the child is weak', in which case the rubric states 'it shall suffice to pour water upon it'. According to his *Journal*, Wesley quoted the exact words of the 1662 prayer book rubric to Anne Parker and, therefore, was fully justified in declining to baptize the child, since she would not affirm that the child was weak but was merely opposed to it being immersed. However, the rubric also says that the child can be dipped in the water 'if they [the godparents] shall certify him [the clergyman] that the Child may well endure it'. Even the High Churchman Charles Wheatly admitted that the rubric requires the clergyman not to dip without express permission from the godparents. Therefore, Wesley either misinterpreted the 1662 prayer book, or probably more likely was following the 1549 rubric that does not ask for anyone to certify whether the child can endure immersion.[23]

In concluding his account of his exchange with the Parkers, Wesley made the highly significant claim that 'the child was baptized by another person'.[24] Other clergy in the area included Ingham, Anton Seiffert amongst the Moravians, Johann Boltzius and Israel Gronau amongst the Salzburgers, and Edward Dyson, a roving military chaplain.[25] Unfortunately, there is no evidence to suggest whether any of these clergy might have been involved or who this person might have been.

The Parkers may have held what seems to have been a common aversion to immersion perceived as an unhealthy practice, which was angrily voiced by the chief magistrate and keeper of the Trustees' store, Thomas Causton, who called Wesley 'a murderer of poor infants by plunging them into cold water'.[26] Although these are the only two references to immersion in Wesley's journals and diary, the re-emergence of this issue in the August 1737 Indictments of the Grand Jury against Wesley indicates that this practice was maintained.[27] The June 1738 testimony of William Stephens, who arrived in the colony in

[22] BIJ, 14 April 1736, Lincoln Cathedral Library MS 299. This entry is found in the Lincoln Cathedral Library manuscript only.

[23] JWJ, 5 May 1736; cf. JWJ, 5 May 1736 n. 84; Wheatly, 339. The minority report of the Grand Jury cited the BCP in defence of Wesley's actions: JWJ and JWMSJ, 12 September 1737.

[24] JWJ and JWD, 5 May 1736.

[25] It is unclear whether Henri François Chiffelle, a Reformed French-Swiss minister in Purrysburg, South Carolina had taken up his post before 1737.

[26] JWMSJ, 10 August 1737.

[27] After he had given public notice that he would be leaving the colony Wesley was pleased to baptize five children, one of 'whose parents had been Anabaptists': JWMSJ, 30 November 1737.

October 1737 as 'Secretary of the Trustees in Georgia', affirmed Wesley's commitment to immersion and the controversy surrounding it. Stephens noted that George Whitefield, who departed for Georgia at nearly the same time as Wesley arrived back in England with the intention of joining Wesley in Georgia as a volunteer missionary, administered baptism 'by sprinkling; which gave great Content to many People, that had taken great Distaste at the Form of Dipping, so strictly required, and so obstinately withstood by some Parents, that they have suffered their Children to go a long while without the benefit of that Sacrament, till a convenient Opportunity could be found of another Minister to do that Office'.[28] It seems that there would have been an inevitable clash of personalities if Wesley and Whitefield had ministered in the colony at the same time, since Whitefield was opposed to the fact that Wesley's friend, Commissary Alexander Garden of Charlestown, was 'strict in the outward discipline of Church' while Wesley was even stricter at least in the case of Canon twenty-nine (1604), requiring godparents to be communicants.[29]

Because of opposition to Wesley's resolve to strictly observe the Church's rubric, there appears to have been a backlog of children awaiting baptism. Following his return in September 1736 from three weeks in Frederica, Wesley was dismayed to discover that Edward Dyson (d. 1739) had been baptizing 'strong, healthy children in private houses', which he told Dyson he 'had entirely broke through.' This common problem in England and America of persuading parents 'to bring their Children to Church for Public Baptism' was his father's 'biggest struggle' in Epworth.[30] Wesley noted that Dyson promised to discontinue this custom but disingenuously resumed this practice the next day. In his interpretive gloss, Wesley decried the undermining of his ecclesial discipline, which he was convinced was essential to reviving the spirit of the primitive church. He wrote: 'O discipline! Where art thou to be found? Not in England, or (as yet) in America.'[31]

In addition to immersion and the challenge to his authority posed by Dyson, Wesley's determination to rebaptize Dissenters naturally aroused debate in the colony. Although we have no indication that either Ambrose Tackner or other passengers voiced objections to him being rebaptized just before the *Simmonds* set sail,[32] Wesley's belief was not accepted without

---

[28] Stephens, *Journal*, 18 June 1738, *CRG*, 4:157–8.

[29] *George Whitefield's Journals* (Edinburgh, 1960), 9 January 1740, p. 389; see the letter from Garden to the SPG extracted in the SPG Journal, 19 July 1734, vol. 6; cf. the discussion of this issue regarding Wesley in the following text. See also Wesley's praise of Garden: JWJ, 17 April 1737 and JWMSJ, 18 April 1737.

[30] Wesley, *Advice to a Young Clergyman*, 66; cf. Wall, *History of Infant Baptism*, 1:228. Nicholas Beasley has noted that private baptism was common in British plantation colonies and disputes occasionally arose between clergy who insisted on church baptism and clergy who were willing to privately baptize people from outside of their parish: 'Domestic Rituals', 346–7, 350–1.

[31] JWMSJ, 6 September 1736; JWD, 7 September 1736.

[32] JWMSJ, 18 October 1735; JWD, 17–18 October; BIJ, 18 October 1735, p. 68.

question by his parishioners in Savannah. Early on in his ministry, Wesley discussed the issue of 'lay-baptism' with William Gough, Jr. From opponents of Wesley's principles, we know Gough had received communion from Wesley in March 1736 and was not long thereafter denied admission to the Lord's Table after Wesley had discovered he was baptized by a Presbyterian minister and would not submit to rebaptism. Evidently there was no irreconcilable enmity between Wesley and Gough, since Gough signed the minority report disputing the validity of the Grand Jury's Indictments and fled to South Carolina with Wesley in December 1737.[33]

Wesley failed to convince Gough, but he persuaded Richard Turner and his fourteen-year-old son Thomas to be publicly rebaptized at the conclusion of morning prayer on Trinity Sunday 1737.[34] Patrick Tailfer and his fellow authors of *A True and Historical Narrative* cited these two cases as the first of four reasons why they believed Wesley was a Roman Catholic.[35] While baptismal method was the cause of Wesley's disagreement with the Parkers, it was rebaptism that evoked the most vociferous opposition.

Occurrences such as those cited by Tailfer were used against Wesley in the Grand Jury's Indictments during the Sophia Williamson case. While the rebaptism of the Turners does not appear, the cases of the Parkers and Gough are cited in the Indictments, along with three other controversies concerning baptism.[36] One of these occurrences related to burial rites. Wesley was accused of refusing to read the prayer book burial office at the funeral of the Anabaptist (i.e. Baptist) Nathaniel Polhill.[37] In Wesley's defence, a minority of the jurors claimed that Polhill had declared while alive that he did not desire to be buried according to the Anglican rite. While this Indictment does not claim that Wesley refused to read the burial office over all Dissenters, it would not have been out of character with his convictions if this were the case. The 1662 prayer book rubric states that the office 'is not to be used for any that die unbaptized', while Deacon's *Devotions* add the stringent clause 'or out of the communion of the Church'.[38] Deacon's rubric would certainly suggest that baptized Dissenters

---

[33] JWD, 27 March 1736; JWMSJ, 1 September 1737; Tailfer, 41; JWMSJ, 12 September 1737; *LES*, 76. Gough was considered by Egmont to be 'an idle fellow': *LES*, 76.

[34] JWMSJ and JWD, 5 June 1737.

[35] Tailfer, 41.

[36] These Indictments and the discussion of those that follow can be found in Wesley's manuscript journal for 1 September 1737 and in summary and in his *Journal* for the same date. The minority report of the jurors can be found in his journals under the date 12 September 1737.

[37] Nathaniel Polhill is not mentioned in Wesley's journals or diary prior to these Indictments. Egmont added the interesting interpretive gloss that the refusal was 'because he was not of his opinion, a Methodist': *The Journal of the Earl of Egmont... 1732–1738*, ed. Robert G. McPherson (Athens, 1962), 7 December 1737, p. 322. Thomas Causton also accused Wesley of refusing to bury Paul Cheesewright, who is not mentioned in Wesley's journals and diary: JWMSJ, 11 August 1737.

[38] BCP, 'The Order for the Burial of the Dead'; Deacon, 186; cf. Canon 68 (1604).

be refused the burial service. However, if Polhill was baptized, then provided he was not excommunicated and had not committed suicide, Wesley was required to read the burial office at his funeral.[39]

The other two Indictments relating to baptism have to do with sponsorship of the child by godparents.[40] One of the bills alleged that Wesley would not allow William Aglionby, an attorney from Westminster, to stand as a godparent at the baptism of Henry and Sarah Manly's son because he was not a communicant.[41] The legality of Wesley's refusal in this instance is difficult to determine because, while the Grand Jury report asserted that Aglionby had received the sacrament at some unspecified time, the minority report claimed that this had not been 'certified' by Wesley. The prayer book rubric requires that godparents be baptized and confirmed (although the requirement of confirmation might be waived at the discretion of the minister), while Canon twenty-nine adds '...neither shall any person be admitted godfather or godmother to any child at christening or confirmation, before the said person so undertaking hath received the Holy Communion.'[42] Ultimately, Aglionby's professed deism may have been a major reason for Wesley's action.[43]

The final charge stated that Wesley baptized the child of the Indian trader Thomas Jones with only one godmother and godfather in spite of the offer of Jacob Matthews and his wife Mary née Musgrove to stand as sureties. Part of this Indictment is identical to that relating to Aglionby, since Matthews was also not a communicant; however, a portion of the accusation ironically asserts that Wesley did not apply the rubric strictly enough, since the prayer book requires three godparents. Wesley duly noted this in his *Journal*, with the

---

[39] Spaeth, *Church in An Age of Danger*, 201. John White, vicar of Avebury in Wiltshire, refused to bury a Presbyterian in 1710 and was later censured in court: Spaeth, *Church in An Age of Danger*, 201.

[40] In his *Advice to a Young Clergyman*, Samuel Wesley urged clergy to ensure that godparents were present at baptisms (p. 65).

[41] The Indictment states that this incident took place 'on or about the Tuesday in Whitsun Week last' and Wesley's diary records that he had religious talk with Mrs Manly on that day: JWD, 31 May 1737. The lack of evidence that a baptism ensued suggests that a disagreement occurred. Aglionby worked with the Grand Jury that accepted the Indictments against Wesley as true bills by travelling to Charlestown to enquire about the extent of the rights of a Grand Jury: Thomas Causton to Trustees (25 July 1738), *CRG*, 22.1:207.

[42] BCP, 'The Ministration of Publick Baptism of Infants to be used in the Church'; *Canons* (1604). In the case of infant baptism, Deacon's rubrics are less stringent than those of the BCP. In his study of lay–clerical conflict in the Church of England, Donald Spaeth cited a similar refusal in Dorset as an example of 'Clerical inflexibility that did the Established Church considerable harm, provoking hostility and widening the gap between the clergy and an uncomprehending laity': *Church in An Age of Danger*, 202. This issue also arose in America; Commissary Alexander Garden reported to the SPG the consequences of the determination of Andrew Leslie of St Paul's Parish, South Carolina, who was 'voted against and rejected' by the people of his parish for taking a stand on this same matter: SPG Journal, 19 July 1734, vol. 6.

[43] *LES*, 61. Aglionby declined to have George Whitefield pray for him on his deathbed, consequently leading to Whitefield's refusal to administer the burial office over him: Stephens, *Journal*, 23 August 1738, *CRG*, 4:188–9. As with Polhill, Wesley's journals and diary gives no firm evidence that he knew Aglionby.

sarcastic comment that '(This, I own, was wrong; for I ought at all hazards to have refused baptizing it till he had procured a third).'[44]

Social status may have been a factor in the Grand Jury's use of these five men in their Indictments. All of the names except for Henry Parker (who held a dignified office as Second Bailiff) are found in Egmont's list of 'Persons who went from Europe to Georgia on their own Account' (i.e. at their own expense).[45] Therefore, these men were not debtors or servants and were not amongst the poorest of Georgia's colonists. They were men with social standing who would have been expected to be treated in a manner appropriate to their status by a clergyman. The public humiliation that each of them faced, coupled with their social status, may go some distance in explaining the jury's citation of their cases.

We might logically ask at this point how Wesley dealt with the issue of confirmation. Despite his rigid adherence to the prayer book rubric on baptism, Wesley evidently operated with a measure of flexibility as he accepted baptism apart from subsequent confirmation as a complete rite of initiation into the Church.[46] Thus, in violation of the prayer book rubric, he admitted four unconfirmed children to the Lord's Table.[47] This was a necessary modification of Church polity in America because there were no bishops there to administer the rite of the confirmation, which would normally take place before a baptized member of the Church would receive his or her first communion. Though the ideal in England was for confirmation to precede communion, numerous obstacles to the effective performance of the rite meant that this was not always the case.[48] According to the High Churchman Charles Wheatly, whose *Rational Illustration of the Book of Common Prayer* Wesley reread in Georgia, Wesley's practice could have been justified as an extraordinary circumstance due to 'the want of a Bishop near the place.'[49]

In sum, Wesley's contention that in Georgia he 'observed all the rubric in the liturgy; and with all possible exactness' veils the fact that this tells only part

---

[44] JWJ, 1 September 1737. See 'Serious Thoughts Concerning Godfathers and Godmothers' (1752) for Wesley's valuation of the importance of baptismal sponsorship: *Works* (Jackson), 10:506–9.

[45] See *LES*.

[46] Holland, *Baptism in Early Methodism*, 28.

[47] BCP, 'The Order of Confirmation'; JWJ, JWMSJ, and JWD, 29 May 1737. Thomas Deacon omitted the BCP requirement that confirmation must come before Communion. Nonetheless, he adopted the position (similar to Eastern Orthodoxy) that baptized infants may be confirmed: 'The Order of Confirmation', in *Devotions*, 134–8.

[48] See Robert Cornwall, 'The Rite of Confirmation in Anglican Thought during the Eighteenth Century', *Church History*, 68 (June 1999), 359–72.

[49] JWD, 4, 12, 21 May 1737 (also read October 1731); Wheatly, 384. Though the earlier editions entitled *The Church of England Man's Companion, or, A Rational Illustration of the Harmony, Excellency, and Usefulness of the Book of Common Prayer* (1710) do not contain this material, it is more likely that Wesley would have read one of the enlarged editions—that is, the third or more recent editions.

of the story.[50] As far as it applies to his insistence on immersion when possible, his refusal to privately baptize his parishioners, and his rejection of godparents who were not communicants, this statement is accurate. However, Wesley might have added that 'I went beyond the rubric and applied the practices of the primitive church which I had learnt from the Essentialist Nonjurors.' In so far as he divided public prayers, required trine immersion, and forced Dissenters to be rebaptized before being admitted to the Lord's Table, he was adhering not to the rubric of the Church of England but the principles of the Nonjurors.[51]

HOLY COMMUNION

Wesley's habit of offering the sacrament weekly was rare though not unique in the eighteenth century, when three to four times a year and sometimes monthly celebration was observed in rural parishes.[52] In England, weekly observance was more common in cathedrals, collegiate churches, and colleges, where the prayer book rubric required it, than small parish churches. Wesley's practice was grounded in his conviction that the primitive church celebrated the Lord's Supper on a weekly, if not daily, basis and his personal habit of communicating weekly since 1725.[53] In actual fact, the sacrament was offered slightly more often than weekly due to Wesley's observance of the Church's festivals and special celebrations relating to Georgia.[54] Worship on these feast days began at about 10.30 in the morning and incorporated prayers along with a sermon and sacrament in the same pattern as on Sundays. Festivals on which the sacrament was offered included: the Circumcision of Christ (1 Jan. 1736); the Conversion of St Paul (25 Jan. 1736 and 1737); the anniversary day of the

---

[50] 'Farther Thoughts on Separation from the Church' (1789), *Works*, 9:538.

[51] Cf. the conclusions of Holland, *Baptism in Early Methodism*, 33–4.

[52] F. C. Mather has shown that monthly communion (observed by Samuel Wesley, Sr) was not uncommon in the eighteenth century: 'Georgian Churchmanship Reconsidered', 269–75. He argued that if clergyman had not been hindered by 'the reluctance of the laity to communicate', observance would have been more frequent (p. 272). Wesley announced his intention to celebrate the sacrament weekly to the congregation on 14 March 1736: JWJ. Although not specifically High Church colloquialisms, Wesley's terming of the sacrament as 'the Sacrifice of Thanksgiving' and 'the mysteries of God' affirms the persistence of his high view of the Eucharist: JWMSJ, 22 January 1737; JWMSJ and JWJ, 11 August 1737.

[53] On his continuing belief in daily communion in the early church, see John and Charles Wesley, *Hymns on the Lord's Supper*, VI.2, 124, 137, 164, 166; JWJ, 27 June 1740 and 25 December 1774, 19:158 and 22:441; 'Upon our Lord's Sermon on the Mount: Discourse the Sixth' (1748), *Works*, 1:584. On Wesley's practice, see 'Wesley's Theology of the Eucharist in His Early Writings' in chapter 2.

[54] William Stephens noted that Wesley offered the sacrament 'on most Saints days': Stephens to Trustees (20 December 1737), *CRG*, 22.1:34. Nicholas Beasley has argued that 'the re-creation of English ritual ways [was] central to . . . the colonial experience' of Barbados, Jamaica, and South Carolina and colonists 'found more meaning in Christian ritual than we have realized': Nicholas

'first convoy's landing in Georgia' (1 Feb. 1737); the Purification of the Blessed Virgin (2 Feb. 1737);[55] the Annunciation (25 Mar. 1736 and 1737); St Philip and St James the Apostles (1 May 1736 and 1737); Ascension Day (3 June 1736 and 19 May 1737);[56] St Barnabus (11 June 1737); The Nativity of St John the Baptist and feast day for the Savannah Freemasons (24 June 1737);[57] St Peter the Apostle (29 June 1736 and 1737); the anniversary day of the establishment of the court in Georgia (7 July 1737);[58] St Bartholomew the Apostle (24 Aug. 1736 and 1737); St Matthew the Apostle (21 Sept. 1736); St Michael and All Angels (Michaelmas) (29 Sept. 1736); All Saints' Day (1 Nov. 1736); St Andrew the Apostle (30 Nov. 1736); Oglethorpe's birthday (21 Dec. 1735 and 1736); Christmas Day (25 Dec. 1735 and 1736); St Stephen the Martyr (26 Dec. 1735 and 1736); St John the Evangelist (27 Dec. 1736); and The Holy Innocents (28 Dec. 1735 and 1736). Wesley also made particular note of observing Easter (25 Apr. 1736 and 10 Apr. 1737), Whitsunday (Pentecost) (13 June 1736 and 29 May 1737 [also Restoration Day]), and Trinity Sunday (5 June 1737), as well as the holy days of Ash Wednesday (23 Feb. 1737) and Good Friday (23 Apr. 1736 [also St George's Day] and 8 Apr. 1737).[59] During Holy Week in 1737, Wesley preached and administered the sacrament on every day of the week leading up to Easter Sunday.[60] Significantly, Wesley observed the five 'Greater Festivals' singled out in Deacon's *Devotions*.[61]

Wesley expressed his pastoral instincts and conviction about the centrality of the sacrament in the Christian life by resolving to speak to his communicants at least once a week and occasionally administering communion to sick parishioners in their homes, as he had previously done with passengers on the *Simmonds*.[62] Communion was considered the pinnacle of worship for

---

M. Beasley, 'Ritual Time in British Plantation Colonies, 1650–1780', *Church History*, 76 (2007), 541, 568.

[55] This feast day is now commonly called The Presentation of Christ in the Temple.

[56] Wesley made a special note in his *Journal* that he administered the sacrament on Ascension Day 1736.

[57] JWD and Causton, 'Journal', 262.

[58] Causton, 'Journal', 6–7 July 1737, pp. 266–7.

[59] See Wesley's diary under the dates cited for his observance of these feasts and holy days. It should be noted that in most cases Wesley does not explicitly acknowledge his celebration of these festivals, therefore in some cases the sacrament may have been offered on a festival day that Wesley did not consciously observe. It does not seem that he celebrated the specifically English festival days such as the martyrdom of Charles I, St George's Day, Restoration Day, Gunpowder Treason Day, and the ascension, coronation, and birth of George II.

[60] See JWD 3–10 April 1737; JWJ and JWMSJ 3 April 1737. He recorded attendance at all services except one, which overall averaged an attendance of thirty-eight, with twenty-one receiving the sacrament on Good Friday.

[61] Deacon, xxx. These were: Easter Day, the Sunday after Easter, Ascension Day, Whitsunday, Christmas Day, and all Lord's Days. In his celebrations, Wesley may have drawn on the prayers in Nelson's *Companion for the Festivals and Fasts of the Church of England*.

[62] JWMSJ, 7 March 1736. On 23 April 1736 Wesley administered the sacrament to John Dearn, whom he buried on 1 July 1737: JWD. The context of Wesley's diary makes it appear that Jacob

Wesley as for High Churchmen in general. As a result, he kept a parish register, which William Stephens observed after Wesley's departure from the colony was 'filled with the Names of Communicants at the Sacrament, where their Number and Day of receiving was carefully preserved.'[63] Stephens went on to comment that generally the same number and persons were repeated week after week. Although no list of Wesley's communicants has survived, we can compare Stephens's comment that he had a consistent number of communicants with evidence from Wesley's diary.

Overall, Wesley's diary contains notes on the number of communicants in Savannah for twenty-seven Sundays and on ten other days, several being significant dates on the Church calendar such as Good Friday and Ash Wednesday. These figures vary from a high of 35 at Easter 1736 to a low of 10.[64] The average number of communicants on Sundays was 18, as compared to 15 on other days and 15 on the *Simmonds* voyage.[65] These statistics are approximately three times more than Samuel Quincy's average of five to six communicants.[66] An average of about 18 communicated on Sundays out of a congregation that averaged 49 people—a ratio of 37 per cent. It remains to ask whether the number of communicants remained static during Wesley's ministry in Georgia, as Stephens claimed. While one could make a case that the figures were fairly consistent, they were not altogether unvarying. Although twenty of the twenty-seven records come from 1736, there is substantial evidence that Wesley had admitted more parishioners to the Lord's Table by the latter stages of his ministry in Georgia than at the beginning. During 1736 there was an average of 16 communicants, which increased by over five to 22 in 1737. This was likely because of the retention of his regular communicants coupled with the addition of new communicants. Indeed, on Whitsunday 29 May 1737 Wesley noted in his diary the admission of '4 new communicants!'[67] In sum, this rise in communicants mirrors the

Charles, John Brownfield, and Sarah Turner were ill when he gave them the sacrament: JWD, 14 September and 12 November 1736, 28 May 1737. This practice was sanctioned by Canon 71 (1604). Wesley, Ingham, and Delamotte apparently privately celebrated communion together on one occasion (JWD, 11 October 1736; cf. BD, 15–16 October 1735, p. 68); see Deacon's 'Office' for private communion: *Devotions*, 327–37. See BCP, 'The Communion of the Sick'; cf. the liturgy in Deacon's *Devotions*, 174–85.

[63] Stephens, *Journal*, 3 July 1738, *CRG*, 4:166. Stephens commented that this register did not contain 'an Account of the Births and Burials, &c.' as was customary: Stephens, *Journal*, 3 July 1738, *CRG*, 4:166; Canon 70 (1604). Wesley referred to this record in his manuscript journal: JWMSJ, 3 July 1737. The SPG directed its missionaries to keep a register for their own use containing records of baptisms and communicants: *A Collection of Papers*, 25, 27.

[64] William Stephens reported that Wesley's successor, William Norris, had about thirty communicants on Easter Sunday 1739: *CRG*, 5:219.

[65] All numbers 0.5 and above are rounded up. This seems like a very slight increase on communicants compared to the voyage to Georgia; however, it should be remembered that a number of his regular communicants settled in Frederica.

[66] Quincy to Harman Verelst (28 June 1735), *CRG*, 20:407.

[67] Cf. JWJ and JWMSJ, 29 May 1737.

increase in congregants at public worship, which supports the conclusion that on the whole Wesley's ministry contributed to a moderate advance in attendance at Savannah's parish church.[68]

August Spangenberg on Wesley's Eucharistic Theology

August Gottlieb Spangenberg's 1737 letter to Herrnhut supplies important information regarding Wesley's determination to uphold the rubric and canons of the Church. It also reflects the contemporary opposition being voiced about Wesley's ministerial practice at the time the controversy over his denial of communion to Sophia Williamson was brewing.[69] In his report to his brethren in Herrnhut, Spangenberg explained that in England one who does not adhere to the minimum canonical requirement of participating in the Lord's Supper three times per year is '*Civiliter mortuus*' (dead in the civil sphere); they cannot be a godparent or guardian, hold civil office, or be a witness in court.[70] However, Spangenberg implied that the canons encourage hypocrisy, since only the 'notoriously godless' can be denied communion and this can only be applied when one is charged in court, convicted, and brought to punishment. In actual fact, the prayer book rubric (cited later) allowed a wider scope for denying communion to parishioners than Spangenberg's opinion permits and a court case was not needed for this to be enforced. Spangenberg went on to explain that Wesley viewed communion as 'a means of grace' and a possible means of conversion, providing evidence of his early thoughts on communion as a converting ordinance.[71]

According to Spangenberg, Wesley also believed that communion could be administered to children but there is no evidence that by this he meant infant communion as practised in the Orthodox Church and supported by the *Apostolic Constitutions* (VIII.13).[72] One of the August 1737 'Grievances' of the Grand Jury against Wesley provides evidence that Wesley administered 'the Sacrament of the Lord's Supper to boys ignorant and unqualified, and that notwithstanding of their parents and nearest friends remonstrating against it, and accusing them of disobedience and other crimes, etc.': this may have been inspired to some degree by the Moravians, since Spangenberg told Wesley that

---

[68] On the rise in attendance at public worship see Hammond, appendix 11.

[69] See Wesley's journals from 7 August to 2 December 1737 and 'The Sophia Williamson Controversy in Context: Opposition to Wesley's Ministry to Women' in chapter 5.

[70] See the 1662 BCP communion rubrics and Canon 21 (1604) on the canonical requirement.

[71] See note 135 in chapter 2.

[72] Spangenberg asserted that Wesley's practice was like that of the 'Greek Church' while failing to distinguish between infant and child communion. This may perhaps reflect Wesley's lack of clarity about this distinction. William Wall concluded that in the time of Cyprian and St Augustine, communion was sometimes given to infants/children: *History of Infant Baptism*,

he had 'known a child of eight years old admitted to communicate.'[73] However, the record of this conversation appears two months after Wesley's journal note that 'four of our scholars, after having been daily instructed for several weeks preceding, were at their earnest desire, frequently expressed, admitted to the Lord's Table.' These were most likely boys who attended the school run by Delamotte. They were probably the boys referred to in the Grievances.[74]

Spangenberg explained that, on the one hand, Wesley admonished all parishioners to receive communion, which he made available weekly and often several times each week. However, on the other hand, he was thoroughly convinced that communicants must live holy lives.[75] Therefore, his solution was to publicly announce that he would restrict the Lord's Table to those he had examined beforehand. This was similar to the views of Zinzendorf, as well as the practice of the Moravians in Georgia.[76] Spangenberg may have helped inspire and/or strengthen Wesley's resolution in this regard, since a factor in Spangenberg's dismissal from Halle was his contention that the converted should not receive communion with the unconverted.[77] In one sense Wesley's practice was not as radical as it might sound, since the SPG instructed its missionaries to 'duly consider the Qualifications of those adult Persons…whom they admit to the Lord's Supper, according to the Directions of the Rubrics in our Liturgy'.[78] However, if the Grievances of the Grand Jury are accurate, Wesley went beyond the prayer book by asking non-communicants to withdraw before pronouncing the benediction. For this practice Wesley drew on the teaching of the *Apostolic Constitutions* and Deacon, which went further than the Grievances by declaring that communion should be reserved for the faithful and be administered after all non-communicants had departed.[79] In confining the Lord's Supper, Wesley could also appeal to the prayer book rubric that those who wish to partake must inform the curate at least a day in advance. If a clergyman was convinced that a person was guilty of 'malicious and open contention with his neighbours, or other grave and open sin without

2:446. Thomas Deacon believed in infant communion: Quantin, *Church of England and Christian Antiquity*, 407.

[73] JWMSJ, 22 August 1737; 31 July 1737; cf. Hunter, 35–6.

[74] JWJ, JWMSJ, and JWD, 29 May 1737.

[75] The BCP communion rubrics and Canon 22 (1604) obliges ministers to urge their parishioners at morning prayer on the Sunday prior to administering communion to prepare themselves for receiving the sacrament.

[76] In his letter to Wesley in Georgia, Zinzendorf stated his conviction that communion brings nothing but condemnation to the ungodly and that only 'regenerate' Christians 'who specifically on that occasion of communion are neither distracted nor interrupted in their holy struggle' should be admitted to partake of the sacrament: [23 October 1736], *Works*, 25:479–83. On the practice of the Moravians, see 'Töltschigs Diarium', 18, 20 April and 18 May 1736 and (NS), fos 416, 418.

[77] Atwood, 'Spangenberg', 12. On Spangenberg's dismissal from Halle, see Ward, *Protestant Evangelical Awakening*, 139–41.

[78] *A Collection of Papers*, 24; cf. Humphreys, *Historical Account*, 70.

[79] JWMSJ, 22 August 1737; *Constitutions* VIII.12; Deacon, *Devotions*, 74.

repentance' he was to submit this case before the ordinary (usually a bishop) and abide by his order. To prevent public embarrassment, the minister was asked to warn the prospective communicant not to present him or herself at the Lord's Table until the ordinary had sent his decision. 'In case of a grave and immediate scandal to the Congregation', the minister was permitted to deny communion to a parishioner provided that he submit the case before the ordinary within seven days. Anyone was to be afforded an opportunity of an interview before the ordinary before a final decision was given.

In reality, the prayer book rubric provided little practical guidance for Anglican clergy in the American colonies, especially colonies like Georgia that lacked a commissary commissioned by the bishop of London.[80] The reality was that Wesley was curate, parish priest, and *de facto* ordinary. Therefore, there was no one to mediate potential disputes between him and parishioners and no ecclesiastical court equipped to judge ecclesial matters.[81] All parishioners knew that complete day-to-day ecclesial power was vested in Wesley. The ongoing dispute over ecclesiastical jurisdiction between the Trustees and the bishop of London meant that the situation was extremely ambiguous. While the Trustees effectively prevented the bishop of London from exercising ecclesiastical jurisdiction in Georgia, such obstructionism was of questionable legality. The Trustees believed that they were the 'Ordinaries' of Georgia with jurisdiction in ecclesiastical matters.[82] However, their distance from the colony made their actual authority negligible. Most Trustees had neither the expertise in canon law nor the experience necessary to effectively solve ecclesiastical disputes; their consistent solution was to revoke the license of their ministers and choose a replacement.

Given the uncertainty surrounding Wesley's authority, Spangenberg accurately discerned that Wesley was playing with fire by insisting on imposing strict ecclesial discipline. Technically speaking, he should have presented any cases for excluding parishioners from the Lord's Table to the Trustees or the bishop of London or, at the very least, Alexander Garden, the bishop's commissary to South Carolina. Spangenberg was of the opinion that Wesley was actively exceeding his ecclesial authority and 'must either do what the English Church orders or he cannot be its minister.' He noted the danger that the Church might 'cast him out', allowing him to 'become a free servant of Christ.'

---

[80] Traditionally the bishop of London held authority over the Church of England in the American colonies. The bishop of London, Edmund Gibson, was granted a royal patent to exercise authority in America. His practise was to send commissaries to act on his behalf in the colonies: Robert G. Ingram, *Religion, Reform and Modernity in the Eighteenth Century: Thomas Secker and the Church of England*, Studies in Modern British Religious History, 17 (Woodbridge, 2007), 240–1.
[81] As chief magistrate, Thomas Causton recognized that the lack of an ecclesiastical court made minor community disputes difficult to solve: Causton, 'Journal', 31 May 1737, p. 247.
[82] Egmont, *Journal*, 12 July 1738, *CRG*, 5:48.

Spangenberg relayed that he had ordered the Moravians not to 'meddle' in cases dealing with Wesley's office. However, if indeed he was cast out, Spangenberg informed his colleagues in Germany that he instructed the Moravians to 'take him in our house.'[83]

A True and Historical Narrative of the Colony of *Georgia* on Wesley's Eucharistic Practice

In Georgia, even colonists outside Wesley's circle of disciples were well aware of his liturgical innovations, which Tailfer and the authors of *A True and Historical Narrative* noted 'he called *Apostolick Constitutions*.' The comments relating to Wesley from this polemical work aimed at what the authors saw as the failure of the Georgia colony as a whole provides substantial evidence of Wesley's ministerial practice from the perspective of his opponents. This account overlaps to a degree with the Grievances and Indictments of the Grand Jury because of the authors' involvement in that jury. Because we have few descriptions of Wesley's ministry from his supporters, we are left to critically evaluate those of his opponents alongside the clues provided by Wesley's journals and diary. Significantly, Tailfer's criticisms of Wesley confirm that Wesley did in fact carry out his apostolic practices in Georgia.[84] Relating to communion, he specifically referred to Wesley's habit of 'Mixing Wine with Water in the Sacrament, and Suppressing in the Administration of the Sacrament, the Explanation adjoined to the Words of communicating with the Church of England, to shew that they mean a Feeding on Christ by Faith, saying no more than "The Body of Christ; The Blood of Christ"'.[85]

The mixing of wine with water in the sacrament was one of the Nonjurors' four primitive usages based on the 1549 prayer book and the *Apostolic Constitutions*. The words of the prayer book liturgy to be spoken before the administration of the sacrament that Tailfer accused Wesley of suppressing were:

> The Body of our Lord Jesus Christ, which was given for thee, preserve thy body and soul unto everlasting life: Take and eat this in remembrance that Christ died for thee, and feed on him in thy heart by faith with thanksgiving. *And the Minister that delivereth the Cup to any one shall say,* The Blood of our Lord Jesus Christ, which was shed for three, preserve thy body and soul unto everlasting life: Drink this in remembrance that Christ's Blood was shed for thee, and be thankful.[86]

---

[83] Spangenberg, 'A Moravian's Report', 407–8.
[84] Cf. Wesley's criticisms of Tailfer's immoral life: JWMSJ, 12 November 1736.
[85] Tailfer, 42. Egmont called the section of this book dealing with Wesley 'tedious' and 'impertinent': Ver Stegg (ed.), *True and Historical Narrative*, 67.
[86] The 1549 BCP liturgy is the same except for the absence of 'Take and eat...' and 'Drink this in remembrance...'

If Tailfer's testimony was accurate, and we have no reason to believe it was not, this truly was a suppression of the liturgy. Wesley's modified practice was based on the precedent of the primitive church, which formed the inspiration for Deacon's liturgy. In Georgia, Wesley read Claude Fleury, who quoted the testimony of 'one of the earliest writers' that the bread and wine is taken to be 'the flesh and blood of the incarnate Jesus.'[87] As a Catholic, Fleury was inclined to link the doctrine of transubstantiation with the Church Fathers; Wesley seems to have also wanted to maintain a close connection between the elements and Christ's body and blood. In this way, the real presence of Christ in the Eucharist could be maintained without necessarily affirming any transformation in the elements. The words at the distribution of the elements in the *Apostolic Constitutions* (VIII.13) are: 'The body of Christ' and 'The blood of Christ, the cup of life.' Deacon's liturgy called for the priest to say 'this Bread and Body of thy Christ' and 'this Cup the Blood of thy Christ' during the prayer for the invocation of the Holy Spirit on the elements, followed by the exact words of the *Constitutions* when administering the Eucharist to communicants.[88] Given Wesley's penchant for following the *Constitutions* and Deacon's liturgy, it is not surprising that Tailfer's report of Wesley's practice is very close to the language they used. Both Deacon and Wesley avoided the prayer book language of remembrance, which could lead to a memorialist interpretation of the sacrament. It is likely that a minority of Anglicans interpreted the Lord's Supper as merely a symbolic memorial; however, Wesley wanted to maintain a close link between the elements and Christ as the elements were seen by him to be instruments through the agency of the Holy Spirit to convey Christ's presence to the faithful. Assuming that Tailfer's account faithfully recounts Wesley's precise words at the distribution, it is worth noting that Wesley's practice foreshadowed that of Thomas Rattray (1684–1743), leader of the usager party of Scottish Episcopalians, whose communion office published in 1744 contains the exact words that Wesley purportedly used at the distribution of the elements.[89]

The Grand Jury's Grievances and Indictments Relating to the Eucharist

The thirteen Grievances and ten Indictments of the Grand Jury against Wesley contain several items that shed important light on his Eucharistic theology.

---

[87] Fleury, 18–19.
[88] Deacon, *Devotions*, 92–3, 97.
[89] *The Ancient Liturgy of the Church of Jerusalem*, in Grisbrooke, 330–1. The Usagers became the majority in the Scottish Episcopal Church in the latter half of the eighteenth century: Buxton, *Eucharist and Institution Narrative*, 189.

The Grievances, minus the charge of admitting unqualified boys to the Lord's Table discussed earlier, were:

> 5. By restricting the benefit of the Lord's Supper to a small number of persons, and refusing it to all others who will not conform to a grievous set of penances, confessions, mortifications and constant attendance of early and late hours of prayer, very inconsistent with labours and employments of this Colony;
> 7. By refusing to administrate the Holy Sacrament to well-disposed and well-living persons, unless they should submit to confessions and penances for crimes which they utterly refuse, and whereof no evidence is offered;
> 8. By venting sundry uncharitable expressions of all who differ from him, and not pronouncing the benediction in church until all the hearers except his own communicants are withdrawn;[90]

In addition to the evidence that Wesley turned away prospective communicants such as William Gough, he generally restricted the potential number of communicants by enforcing the prayer book requirement that they submit their names to him at least the day before partaking. While when observed this would commonly have been a routine procedure, Spangenberg recalled that if Wesley had 'seen any with whom he is not satisfied, he has said to them that they should wait awhile and he would see whether they have improved.'[91] The inevitable tension this would cause in an infant colony with a single clergyman in control is obvious. As genuine as Wesley's concerns might have been, many colonists predictably took this as an affront to their character rather than an opportunity to reform their lives. Indications are that Wesley was aware of the possible consequences, but believed that restricting the sacrament to the 'faithful' was the true primitive way.

The eighth charge, which could be deduced as probable from Spangenberg's letter, is confirmed in the Grievance. The practice of asking his non-communicants to withdraw before pronouncing the benediction cannot be found in either the 1549 or 1662 prayer books. As noted, this was inspired by the *Apostolic Constitutions* (VIII.12) and Deacon's *Devotions*. Deacon's rubric prefaced to his communion office states '*none but the Faithful are to be present at this office*' and he specified that before the offertory and words of institution the deacon is to say: 'If there be any here, who are not of the number of the Faithful, let them depart.'[92] Here Deacon followed the liturgy in the *Constitutions*, which instructs the deacon to announce that the catechumens, hearers, unbelievers, and heterodox are to depart. Therefore, Wesley may have gone further than the Grievance states by asking all but communicants to depart prior to reciting the communion office. However, the Grievance may indicate that Wesley did not fully follow Deacon's liturgy

---

[90] JWMSJ, 22 August 1737.   [91] Spangenberg, 'A Moravian's Report', 408.
[92] Deacon, 74, 80.

by allowing non-communicants to remain in the church until the time of the benediction.[93] In any case, this charge provides firm evidence that Wesley drew on the liturgies of the *Apostolic Constitutions* and Deacon in Georgia. As a High Church rigorist who saw the Eucharist as the centre of worship, he evidently wanted to maintain a level of distinction between communicants and non-communicants. Wesley shared Deacon's conviction that only those who lived holy lives should communicate.[94] Depending on one's perspective, Wesley's Eucharistic practice in Georgia might be called High Church legalism or High Church sacramental piety.

All of these general Grievances were dropped in favour of more specific charges in the Indictments composed by the Grand Jury less than two weeks later. The one Indictment dealing specifically with communion cited Wesley for declining to offer the sacrament to Sophia Williamson 'without any apparent reason for so doing, much to the disquiet of the mind of the said Sophia Christiana Williamson, and to the great disgrace of her character.'[95] In this Indictment, the consequences of Wesley's resolutions to obey all of the Church's rubrics came full circle. The charges of confessions, penances, and mortifications were left out of the Indictments, but are scrutinized in the next section.

CONFESSION AND PENANCE

The accusations of Tailfer and the Grievances of the Grand Jury allege that Wesley sought to enforce a system of confession and penitential discipline on his parishioners. Echoing the Grand Jury's Grievances, Tailfer and friends believed that Wesley hoped to enslave the minds and bodies of colonists by his 'Endeavours to establish Confession, Penance, and Mortifications', as well as attempts to suppress people's minds and liberty by 'Fastings.'[96] Are these sources reliable, and can the claims they made be substantiated?

Tailfer's critical remarks contain a good deal of truth mixed with some exaggeration. Taking into account the polemical nature of the *Narrative*, it nonetheless compares closely with the list of Grievances reported in Wesley's manuscript journal adding weight to its reliability as a historical source. The claim that Wesley termed his liturgical preferences 'Apostolick Constitutions'

---

[93] In Deacon's liturgy, the benediction is the concluding act of the service of communion, which is followed by the deacon's words 'depart in peace': *Devotions*, 100.

[94] After his arrival in the colony, William Norris learned that Wesley 'excluded' people from communion, a practice he condemned: Norris to Trustees (12 December 1738), *CRG*, 22.1:351.

[95] The sixth, ninth, and tenth Indictments that relate both to baptism and communion are discussed in 'Resolutions Relating to Baptismal Practice' in this chapter.

[96] Tailfer, 42. Some parallel can be found between Tailfer's comments and those of the Non-Usager bishop of the Nonjurors, George Smith (1693–1756). Smith accused the Usager

matches Wesley's own statements about his intention to revive primitive Christianity in the Georgia wilderness. Wesley's own self-understanding was that he was restoring the practices and discipline of the primitive church; however, Tailfer saw things differently. For him, Wesley's practices were reminiscent of the tyrannical behaviour displayed by Roman Catholic priests.

The probability that the claims of the Grand Jury and Tailfer were substantially accurate is increased by an informative section of a letter written by William Norris, a successor to Wesley as missionary in Georgia, who informed the Trustees that

> a separate nightly Assembly was formed at the Minister's House, which made up a Communion of Saints; & were distinguished by the Name of the Faithful: but were indeed such Members as neither contributed to the Credit of Religion, nor Society; these observed particular Forms of Worship & Duties such as publick Confession, Pennance [sic], Absolution &c; & many believed that an Avenue was herein opening for the Introduction of Popery.

For Norris, Wesley's religious societies invited suspicion with their implication of holy group separatism. These meetings were seen as a pretext for encouraging the 'Judaising spiritual Pride' of false religion.[97] Notable is the claim that the people called one another 'the Faithful'. This suggests a deliberate imitation of the language used in the *Apostolic Constitutions* and *Canons* and in Deacon to differentiate communicants from the rest of the congregation. Norris's second-hand testimony coupled with the Grievances and Tailfer prove that there were more than one or two colonists who believed Wesley might be part of a conspiracy to introduce popery in Georgia.

Tailfer perhaps observed (or heard of) confession, penance, mortification, and fasting amongst the missionaries and a select few colonists to whom Wesley devoted the bulk of his pastoral care. These accusations also may have been derived from colonists who, like Emily Wesley (John Wesley's sister), saw confession as a form of 'church tyranny.'[98] In the context of Tailfer's overall criticism of Wesley, he charged that Wesley specifically targeted women for confession.[99] Whether Wesley required confession as a prerequisite to receiving the sacrament is uncertain. It is unclear whether Wesley systematically required his parishioners to participate in private confession, although he

party as advocating the usages 'under the pretence of setting up *Primitive Christianity*', which he proclaimed was 'the readiest and smoothest way to lead your deluded admirers to the embracing of the Romish Religion': George Smith to Thomas Brett, 31 January 1731, quoted in Sharp, '100 Years of a Lost Cause', 46.

[97] Norris to Trustees (12 December 1738), *CRG*, 21.1:352.

[98] Emily Wesley to JW [13 August 1735], *Works*, 25:431. Another possibility is that Tailfer may have been thinking of Wesley's attempt to convince Sophia Williamson to confess her faults in a penitential fashion after her failure to keep her word to consult with Wesley before marrying and her neglect of public worship following her marriage to William Williamson.

[99] Tailfer, 42.

often met privately particularly with receptive parishioners to exhort them to live holy lives. This may have led to some confessional sessions, but was not specifically designed to elicit confessions. Similarly, his summary state-ment on the Methodist plan for promoting and supporting religious societies in Savannah mentioned 'conversing singly with each' person.[100] Here again we would be on shaky ground to conclude that this refers to a method for private confession, although the kind of voluntary confession recommended in *The Country-Parson's Advice to his Parishioners* (1680) would have been quite wel-come at such sessions.[101]

Although neither the Grievances nor Tailfer specified whether the confes-sions required were public or private, Norris claimed that they were public. Therefore, it is worth asking whether Wesley might have tried to imple-ment a programme of public confession like the one Nathaniel Marshall had recommended in his proposal to Convocation.[102] Deacon's *Devotions* provide a 'Form of admitting a Penitent to Penance' and a 'Form of absolv-ing a Penitent' as a required disciplinary system before partaking of com-munion. The former liturgy requests that the penitent confess his or her sins while kneeling before the priest (presumably within the hearing of the con-gregation) and receive the penance required by the bishop. The *Apostolic Constitutions* (VIII.9) require penitents to depart before the communion office, but they do not contain a programme for conducting confession. It is probably significant that Tailfer complained of Wesley's 'endeavours' rather than of his programme or system. Mutual confession practiced by the Moravians and later by Methodist societies would have no doubt been an element of Wesley's religious societies in Georgia, even if they may have more commonly involved the reading of confessional prayers and the sing-ing of confessional psalms and hymns than personal confessional testimo-nies.[103] While Wesley insisted that certain parishioners amend their lives before partaking of the sacrament, there is insufficient evidence to conclude that he obliged all prospective communicants to submit to confession and penance. Nonetheless, at least in the case of Sophia Williamson, Wesley, as his father had done on similar occasions, demanded repentance (apparently public repentance) as authorized by the prayer book before readmitting her to the Lord's Table.[104]

---

[100] JWJ, 20 April 1736.

[101] See '*Country Parson's Advice*', 26:520. See *Diary of an Oxford Methodist*, pp. 14, 17, 26 on the importance of this work to Wesley.

[102] Wesley had read Marshall's *The Penitential Discipline of the Primitive Church* in July 1734.

[103] In this respect, Deacon's 'Penitential Prayers' might have been used: *Devotions*, 299–306.

[104] JWMSJ, 11 August 1737. In the *Apostolic Constitutions* (VII.26), holiness is required before partaking of the Eucharist, but if one is not holy they can be made so by repentance.

Tailfer's polemic may reflect a controversy over confession that broke out two months after Wesley's departure from the colony. Charles Delamotte wrote to Wesley:

> there went a great cry through the streets, 'News concerning the saints',[105] that now there was proof of the horrid proceedings of that monster Wesley and his crew— Mr [James] Campbell had committed adultery with Mrs. Mears,[106] and had made confession, and had received absolution from you. 'What need have we of further proof of his being a Roman priest, and all his followers Roman Catholics?'

Delamotte related that this led Thomas Causton to make 'a second Sophy's affidavit of two sheets of paper full of the horridest [*sic*] lies and nonsense that ever were put together'. James Campbell and probably Mrs Mears were involved in Wesley's Savannah religious societies and Wesley read, prayed, and sang with Campbell on a number of occasions.[107] Their inclusion amongst Wesley's pious parishioners seems to be reflected in the affidavit's claim that they 'greeted each other with a holy kiss, and sang a Psalm' after sleeping together. The affidavit describes 'the posture we all sat in at the time of confession, Mr B—[urnside?] upon the stairs, hanging down his head, Mrs. [Margaret] Gilbert clapping her daughter upon the back and saying, Speak up, Betty, never fear, when it is out there is an end of it, etc., and much more nonsense of the same import'.[108] Although Delamotte disputed the details of these claims, he did not deny that there was a 'time of confession'.[109] Therefore, we may cautiously conclude that Wesley encouraged public confession.[110] In the context of Delamotte's letter, it seems that confession was incorporated within Wesley's Savannah religious societies. This affidavit brings together the chief complaints against Wesley found in other polemics, namely, that he was a divisive figure, a Roman Catholic, an enthusiast, a disrupter of proper social order, and a manipulator, particularly of women.[111]

There is no doubt that Wesley's strict conception of ecclesial discipline contributed to conflicts with his parishioners. Confession and penance, in particular, provoked accusations of popery. Like his father before him, he was more interested in obeying the Church rubrics (when they agreed with his conception of primitive Christianity) than in promoting harmony in his parish through compromise. He was faithful to his father's advice to utilize all the 'Coercive' discipline the Church allows.[112]

---

[105] Cf. William Norris's report that Wesley's followers 'were distinguished by the Name of the Faithful': Norris to Trustees (12 December 1738), *CRG*, 21.1:352.

[106] This seems to have been Elizabeth, daughter of Margaret Gilbert: *LES*, 75, 88.

[107] JWD, 4, 15, 21 March, 4, 5 April, 6, 24 June 1737.

[108] Betty may have been Elizabeth Gilbert.

[109] Delamotte to JW (23 February 1738), *Works*, 25:530.

[110] Cf. Dearing, *Wesleyan and Tractarian Worship*, 62.

[111] These polemical complaints are discussed in chapter 5.

[112] Wesley, *Advice to a Young Clergyman*, 70.

ASCETICISM: EATING AND SLEEPING

While in Georgia, Wesley frequently reminded himself that he came to the New World desiring nothing but food and raiment.[113] Indeed, for several months prior to November 1737, he survived without having a single shilling, but claimed he lived in 'peace, health, and contentment'.[114] The asceticism displayed by the Georgia Methodists was likely to have been behind the charges of requiring 'mortifications' before reception of the Lord's Supper in the Grand Jury's Grievances and Tailfer, as well as the allegation of fasting in Tailfer. The accusation of mortifications seems to have been used as a blanket term that encompassed fasting and other unspecified disciplines, as in the charge that Wesley taught 'wives and servants that they ought absolutely to follow the course of mortification, fastings, and diets of prayers prescribed by him, without any regard to the interest of their private families, or the commands of their respective husbands and masters.'[115] It would not have escaped the colonists' notice that the Georgia Methodists experimented with a vegetarian diet and rigorously observed days of fasting. According to Ingham, in Georgia, he alone stuck with the voyage experiment of not eating supper, while his colleagues resumed eating the evening meal. Nonetheless, Wesley and Delamotte continued to regularly fast until three in the afternoon and, to a degree, they took their strict dietary regulations a step further by trying 'whether life might not be as well sustained by one sort as by a variety of food.' Accordingly, they adopted a diet of bread as their only food 'and were never more vigorous and healthy than while we tasted nothing else.' Immediately after this statement Wesley quoted the biblical passage: 'Blessed are the pure in heart', linking this verse to his belief in fasting as a means of purification.[116]

---

[113] JW to George Whitefield and the Oxford Methodists [10 September 1736], *Works*, 25:472; JW to Richard Morgan, Jr [16 February 1737], *Works*, 25:491; JW to the SPG [23–6 July 1737], *Works*, 25:516. Wesley's stated goal proved impossible to fulfil, since money was needed for the upkeep of the parsonage and travel to and from Frederica. He was certainly anxious for authorities in London to be satisfied that he was living frugally. Therefore, Ingham's report of the rumour that the bishop of London was 'offended' by his expenditure would have troubled him: JWMSJ, 4 March 1737; JW to the Trustees [4 March 1737], *Works*, 25:496–7; Ingham to JW (19 October 1737), *Works*, 25:521.

[114] JWMSJ, 1 November 1737.

[115] JWMSJ, 22 August 1737; cf. the affidavits of Sophia Williamson and Charles Delamotte: JWMSJ, 16 August 1737. Deborah Madden has rightly pointed out that 'Wesley did not endorse extreme asceticism': '*A Cheap, Safe and Natural Medicine*', 42. However, it may be that Wesley's asceticism in Georgia, which manifested itself in practices of bodily austerity, could understandably have been seen by some colonists to be extreme enough to be labelled as mortification.

[116] BIJ, 7 December 1735, p. 71; JWMSJ, 16 August 1737; JWJ, 31 March 1736; Matthew 5:8. There is evidence that Charles Wesley stuck with his vegetarian diet in Georgia: see CWJ, 4 April 1736, p. 19.

Wesley's account of the beginning of this experiment contains the unstated implication that this may have been more than simply a temporary trial. From the date of this entry (31 March 1736) through the following week, the word 'bread' is found in Wesley's diary at least once a day. Although he declared that this diet was met with at least short-term success, we are left with uncertainty as to how strict the regime was and long it lasted.[117] After this period the reader of Wesley's diary can only spot the occasional reference to bread, bread and butter, or bread and cheese. A few other food items appear in the diary including fish, oysters, eggs, rice, chocolate, and 'barbecued bear flesh.' The first item appears under the date 7 April 1736, showing that the initial trial was not exclusively adhered to, while the reference to eating bear flesh was printed in Wesley's *Journal*.[118] Therefore, while there is solid evidence to suggest that Wesley kept an ascetical diet as a matter of religious expression, it was not an uncompromising vegetarian diet.[119] This conclusion is supported by the anecdote Henry Moore heard from Wesley decades later. Oglethorpe asked Wesley to dine and said: 'Mr. Wesley, there are some here who have the wrong idea of your abstemiousness. They think you hold the eating of animal food and drinking wine to be unlawful. I beg that you will convince them of the contrary.' Wesley obliged, but found himself afterwards to be struck by a fever for five days.[120]

Fortunately, we also have accounts from contemporary witnesses to Wesley's ascetic diet. Johann Töltschig observed that the English missionaries

> practice the greatest self denial... They do not lie on a bed but upon the bare floor or ground.[121] They come to table and eat hominy and hominy bread with us (a dish made of Indian corn or else Indian corn and Welsh corn and rice). Here they surely could and should have the best food from the [Trustees'] storehouse. When we accordingly wish to give them something better they aren't able to accept it.[122]

The Lutheran minister Israel Gronau reported to Halle that 'he has many a legalistic practice which I cannot imagine for myself, such as sleeping on the bare ground like the Indians, with a fur under him and his clothes on, or eating foods without salt or fat, or wearing long linen trousers which reach to

---

[117] Wesley noted that he returned to his 'old simplicity of diet' on his voyage back to England, perhaps suggesting that his abstemiousness had lapsed at some point: JWJ, 26 December 1737.

[118] JWJ, JWMSJ, JWD, 1 January 1737.

[119] At the least, Charles Wallace's statement that his vegetarian diet began on the *Simmonds* and 'lasted for two years' should be modified: Wallace, 'Eating and Drinking with John Wesley', 145. Wesley regularly drank tea, coffee, and sassafras. He may have drank sassafras as root beer made by boiling the roots of the sassafras tree with molasses and/or sassafras tea produced by steeping the bark of the tree: see JWD, 18 March 1736.

[120] Moore, *Life of the Rev. John Wesley*, 1:311. This was probably a recollection of the fever he suffered under at Frederica: JWMSJ and JWD, 16 August 1736.

[121] This practice was confirmed under oath by Charles Delamotte: JWMSJ, 16 August 1737.

[122] Töltschig's Diary, 1 June 1736 (NS), in Nelson, 32–3.

his shoes and, therefore, no stockings, etc'. What Gronau did not mention is that at least on occasion Charles Wesley, Ingham, and Delamotte joined John Wesley in sleeping without a bed.[123] Before Gotthilf Francke received this letter, Philipp von Reck had told him that Wesley was 'so ascetic in diet and the like because he is considering work among other heathen in the future, and hopes thereby that their lifestyle might not seem so unfamiliar to him'.[124] The accounts of Töltschig and Gronau provide important insights into the holistic nature of Wesley's ascetic spirituality. It spread not only to eating and clothing, but also to sleeping habits. Additionally, von Reck's testimony is highly valuable because it shows that long into the Georgia mission Wesley continued to conceive of his mission as a means to convert the Indians to Christianity.

Wesley was fully committed to undergoing what he believed were the necessary hardships of a pioneer missionary. Part of this programme of emulating the poverty of Christ and the primitive church was to be content and indeed count it a blessing to sleep rough. In this practice, Gregorio López may have been an inspiration.[125] This process began on the *Simmonds* when Wesley was forced to sleep on the floor on a night when his bed became wet in a storm. In his *Journal*, he remarked 'I believe I shall not find it needful to go to bed (as it is called) any more'.[126] Sleeping was not always a pleasant experience for Wesley. On occasion he could not sleep because of fleas and flies.[127] Particularly on journeys via the intracoastal waterway to Frederica, at times he had to sleep on the piragua (a flat-bottomed boat with two masts) wrapped in a cloak to avoid being attacked by sand-flies.[128] Gronau would only have been aware of his sleeping habits as they applied to Savannah, therefore, Wesley's remark that he laid 'without bolster' in Frederica is especially valuable.[129] It may have been his experience in Frederica where all colonists spent their first weeks in tents that trained him for austere sleeping in Savannah's parsonage. On his first return journey to Savannah he thought his experience of sleeping on the ground noteworthy enough to add an exclamation mark after this comment in his diary.[130] According to Wesley, it was during his third visit to Frederica

---

[123] CWJ, 16 May 1736, p. 34.

[124] Gronau to Francke (9 June 1737) and Francke to Gronau (23 December 1737), in Zehrer, 'Relationship between Pietism', 214; cf. Johann Martin Boltzius and Israel Christian Gronau to Heinrich Alard Butjenter (20 January 1738), in Boltzius, *Letters*, 1:226. Delamotte also cited the planned mission to the Indians as the 'chief reason' for his ascetic practices: JWMSJ, 16 August 1737.

[125] Losa, *Life of Gregory Lopez*, 27:391–2. Was Wesley aware that his practice of sleeping on the floor agreed with that of some early Christian ascetics (e.g. Origen)? See J. Stevenson and W. H. C. Frend (eds), *A New Eusebius: Documents Illustrating the History of the Church to AD 337*, 2nd edn (London, 1987), 191.

[126] JWJ, 30 January 1736.

[127] JWD, 15 April, 26 May, 7 June 1736.

[128] JWJ and JWD, 4 April 1736.

[129] JWD, 24 May 1736.

[130] JWD, 19 April 1736.

in August 1736 that he was providentially forced to overcome his fear of lying in the woods when he got lost in the surrounding forest.[131] In this instance, he had to sleep covered in dew, but this was a minor trial compared to a journey to Cowpen (a few miles from Savannah) in December 1736. The guide leading Wesley and Delamotte got lost, forcing them to wade through a creek followed by walking through a cypress swamp nearly neck high. By sunset they had still not found their way and were compelled to lie down in a pine grove where they could not make a fire due to the dampness of the place. Already being wet with dew, the overnight frost covered them so that they awoke covered 'as white as snow.' In his *Journal*, Wesley simply recounted that he 'slept till six in the morning.' Without examining the content of the diary one is left with the impression that he possessed almost superhuman strength and endurance. More realistically, the diary reads '9 Waked by frost and cramp many times. 10 Heavy dew, froze over; ground and cloths wet beneath; almost dispirited.' These two heroic stories became important to the public narrative of his Georgia mission because they were incorporated into his *Journal*.[132]

We also have two testimonies to Wesley's ascetic sleeping from English colonists. Philip Thicknesse recalled that he 'slept rolled up in a blanket (at least he told me he did)', which he mentioned together with Wesley's wearing of Indian '*Maugazeens*' (moccasins).[133] Yet another opinion on his ascetic sleeping was expressed in a letter sent to England by William Williamson two months after he had married Sophia Hopkey.

> I cant help Adding a particular which my Sister Informed me of in London which sometimes affords me no small Diversion; Upon Asking her how she Came to provide me such Ordinary Linen Bedding &a As to Linen; She told me if it was finer or Ruffled Mr Oglethorpe would take it from me And As to Bedding &a It was as good as Even the parson had. (the last Mistake indeed is on the right side, for the Parson (being a strict Primitive) Lyes on the Ground).[134]

In this letter Williamson revealed that his addressee (likely a Trustee) wanted to keep 'the Seeds of Luxury & Idleness' out of Georgia. The tone of the letter shows that Williamson was becoming disillusioned with what he saw as the failure of the Trustees' well-meaning plan to make Georgia into a 'primitive' economy. In this endeavour, he viewed Wesley as an exemplar of this oppressive primitivism encouraged by the Trustees. Williamson foreshadowed the complaints of Tailfer, who mocked the Trustees for affording them 'the opportunity of arriving at the integrity of the Primitive Times' and Robert Williams's

[131] JWJ, JWMSJ, JWD, 28 August 1736.
[132] JWJ, JWMSJ, JWD, 22 December 1736.
[133] Letter to *The Gentleman's Magazine* (1791), in Heitzenrater, *Elusive Mr. Wesley*, 256; cf. *The St. James's Chronicle*, 5 October 1780, in Baine, 'Thicknesse's Reminiscences', 690.
[134] Letter of 8 May 1737, in *CRG*, 21:463–4.

charge that Wesley '*seduced the common Persons there settled* [in Georgia], *to Idleness*'.[135]

Like the gossip that Wesley had 'a more than ordinary call to go to Georgia', rumours about his asceticism spread to interested clergymen in England.[136] Not surprisingly, such reports centred on Wesley's desire to convert the Indians to Christianity, which had received attention in London newspapers.[137] In August 1738, William Warburton penned the following satire to Dr Conyers Middleton:

> [John] Westley [*sic*], told a friend of mine that he had been last summer in Georgia where he had lived most divinely, feeding on boiled maize with the sauce of Oak-ashes, and sleeping in Fresco, under Trees: That he intends to return thither, and that then he will cast off his English habit, and wear a dried-skin like the Savages, in order to ingratiate himself the better with them.[138]

By the time of Wesley's death, it was his followers rather than detractors for whom his asceticism in Georgia became legendary. In his sermon on the death of Wesley, Thomas Coke made the exaggerated claim that when Wesley made 'the sacrifice' of going to Georgia, 'he lived on nothing but vegetables, milk, and water' and 'would endure exquisite hardships for want of food, even to the supporting of himself, and his companion who travelled with him, on the very berries which grew upon the hedges of the field.' Coke also conveyed to his fellow Methodists the heroic story of Wesley sleeping in the woods overnight 'when he was almost frozen to death.' In retelling these anecdotes as didactical exhortations, Coke described Wesley's work in Georgia as an act of self-denial in a manner faithful to Wesley's own self-understanding and the original purpose of Wesley's journals.[139]

Coke's attitude contrasts sharply with the uniform criticism of Wesley's contemporaries. Nonetheless, the type of ascetic spirituality the Methodists modelled would have encouraged their followers to follow suit. These were ordinary

---

[135] Tailfer, v; 'Robert Williams's Affidavit', in *Progress of Methodism*, 44. For more on the views of the Trustees, see 'The Georgia Trustees' Ideal of Economic Primitivism' in Hammond, appendix 2.

[136] Wilson, *Diaries*, 5 November 1735, p. 137.

[137] See *The London Evening-Post*, 14–16 October 1735; *The Daily Gazetteer*, 15 October 1735; *The Daily Journal*, 15 October 1735; *The Weekly Miscellany*, 18 October 1735; *Read's Weekly Journal, Or, British-Gazetteer*, 18 October 1735; *The Gentleman's Magazine* 5 (October 1735), 617; and Wesley's letters published in *The Gentleman's Magazine*, May 1737, pp. 318–19, September 1737, p. 575.

[138] Egerton MS 1953 (27 August 1738), in M. Lawrence Snow, 'Methodist Enthusiasm: Warburton Letters, 1738–1740', *MH* 10 (1972), 39. This gossip was repeated in a 16 September 1738 letter to Peter des Maizeaux: Snow, 'Methodist Enthusiasm', 38 n. 26. Wesley's uncle, Matthew, also ridiculed his nephew's 'apostolical project': CWJ, 21 December 1736, p. 70. Both Warburton and Middleton later became opponents of Wesley and the Methodists.

[139] *The Substance of a Sermon Preached...On the Death of the Rev. John Wesley*, 2nd edn (London, 1791), 9–11, 17.

Georgians whose voices have been largely lost to history. It may not have been a coincidence that Wesley met for group fellowship with his Savannah religious societies on the eves of Pentecost, St Bartholomew's Day, and the three Rogation Days, dates defined as Fast Days in the Book of Common Prayer.[140] He recommended ascetical living to close friends like Sophia Hopkey, and the levelling of these accusations makes it probable that other regular attendees of the religious societies joined the Methodists in their spiritual practices.[141] Overall, observers of Wesley in Georgia confirm that he carried out the spirit of his commitment expressed to John Burton to dismiss 'worldly desires and worldly cares' and content himself with nothing more than 'food to eat and raiment to put on.'[142]

DEACONESSES

Tailfer's complaints contain the accusation that Wesley violated orthodox Anglican practice by taking the extremely radical step of 'appointing Deaconesses, with sundry other Innovations, which he called *Apostolick Constitutions.'* Deaconesses could have been appointed based on the *Apostolic Constitutions* (II.57, 58, III.14–16, VI.17, VIII.19–20, 28) and *Deacon's Devotions*, but were not introduced into the Church of England until the 1860s.[143] According to the *Constitutions*, deaconesses were to be virgins or widows and assist in such ministries as the distribution of charity and the baptism of women.[144] That there was certainly some substance to Tailfer's claim is shown by August Spangenberg's journal entry on the day that he posed his well-known questions to Wesley regarding the state of Wesley's soul.[145] Spangenberg noted that Wesley's vision for his mission to the Indians included the ordination of deaconesses to allow for the ancient practice of baptism by immersion for women.[146] For this purpose he hoped to recruit some Moravian women to work alongside him amongst the Indians.

[140] JWD, 12 June 1736 and 28 May 1737; 23 August 1736 and 1737; 16–18 May 1737.

[141] JWMSJ, 16 August 1737.

[142] JW to Burton (10 October 1735), *Works*, 25:442. His conception of disciplined living was more strict than the SPG instructions that missionaries be 'contented with what Health requires' and live in a 'Frugal' manner: *A Collection of Papers*, 22.

[143] See Deacon's 'Form and Manner of Ordaining Deaconesses', 240–6. Wesley also read about deaconesses in the early church in Cave's *Primitive Christianity* and Horneck's 'Letter to a Person of Quality': *Christian Library*, ed. JW, 31:199–200; 29:115, 120 (Bristol, 1753).

[144] Deacon did not require deaconesses to be virgins or widows and defined their role in terms of overseeing the women of the church: *Devotions*, 244.

[145] JWJ, 7 February 1736.

[146] 'Spangenberg's Diary', 8 February 1736, in Schmidt, *John Wesley*, 152.

Although this shows that Wesley was thinking along these lines, there is less evidence to substantiate Tailfer's assertion that he actually appointed deaconesses. However, this allegation should be taken seriously, especially since he correctly understood that the *Apostolic Constitutions* were central to Wesley's 'Innovations'. First of all, there is no proof that Wesley convinced the Moravians to adopt his scheme, although in September 1736 they did send a married couple, Peter and Catherine Rose, to work alongside Ingham at the Indian school Irene. They received a sort of consecration rite from Anton Seiffert in front of their congregation and Catharine was assigned to teach Indian girls to read at the school, but there is no indication that either Wesley or the Moravians saw her as the type of deaconess he had envisioned.[147]

The specific nature of Tailfer's testimony adds weight to the near certainty that Wesley used the term 'deaconess' in the context of his ministry in Georgia. His close friend Margaret Bovey (d. 1742) was likely being prepared by him to be a deaconess to minister to Indian women. Bovey, from the parish of St James's, Westminster seems to have been from a fairly prominent family because of her friendship with Wesley's friend Ann Granville, the sister of Mary Pendarves.[148] Wesley became close with Bovey after the mysterious and sudden death of her younger sister Rebecca on 10 July 1736. Tailfer was the physician who declared that Rebecca was dying, although Wesley believed 'she might only be in a swoon'. He probably would have noted the friendship between Wesley and the Bovey sisters, but it is unlikely that talk of deaconesses would have come up on this occasion. Through the whole ordeal Wesley was moved by the firm reliance of the sisters on God's mysterious providence.[149]

In the coming weeks, Wesley frequented Bovey's home and noted that they became 'close' and had religious discussions on topics such as 'dress and company'. Wesley read to her one of his sermons, which brought her to tears and continued with Henry Scougal's popular work *The Life of God in the Soul of Man*, whose central theme of the union of the soul with God was a consistent feature in Wesley's early sermons. On the second Sunday after Rebecca's death, Wesley noted in his diary with an exclamation mark that Bovey attended morning prayer and he also recorded her reception of the sacrament, indicating his stamp of approval on her spiritual state following the loss of her sister.[150] Upon Wesley's return from his third visit to Frederica in September, on weekday afternoons he began to regularly tutor Bovey in the French language at her home.[151] In the period prior to his fourth visit to Frederica beginning on 13 October 1736,

---

[147] 'Töltschigs Diarium', 25 October 1736, fo. 447.
[148] JW to Ann Granville [24 August 1736], *Works*, 25:475–6.
[149] JWJ and JWD, 10 July 1736.
[150] JWD, 14, 15, 18–20, 22–3, 25 July 1736.
[151] From November there are indications that Sophia Hopkey occasionally joined their lessons, but there is also evidence that he met with them separately.

Wesley spent time with Bovey on every weekday. This is significant because it is a story that cannot be told apart from Wesley's diary. Wesley's journals disguise the fact that his relationship with Bovey was equally as close as with Sophia Hopkey, who receives disproportionate attention in his journals (and in subsequent historiography) because they were retrospectively written in light of the conflict that broke out in the following year. A fluid combination of French lessons, religious talk, devotional reading, and religious society meetings continued on an almost daily basis with Bovey for the entirety of Wesley's stay in Georgia, continuing even after her marriage to Irish emigrant James Burnside (1708–55).

The available evidence allows for a strong possibility that Bovey was being trained as a deaconess, based on Wesley's close friendship with her and his objection to her getting married.[152] He may have hoped that she would remain single in accordance with the *Apostolic Constitutions* (VI.17), which requires deaconesses to be virgins or widows. The probability of this is somewhat strengthened by the fact that Wesley subsequently continued to esteem the deaconesses of the early church, whom he believed Methodist women imitated by visiting the sick.[153]

Apart from the deaconess issue, Wesley obviously had a deep respect for Bovey's faith. He trusted her to the extent of allowing her to play an important role in the religious societies. Therefore, it is fair to conclude that he was indeed training her to exercise lay leadership. In this respect, Bovey was not the only woman allowed this liberty. The home of Margaret Gilbert was used by Wesley as a place for prayer, singing, and the reading of religious books.[154] Wesley's diary note 'Mr Hows, etc.; read; sang; prayed. 8:45 Mrs Gilbert, etc. 9 They explained' seems to indicate that along with her son-in-law, Robert Hows, Gilbert exercised leadership in the Saturday evening communion preparation class.[155] Wesley consistently mentioned Mrs Gilbert rather than her husband Robert in connection with the society meetings. This illustrates his willingness to develop close friendships with women whether married or single.[156] At a minimum, there is clear evidence that Wesley used women in pastoral roles, although formal ordination as discussed with Spangenberg does not seem to have been attempted.[157] He was taking advantage of the lack of

---

[152] On Bovey's marriage, see Hammond, appendix 10. Without the benefit of the *Detailed Reports* or the diary of Spangenberg, Curnock surmised that Bovey was being trained as a deaconess: JWJ (Curnock), 1:272.

[153] *A Plain Account of the People Called Methodists* (1749), in *Works*, 9:274; cf. his comments on Romans 16:1 regarding deaconesses in the early church in his *Explanatory Notes upon the New Testament*.

[154] See JWD, 11 September, 6 October 1736, 20 February, 16 July 1737.

[155] JWD, 7 May 1737.

[156] Mrs Mary Vanderplank was yet another woman whom Wesley highly regarded. They met at her home on several occasions, where in one meeting they read Fleury's *Manners of the Antient Christians* and sang: JWD, 28 March 1737.

[157] Baker, *John Wesley*, 355 n. 41.

episcopal oversight in Georgia to encourage women to engage in ministry to an extent that was far from customary within the Church of England.

WESLEY'S RELIGIOUS SOCIETIES IN GEORGIA[158]

In a letter to *The London Magazine* (1760), Wesley credited the foundation of Oxford Methodism to his reading of *The Country-Parson's Advice to his Parishioners*, despite the fact that he had not read the book until 1733, when the Oxford Methodists had already been established. Wesley reported:

> I read these words: 'If good men of the Church will unite together in the several parts of the kingdom, disposing themselves into friendly societies, and engaging each other in their respective combinations, to be helpful to each other in all good, Christian ways, it will be the most effectual means, for restoring our decaying Christianity to its primitive life and vigour, and the supporting of our tottering and sinking church.' A few young gentlemen then at Oxford, approved of and followed the advice. They were all zealous Churchmen, and both orthodox and regular to the highest degree. For their exact regularity they were soon nick-named Methodists.[159]

Wesley also seems to have perpetuated an anachronism originally implied in his *Journal* by claiming in *A Short History of the People Called Methodists* (1781) that the second phase of Methodism began in Savannah,[160] when his diary shows that he first regularly led religious societies in Frederica. These meetings were initially held with the assistance of Charles Delamotte in June 1736. According to Wesley's *Journal*,

> We began to execute at Frederica what we had before agreed to do at Savannah. Our design was, on Sundays in the afternoon and every evening after public service, to spend some time with the most serious of the communicants in singing, reading, and conversation. This evening we had only Mark Hird. But on Sunday Mr. Hird and two more desired to be admitted. After a psalm and a little conversation, I read Mr. Law's *Christian Perfection* and concluded with another psalm.[161]

Wesley's diary entry for 10 June 1736 reads 'Mark Hird, began singing', suggesting something more spontaneous than the *Journal* record. In any case, three

---

[158] On Wesley's 'Devotional Reading Societies' on the *Simmonds* as a foreshadowing of his religious societies, see Hammond, 107–13.

[159] Wesley, 'To Mr. T. H. *alias* Philodemus, *alias* Somebody, *alias* Stephen Church, *alias* R. W', *The London Magazine* (December 1760), 651; *Letters* (Telford), 4:119–20; 'Country Parson's Advice', 26:464.

[160] *Works*, 9:430.

[161] JWJ, 10 June 1736.

days later, on Whitsunday, the devotional society began in earnest with the addition of three new members: Mark's mother Grace, his sister Phoebe, and her eighteen-year-old friend Betty Hassel.[162] Mark Hird remained a core member of the Sunday afternoon group that met on each of the next six Sundays that Wesley was in Frederica until 24 October 1736, encompassing his third and fourth visits to the southern outpost. In Wesley's diary entry for 15 August four new names are mentioned in connection with this group: Mark's father Thomas, Ambrose Tackner, Sophia Hopkey, and Elizabeth Fawset. Through this devotional group Wesley continued to disciple the Hirds and Tackner, all of whom he had baptized on the *Simmonds*. For all but one meeting at which they read Ephraem Syrus, Wesley read to the group from Law's *Christian Perfection*.[163] This was an obvious choice for him, since it was the book he used in his first devotional reading society on the *Simmonds*, which he believed had a spiritually awakening effect on his hearers.[164]

Wesley's diary indicates that they were fairly successful in their endeavour to meet with their 'most serious' communicants each evening after prayers. This was accomplished on the nine evenings Monday to Saturday from Whitsunday to the end of Wesley's second visit to Frederica and on about seventeen days during his third and fourth visits, representing nearly every day of those visits. These gatherings seem to have been composed of largely the same people who attended the Sunday group with Mark Hird.[165] However, he attempted to institute a second (or third) group consisting of Will Reed,[166] Samuel Davison[167] and Thomas Walker[168] in the afternoon on the primitive fast days of Wednesday and Friday. Nonetheless, his diary gives no indication that this group continued to meet after their two initial meetings.[169] The reading of these groups was the same as on Sundays, with Law mentioned in Wesley's diary seven times and Ephraem cited on five occasions. When recording the meetings, Wesley typically noted that the order of activities was 'sang, read, sang' in his diary and often on Sundays 'sang, read, sang, prayed, sang.' Although religious discussion played a role, these devotional groups were structured around singing psalms.

---

[162] JWD, 13 June 1736.

[163] JWD, 17 October 1736.

[164] See the section on 'Devotional Reading Societies' in Hammond, 107–13.

[165] Wesley mentioned the same names as for Sunday except for Grace Hird, Tackner, and Hassel; however, this does not prove that they were not involved, since his usual practice was only to mention one name followed by 'etc.' [John] Robinson, an accompt (i.e. accountant) who sailed with Wesley on the *Simmonds* is the one new name that appears: JWD, 17, 23 August and 1 September 1736.

[166] For other references to Reed in Wesley's diary, see JWD, 2, 12–13 December 1735; cf. CWJ, 30 March 1736, p. 17.

[167] On Davison, see JWD, 5 November 1735; CWJ, 6 April 1736, p. 19; Egmont, *Diary*, 8 December 1736, 2:313.

[168] On Walker, see CRG, 5:655.

[169] JWJ, 16 June 1736; JWD, 16 and 18 June 1736.

Before returning to Savannah after his third visit to Frederica in August 1736, Wesley persuaded Will Reed 'to read Evening Prayers' in his absence. He also noted that 'five or six persons agreed to spend an hour together every day in singing, reading, and exhorting one another.'[170] Knowing that Charles Wesley had left the colony, and that he would not be able to spend much time in Frederica, he made a pragmatic decision intentionally to train Will Reed and Mark Hird as lay pastors to serve Frederica's citizens and the small circle of disciples Wesley had gathered around him. This action could be justified based on the *Apostolic Constitutions*, which state 'Let him that teaches, although he be one of the laity, yet, if he be skillful in the Word and grave in his manners, teach; for, "They shall all be taught of God".'[171] When he returned to Frederica in October Wesley discovered that Reed had stopped reading prayers, although the religious society may have been maintained.[172] During his final visit to the southern frontier village in January 1737, Wesley made no mention of the religious society meeting together.[173] Nonetheless, he maintained his friendship with the prominent religious society member, Mark Hird.[174]

According to Wesley's retrospective thoughts, 'The second [rise of Methodism] was at Savannah, in April 1736, when twenty or thirty persons met at my house.'[175] Wesley's *Journal* gives more detail about the ministry strategy he and his co-labourers Delamotte and Ingham decided on:

> Not finding as yet any door opened for the pursuing of *our* main design [the mission to the Indians], *we* considered in what manner *we* might be most useful to the little flock at Savannah. And *we* agreed: first, to advise the more serious among them to form themselves into a sort of little society, and to meet once or twice a week, in order to reprove, instruct and exhort one another; second, to select out of these a smaller number for more intimate union with each other, which might be forwarded, partly by *our* conversing singly with each, and partly by inviting them all together to *our* house; and this accordingly *we* determined to do every Sunday in the afternoon.[176]

It seems that the religious society of Wesley's predecessor Samuel Quincy, which was led by Robert Hows, the parish clerk, remained active during the year between his letter to Henry Newman, Secretary of the SPCK, and Wesley's comments.[177] This society was actually discovered by Ingham while

---

[170] JWMSJ, no date, p. 418.

[171] VIII.32; John 6:45.

[172] JWJ and JWMSJ, 16 October 1736. In December 1736, Elisha Dobree noted in a letter to the Trustees that Mr Hird (either Mark or Thomas) read prayers on Sundays: *CRG*, 21:286.

[173] In his retrospective *Journal*, Wesley testified to his 'despair of doing good' in Frederica (26 January 1737). However, August Spangenberg reported that 'the people were so hostile towards him that he was no longer sure of his life, and was compelled to withdraw from them': Spangenberg, 'A Moravian's Report', 407.

[174] See Wesley's mention of the letters he sent to Hird: JWD, 21 February and 7 May 1737.

[175] *A Short History of the People Called Methodists* (1781), *Works*, 9:430.

[176] JWJ, 17 April 1736 (italics added).

[177] Samuel Quincy to Henry Newman (4 July 1735), *CRG*, 20:419 and Robert Hows to Thomas Coram (16 May 1735), *CRG*, 21:164–5. For further details, see Hammond, 306–8.

Wesley was away in Frederica, and there is no evidence that Newman told the Methodist missionaries of its existence. Ingham 'found their design was good, they read, prayed and sung psalms together; accordingly I exhorted them to go on, promising myself to meet with them sometimes and give them such helps and directions as I could.'[178] Evidently the society was formed directly from Quincy's society, with Hows remaining a key participant, although we do not know the extent of continuity in membership. Wesley's *Short History* makes it appear that he was solely responsible for the founding and organization of this society, but by using the words 'we' and 'our' in his *Journal* account Wesley emphasized the collective action of his colleagues. Taking this into account, his *Journal* is still misleading, since he wrote as if the society was founded in April 1736 when it had in fact been established nearly a year earlier by Quincy at the instigation of Robert Hows.

Richard Heitzenrater has noted that in all three rises of Methodism outlined in Wesley's *Short History* he tended to:

1. Set a date of origin that is more precise than is warranted.
2. Incorporate later developments into the description of the initial instance.
3. Give himself a more central role than was apparent at the time to others or even himself.[179]

The first point has already been partially discussed in terms of the establishment of the society in 1735; however, Wesley's *Journal* extract is also misleading, since there is no evidence from his diary that he interacted with a Sunday religious society until November of that year. Heitzenrater's third statement is accurate regarding the *Short History* but not the *Journal* account, and as to his second argument it seems that when Wesley published his *Journal* three years later he was thinking of these developments in November 1736, which he wrote back into his account of the origins of the society in April 1736.

Although the Sunday society did not begin until November, from September a group began to meet every Saturday evening that Wesley was in Savannah. These developments were reflected by Wesley in a February 1737 letter to Dr Bray's Associates:

> Some time after the [Sunday] Evening Service, as many of my parishioners as desire it meet at my house (as they do likewise on Wednesday evening) and spend about an hour in prayer, singing, reading a practical book, and mutual exhortation. A smaller number (mostly those who desire to communicate the next day)

---

[178] BIJ, 11 April 1736, p. 79.

[179] Heitzenrater, 'John Wesley as Historian of Early Methodism', in Neil Semple (ed.), *Papers of the Canadian Methodist Historical Society*, 7 (Toronto, 1990), 39.

meet here on Saturday evening; and a few of these come to me on the other evenings, and pass half an hour in the same employments.[180]

The pattern of prayer, singing, reading, and exhortation can be compared to Johann Boltzius's report that when he was present at one of the meetings they sang a psalm, read, and prayed. Boltzius commented that he thought discussion and 'a simple catechetical lesson' would have been more edifying.[181] The letter to Dr Bray's Associates and other evidence from Wesley suggests that discussion was a regular feature of the meetings.

Wesley's diaries make it clear that his leadership of a religious society in Savannah originated with a group that met on Saturdays immediately after evening prayer. This meeting was designed as a communion preparation class. Wesley may have been aware that this followed the pattern of his father's Epworth society, which met on Saturday evening 'in order to prepare for the Lord's Day'.[182] Wesley's diary entry for the date the society first met reads '7.45 Communicants came, began Patrick. 8 Patrick; religious talk; sang; prayed (lively zeal).'[183] This indicates that for their meetings Wesley returned to Simon Patrick's *The Christian Sacrifice* (1671), which he had used for a Sunday reading group on the *Simmonds*.[184] Patrick is mentioned as the book read during the first nine society meetings through to 18 December 1736.[185] William Law is cited on 25 December and Brevint on 30 April 1737, being Daniel Brevint's *The Christian Sacrament and Sacrifice*. Overall, for the majority of Saturdays Wesley does not specify what was read, although there is sufficient data to conclude that the society focused on works relating to Holy Communion.

Who were Wesley's communicants? Unfortunately, he does not provide a list of them, and only four names are mentioned in association with the Saturday evening society: Sophia Hopkey, Robert Hows, Margaret Gilbert, and Mrs Anne.[186] If anywhere near his average of fifteen communicants frequented this society, there were more than four people associated with it. As will be noted, there were ten additional names Wesley mentioned in connection with

[180] JWMSJ, 26 February 1737; also printed in JWJ, 26 February 1737; *Works*, 25:495; *A Short History of the People Called Methodists* (*Works*), 9:429. Immediately following his citation of this letter in his *Short History*, Wesley noted, 'I cannot but observe that these were the first rudiments of the Methodist Societies. But who could then have even formed a conjecture whereto they would grow?'

[181] Johann Martin Boltzius and Israel Christian Gronau to Gotthilf August Francke (29 July 1737), in Boltzius, *Letters*, 1:205.

[182] W. O. B. Allen and Edmund McClure, *Two Hundred Years: The History of the Society for Promoting Christian Knowledge, 1698–1898* (London, 1898), 90–1.

[183] 18 September 1736.

[184] Hammond, 110–11.

[185] Wesley probably read to the society the meditations and prayers designed to be used before receiving the sacrament.

[186] Sophia's name appears on 6, 13, 27 November and 11 December 1736; Hows is mentioned on twenty-four occasions between 4 December 1736 and 27 August 1737; Margaret Gilbert is named five times from 16 July 1737; Mrs Anne is cited once on 14 June 1737.

all religious societies that met in Savannah and it is highly likely that some of these were also regularly present at the Saturday meetings. The Saturday society was a stable institution that met on all forty Saturdays (with one possible exception)[187] that Wesley was in Savannah between 18 September 1736 and 27 August 1737. This group was the foundation and (along with the Sunday society) most consistent of all Savannah societies.[188] When the Sophia Williamson controversy broke out, her aggrieved uncle, Thomas Causton, strategically tried to turn Wesley's communicants against him.[189]

The Sunday society, which met after evening prayer (which generally began between two and three in the afternoon), commenced on 14 November 1736 with 'Miss Sophy [Hopkey], Mr [James] Houston, [Mrs Margaret] Gilbert, etc.' A sermon was read from Edward Young's two-volume *Sermons on Several Occasions* (1702–3), followed by religious talk and singing.[190] A week later 'Potter' (either Robert Potter or his wife) was mentioned in association with the group, and subsequently [Robert] Hows two weeks later. These are the only names cited and they all occur only once expect for Gilbert (eight times) and Hows (twenty-six times). Here again there were certainly a number of other attendees whom Wesley referred to only by the designation 'etcetera.' Although this group began nearly two months after the Saturday society, it met with the same regularity, never failing to assemble during the thirty-five Sundays that Wesley was in Savannah between 14 November 1736 and 28 August 1737. These gatherings followed the same basic pattern as Saturday meetings, opening and closing with singing separated by devotional reading and prayers. We have limited knowledge of what the society read, since Wesley ceased to record this information after 26 December. On the four Sundays after the initial reference to Young's *Sermons*, Wesley noted they read a sermon, which may have been a continuation of their reading from Young. He subsequently began Law's *Christian Perfection* with them, which may have remained the text for the Sunday society for the remainder of its duration.

The seventy-five meetings that took place on Saturdays and Sundays represent forty per cent of the 185 religious society gatherings in the nine months Wesley was in Savannah between September 1736 and August 1737.

[187] 20 November 1736.

[188] For a time, Wesley appears to have attempted to convene the communicants' society more than once a week: see JWD, 20 and 28 September 1736. It is a testament to the strength of this society that it continued to meet as normal after Wesley's absence from Savannah during three Saturdays in October 1736, all five Saturdays in January 1737, and two Saturdays during April of that year. This may indicate that the society met in Wesley's absence, perhaps under the direction of Ingham on the first two occasions.

[189] JWMSJ, 15 August 1737.

[190] Young (1641/2–1705), best known for his sermons, served as dean of Salisbury and was the father of a son of the same name who became famous for his poem *The Complaint, or, Night-Thoughts on Life, Death, and Immortality* (1742–6), which was popular with evangelicals because of its praise of conversion.

Wednesday was the most common weekday on which these assemblies were held. Therefore, Wesley accurately highlighted the Wednesday meetings in his letter to Dr Bray's Associates, although a close reading of his diary shows that consistent weekly gatherings on Wednesdays were just developing at the time he penned this report. From March 1737, the religious societies reflected Wesley's conception of the primitive pattern by meeting every Wednesday (fast day), Saturday (Sabbath), and Sunday (Lord's Day) Wesley was in Savannah, closely following the structure of his *Collection of Psalms and Hymns*. While meetings developed into a set pattern on these days, fluid and varied gatherings were often held on other days of the week.[191]

Wesley's mention of Margaret Bovey on fifty-seven occasions in association with weekday meetings plainly reveals the central place she had amongst Wesley's most committed parishioners. James Burnside, who married her in March 1737, also became involved after their wedding. Of those already mentioned, especially Hows, and also Gilbert, and Hopkey, and to a lesser extent John Robinson and Will Reed (when in Savannah), took part in these gatherings. In addition to James Burnside, six names not mentioned in connection with the Saturday or Sunday societies are noted in Wesley's diary.[192] Overall, sixteen parishioners at some time or another were present at a Savannah religious society. The data available in Wesley's diary makes it seem likely, but not certain, that his estimation of twenty or thirty religious society adherents given in his *Short History* was higher than the number he averaged in Savannah. Wesley highlighted Hows,[193] Gilbert, Bovey, and Hopkey (before her marriage in March 1737) far more often than any other parishioners, indicating that he saw them as valuable and faithful members of the societies. Unfortunately, we do not know what level of leadership they might have exercised in the societies, but we can assume that he expected fervent participation of all who attended and this would have provided some leeway for spiritually mature parishioners to exhort their fellow Georgians to live holy lives.

Regarding weekday meetings Wesley made reference to seven (or eight) distinct sources. These include two devotional biographies: *Memoirs of the Life of the Reverend Mr. Thomas Halyburton* (1714) and John Fell's *The Life of the most*

---

[191] There were eighteen meetings on Mondays, twenty-four on Tuesdays, twenty-two on Thursdays, and seventeen on Fridays. Relying on Wesley's *Journal*, Schmidt emphasized Wesley's testimony that he selected the members, which set these societies apart from more voluntary models. However, the fluidity of the gatherings indicates that participation was not as rigidly controlled as this suggests: Schmidt, *John Wesley*, 191–2; cf. Rack, 120, who cited Schmidt's conclusion with approval.

[192] Sir Francis Bathurst, [James] Campbell, [Elizabeth] Fallowfield, John [?], [Richard] Turner, and [Mary] Vanderplank.

[193] Hows's continuing importance is revealed in Delamotte's claim that Causton called him 'a principal man' and told him that the society(s) 'will break up by degrees' 'if you don't set the Psalm': Delamotte to JW (23 February 1738), *Works*, 25:530.

Learned, Reverend and Pious Dr. H[enry] Hammond (1661).[194] Halyburton's
Memoirs detail his mental anguish as a young man who struggled to find
philosophical arguments to answer the threat posed to Christianity by deism.
Eventually he underwent a life-changing conversion that brought with it a
conviction that philosophy and faith were incompatible. The *Memoirs* found
a ready audience amongst evangelical clergy drawn to Halyburton's promotion of heart religion, such as Isaac Watts, who added a preface to editions
published after 1718, and George Whitefield and Wesley, who each wrote a
preface to an abridgement they jointly published in 1739.[195] Fell's biography
portrays Hammond as a devout and charitable Christian, and an upholder of
prayer book Anglicanism during the dark days of the Civil War. Additionally,
Wesley read William Tilly's sermons on at least one occasion and August
Hermann Francke's *Nicodemus, or, a Treatise against the Fear of Man* (1706).[196]
Wesley also utilized John Worthington's *The Great Duty of Self-Resignation to
the Divine Will* (1675), whose theme of self-denial was of perennial interest
to him. Worthington's work was heavily influenced by the moral rigorism of
Thomas à Kempis's *De Imitatio Christi*, which Worthington published a version of under the title *The Christian's Pattern* (1654). Being associated with
several of the Cambridge Platonists, Worthington shared with Wesley not only
a stress on ascetical discipline, but also a hatred of superfluous doctrinal disputes, which he believed were merely a mask for more sinister errors.[197]

The model of the early church was utilized by Wesley to inspire religious
society participants. On two occasions he referred to reading 'Clement.'[198] This
may have been either a reference to the epistles of Clement of Rome or the
Clementine Liturgy, i.e. the *Apostolic Constitutions*. Although the *Constitutions*
are heavily liturgical, the lengthy prayers contained therein make them suitable for devotional use. If he read the epistles of Clement, he probably would
have read them from William Wake's translation: *The Genuine Epistles of the
Apostolical Fathers...and the martyrdoms of St. Ignatius and St. Polycarp*—a
work he read during one religious society gathering. Wesley revisited his

---

[194] Halyburton: JWD, 1, 15 February 1737; cf. 4, 6–15, 20 January, 7, 9, 14 February 1737;
Hammond: JWD, 1 March 1737. Halyburton was probably introduced to Wesley during his
January visit to the Scottish Presbyterian Highlanders at Darien.

[195] *An Abstract of the Life and Death of the Reverend Learned and Pious Mr. Tho. Halyburton,
M.A.* (London). It is noteworthy that Wesley copied a substantial portion of the title of Fell's
biography of Hammond: see M. A. Stewart, 'Halyburton, Thomas (1674–1712)', *ODNB*.

[196] Tilly: JWD, 3 March 1737; Francke: JWD, 20 December 1736; cf. 5, 7–11, 13–18, 21–4
December 1736, and 10, 12, 17 August 1737. While at Oxford, Wesley abridged five of Tilly's
sermons from his *Sixteen Sermons...upon Several Occasions* (1712) into a notebook and used
them as sermon material: see MARC, Colman MS Collection, 19. Wesley published an abridged
version of *Nicodemus* in 1739 and later in his *Christian Library*.

[197] JWD, 10 March 1737; cf. JWD, 2–3 September 1736 and 17 March 1737; John T. Young,
'Worthington, John (*bap.* 1618, *d.* 1671)', *ODNB*.

[198] JWD, 22 September, 6 October 1736; cf. JWD, 9 November 1736, 8–9 March, 2, 4, 7
July 1737.

favoured translation of the Apostolic Fathers on a number of occasions in Georgia and he would have hoped their piety would inspire his parishioners to live lives modelled after the holiness of the leaders of the early church.[199] A fondness for the ancients was displayed in Wesley's only non-Christian choice: Plato's *Phaedo*. It would have been particularly surprising to find that he used a contemporary work whose primary focus was anything other than religious piety, but *Phaedo* was presumably acceptable because of the ancient wisdom it portrayed on the immortality of the soul.[200]

The books utilized in society meetings illustrate Wesley's passion for devotional treatises on holy living by recent and ancient authors. Like the author of *The Country-Parson's Advice*, he saw religious societies as a means to restore primitive Christianity. Wesley's diary shows that Wednesday, Saturday, and Sunday societies developed into a regular pattern probably with fairly steady attendance, while meetings on other days were more fluid and spontaneous. Therefore, Wesley's religious societies in Georgia should be conceived of as an evolving web of related and overlapping gatherings. These societies had not reached the climax of their regularity when Wesley's diary abruptly ended on 31 August 1737. They continued to meet after his departure from the colony, with support from the leadership supplied by Delamotte, in spite of the persistent efforts of Causton and the magistrates to stop them.[201] After his return to England, one of Wesley's purposes for continuing to write to several Georgians who frequented his societies was probably to encourage them to carry on the societies.[202]

Wesley's leadership in this 'rise' of Methodism had its roots in a variety of experiences, including Oxford Methodism and his knowledge of Anglican societies and Moravian bands. His reading and account of the establishment of the societies show that he was actively reflecting on the primitive church and imitating the Moravian method of cultivating piety through intimate bands of committed Christians.[203] Through Moravian influence, he introduced hymn singing into society meetings. However, Wesley's societies seem to have been formed in an experimental manner, making them different from all of

---

[199] JWD, 7 March 1737; cf. JWD, 3–5, 8, 18–19 March, 1, 8, 27 July 1737. See 'The *Apostolic Constitutions* and *Canons* and the Apostolic Fathers' in chapter 1 on Wesley's reading of Wake at Oxford.

[200] JWD, 23 March and 17 December 1736. Wesley probably used the 1713 translation published in London under the title *Plato's Dialogue of the Immortality of the Soul*.

[201] Charles Delamotte to JW (23 February 1738), *Works*, 25:529–30.

[202] See, for example, his diary records that he wrote to James Burnside on 16 May, 25 August, 16 December 1738, and 28 June 1740: *Works*, 25:750, 51, 52 and 26:624.

[203] At this time, the Moravians had separate bands for married men, unmarried men who were communicants, and unmarried non-communicants: Fries, 129. Since there were fewer women, they may have all been placed in the same band. Curnock's conclusion that the Savannah plan was implemented after close consultation with the Moravians is unsubstantiated: JWJ (Curnock), 1:198.

these precedents as well as the more systematic plan of later Methodist societies. Whereas the Oxford groups (with the possible exception of the society
amongst the townspeople) involved academic study and promoted ministry to
the surrounding community, the Georgia societies were primarily devotional.
And unlike Moravian bands and Anglican societies, Wesley included women
and men together in the same gatherings.

THE INDIAN MISSION

Although Wesley went to Georgia explicitly to convert the Indians to
Christianity,[204] and it was widely reported in the London press that two of the
missionaries planned to go amongst the Indians, his intended Indian mission
did not take place.[205] While Ingham devoted several months to teaching the
Yamacraw Indian children, Wesley accomplished nothing other than having a
few interesting conversations with various Indian chieftains.[206] On the whole,
his interactions with Indians were only of a brief and occasional nature. This
was likewise the common experience of the Moravians and Salzburgers, who
also intended to establish Indian missions. Despite the lack of progress, Wesley
continued to see himself as first and foremost a missionary to the Indians.
Incidentally, his self-perception may have freed him to experiment with 'primitive practices' more than he might have otherwise done, since he believed
his care for Savannah parish was only a temporary position. In any case, he
chose not to disobey Oglethorpe's wish that he continue in his role as missionary to Savannah even after Oglethorpe had returned to England in November
1736.[207] We can be assured that had Wesley been able to preach to the Indians
he would have implemented his plans, in Johann Boltzius's words, to use 'the
methods of the apostles that we learn from Acts and the Epistles of Paul.'[208]
However, because of his fleeting contact with the Indians, our focus will be
on the extent to which his view of the Indians as ideally suited for renewing

[204] See Hammond, 'John Wesley's Mindset', 16–25.

[205] See note 137. Nonetheless, some of Wesley's contemporaries continued to believe that he
had ministered to the Indians; for example, *Pulpit Elocution: Or Characters and Principles of
the Most Popular Preachers, Of Each Denomination, in the Metropolis and its Environs* (London,
1782), 50. Wesley's plan was hindered by the fact that his brother-in-law, the Revd Westley Hall,
who was appointed as minister of Savannah, decided against going to Georgia at the last min-
ute: JW MS in JWJ (Curnock), 8:152 and Egmont, *Diary*, 14 October 1735, 2:200.

[206] On Ingham's work see 'Töltschigs Diarium'; Ingham to Sir John Philipps (15 September
1736), *CRG*, 21:221–3; Johann Martin Boltzius to Gotthilf August Francke (1 March 1737), in
Boltzius, *Letters*, 1:193; Scott, ' "Next to Nothing?" '.

[207] For more on 'Wesley and Oglethorpe on the *Simmonds* and in Georgia', see Hammond,
appendix 7.

[208] Johann Martin Boltzius and Israel Christian Gronau to Gotthilf August Francke (29 July
1737), in Boltzius, *Letters*, 1:205.

primitive Christianity and as 'noble savages' was modified during his Georgia sojourn.[209] For this task, his reading and journal comments form the most relevant sources.

Wesley's interest in foreign missions predated the founding of Georgia.[210] While in the colony he reread the account of the Pietist mission to the East Indies (partly sponsored by the SPCK) titled *Propagation of the Gospel in the East*.[211] Of the seven missionary tracts Wesley read in Georgia, five dealt with the conversion of the Indians to the Christian faith. His close connection with the SPCK and interest in the SPG prompted him to examine the missionary strategy of Thomas Bray, the founder of both societies. He first read 'Dr Bray's circular letters', which may indicate Bray's *Several Circular Letters to the Clergy of Mary-land* (1701), but since he read Bray to Delamotte, Hopkey, and Mary Musgrove's household, Bray's sermon *Apostolick Charity* (1699) with his appended circular letter to the clergy in Maryland may have been more appropriate. Both works emphasize the importance of understating the tenets of the Christian faith through catechetical instruction and reading devotional tracts. In *Apostolick Charity* the need for Indian schools was stated, while the *Circular Letters* stressed ministry to Africans in the American colonies.[212] After reading the circular letters, Wesley turned to 'Dr Bray's tracts', which was probably his *Missionalia: or, a Collection of Missionary Pieces Relating to the Conversion of the Heathen; both the African Negroes and American Indians* (1727).[213] In his advice to the clergy of Maryland, Bray recommended that after completing a period of probationary training they should focus first on the instruction and conversion of African slaves, followed by the more difficult task of civilizing and converting the Indians.[214]

In connection with his vocation as a missionary (though his relationship with the SPG was ambiguous) Wesley consulted David Humphreys's *An Historical Account of the Incorporated Society for the Propagation of the Gospel in Foreign Parts* (1730) on the history of the Society's work.[215] Humphreys's

---

[209] The most extensive study on Wesley and the Georgian Indians is Martin Schmidt, *The Young Wesley, Missionary and Theologian of Missions*, trans. L. A. Fletcher (London, 1958), who notes that Wesley was motivated by the desire to restore the primitive church. Other studies include J. Ralph Randolph, 'John Wesley and the American Indian: A Study in Disillusionment', *MH* 10 (1972), 3–11 and Julie Anne Sweet, *Negotiating for Georgia: British-Creek Relations in the Trustee Era 1733–1752* (Athens, 2005), 78–94.

[210] See Hammond, appendix 1.

[211] JWD, 15–7, 26 March 1737; Wesley first read this work in 1730. In a letter to Halle, Johann Boltzius noted that Wesley 'appreciates the mission reports from the East Indies': Letter dated 29 July 1737, in Zehrer, 'Relationship between Pietism', 214. Wesley and Ingham read several of Oglethorpe's letters on the Indians prior to embarking on the mission: BIJ, 65.

[212] JWD, 20–1, 25 November 1736; Thomas Bray, *Apostolick Charity...Preached at St. Paul's, at the Ordination of some Protestant Missionaries to be sent into the Plantations* (London, 1700), 7, 19–22; *Circular Letters*, 2–21.

[213] JWD, 27–8 November and 1, 7–8 December 1736.

[214] *Missionalia*, 'The Dedication', unpaginated; 5–13.

[215] JWD, 12 July 1737.

history prompted Wesley to note in his manuscript journal that ninety per cent of the Society's missionaries in America died within four years and all but two or three were 'well spoken of by all men.' According to Wesley, this was not the way of the primitive Christians, who magnified 'the scandal of the cross' in martyrdom. He followed up his reading to pen a letter to Humphreys mildly criticizing the zeal of the Society's missionaries by rhetorically asking 'Where is the seed sown, the *sanguis martyrum* [blood of the martyrs]?' By citing Tertullian's proverbial phrase, Wesley implicitly condemned the unwillingness of SPG missionaries to follow in the footsteps of the early Christian martyrs and make the ultimate sacrifice for the faith. Wesley's conclusion after reading the *Account* was that until God has chosen one or more of his willing servants to be martyred 'not with a stoical or Indian indifference, but blessing and praying for their murderers, and praising God in the midst of the flame' the kingdom of Satan will not be defeated.[216]

On the subject of the Indians as well as African slaves, Wesley perused Morgan Godwyn's, *The Negro's & Indians Advocate, Suing for their Admission to the Church: or, A Persuasive to the Instructing and Baptizing of the Negro's and Indians in our Plantations* (1680).[217] He also read an 'account of Indian Christians', which was possibly Cotton Mather's *An Epistle to the Christian Indians, giving them a Short Account, of what the English Desire them to Know and to do, in order to their Happiness* (1700).[218] Wesley's interest in the conversion of African slaves was illustrated through his reading of Edmund Gibson's *Two Letters of the Lord Bishop of London* (1727) on this subject.[219] In addition to his primary interest in the Indians, Wesley developed a concern for the souls of Africans. His two journeys to South Carolina clearly indicate that he made a concerted effort to interact with Africans. During his first visit in July and August 1736, he was pleased to see several Africans in church and conversed with an African woman who knew nothing about the existence of the soul, which caused him rhetorically to remark in his *Journal*, 'O God, where are thy tender mercies?' A few days later he was unable to fulfil his plan of visiting the plantation of the Scotsman Alexander Skene, who had about fifty Christian slaves whom he had allowed SPG missionaries to convert.[220]

Throughout his second trip to South Carolina Wesley took advantage of every opportunity to converse with Africans. In separate discussions, he found himself impressed by the willingness of a young woman, an old man, and a young lad to be taught the Christian faith. Reflecting on his experiences,

---

[216] JWMSJ, 12 July 1737; cf. *The Gentleman's Magazine*, September 1737, p. 575. See also Wesley's later critique of SPG missionaries: Wesley to Bishop Robert Louth (10 August 1780), *Letters* (Telford), 7:30–1.

[217] JWD, 20 August 1736.

[218] JWD, 18 April 1737.

[219] JWD, 18 November 1736.

[220] JWJ, 31 July, 2 August 1736.

including the cruelty of slavery, Wesley exclaimed, 'O earth! How long wilt thou hide their blood? How long wilt thou cover thy slain?'[221] After these encounters he noted that he believed the easiest way to convert the Africans would be to send out itinerant teachers to travel between plantations with owners sympathetic to having their 'best inclined' slaves instructed in the faith.[222]

Though he was probably aware of the visit of Tomochichi and some of his family members to England in 1734,[223] Wesley's first contact with the Indians in Georgia came when a party of Yamacraws came on board the *Simmonds* while it was anchored at Pepper Island. He responded to the welcoming yet apprehensive greeting of their chief, Tomochichi, with the fairly obscure remark 'There is but One, he that sitteth in heaven, who is able to teach man wisdom. Though we are come so far, we know not whether he will please to teach you by us or no. If he will teach you, you will learn; but we can do nothing.'[224] To a learned scholar Wesley's statement invoking the doctrine of election would have made sense, but Tomochichi was probably hoping for a more practical response. Wesley's reply appears to indicate that he believed an extraordinary work of God was required to enable the Indians to profit from the Methodists' evangelistic efforts. His answer to Tomochichi's speech seems to have been tied to his random opening of his Greek New Testament to I Thessalonians 2:14–16 before meeting the Indians. Just as the churches of Judea were persecuted by the Jews in an effort to prevent them from preaching to the Gentiles, the Thessalonians were suffering at the hands of their own countrymen. Wesley's belief that God led him to specific scriptures that spoke to his present situation caused him at this juncture to interpret his mission through the paradigm of the New Testament church. In this instance, I Thessalonians convinced him that only God could effect the conversion of the Indians, and even if this were to be realized, God's instrument (i.e. the missionary) would be persecuted.

In the coming months, Wesley was kept busy with his work as minister of Savannah. During this period he was confronted with a common problem for SPG missionaries of balancing the expectation placed on them of ministering to the European and native populations.[225] An Indian mission in Savannah parish

---

[221] See Isaiah 26:21.

[222] JWJ and JWMSJ, 23, 27, 29 April 1737; cf. CWJ, 2 August 1736, pp. 46–7 and John Wesley's, *Thoughts upon Slavery* (London, 1774), III.11. His first sustained attempt to teach Africans came on his journey back to England: JWJ, 26 December 1737 and 7 January 1738.

[223] On this episode, see Sweet, *Negotiating for Georgia*, 40–60. According to V. H. H. Green, Wesley had gone to visit some 'Indians kings' at Lincoln in 1730, which he speculated may have been the Cherokee chieftains brought to England by Sir Alexander Cuming: *John Wesley*, 39.

[224] JWJ and JWMSJ, 14 February 1736. The missionaries' arrival and meeting with Tomochichi was reported in the South Carolina *Gazette* in March 1736: A. M. Barnes, 'Americana. The South Carolina Gazette', *PWHS* 16 (1927), 59–60.

[225] The life of Francis Le Jau, SPG missionary in South Carolina, provides an informative case study on this daunting challenge with the added feature of ministering to African slaves: see 'The Carolina Chronicle of Dr. Francis Le Jau 1706–1717', ed. Frank J. Klingberg, *University of California Publications in History*, 53 (1956) and Klingberg's 'The Indian Frontier in South Carolina as Seen by the S.P.G. Missionary', *Journal of Southern History*, 5 (1939), 479–500.

was difficult to establish during his first year in the colony, since Tomochichi and many of his men were assisting Oglethorpe against the Spanish in Frederica. Nonetheless, he did not forget his first design of ministering to the 'poor *hea-thens*.'[226] He initially desired to go to the Choctaw Indians, whom he believed were 'the least polished, i.e., the least corrupted, of all Indian nations'. He met their chieftain, Chigilly, and told him that he must be 'taught by him that is above; and he will not teach you unless you avoid what you already know is not good'.[227] Wesley's conviction was that the most primitive Indians were the most likely to be converted, but any progress was entirely dependent on God's supernatural intervention. His wish to establish a mission to the Choctaws was frustrated by Oglethorpe's refusal to release him from his duties in Savannah.[228]

Wesley had another religious conversation with five Chickasaws, which was published in *The Gentleman's Magazine*.[229] When Oglethorpe departed for England in November 1736 Wesley reported that he had asked for his permission to preach to the Indians numerous times to which Oglethorpe always replied, 'You cannot leave Savannah without a minister'. Wesley declared that before coming to Georgia he had made it clear that his sole intention was the Indian mission. He explained that he was appointed minister of Savannah by the Trustees without his knowledge or approval. As disappointed as Wesley was, he acknowledged that his services were needed in Savannah, and in reference to his conversation with the Chickasaws, he concluded that it was not currently the right time for the Indian mission, since many nations were at war.[230] In a letter dated 10 September 1736 to George Whitefield and the Oxford Methodists, Wesley solicited his English friends for help so that he could be freed for the Indian mission.[231] Although the call was answered by Whitefield, the Anglican missionaries did not receive the response they hoped for, therefore they decided to send Ingham back to England in February 1737

---

[226] See his journal entry for 17 April 1736 and his letter to John Burton [10 May 1736], *Works*, 25:461–2. In using this terminology, Wesley identified himself with the prevalent transatlantic rhetoric and feeling of pity towards the Indians: see Laura M. Stevens, *The Poor Indians: British Missionaries, Native Americans, and Colonial Sensibility* (Philadelphia, 2004).

[227] Julie Anne Sweet used this remark to make the misleading statement that 'Wesley... wanted both conversion and civilization combined into one process': *Negotiating for Georgia*, 91. Wesley's words are best understood in the context of his belief that moral virtue enabled by God's prevenient grace helped prepare one to receive God's gift of salvation.

[228] JWJ, 27 June 1736. It seems that Wesley, Ingham, and Delamotte planned to go on a joint mission to the Indians: see JWJ, 23 November 1736.

[229] May 1737, pp. 318–19; cf. JWJ, 20 July 1736; Egmont, *Journal*, ed. McPherson, 10 July 1736, pp. 177–8. For the historical context of this Chickasaw visit to Savannah, see Edward J. Cashin, *Guardians of the Valley: Chickasaws in Colonial South Carolina and Georgia* (Columbia, SC, 2009), chapter 3. This interview initially inspired Wesley to contemplate a mission to the Chickasaws: JW to James Vernon [11 September 1736], *Works*, 25:473–4.

[230] JWJ, 23 November 1736. Charles Wesley reported and apparently believed Mr Appee's claim that Oglethorpe told him he 'never intended' his 'brother's going to the Indians', but was intent on making 'his own use of him': CWJ, 27 August 1736, p. 49.

[231] *Works*, 25:472.

to try to persuade some of their friends to join them in Georgia.[232] Ingham's departure left Wesley with no real possibility of going to the Indians.

Although Wesley had no meaningful contact with Indians in 1737, the planned Indian mission nevertheless affected his personal decisions. As noted, his ascetical practices such as sticking to a simple diet and sleeping on the ground were continually observed, in part, to prepare for life amongst the Indians. Likewise, his commitment to preaching to the Indians was cited by him as one of three reasons why he was reluctant to marry Sophia Hopkey.[233]

At the same time as these preparations were being made, and although he did not have much first-hand experience with Indians, Wesley's idealistic notions of them began to give way to bitter denouncements of their moral corruption and unwillingness to receive the gospel. He partially revised his romantic European view with scepticism typical of colonists.[234] In July 1737, he spoke with a Frenchman who had spent a few months living with the Chickasaws. After hearing of the brutal treatment of the French by the Chickasaws, Wesley added, 'See *The Religion of Nature* truly *Delineated!*'[235] In his summary observations about the colony of Georgia, he drastically modi-fied his view of the noble savages by severely criticizing the Chickasaws, the Cherokees, the Yuchis, and the Creeks. His analysis, however, reveals some of the common mistakes made by observers of the Native Americans with lit-tle first-hand experience of them.[236] Despite Wesley's contentions, the Indians did have religious beliefs and observed religious rituals, and they had forms of government, although Europeans often failed to recognize them.[237] Unlike many of his contemporaries, Wesley did not censure the Indians in order to praise the superiority of civilized England (or Europe); he instead blamed 'European vices' such as drunkenness as being partly responsible for their moral degradation.[238] Notwithstanding the vehement nature of his condem-nations, he seems to have wanted to continue to believe in the noble savage. The Choctaws, whom he had previously labelled 'the least corrupted', were exempted from his denunciations.[239]

---

[232] According to Johann Töltschig, this was also Charles Wesley's task when he left Georgia in July 1736: 'Töltschigs Diarium', 6 August 1736, fo. 439.

[233] JWMSJ, 5, 8 February 1737.

[234] Glyndwr Williams, 'Savages Noble and Ignoble: Concepts of the North American Indian', in P. J. Marshall and Glyndwr Williams (eds), *The Great Map of Mankind: British Perceptions of the World in the Age of Enlightenment* (London, 1982), 221.

[235] JWJ, 9 July 1737. Here Wesley was referring to William Wollaston's *The Religion of Nature Delineated* (1722), in which the author tried to promote religion without the need for divine revelation. Wesley had read this work in 1733.

[236] Williams, 'Savages Noble and Ignoble', 192.

[237] Williams, 'Savages Noble and Ignoble', 192–3, 198. Wesley later repeated these assertions in his sermon 'The Imperfection of Human Knowledge' (1784), *Works*, 2:580.

[238] Williams, 'Savages Noble and Ignoble', 197, 213–16, 190, 194–5.

[239] JWJ, 2 December 1737. Richard Heitzenrater has pointed out that later in his life Wesley continued to be interested in the conversion of the Indians: 'Wesley in America', 109.

WESLEY'S REFLECTIONS ON THE PRIMITIVE
COUNCILS AND CANONS

Wesley's Georgia mission was a time for both the application of his clerical/
missionary convictions and for theological reading and reflection.[240] His motivating vision of restoring the primitive church in a primitive environment
did not proceed without periods of reflection on the viability of his view of
the early church. Wesley's willingness to question his perception of primitive
Christianity led him to re-evaluate the early church councils and canons.[241]

According to his journals, Wesley's opinion about the unity and authority of
the primitive church began to change with his reading of William Beveridge.
Ironically it was Beveridge's work that led Wesley to question the antiquity and
reliability of the *Apostolic Canons*, although John Clayton had recommended
he read Beveridge's defence of these documents three years earlier.[242] Wesley's
journals note that he read *Pandectae Canonum Conciliorum* (the subtitle of
Synodikon 'Summaries of the Canons and Councils') with Charles Delamotte
in September 1736.[243] However, it is quite possible that he had some previously
held doubts about the authority of the primitive documents he highly prized.
Along with the Nonjurors, he probably did not believe that the *Canons* and
Constitutions were of apostolic authorship but that they were derived from
apostolic tradition. Even the Usager Nonjuror, Bishop Jeremy Collier, openly
admitted that the *Apostolic Constitutions* 'won't answer quite up to the Title'.[244]
William Cave had rejected the view that they were of apostolic authorship.[245]
And Wesley had recently read Laurence Echard's *General Ecclesiastical History*
(1702), which dismissed the hypothesis of the early authorship of the *Apostolic
Canons*.[246] Whether or not seeds of doubt were planted in his mind prior to
1736, Beveridge's study of the ancient canons and councils convinced Wesley
that 'general councils may err and have erred'. These words were taken from
Article XXI, which decrees that councils have authority only in so far as they
are 'taken out of Holy Scripture'.[247] However, it is important to note that Article

---

[240] On Wesley's reading, see Hammond, appendix 8.

[241] At the same time, he was also re-evaluating his view of mysticism in light of Christ and the
primitive church: see Hammond, 222–5.

[242] Clayton to JW (10 September 1733), *Works*, 25:356; cf. Doll, 'Architectural Expression', 299.

[243] The first fifty-eight pages of this work reproduce the *Apostolic Canons* with comments from
three twelfth-century Greek historians of canon law: Theodore Balsamon, Johannes Zonaras,
and Alexius Aristenus.

[244] Collier, 6; cf. Brett, *Collection of the Principal Liturgies*, 426. If Wesley had read Cotelier's
Patres Apostolici prior to October 1736, Cotelier's vague claim that they were written before 'the
latter end of the Fourth *Century*' may been a factor: Collier, 7 quoting *Patres Apostolici*, 1:195;
JWD, 5 October 1736.

[245] Cave, *Primitive Christianity*, Preface (no pagination); cf. Wheatly, 14–15.

[246] JWD, 16–26, 29 March, 2 April 1736; Echard, (London, 1702), 183.

[247] JWJ and JWMSJ, 13 September 1736.

XXI was in no way intended to repudiate the authority of councils to interpret scripture for the Church.

Wesley's thoughts on councils were further clarified in his January 1738 reflection written in the midst of his journey back to England. He commented that he erred 'by not considering that the decrees of one provincial synod could bind only that province, and the decrees of a general synod only to those provinces whose representatives met therein' and 'by not considering that most of those decrees were adapted to particular times and occasions, and consequently when those occasions ceased, must cease to bind even those provinces.'[248] From these comments, it is evident that his faith in the unity of the early church and its councils was disrupted by Beveridge's work. The door was cracked open for further questioning of the viability of renewing the church universal along primitive lines.

Wesley's journal entries for a week later state that they read Beveridge's *Codex Canonum Ecclesiae Primitivae Vindicatus ac Illustratus*. Therefore, it appears that he read both of Beveridge's works at this time. In his comment on the book, Wesley noted that Beveridge showed that the *Canons* were termed apostolic because they were 'partly grounded upon, partly agreeing with, the traditions they had received from the apostles.' Wesley also discovered that they were collected by several people at different times up to the year 500, when they were codified. However, according to Beveridge, many of them were already obsolete at the time the Council of Nicaea (325) met. Although clearly there is evidence here of a modification of Wesley's enthusiasm for the *Canons*, his note 'I must confess I once thought more highly than I ought to think' of them is found only in his *Journal* published in 1740.[249] Ironically, although Beveridge's overall purpose was to vindicate and illustrate the *Canons* and promote their usage in the Church of England, his study led Wesley to doubt their authority.

In any case, it is evident that Beveridge's books caused Wesley some anxiety over the ancient councils and *Apostolic Canons* (the *Apostolic Constitutions* are not specifically mentioned). By the time of his January 1738 reflection, Wesley concluded that he had valued the authority of 'antiquity' too highly by making it 'a co-ordinate (rather than subordinate) rule with Scripture.' In addition to modifying his view of scripture and tradition, on the whole his comments seem to reveal that he reached the conclusion that he had less support for his views of ancient liturgical and disciplinary practices than he had once imagined. Even so, this 'modification' had little if any immediate impact on his liturgical practice, since most of Thomas Causton's Grievances and the

---

[248] JWJ, 25 January 1738.
[249] JWJ and JWMSJ, 20 September 1736. This book was first read by Wesley in February 1735. Wesley's Georgia diary reveals that his intense study of the *Canons* continued until 4 October and it appears that some of the Moravians joined him in this study, as it frequently took place at eight in the evening, immediately after he had attended the Moravian service.

Grand Jury's Indictments refer to events that took place in 1737. This was an adjustment of Wesley's view of authority in the Christian life rather than a rejection of Christian tradition in favour of scripture. Wesley later claimed that by 1730 he was a *homo unius libri* ('man of one book'), and this was true in the sense that he consistently prioritized the authority of scripture and reading scripture over any other book.[250] One change that gradually took place was that Wesley could no longer adhere to the conviction of the Usager Nonjurors that primitive tradition was binding when a matter was not able to be resolved by scripture. Nonetheless, his clerical practice and publications show that he evidently continued to see a number of debated apostolic traditions such as the rebaptism of Dissenters and the usages of the Nonjurors as scriptural.[251]

One of Wesley's two manuscripts that deal with the *Apostolic Constitutions* and *Canons* appears to align closely with the doubts he was having at this time.[252] The manuscript consists of three pages on one sheet folded in half. Their chronological progression from book five of the *Constitutions* to the *Canons* suggests that there was probably another (now lost) manuscript with notes on the *Constitutions* books one to four. The first page contains three abbreviated and cryptic quotations that have not been traced. Following this are seven Greek words, which Frederick Hunter has stated are from book V.15 of the *Constitutions* on the stationary fasts.[253] Page two and the top of page three contain comments on eleven items from the *Constitutions* VI.24 to VIII.21. Wesley's remark on VII.23 shows that he had begun to doubt the claim found in this section that fasting should take place on the fourth day of the week (Wednesday) because Judas betrayed Christ on that day. Based on the testimony in the Gospel of John chapter thirteen Wesley concluded that the betrayal took place on the sixth day. He did not mention that some scholars such as Claude Fleury justified Wednesday fasting because Christ was brought to trial on a Wednesday.[254] Other notes in this section are generalized and do not contain his judgment on the *Constitutions*.

The remainder of page three has critical comments expressing doubt about the authority of five *Apostolic Canons* because of his conclusion that they were not extant during the apostolic era. Questioned is Canon 27 forbidding unmarried clergy to marry (cf. VI.17); Canon 52 commanding clergy to receive reformed penitents into the church; Canon 68 declaring baptism by heretics null and void; Canon 69 commanding that clergy and laity

---

[250] JWJ, 14 May 1765, 21:510. An example of Wesley's redirected focus can be seen in this letter, where he claimed that his *Collection of Forms of Prayer* contains his teaching on Christian perfection, although he 'should have started at *the word*': JWJ, 14 May 1765, 21:511.

[251] On rebaptism, see note 51 in the 'Conclusion' of this book, and on the usages see John and Charles Wesley's *Hymns on the Lord's Supper* (1745).

[252] Wesley's Chapel, City Road, London, MS, LDWMM/1994/2067.

[253] Hunter, 52.

[254] Fleury, 14.

observe the stationary fasts and Lent;[255] and Canon 85 declaring Judith's and Clements's epistles to be part of the canon of scriptures. While Wesley's notes on page one to the top of page three are general rather than sceptical, his reservation regarding five of the *Canons* on page three almost certainly indicates that this part of the manuscript was written around the time he was studying Beveridge's work in September 1736. Because of the extremely brief nature of the comments, they are difficult to definitively interpret. Did he, for example, still believe it was prudential to observe Lent and the stations, although they may not have been extant before Tertullian's time? Did he alter his baptismal practice after this time based on his remark that the first testimony concerning the invalidity of baptism by heretics comes from St Cyprian? On both of these issues we may doubt that his observations represent the beginning of a major change in devotional and liturgical practice.[256] Wesley certainly continued to regularly fast for the remainder of his life and in Georgia and possibly later in life he persisted in rebaptizing Dissenters. While his notes on Canons 68 and 69 seem to indicate a movement to a less rigid devotional and liturgical practice, the annotation on Canon 52 is ambiguous and does not seem to suggest a lowering of disciplinary standards, although he may have intended to call into question discipline through penance.[257]

Taken as a whole, these notes seem to indicate more of a tempering of his confidence in the apostolicity of portions of the *Constitutions* and *Canons* than a major shift in his belief that they were an authoritative source of ancient liturgical tradition. Nonetheless, although he retained some of the practices prescribed in the *Constitutions* and *Canons*, after the Georgia mission Wesley turned more often to writers such as Cave, Horneck, and Fleury, rather than the *Constitutions* and *Canons* as authorities on primitive Christian practice.[258]

In conclusion, Wesley's recollection that he strictly observed the rubrics of the Church of England is true to some degree, but is also somewhat misleading. Exact adherence to the rubrics in England was not unusual, and was regularly a source of lay–clerical conflict.[259] However, in Georgia, Wesley took advantage of the lack of ecclesiastical oversight to implement forms of worship encouraged by the Usager Nonjurors. By dividing public prayers, and

---

[255] Hunter concluded that this manuscript was written prior to the manuscript containing Wesley's liturgical resolutions because his questioning of Canon 69 may have been the reason he included the stationary fasts and Lent under the heading of 'prudent' practices (p. 52). While this is a possibility, there is insufficient evidence to prove this assertion. I agree with Frank Baker that this second manuscript was probably the latter of the two documents: *John Wesley*, 354 n. 24.

[256] Cf. Bowmer, 235; Lawson, *John Wesley*, 14, 17. There is insufficient evidence to support the argument of Baker and implication of Keefer and Campbell that the changes in Wesley's conception of the primitive church occurred fairly rapidly: Baker, *John Wesley*, 49–50; Keefer, (1982), 81–6; Campbell, 40, 114.

[257] Hunter, 50.

[258] Campbell, 41.

[259] Spaeth, *Church in An Age of Danger*, 200.

insisting on trine immersion, he rejected the 1662 prayer book in favour of the 1549 book. In other respects, he discarded the Book of Common Prayer and the Canons of the Church of England in favour of the practices of the primitive church as outlined in the *Apostolic Constitutions* and *Canons* and by the Essentialist Nonjurors in Thomas Deacon's *Devotions*. Colonists' complaints about Wesley's conduct show that they were aware that in several respects his clerical practice went beyond the Church's rubrics. Nonetheless, historians have generally failed to note that Wesley's overarching concern for reviving the discipline and practice of the primitive church led him to prioritize his conception of the primitive church over the rubrics of the Church of England. His passion for restoring primitive Christianity was the driving force behind all of the major subjects discussed in this chapter, namely, prayer book revision, precise sacramental observance, confession and penance, ascetical discipline, deaconesses, religious societies, mission to the Indians, and re-assessment of the primitive councils and canons.

5

Opposition to Wesley's Primitive Christianity in Georgia

There are three principal reasons why Wesley failed to unify Georgian society. First of all, as noted, some colonists were opposed to his implementation of High Church Anglican practices. Opposition to Wesley's churchmanship inspired various polemical caricatures of Wesley as an enthusiast, a Roman Catholic, and a divisive clergyman. Second, Wesley interacted with women in a way that many male colonists found repulsive. Third, Wesley helped undermine the authority of the magistrates by publicly defending himself in the Williamson case and opposing them in several other legal disputes. The purpose of this chapter is to examine the opposition to Wesley's ministry in Georgia. With this in mind, new light can be shed on the Williamson affair when understood in the context of colonists' antagonism towards Wesley's relationships with women. This may be seen as an alternative methodology and implicit challenge to those who have sought to understand the Williamson controversy through the lens of the modern interest in sex and psychology.[1] His conflicts with the magistrates of Savannah over his denial of communion to Williamson and his advocacy for Captain Joseph Watson and William Bradley in their legal cases are interpreted within the framework of his support of ordinary Georgians. The combined strength of these controversies fuelled by the Williamson controversy became the primary reasons for Wesley deciding he had little choice but to leave the colony.[2]

---

[1] See Willie Snow Ethridge, *Strange Fires: The True Story of John Wesley's Love Affair in Georgia* (New York, 1971); John W. Drakeford, *Take Her, Mr. Wesley* (Waco, TX, 1973); Robert L. Moore, *John Wesley and Authority: A Psychological Perspective* (Missoula, MT, 1979), chapter 3. See also the unsubstantiated claim by Aaron Spencer Fogleman that 'Wesley was caught in a sex scandal and had to leave the colony': *Jesus is Female: Moravians and the Challenge of Radical Religion in Early America* (Philadelphia, 2007), 58.

[2] As controversial as his High Churchmanship was, it was his denial of communion to Sophia Williamson that was the most direct cause of his departure from Georgia.

WESLEY AS AN ENTHUSIAST

Although in the early eighteenth century charges of enthusiasm most often referred to fears of Puritan sectarianism and Roman Catholic superstition, accusations of enthusiasm were occasionally geared towards fervent High Churchmen. For example, William Law was placed in this category by some who considered him to be a fanatical forerunner of Methodism.[3] The High Church devotion of the Methodists led the anonymous letter-writer to *Fog's Weekly Journal* to criticize them as melancholy 'sons of sorrow' whose spiritual-ity mimicked that of the Puritans in the Civil War era. According to this writer, their overzealousness might be judged 'enthusiastic madness' and should be considered a threat to innocent social pleasures and to religion itself.[4] Similar charges were levelled at Wesley by the Earl of Egmont who, reflecting on Wesley's time in Georgia, remarked that 'the New Sect call'd Methodists' were enthusiasts influenced by Quakerism to 'fancy themselves led by the Spirit in every Step they take'. Nonetheless, he noted that they were 'Strict adherers to the Church of England'.[5] In Georgia, colonists opposed to Wesley's cleri-cal practice interpreted matters along similar lines. Philip Thicknesse, in his *Memoirs*, characterized the Georgia Methodists (and later Methodism) as sec-tarian enthusiasts who relied on enthusiastic women to promote their move-ment.[6] Instead of defining enthusiasm as overzealousness, Wesley inverted the typical contemporary understanding by associating enthusiasm with the spiritually lazy attitude of hoping 'to attain the end without the means [i.e. spiritual discipline and the sacraments]'.[7]

The earliest insinuation that the Anglican missionaries had enthusiastic ten-dencies comes from Captain Dunbar's report to the Trustees in June 1737 that 'These Methodical Gentlemen, or Methodists as they call themselves are for the general pious and zealous for advancing the cause of Religion, but what ever they deliberate on and afterwards resolve, they fancy to be a motion of the Holy Spirit'.[8] William Norris, Wesley's successor in Savannah, who prob-ably never met him, concluded that Wesley and his fellow missionaries were enthusiasts.[9] The controversial events of the summer and autumn of 1737, which were not quickly forgotten by some of Wesley's contemporaries, fuelled charges of enthusiasm against Wesley. Tailfer argued that Wesley's enthusiasm

---

[3] See Joseph Trapp, *The Nature, Folly, Sin, and Danger of Being Righteous Over-much* (London, 1739), 23.

[4] *Fog's Weekly Journal*, 9 December 1732, in Heitzenrater, *Elusive Mr. Wesley*, 226–9.

[5] *Journal*, ed. McPherson, 17 September 1735, p. 107.

[6] Thicknesse, *Memoirs and Anecdotes of Philip Thicknesse* (Dublin, 1790), 24–5.

[7] JW to Mary Chapman [29 March 1737], *Works*, 25:504.

[8] Egmont, *Journal*, ed. McPherson, 6 June 1737, p. 277. Dunbar is not mentioned in Wesley's journals and diary.

[9] Norris to Trustees (12 December 1738), *CRG*, 22.1:352.

for frequent and irregularly timed services led to 'indolence' and 'hypocrisy' among the poorest settlers as they neglected manual labour in favour of 'an affected Shew of Religion'. The charge that Wesley's followers displayed affection and showy religion seems to be a veiled accusation that they were, in fact, religious enthusiasts.[10]

WESLEY AS A ROMAN CATHOLIC

While Wesley displayed many characteristics of a zealous High Churchman, his devotional reading and attitude towards Roman Catholicism was substantially catholic. Nonetheless, it would not have been surprising had Wesley adopted the prevalent anti-Catholicism of his High Church and Nonjuror mentors. Wesley probably would have agreed with Thomas Deacon that the Roman Church is 'a large Unorthodox Schismatical branch of the Universal Church'.[11] And in Georgia he 'occasionally preached of the grievous errors that Church was in, and the great danger of continuing a member of it'.[12] Wesley's statement goes on to suggest that he had successfully convinced several colonists of 'errors' of the Catholic Church, seemingly indicating that some Catholics were entering the new colony despite the prohibition of this enshrined in the Colony's Charter.[13] However, in agreement with Egmont, he alleged that there was not more than one Catholic in the colony, except perhaps an Italian or two.[14] His efforts to combat Catholicism should be read in the context of his comments made a few months prior to setting off to Georgia declaring that he could 'by no means approve of the scurrility and contempt with which the Romanists have often been treated'.[15]

The accusation that Wesley was 'a Papist, if not a Jesuit' by Thomas Causton and friends during the controversial Sophia Williamson case should probably be partially attributed to the prevalence and effectiveness of anti-Catholic rhetoric in English culture.[16] This memory of Wesley by his enemies was still fresh in 1742 when Thomas Christie, in his letter in support of Robert Williams's affidavit against Wesley, called the former missionary in Georgia 'a base and Jesuitical Man'.[17] According to *A True and Historical Narrative*, Wesley was

---

[10] Talifer, 41. Here we have an interesting precursor to the multitude of accusations levelled in ensuing years that Wesley and the early Methodists were enthusiasts.

[11] Deacon, *Doctrine of the Church of Rome Concerning Purgatory*, 140.

[12] JWJ, 25 May 1737.

[13] *CRG*, 1:21–2.

[14] JWMSJ, 25 May 1737; Ver Stegg (ed.), *True and Historical Narrative*, 69.

[15] JW to a Roman Catholic Priest [? May 1735], *Works*, 25:429.

[16] JWMSJ, 10 August 1737; Colin Haydon, *Anti-Catholicism in Eighteenth-Century England, c.1714–80: A Political and Social Study* (Manchester, 1993).

[17] *Progress of Methodism*, 60. In 1737, Christie was the court Recorder in Savannah.

commonly suspected to be a Roman Catholic for four reasons: he 'unmerci-
fully damned all *Dissenters*', 'Persons suspected to be *Roman Catholicks* were
received and caressed by him as his First-rate saints', he endeavoured 'to establish Confession, Penance, and Mortifications, mixed wine with water in the
Sacrament', as well as modified the words of institution in the communion
service, and appointed deaconesses. Finally, his overall plan was 'to break any
Spirit of Liberty' and prepare the people for 'Civil or Ecclesiastical Tyranny'.
The authors continued on with the claim that Wesley used '*Jesuitical* Arts...to
bring the well concerted Scheme to Perfection.'[18] These accusations have been
discussed, but the fourth allegation will be expounded upon in 'Wesley as a
Divisive Clergyman' in this chapter. Although the second charge is difficult
to fully unpack, it may reveal that Wesley was eager to reach out to colonists
who might have been shunned by a clergyman less interested in the unity of
the universal church. Georgians influenced by Catholicism may have been
drawn to Wesley's liturgically oriented ministry, particularly his focus on the
Eucharist as the centre of worship.

Tailfer knew that the Georgia Charter excluded Catholics from the colony,
so the fact that he observed in Wesley an extreme form of High Church practice that he (and several other colonists) interpreted as Roman Catholic rather
than Anglican practice must have been shocking for a man who would not
have expected to have encountered this sort of clerical behaviour in the New
World. Georgia was conceived of as a buffer zone between South Carolina and
Spanish Florida, and colonists' sense of communal identity was set in juxta-
position to popular depictions of the brutal Catholic Spaniards. If anything,
the constant danger that Georgia would be raided by the Spanish must have
made Wesley's 'Catholic behaviour' all the more suspect in the minds of some
colonists.

Wesley's Georgia *Journal* contains one extremely revealing comment on
his moderate views towards Catholicism. Fortunately, we have the comment
in his manuscript journal, which is more strongly worded than his published
Journal. Portions of the account not included in the published *Journal* are
given in italics.

> I was sent for by one who had been a convert to the Church of Rome,[19] *but desired
> to return to the Church of England. Upon this occasion I can't but observe the sur-
> prising infatuation that reigns in England, and especially in London.* Advice upon
> advice did we receive there to beware of the increase of popery, but not one word
> do I remember to have heard of the increase of infidelity. *Now this overgrown zeal
> for Protestantism, quite swallowing up zeal for our common Christianity, I can't
> term anything better than infatuation, for these very plain reasons:* (1) Because as
> bad a religion as popery is, no religion at all is still worse, a baptized infidel being

---

[18] Tailfer, 41–2.
[19] W. R. Ward commented that this was 'Apparently Mrs. Elizabeth Fallowfield': JWJ, 182 n. 77.

twofold more a child of hell than the fiercest Papist in Christendom; (2) Because as dangerous a state as a Papist is in, with regard to eternity, a Deist is in a far more dangerous state, if he be not rather an assured heir of damnation; and (3) Because as difficult as it is to recover a Papist, 'tis far more difficult to recover an infidel. *This I speak from the strongest of all proofs, experience.* I never yet knew one Deist re-converted; *whereas, even in this place, I do not know of more than one Papist remaining, except an Italian or two, whom I cannot yet speak to.*[20]

It looks as if Wesley was referring to the advice that he and his friends received in London just before their departure for Georgia. This counsel probably came from both the Trustees and the SPCK, but was likely emphasized to a greater extent by the SPCK, which was then in the midst of a nationwide campaign to curb the influence of Popery.[21] This effort was highlighted in the Society's 1735 *Circular Letter*, a publication Wesley received as a corresponding member of the Society.[22] It is possible that his opposition to overzealous anti-Popery was strengthened by Sir John Philipps's vociferous rejection of his translation of à Kempis's *The Christian's Pattern*.[23] If he was made aware of this, it would not have increased his confidence that the SPCK's fears of Popery were reasonable. While the account of Wesley's views in his *Journal* reveals that he occasionally preached against the errors of the Church of Rome, he was clearly convinced that the threat of 'infidelity' was a greater problem. If Wesley was not given anti-Popery tracts by the SPCK before departing for Georgia, he would have found plenty awaiting him upon his arrival in the colony, as Samuel Quincy was sent '300. Sheets of the View of the Articles of the Protestant and pop-ish Faith[24] 100. Short Refutations of Popery[25] 100. Questions and answers about the two Religions[26] 100. Dialogue between a Protestant Minister and a Popish Priest'[27] in February 1735. The Society assured both Quincy and the Salzburgers that they stood ready to provide more tracts if desired.[28] Wesley

---

[20] JWMSJ, 25 May 1737; cf. JWJ, 25 May 1737. On 18 May 1737, Wesley noted that he discovered 'the first convert to Deism' in Georgia: JWJ and JWMSJ. That this was the physician Dr Henry Garret whom he spoke to on that day is confirmed by Wesley's conversation with Thomas Causton: JWD; see Causton, 'Journal', 17 June 1737, p. 257 and *LES*, 75.

[21] See, for example, Minutes of the SPCK, 4 February 1735, vol. 16, 1734–36, SPCK Archives, Cambridge University Archives.

[22] *A Copy of the Circular Letter from the Society*...(Dublin, 1735). The Society forwarded a copy of the letter to Wesley just before the *Simmonds* was due to set sail for Georgia: Newman to Wesley (13 October 1735), *Henry Newman's Salzburger Letterbooks*, 179.

[23] Wilson, *Diaries*, 22 July 1735, pp. 128–9. Philipps was a supporter of the Oxford Methodists and a leading authority in the SPCK.

[24] *A View of the Articles of the Protestant and Popish Faith* (London, 1735).

[25] *A Short Refutation of the Principal Errors of the Church of Rome* (London, 1714).

[26] [Anthony Horneck], *Questions and Answers Concerning the Two Religions* (London, 1727).

[27] Perhaps Matthew Poole's *A Dialogue between a Popish Priest, and an English Protestant* (London, 1735).

[28] Minutes of the SPCK, 18 February 1735.

may have agreed with Samuel Quincy, who told the SPCK in July 1735 that their fears of Catholicism gaining a foothold in the colony were misplaced, since 'Religion seems to be the least minded of anything in the place.'[29]

WESLEY AS A DIVISIVE CLERGYMAN

Wesley's conviction that following Christ inevitably led to suffering did not make him a model of an accommodating parish priest. As he was beginning his public ministry in Georgia, he read of the sufferings of John the Baptist, Jesus, and the disciples, and evaluated these scriptures in the light of the persecution he expected to receive. On his first Sunday in Savannah, he boldly told his congregation 'that offenses would come' in the context of his speech on the rigid principles by which he intended to carry out his ministry.[30] Also upon his arrival in the colony he exhorted Johann Boltzius and Israel Gronau not to 'be alarmed by these sufferings of ours, to which we are called', and although his ministry in Savannah began smoothly, a few weeks later, he expressed his opinion that it would not last. He subsequently conveyed his disappointment of being 'in ease and honour and abundance', which contrasted sharply with the suffering of the primitive Christians and his belief that martyrdom would probably follow ministry to the Indians. Wesley used the theme of persecution as a badge of honour in an effort to challenge Richard Morgan, Jr to join him in Georgia. The writings of Wesley's missionary colleagues share the common theme that persecution and suffering are essential parts of the Christian life and a divinely ordained means for growth in holiness.[31] This expectation of persecution created an environment in which peace and compromise were not high priorities.

Somewhat related to the accusation that Wesley was an enthusiast was the contention that he sowed divisiveness. This argument was made by William Horton, a magistrate and commander of the militia at Frederica (in effect the counterpart of Thomas Causton in Frederica), during Wesley's second visit there in June 1736.[32] In his sermon on Sunday 20 June Wesley gave a

[29] Quincy to Henry Newman (4 July 1735), *CRG*, 20:419 and *Henry Newman's Salzburger Letterbooks*, 588.
[30] JWJ, 6 February, 7 March 1736; JWMSJ, 7 March 1736; cf. 11 September 1737.
[31] JW to Boltzius and Gronau [13 March 1736], *Works*, 25:449; JW to Charles Wesley (22 March 1736), *Works*, 25:452; JW to Dr Timothy Cutler [23 July 1737], *Works*, 25:515; JWMSJ, 25 October 1736; JW to [Richard Morgan, Jr] [16 February 1737], *Works*, 25:491; Charles Wesley to JW [1–6 and 15–25 October 1736], (2 January 1738), *Works*, 25:477, 484, 524–5; Ingham to Wesley (17 June 1735), MARC, Letters to John Wesley Box, Folder I; Delamotte to JW (23 February 1738), *Works*, 25:530.
[32] Their close identification with each other can be seen in a 7 May 1737 letter of Horton to Causton: *CRG*, 21:459–62.

summary of what he 'had seen or heard at Frederica [that was] inconsistent with Christianity', and two days later Horton pointedly told Wesley:

> I like nothing you do. All your sermons are satires on particular persons. Therefore I will never hear you more. And all the people are of my mind. For we won't hear ourselves abused. Beside, they say they are Protestants. But as for you, they can't tell what religion you are of. They never heard of such a religion before. They don't know what to make of it. And then your private behaviour—All the quarrels that have been here since you came have been 'long of you.[33]

Horton's angry polemic provides evidence that Wesley's clerical style was a topic of conversation in Frederica. There is no reason not to trust the accuracy of Horton's contention that many colonists found Wesley's ministerial practice unfamiliar and strange. Horton's position arguably made him the highest rank-ing and most important resident of Frederica, placing him in a prime position to be an arbiter of public opinion. The fact that he delivered this indictment in a fit of anger should not detract one from seriously considering what he said. However, it should be kept in mind that Horton's ambition was to wield mili-tary and civil power in Frederica.[34]

Horton's comment that Wesley's sermons were 'satires on particular per-sons' is extraordinarily provocative.[35] His sermons were clearly aimed at iden-tifying and reproving the unchristian behaviour he saw in individuals and in the culture at large. However Wesley delivered his sermons aimed at moral ref-ormation, his direct approach of confronting moral shortcomings made some parishioners uncomfortable and others offended and angry. Horton clearly felt that Wesley was not treating him and his fellow citizens with the dignity and respect he deemed they deserved. The second primary contention of Horton's polemic reveals that Wesley's clerical manner confused the colonists. This is certainly a reference to his extreme form of High Churchmanship. The colo-nists did not know what to make of his liturgical practices and ascetical disci-pline. For some people who were walking a thin line between living at a bare

---

[33] JWJ, 20 June 1736; JWJ and JWD, 22 June 1736. During Wesley's August visit he tried unsuccessfully to convince Horton that he 'was not his enemy.' Horton 'had heard stories which he would not repeat, and was consequently immovable as a rock. Many things indeed he men-tioned in general, as that I was always prying into other people's concerns, in order to set them together by the ears; that I had betrayed everyone who had trusted me; that I had revealed the confessions of dying men; that I had belied everyone I had conversed with: himself, in particular, to whom I was determined to do all the mischief I could. But whenever I pressed him to come to particulars, he absolutely refused it': JWMSJ, 21 August 1736. See also Thomas Causton's claim that Charles Delamotte's teaching of children was 'a cloak to inquire into everybody's private affairs': Delamotte to JW (23 February 1738), *Works*, 25:529. Horton also wrote a letter to the Trustees (read on 24 November 1737) representing Wesley 'in a very bad light': Egmont, *Diary*, 2:449 and *Journal*, ed. McPherson, p. 320.

[34] Andrew C. Lannen, 'James Oglethorpe and the Civil–Military Contest for Authority in Colonial Georgia, 1732–1749', *GHQ* 95 (2011), 213–14, 222–7.

[35] On the two extant sermons that Wesley delivered in Georgia, see Hammond, appendix 9.

subsistence level and going hungry, at times Wesley must have seemed out of touch with their struggles.

Wesley does not appear to have been sensitive enough to the volatile situation in Frederica to realize that the stress of living in a military colony made the need for social cohesion vital so that colonists had little tolerance for anything that lent itself to social disruption. For this reason, neither John, Charles Wesley, nor Ingham were well liked by the people of Frederica, who came to see them as divisive figures. The missionaries were seen by many as enemies of social stability, therefore their clerical authority was rejected by substantial segments of the community. It is ironic that while the Anglican missionaries wanted to purify the moral shortcomings of the society, the colonists wanted to purify their society by rejecting these clergymen as threats to the stability of the social order.

Similar accusations of divisiveness arose in the wake of the Sophia Williamson affair. Thomas Causton echoed Horton by telling Wesley, 'You are introducing I know not what new religion among us.' In a fit of anger he also called Wesley 'a proud priest, whose view it was to be a bishop, a spiritual tyrant, an arbitrary usurper of illegal power.' He used this same type of polemic to influence the Grand Jury to 'not suffer any person to infringe their liberty, or usurp an illegal authority over them—to beware of spiritual tyranny, to insist upon their ecclesiastical rights and privileges, to oppose the new, illegal authority which was erecting among them, and suffer no one to lord it over their consciences.' The Grand Jury's initial Grievances delved into the issue of divisiveness by charging Wesley with searching 'into and meddling with the affairs of private families, by means of servants and spies employed by him for that purpose, whereby the peace both of public and private life is much endangered.'[36] This explosive rhetoric may have been employed more for effect than out of substance, since this Grievance was not included in the jury's Indictments. Nonetheless, Wesley's determination to impose strict apostolically inspired discipline on his parishioners and his refusal to compromise was interpreted by some colonists as clerical tyranny. From Wesley's perspective, this was precisely the offence leading to persecution that all true Christians must endure in imitation of Christ and the primitive church.

In the opening of his polemic against Wesley, Tailfer commented:

And *Now* to make our Subjection the more compleat, a new kind of Tyranny was this Summer [1737] begun to be imposed upon us; for Mr. *John Wesly* [sic], who had come over and was receiv'd by us as a Clergyman of the *Church of England*, soon discovered that his Aim was to enslave our *Minds*, as a necessary Preparative for enslaving our *Bodies*. The Attendances upon Prayers, Meetings and Sermons inculcated by him, so frequently, and at improper Hours, inconsistent with necessary Labour, especially in an infant Colony, tended to propagate a Spirit of Indolence, and of Hypocrisy amongst the most abandoned; it being much easier for such Persons, by an affected Shew of Religion, and Adherence to Mr. *Wesly's* Novelties, to be provided by his Procurement from the publick Stores, than to use that Industry which *true* Religion recommends: Nor indeed could the Reverend Gentleman conceal the Designs he was so full of, having frequently declar'd, *That he never desir'd to see* Georgia *a Rich, but a Religious Colony.*[37]

In a serious allegation against Wesley's character, Tailfer blamed him for encouraging slothful behaviour by obtaining goods from the public store for his poor followers. The implausibility of Wesley being able to regularly procure goods from the public store for his friends makes this almost certainly an exaggerated accusation. However, this could indicate that Wesley advocated a kind of primitive community of goods shared by all in Savannah. In any case, it seems that he supported a more generous distribution of the Trustees' public goods than Tailfer would have allowed. The overall thrust of the accusation is that Wesley was a subversive citizen of Georgia. According to their interpretation, his actions as a high-ranking and influential resident of Georgia played a role in directly undermining the social unity of the colony by encouraging laziness in the name of religion. When compared with the provision of divine service that many of the colonists would have been exposed to in Britain, the frequency with which Wesley held services may have seemed unusual, and to some, excessive. However, considering that he confined most services to the early morning and evening, it is difficult to accept the insinuation that frequent services at improper hours brought people into church during prime working hours. Nonetheless, prayer services held between five and six in the morning were perhaps scheduled too early to draw large audiences on a constant basis.[38] The small, compact community of Savannah combined with Wesley's strict churchmanship undoubtedly put more pressure on colonists to attend divine service than many of them would have been used to. Others perhaps omitted going because they saw the services as an exclusive club of Wesley's followers.[39]

Tailfer's statement that Wesley 'frequently declar'd, *That he never desir'd to see* Georgia *a Rich, but a Religious Colony*' is completely in keeping with Wesley's view of himself as being in Georgia first and foremost as a missionary whose essential job description was to help mould Georgia into a religious colony. In this case, the accuracy of Tailfer's claim can be certified through Wesley's letter of 11 September 1736 to the Trustee James Vernon, in which he stated, 'My heart's desire for this place is, not that it may be a famous or a rich, but that it may be a religious colony.'[40] He would not

[37] Tailfer, 40–1.
[38] See Thicknesse, *Memoirs*, 16.
[39] See Thicknesse's comment in *The Gentleman's Magazine* (1791), in Heitzenrater, *Elusive Mr. Wesley*, 255.
[40] *Works*, 25:474.

necessarily have been opposed to some degree of economic prosperity in Georgia but he was, of course, far more concerned for the colony's spiritual welfare and so would have preferred a poor yet religious colony over a rich colony indifferent to religion. However an individual colonist interpreted Wesley's words, the colonist's lens for interpretation would surely have been shaped by whether they were hearing his words as one of a small number of his disciples or whether the statement was heard by one on the outside looking in on Wesley's group of followers.

Related to the issue of divisiveness was the subject of the nature and extent of Wesley's authority, which, as noted, was ambiguous. Both the Grievances and Indictments of the Grand Jury contained the claim that Wesley 'called himself, "Ordinary", and thereby claiming a jurisdiction which we believe is not due to him, and whereby we should be precluded from access to redress by any superior jurisdiction.'[41] Wesley later discovered that this contention was engineered by Hugh Anderson, one of the authors of *A True and Historical Narrative*, 'who had asserted that I went from house to house to stir up the people to mutiny, and that I had publicly affirmed myself to be Bishop and Ordinary of this place.'[42] In the Church of England, the term 'ordinary' referred to the ecclesiastic holding the jurisdiction affixed to an office. Therefore, the term usually applied to the bishop of the diocese, although a parish priest had some level of inferior jurisdiction, which could not be exercised in opposition to his superior ordinary. Although Wesley seems to have denied this charge since he wanted Anderson to prove or retract his statement before the court, he attempted to evade the Indictments presented against him by claiming that there was no authority in Georgia to judge ecclesiastical matters.[43] This may have struck those hostile to him as a declaration that he was, at least *de facto*, the ordinary of the province. The confused situation of jurisdiction over ecclesiastical affairs in Georgia made him susceptible to charges that he demanded absolute authority to his will.

While charged with exceeding his authority as an Anglican clergyman, Wesley was also accused of disloyalty to the Church. According to one of the bills of Indictment, 'Wesley hath not since his arrival at this town emitted any public declaration of his adherence to the principles and regulations of the Church of England, contrary to the laws established, and to the peace of our Sovereign Lord and King, his crown and dignity.' Such a declaration was

[41] JWMSJ, 22 and 31 August 1737.

[42] JWMSJ, 3 November 1737. William Horton similarly accused Wesley of stirring up mutiny: Horton to Causton (7 May 1737), *CRG*, 21:460; Egmont, *Journal*, ed. McPherson, 23 November 1737, p. 320.

[43] JWMSJ, 2 September 1737. On the question of the legality of the Grand Jury's proceedings, Alexander Garden declared that they should be presented for making presentments against Wesley, since civil courts have no authority in ecclesiastical matters: Letter to JW [September 1737], *Works*, 25:520.

required for clergymen inducted to livings, but as the minority report correctly stated, 'a formal declaration is not required but from those who have
received institution and induction.' As a missionary, Wesley was not inducted
into a living and, therefore, he declared that he did not contemplate that
there was any need for him to make a formal declaration of adherence to the
Established Church (although, of course, he would have made this avowal at
the time of his ordination). Indeed, this charge is somewhat ambiguous in that
the Church of England was not established as the official church in Georgia.
Being the senior ecclesiastic in Georgia operating under the license of the
Trustees, Wesley had no one in the colony such as a higher-ranking clergyman or patron of Savannah parish to institute and induct him into a living.
Additionally, Wesley saw himself as a temporary minister of Savannah until
a door opened for him to live amongst the Indians. The minority of jurors
believed that 'he had declared his adherence to the Church of England in a
stronger manner than by a formal declaration, by explaining and defending
the Apostles', the Nicene, and the Athanasian Creeds, the Thirty-nine Articles,
the whole Book of Common Prayer, and the Homilies of the said Church.'[44]
While he chose to violate the rubrics of the 1662 prayer book in favour of the
Apostolic Constitutions and *Canons*, the 1549 prayer book, and the principles
of the Essentialist Nonjurors, there is no evidence that he deliberately sought
to avoid making a public declaration.[45]

   In general, it can be argued that the Grand Jury attempted to use its power
to question and limit the authority of the Church of England in Georgia.
According to Wesley, twenty-one or twenty-two of the forty-four jurors
were Dissenters, most being Scottish Presbyterians who rarely attended
church.[46] From what we know of Wesley's relationship in Georgia with some
of the jurors, it appears that Wesley's opinion was probably accurate that the
majority of jurors signed on to the Indictments against him either because
they were persuaded by Causton or were personally hostile towards him or
the Church of England.[47] In a set of Grievances against Causton, the jury

[44] JWMSJ, 31 August, 11 and 12 September 1737; cf. Thomas Causton's claim that Wesley was
a 'denier of the King's supremacy', which may have been aimed at his failure to declare his adherence to the Church, or, perhaps, his neglect in implementing George II's order to pray for the
princess of Wales: Benjamin Martyn to Oglethorpe (17 June 1736), *CRG*, 29:146.
[45] Curnock claimed that Wesley's diary for 1 May 1737 contains the words 'subscribed the
Prayers'—JWJ (Curnock), 1:353—which may have been a reference to a declaration made by
an incumbent; however, this seems to have been a misreading of Wesley's shorthand, since no
such words appear in the edition of his diary in the *Works* edited by Heitzenrater. Interpreters
subsequent to Curnock, such as Hunter, were misled by Curnock (p. 33). William Norris later
claimed that Wesley 'abridged & contracted' the 'Prayers for the Royal Family': Norris to Trustees
(12 December 1738), *CRG*, 22.1:351.
[46] This was irregular, since a jury was supposed to consist of ten men: see Phinizy Spalding,
Oglethorpe in America (Chicago, 1977), 15; cf. JWJ, 12 September 1737.
[47] Their names can be found in 'The Humble Representation of the Grand Jury for the Town
and County of Savannah', MARC, MAW MS 260 fo. 8.

unanimously accused him of intimidating them, obstructing their business, and refusing to help them understand the law.[48] The jury's prefatory statement to one of the Indictments against Wesley affirms that relations between the Church of England and Dissenters were a significant concern to them. Given that Wesley believed that only one-third of his parishioners were adherents of the Church, it is no surprise that this was a live issue. Their statement that Georgia was made up of both Dissenters and members of the Church of England reveals perhaps a measure of prejudice against the Church, and a definite assertion that Wesley was too divisive for the religiously diverse colony.[49]

We have several favourable assessments of Wesley's ministry that contrast heavily with the severe criticisms found in *A True and Historical Narrative*. In a July 1736 letter to the Trustees, James Oglethorpe noted that 'The change since the Arrival of the [Methodist] Mission is very visible, with respect to the Increase of Industry, Love and Christian Charity' amongst the people.[50] Wesley had a number of supporters, including Elizabeth Stanley, a midwife at Savannah, who left the colony in October 1736 and gave the Trustees 'an extraordinary good account of the people's industry and attendance at Divine worship, greatly commending Mr. John Wesley, our minister at Savannah, who goes from house to house exhorting the inhabitants to virtue and religion.'[51] After his departure from the colony, Elizabeth Fallowfield wrote: 'How shall I return you sufficient thanks for your good advice, or enough regret the loss of such a friend, since I need never hope to see you here again. No, you have met with too much ingratitude from thoughtless, wicked people, who knew not the value of that blessing heaven had lent them.'[52] Philip Thicknesse questioned aspects of Wesley's character, but thought that he was generally upstanding. He recalled that Wesley's 'Deportment in Publick [was] grave and steady, his language pure, and his preaching captivatingly persuasive.'[53] Equally impressive is the testimony of Alexander Garden that 'no one cou'd be more approv'd, better liked, or better reported of' than Wesley prior to the Williamson controversy.[54]

[48] MARC, MAW MS 260 fos 1–2.

[49] JWMSJ, 17, 21 August, 1 September 1737; cf. JWMSJ, 30 September 1737 on Thomas Causton's possible prejudice. Harold Davis has stated that 'one searches in vain for signs of persecution of dissenters for religious reasons' in colonial Georgia; however, some Dissenters believed that they were persecuted by Wesley: *Fledgling Province*, 196.

[50] *CRG*, 21:198.

[51] Egmont, *Diary*, 16 March 1737, 2:370.

[52] (27 December 1737), *Works*, 25:523.

[53] *The St. James's Chronicle*, 5 October 1780, in Baine, 'Thicknesse's Reminiscences', 690.

[54] Garden to the bishop of London (22 December 1737), in Fulham Papers, American Colonial Section, vol. IX, South Carolina 1703–34.

THE SOPHIA WILLIAMSON CONTROVERSY
IN CONTEXT: OPPOSITION TO WESLEY'S
MINISTRY TO WOMEN

Wesley's comments on his October 1736 journey from Frederica to Savannah with Sophia Hopkey and one of his servant boys reveals the characteristics of Hopkey that he found attractive.[55] During their travel he read to her from Simon Patrick's prayers and Fleury's *Ecclesiastical History*, which he intentionally chose to draw attention to the 'glorious examples of faith and patience in the sufferings of those ancient worthies "who resisted unto blood, striving against sin"'. They conversed about Christian holiness, which 'endeared her' to him. He was pleased by the 'simplicity of her behaviour' and her disregard for fancy dress and social diversions. She embraced his regime of fasting and he saw her as something of a fellow ascetic content to sleep upon the ground, adopt a bread and water diet, and not complain despite suffering from frequent headaches. He also found her to be intelligent, prudent, humble, eager to learn, meek, and peaceful. Therefore, Wesley set before her the model of primitive Christianity and saw the character of a true primitive Christian in her speech and behaviour.[56]

Since Wesley tutored her in French and practical divinity, the two spent a considerable amount of private time together 'to the offense of many people'.[57] Though Sophia, at around eighteen years of age, was about half of Wesley's age, he was clearly falling in love with her.[58] By October 1736, he was considering a proposal of marriage, but hesitated due to fear that his effectiveness as a minister might be greater if he remained single. He certainly would have felt major tensions between his attraction to Hopkey and his stated desire to remain celibate while in Georgia made before he departed for the New World. Although this resolution was made with the thought that he was going to live and minister amongst the Indians, there is evidence that he grappled with the twenty-seventh Apostolic Canon, which required unmarried clergy to

---

[55] I do not attempt here to retell the complete story of Wesley and Sophia Hopkey. The account from Wesley's manuscript journal is summarized in Bufford W. Coe, *John Wesley and Marriage* (Bethlehem, PA, 1996), 72–9.

[56] JWMSJ, 25, 28 October, 1 November 1736. Her only comments on Wesley can be found in her affidavit of 16 August 1737, which may not have been written by her: JWMSJ. In addition to reading William Law's *Christian Perfection* and *Serious Call*, which convinced her that holiness leads to happiness, Wesley also read to her several other works with a primitive theme, including: Ephraem Syrus, Cave's *Primitive Christianity*, and Hickes's *Devotions in the Ancient Way of Offices*: JWMSJ, 19 August, 16 October, 1 November 1736.

[57] Johann Martin Boltzius and Israel Christian Gronau to Heinrich Alard Butjenter (20 January 1738), in Boltzius, *Letters*, 1:224.

[58] It was not unusual in colonial Georgia for men to marry much younger women: see Marsh, *Georgia's Frontier Women*, 73.

remain celibate.[59] The precise level of authority he attached to this prohibition is uncertain; however, it is evident that during and after the Georgia mission he idealized the high level of religious devotion that was attainable for
unmarried clergy and laity.[60] His doubts expressed about the authority and
antiquity of the *Apostolic Canons* in September 1736 may have led him to be
more open to the prospect of courting Hopkey, but much uncertainly and
hesitation remained. The situation came to a head when Wesley told her that
he would not marry her until he had spent some time amongst the Indians.
A month later, on 9 March 1737, Hopkey informed Wesley of her engagement to William Williamson, a clerk who worked for her uncle and guardian
Thomas Causton.[61] The Book of Common Prayer required wedding banns to
be read in church for three consecutive weeks, but three days later the couple
was irregularly married at Purrysburg in South Carolina.[62]

Wesley's hurt and anger over this clandestine marriage increased when
Sophia stopped frequenting his religious society meetings and showed a general decline in religious interest over the following few months.[63] After she
received the sacrament on 3 July, Wesley reproved her for her neglect of public
worship. She refused to admit any wrongdoing and a month later Wesley publicly humiliated Sophia and her family by refusing to administer the sacrament
to her when she presented herself to receive it in church. In addition to her
rejection of the need to confess her faults, Wesley justified his action on the
basis of her neglect of the prayer book rubric requiring her to inform him in
advance regarding her intention to receive the sacrament.

Sophia was not the first person Wesley had repelled from the Lord's Table,[64]
but the controversy over his action in her case was much greater than any
other enforcements of ecclesiastical discipline that he imposed. By taking this
action, Wesley was strictly applying the protocol required by the prayer book.
He probably also believed that he was restricting the Eucharist to 'true believers', as was the custom in the early church.[65] Generally, Wesley's protracted

---

[59] JW to John Burton (10 October 1735), *Works*, 25:440; see Wesley's note on this canon discussed in 'Wesley's Reflections on the Primitive Councils and Canons' in chapter 4.

[60] Henry Abelove, *The Evangelist of Desire: John Wesley and the Methodists* (Stanford, CA,
1990), 49–73.

[61] This news caused Wesley to slip into a serious depression: see JWD, 9 March 1737. Sophia's
decision is not surprising given the unstable environment in Georgia for women. Ben Marsh has
noted that the first recorded instance of a woman in the colony preferring to stay single was in
1753: *Georgia's Frontier Women*, 91.

[62] JWD, 12 March 1737. This was not an unusual choice for Georgians: Marsh, *Georgia's
Frontier Women*, 76. For further context, see Hammond, appendix 10.

[63] See JWMSJ, 5 May, 4 June, and 3–5 July 1737. This contrasted with his friend Margaret
Bovey, who married James Burnside on the same day Hopkey and Williamson were married.

[64] Cf. the case of William Gough, Jr: JWMSJ, 1 September 1737. Johann Boltzius repelled a
congregant from communion for immoral behaviour: Boltzius to Trustees (19 July 1739), *CRG*,
22.2:182–3.

[65] Fleury, 19; see the discussion of this topic in 'Holy Communion' in chapter 4.

struggle as to whether or not he should continue to offer the sacrament to Sophia and his decision to refuse to administer the rite to her illustrates the central importance of the Eucharist to his clerical practice.

As stated in Wesley's letter to John Burton and in his conversations with August Spangenberg, he went to Georgia determined to imitate the apostolic life of celibate asceticism. While his determination 'to have no intimacy with any woman in America' is one of the opening statements in his manuscript journal, this resolution does not feature in the published *Journal*, perhaps due to the controversial nature of celibacy within Anglicanism.[66] His resolve to remain single is presented in the manuscript journal as a central reason why he did not propose marriage to Sophia Hopkey.[67] He probably believed that falling in love with her posed a threat to his commitment to imitating the poverty of Christ and the primitive church.[68] In analysing Wesley's relationship with women in Georgia, the context of Wesley's insistence on living celibate should be kept in mind.

Wesley's relationship with Sophia Hopkey was only the most prominently featured example in his *Journal* of a number of close friendships he developed with women in the colony.[69] Alan Hayes has correctly pointed out that 'his relatively liberated attitude toward women in the church was far more a factor in the opposition to his work in that day than has generally been recognized.'[70] Significantly, conflict over Wesley's ministry to women was first voiced by his missionary colleagues on the *Simmonds*. In this instance, Charles Wesley and Ingham unsuccessfully urged him not to administer communion to Beata Hawkins, whom they believed was a hypocrite who displayed false piety.[71]

Wesley's conviction already seen in his relationship with Sally Chapone née Kirkham ('Varanese') that marriage should be no barrier to spiritual friendship, coupled with his belief that women were in spiritual matters independent of men and equal to them, aroused a significant amount of opposition from male colonists.[72] Tailfer claimed that amongst the '*Jesuitical* Arts' employed by

[66] JW to Burton (10 October 1735), *Works*, 25:439–42; JWMSJ, 31 [July] 1737; Spangenberg, 'A Moravian's Report', 408–9; Apetri, '"The Life of Angels"'.

[67] JWMSJ, 25 October 1736, 1 February, 7 March 1737. Sophia knew this and probably intentionally told Wesley what he wanted to hear when she related to him her view that clergy should be celibate: JWMSJ, 3 February 1737. Wesley's struggle with his feelings towards female friends had emerged a decade previously: Green, *Young Mr. Wesley*, 106.

[68] Schmidt, *John Wesley*, 212.

[69] Wesley's friend Alexander Knox aptly recollected: 'It is certain that Mr. Wesley had a predilection for the female character': 'Remarks on the Life and Character of John Wesley', in Southey, *Life of Wesley*, (London, 1858), 2:295.

[70] 'John Wesley and Sophy Hopkey', in H. F. Thomas and R. S. Keller (eds), *Women in New Worlds: Historical Perspectives on the Wesleyan Tradition* (Nashville, 1981), 1:29.

[71] JWMSJ and JWD, 10 and 12 January 1736. Spangenberg also failed to convince Wesley to heed à Kempis's advice to *Omnes bonas mulieres devita easque Deo commenda* ['Fly from all good women, and recommend them to God']: JWMSJ, 9 February 1736.

[72] Rack, 125. See Wesley's statement to Sophia Williamson that if her husband's 'will should be contrary to the will of God, you are to obey God and not man': JWMSJ, 8 April 1737; Acts

Wesley were to divide families, engage spies, and 'those who had given themselves up to his Spiritual Guidance (more especially Women) were obliged to
discover to him their most secret Actions, nay even their Thoughts and the
Subject of their Dreams.'[73] This serious accusation is laced with insinuation of
manipulation and seduction. In Tailfer's opinion, at first the vulnerable women
may have voluntarily 'given themselves up to his spiritual guidance', but little
did they know that Wesley would manipulate them to such an extent that they
would be 'obliged' to tell him everything, even their most intimate secrets.
The assumption runs throughout this statement that these women innocently
put themselves into a situation that they were helpless to escape from once
they 'had given themselves up to' Wesley's guidance, guidance which Tailfer
suggests really amounted to control. Perhaps the most serious and damaging
part of Tailfer's accusation is the clear insinuation that Wesley seduced these
women, leaving open the possibility that he manipulated them in a sexual
manner (if one is to take the widest possible interpretation). At a minimum,
Tailfer certainly found it repulsive that Wesley pursued what he believed was
a socially unacceptable level of intimacy with these women. Although Tailfer's
language is severe, he was far from the only man who found Wesley's manner
of relating to women suspect.

Given that in the same series of accusations Tailfer outlined Wesley's
Catholic 'Endeavours to establish Confession, Penance, Mortifications' and
'Fastings', it appears that he was attempting to cast Wesley in the stereotypical
mould of a seductive Roman Catholic priest. Tailfer charged that, as was the
case with manipulative popish priests, Wesley persuaded these women to confess everything to him. Tailfer's readers would have easily understood what he
was trying to say—women are vulnerable, women are less rational than men,
therefore women are easy targets for manipulative men and Wesley was fully
exploiting the weaknesses of these women.[74] Part of Tailfer's overall accusation
was that Wesley strayed from proper Church practice by attempting to reinsti-
tute the office of deaconess.[75] As noted, Wesley may have used the term himself
to describe the work of women who were key players in the Savannah religious societies, such as Margaret Burnside, née Bovey and Margaret Gilbert.
It appears that Wesley was training these women to be lay pastors among his
circle of disciples.

5:29. Wesley's attitude towards women was also a theme in later anti-Methodist literature: see, for
example, *Progress of Methodism*.

[73] Tailfer, 42.

[74] Jeremy Gregory has shown that the Catholic Church was often associated with femininity
in eighteenth-century England and female conversion to Catholicism was regularly portrayed as
the result of being seduced by a Catholic priest: 'Gender and the Clerical Profession in England,
1660–1850', in R. N. Swanson (ed.), *Gender and Christian Religion*, Studies in Church History, 34
(Woodbridge, 1998), 246–7, 251.

[75] Tailfer, 42.

Philip Thicknesse was another settler who found himself repulsed by Wesley's 'liberal' attitude towards women.[76] Thicknesse's interactions with Wesley clearly had a lasting impact on him, since in his *Memoirs* (1790) this forms a substantial part of his reflections on Georgia. Thicknesse became aware of Wesley before he sailed to Georgia through his family's friendship with the Hutton family, and carried to Georgia a letter(s) written to Wesley from Mrs Elizabeth Hutton.[77] When he arrived in Georgia on the same ship as William Williamson in September 1736, Thicknesse noted that Wesley 'seemed disposed to admit me among the number of his elect.'[78] However, it appears that this disposition was short-lived, as Thicknesse observed that Wesley seemed to be more concerned with the soul of Hopkey than his own. Thicknesse may have been jealous of Wesley's friendship with a woman of his own age whom he considered to be 'very pretty', since he admittedly 'wanted nothing but a *female friend*', and would have had little hope of competing with a man sixteen years his elder of superior social status.[79] Nonetheless, this criticism may have been justified, since Wesley's diary gives no evidence of interaction with Thicknesse until March 1737, although he had met the young man before this time.[80] From a contemporary letter to his mother, it appears that Thicknesse probably thought more highly of Wesley at the time than he was willing to later admit in his *Memoirs*. After having spent two months in the colony, Thicknesse wrote, that 'He was very civil' when Mrs Hutton's letters were delivered to him 'but has never took any notice of me since. But I believe he has forgot me or else he would [help me], for he is a very good man.'[81]

Convinced that he understood the real motives behind the attention Wesley and his colleagues gave to spiritually inclined women, over fifty years later, Thicknesse wrote: 'those gentlemen were not ignorant, that there never was, nor ever can be, a new sect formed, (and that was their great object) if women were not engaged to promote it.' Thicknesse went on to compare the success of Methodism with the success of Arianism (a heresy which denied the full divinity of Christ) in the early church, fuelled by Arius's strategic conversion of Constantia, the Emperor's sister.[82]

---

[76] He also accused Charles Wesley of trying to seduce James Hutton's sister: *The St. James's Chronicle*, 7 October 1780, in Baine, 'Thicknesse's Reminiscences', 688.

[77] The content of this letter(s) that Wesley appears to have received on 7 September 1736 is unknown, but it seems to have contained a recommendation of Thicknesse to his care from John Hutton: JWD, 7–8 September 1736; Thicknesse, *Memoirs*, 16.

[78] Thicknesse, *Memoirs*, 15; *LES*, 98.

[79] Thicknesse, *Memoirs*, 15, 31.

[80] JWD, 11 March 1737.

[81] Letter dated (3 November 1736), in Mills Lane (ed.), *General Oglethorpe's Georgia: Colonial Letters 1733–1737* (Savannah, 1975), 1:280.

[82] Thicknesse, *Memoirs*, 19. Thicknesse followed up this argument by stating that although the Wesleys and Whitefield began the Methodist movement, it was sustained by Lady Huntingdon.

The male chauvinism that exudes forth from Thicknesse's comments might cause modern readers to dismiss his words as a typical eighteenth-century statement of male prejudice. However, it would be wrong to neglect his point of view for this reason alone, since it was a genuine opinion of several colonists. On one level, the statement is simply false, while on another level, it is highly revealing. The strong link in Thicknesse's mind between women and Methodism was not entirely fanciful. Indeed, recent studies have shown that women made up a numerical majority of early Methodist adherents in both Britain and America.[83] In Georgia, Thicknesse observed first-hand the attraction of some women to Wesley's strong leadership and rigorous spirituality. To both Thicknesse and Tailfer it appeared that women were particularly attracted to Wesley's spiritual guidance. It does not seem that Wesley specifically targeted women over men as objects in need of spiritual direction, but his family background helped prepare him to be at home in the company of women, and he may have found that women in Georgia were more open to his pervasive concern for practising the Christian faith. Although it would be difficult to prove that Wesley had a strategy to specifically attract women to his religious societies, Thicknesse was perhaps hinting at a subtle truth when he insinuated that the Georgia Methodists cleverly catered their message to women.

The logic of Thicknesse's statement is fairly clear: women are irrational; women were needed to promote Methodism because they could best recruit other irrational women; and because women are irrational, they are prone to religious enthusiasm. (As with Tailfer's criticism, Thicknesse appears to imply that women were seduced into the Methodist sect.) It is assumed, of course, that Methodism could not have succeeded without women because men are rational and would not so easily fall into the trap of enthusiasm. Obviously, this is misleading, since several men, such as Robert Hows and James Burnside, were enthusiastic about Wesley's religious societies in Georgia. However, there does seem to have been a general perception in Savannah that it was women who were predominant in the societies.[84] A central problem with Thicknesse's assertion is that there is no evidence that the Georgia Methodists had any design to form a new sect. In forming pious colonists into religious societies, they believed they were being entirely faithful to the Church of England. They did not see their beliefs as distinct from orthodox Anglicanism (and true primitive Christianity), nor did they see the religious societies they promoted as bodies separated from the Church. Nonetheless, they departed from standard Anglican practice by allowing women to take part in religious societies.

As an old man, Thicknesse was still troubled by Wesley's attitude towards women and the way in which the Methodist movement offered women opportunities to exercise religious leadership.

---

[83] David Hempton, *Methodism: Empire of the Spirit* (New Haven, 2005), 137.
[84] William Stephens to Trustees (20 December 1737), *CRG*, 22.1:34.

I thought to have done with this *methodistical* subject, but I cannot lay down my pen, without observing, that however seriously, and in earnest, many of the leaders of those people no doubt are; yet they are all, men of *warm constitutions*, and that if they had been natives of a Mahometan country, where women are excluded, even religious societies, they never would have separated from the established mode of worship.[85]

Thicknesse characterized the leaders of Methodism as 'men of *warm constitutions*' (i.e. enthusiasts), connecting them with the enthusiastic women who promoted the movement. The connotation of his remark was that these men were not true honourable men but effeminate irrational men. In this line of thinking, effeminate enthusiastic men are like parasites who seek out vulnerable irrational women, who all too easily collude with these men to advance their brand of fanatical religion.[86] Since Thicknesse seemingly wrote these words long after his sojourn in Georgia, one must be wary of accepting these sentiments as representative of his views as a young man in the colony. Despite this reservation, his perceptive observation that religious societies were key to Methodist growth rings true for Wesley's period in Georgia and beyond. As an observer of Wesley's religious societies in Georgia, Thicknesse had a unique vantage point from which to comment on the insipient beginnings of Methodism. Thicknesse's comments make it clear that decades after his departure from Georgia, he continued to associate Methodism with religious societies. He astutely contended that if church and state was not so tolerant as to allow religious societies in the first place, there might have been no Methodist movement. What Thicknesse did not mention is that Wesley's experience in Georgia, where he was effectively free from the Church's jurisdiction, played a key role in his continued and expanded use of women in positions of leadership. Women were not tolerated in religious societies in Britain, and if they exercised any leadership, this was generally a development that occurred after the 1730s and was restricted to women of noble birth (e.g. the Countess of Huntingdon) and extraordinary cases (e.g. Mary Fletcher née Bosanquet), primarily in their own households and in Methodist societies. In the new Georgian landscape, the authority of tradition was a distant one and women became more than simply second-class religious society members—they became eligible to exercise spiritual leadership, and some were perhaps seen by Wesley as deaconesses.[87]

---

[85] Thicknesse, *Memoirs*, 24–5.

[86] Effeminacy and religious decline was a larger theme in eighteenth-century literature: Gregory, 'Homo Religiosus', 93–4.

[87] See 'Deaconesses' in chapter 4. Gossip about the conflict between Wesley and Beata Hawkins probably made some male colonists suspicious of his dealings with women: see JWSMJ, 22 August 1736; *The Gentleman's Magazine* (1791), in Heitzenrater, *Elusive Mr. Wesley*, 256; Thicknesse, *Memoirs*, 18.

WESLEY'S ADVOCACY FOR THE POOR AND OPPRESSED

Social relations in early colonial Georgia were volatile. This was particularly true of conflicts involving three crucial institutions—the storehouse, the courthouse, and the jailhouse—and the officials the Trustees appointed to look after them. Wesley confronted all three power structures in his advocacy for select colonists. The Trustees' decision to govern indirectly though appointed colonists, Oglethorpe's conviction that he was the supreme civil and military authority when he was in the colony, and conflicts between civil and military authority when Oglethorpe was absent inevitably led to weak institutional authority in the colony.[88] The dysfunctional court was a perennial centre of conflict when Oglethorpe was absent from the colony.[89]

When Oglethorpe returned to England after his first stint in the colony in May 1734, without agreement from his fellow Trustees he appointed Thomas Causton to fulfil the governmental role he was leaving behind. Not surprisingly, Causton's suddenly increased authority was challenged, particularly by militia officers stationed in Savannah. Numerous accusations of misconduct were levelled against Causton. Upon his return on the *Simmonds* in February 1736, Oglethorpe once again assumed the role of *de facto* governor, effectively undermining the authority of Causton and the other magistrates. The likelihood of conflict rose again when Oglethorpe departed in November 1736, once more leaving Causton (whom the German Pietists were prone to call 'mayor') as the most powerful man in Savannah but with an authority that was often questioned.[90]

Despite the existing power vacuum, all available evidence shows that Wesley's problems with the magistrates did not arise until after the marriage of Sophia Hopkey and William Williamson in March 1737, and not in a severe sense until his subsequent denial of communion to her in August. By this time, he had read in Humphreys's *Account* of the SPG that its missionaries were to 'take a special Care to give no offence to Civil Government, by intermeddling in Affairs not relating to their own Calling and Function: That they should also endeavour to convince and reclaim those who dissent from, or oppose them, with a Spirit of Meekness and Gentleness only'.[91] After Wesley had left the colony, Boltzius and Gronau accurately concluded that 'he is a refuge among all people who are not satisfied with Herr Causton and has become their patron. And it has the appearance as if he wants to take on the cause of those who

---

[88] Lannen, 'James Oglethorpe'; Marsh, *Georgia's Frontier Women*, 9, 33.

[89] J. E. Crowley, *This Sheba, Self: The Conceptualization of Economic Life in Eighteenth-Century America* (Baltimore, 1974), 3, 18, 23, 30, 32.

[90] Lannen, 'James Oglethorpe', 210–13; Müller-Bahlke and Gröschl (eds), *Salzburg—Halle—North America*, 184, 209.

[91] Humphreys, *Historical Account*, 69–70.

suffer in this colony against all those who do violence and injustice against them.'[92] However, prior to August 1737 he lavishly praised the work of the magistrates and in particular Thomas Causton for suppressing 'open vice and immorality' and 'establishing peace and goodwill among men.' Wesley read the royal 'Proclamation against Profaneness' to a congregation of seventy and he believed Causton's leadership was encouraging a genuine reformation of manners.[93] At this stage, it appeared that Wesley and Causton were fulfilling the Trustees' ideal vision for Georgia in which clergy and magistrate would jointly uphold the law and combat vice, while encouraging virtue. Wesley and Causton were undoubtedly friends prior to his denial of communion to Williamson.[94] Boltzius and Gronau commented, 'At least the suspicion is that the grievous things did not receive their beginning on the occasion of the alleged oppression of the poor but in his private matter, and he only intends to be better able to defend himself by this means when he has many on his side who complain against Herr Causton and his helpers.'[95] This very likely reflects a suspicion held by some colonists that was communicated to Boltzius and Gronau.

In any case, tensions began to rise just prior to the communion denial as people began to more readily complain to Wesley about Causton once Sophia was married. Twice in June 1737, Wesley conveyed the people's complaints to Causton, which included the belief that he cheated people by intentionally short-changing them on the weight of goods procured from the public store as an act of revenge against individuals he disliked. From the beginning, Causton suspected Wesley of sympathizing with the colonist's complaints and angrily accused Wesley of conspiring with his 'enemies' and forming 'parties.' Popular animosity towards Causton was amply illustrated when the jury elected to inquire into his conduct immediately following their investigation of charges against Wesley. They also focused two of their Grievances against Causton on his abuse of power as storekeeper and overcharging for goods in the town store. Nonetheless, Causton continued to resent Wesley's candid representation of the people's views, which Wesley came to sympathize with.[96]

---

[92] Boltzius and Gronau to Heinrich Alard Butjenter (20 January 1738), in Boltzius, *Letters*, 1:224.

[93] This may have been *The King's Pious Proclamation, for Encouragement of Piety and Vertue... With an Abbreviate of the Laws to that Purpose* (Edinburgh, 1727).

[94] JW to the Trustees [4 March 1737], *Works*, 25:497; JWMSJ, 27 May 1737; JWJ and JWMSJ, 25 June and 5 July 1737; JWMSJ, 23 July 1737; Causton to JW [10 August 1737], *Works*, 25:517; JWMSJ, 10 August 1737; Causton to Trustees (25 July 1738), *CRG*, 22.1:204–5; cf. JW to Harman Verelst [10 November 1736], *Works*, 25:485–6 and William Williamson to Trustees (28 May 1738), *CRG*, 22.1:180.

[95] Boltzius and Gronau to Heinrich Alard Butjenter (20 January 1738), in Boltzius, *Letters*, 1:224.

[96] JWMSJ, 11 June, 7, 25 August, 2 September 1737; cf. JWMSJ, 10 August 1737; Causton, 'Journal', 9 June 1737, pp. 250–1; 'Humble Representation of the Grand Jury', fos 2–3. Charles Wesley told the Trustees in December 1736 that the criticisms he heard of Causton were unjust: CWJ, 8 June 1736, p. 43; Ver Stegg (ed.), *True and Historical Narrative*, 65. John Wesley's

In the turbulent late summer and autumn of 1737, the Williamson affair was only one part of Wesley's growing conflict with the magistrates. The controversy escalated because of Wesley's involvement in the court cases of Captain Joseph Watson and William Bradley. In Savannah, there was no separation of 'church and state' in the sense that there was no ecclesiastical court, and the town hall building served as the church and court house.[97] Although Wesley believed that the primary duty of a clergyman was to save souls, he wrote to the former MP and friend of the Wesley family, Archibald Hutcheson, in July 1736, that 'I am now satisfied that there is a possible case wherein a part of his [the clergyman's] time ought to be employed in what less directly conduces to the glory of God, and peace and good will among men.'[98] His advocacy for Watson and Bradley placed him in opposition to the magistrates of Savannah and played no small role in his departure from the colony. Wesley's support for them may be viewed within the larger context of his concern for the poor and oppressed, which was a feature of his ministry throughout his life. This was rooted in his belief that Christ voluntarily lived a life of poverty in service to others and the early church followed Christ in especially ministering to the poor both within and outside the Christian community. His conduct in Georgia clearly reveals that he was content to focus his pastoral energies primarily towards ordinary colonists, rather than make special efforts to convert prominent citizens. One notable act of charity occurred after the home of his parish clerk, Robert Hows, burnt down in March 1737. On the following day Wesley helped organize a collection for Hows and was amazed at the willingness of the people to give out of their poverty.[99]

Wesley also began to take some steps to provide for the material relief of poor Georgians, many of whom had arrived in Georgia as indentured servants or had become debtors while trying to establish themselves in the colony.[100] He began work on the three hundred acres of glebe land set aside for the Anglican clergyman at Savannah and commented that 'it would be worth while to make a small garden upon a part of it, which would enable either me or my successor without any expense to give many of these poor people a sort of relief, which in the summer especially is very acceptable to them.'[101] As was characteristic

earlier advice to Oglethorpe on dealing with disputes in the colony may suggest that Oglethorpe had asked him to act as a peacemaker during his absence: CWJ, 31 May 1736, pp. 39–40.

[97] For more on the town house, see Hammond, 298 n. 58 and Reba Carolyn Strickland, 'Building a Colonial Church', GHQ 17 (1933), 276–85.

[98] Letter dated [23 July 1736], *Works*, 25:467; cf. JWJ, 12 June 1736.

[99] JWJ and JWMSJ, 24–5 March 1737; JWD 25–6 March 1737; JW to Trustees [31 March 1737], *Works*, 25:504–5.

[100] Rodney Baine has argued that at least 900 of the 2,831 colonists reported to have arrived in Georgia in the province's first decade were 'identifiable debtors': 'New Perspectives on Debtors in Colonial Georgia', GHQ 77 (1993), 17. For further details and context, see Hammond, appendix 4.

[101] JWMSJ, 3 May 1737 and JWD, 3, 6, 9, 11, 14, 16, 18 May 1737. Causton noted that Wesley asked the surveyor Noble Jones 'to Set out the Glebe Land' on 25 May 1737: Causton, 'Journal', 243.

of Wesley (and William Law), and unlike the Trustees, he made no distinction between worthy and unworthy poor.[102] Wesley's habit of indiscriminately
offering charity seems to have been behind Causton's vindictive charge that
'You [Wesley] don't repel the drunkards and whoremongers that come to your
house, though they only come for a piece or bread.'[103] In imitating Christ,
Wesley conceived of caring for the bodies and souls of the poor as an aspect of
his work in Georgia. Through this activity he believed he was carrying on the
apostolic tradition and continuing the work of the Oxford Methodists.

There is fairly substantial evidence that early on in his Georgia ministry
Wesley became involved in politics. During four days in July 1736 he worked
on 'petitions', covering over eight hours of those days. Although we cannot
know for certain, these were probably petitions written by Wesley on behalf of
colonists to present their concerns about conditions in Georgia to the Trustees.
The petitions were probably carried to the Trustees by Charles Wesley.[104]
Georgians sometimes turned to Wesley with their grievances, as when he
'heard their complaints' at the meeting of one of his religious societies.[105]
Despite his father's advice to keep politics out of the pulpit, Wesley evidently
felt compelled to read his 'Case', (i.e. his defence of his conduct regarding the
Williamson affair) before his congregation at evening prayer.[106]

Patrick Tailfer claimed that Wesley, in collusion with Causton, 'gave his
Opinion in all Civil Causes that came before the Court', despite colonists'
complaints about this.[107] As with the generality of Tailfer's polemic against
Wesley, it contains some truth, particularly in the light of Wesley's defence
of Joseph Watson, which has been neglected by historians.[108] Wesley's concern for Watson should be seen as a continuation of his care for prisoners at
Oxford. He first conversed with Watson, whom the Earl of Egmont considered 'An insolent and vile man' and his fellow Trustees believed was a murderer, a few weeks after he arrived in Georgia and wrote the note 'Strange!'
in his diary.[109] Wesley's comments almost certainly refer to the controversy

[102] James Edward Oglethorpe, *A New and Accurate Account of the Provinces of South-Carolina
and Georgia* (1732), in Rodney M. Baine (ed.), *The Publications of James Edward Oglethorpe*
(Athens, 1994), chapters III and IV, 223; John Munsey Turner, 'John Wesley's Primitive
Christianity', in John Vincent (ed.), *Primitive Christianity*, The Methodist Conference Colloquium
(Blackpool, 2007), 25.

[103] JWMSJ, 11 August 1737.

[104] JWD, 17, 19, 21, 22 July 1736. On 26 July 1736 John Wesley accompanied his brother to
Charlestown on the occasion of Charles's return to England.

[105] JWD, 20 July 1737.

[106] Wesley, *Advice to a Young Clergyman*, 60; JWD, 16 August 1737.

[107] Tailfer, 42.

[108] Wesley's advocacy for Watson is not mentioned in the studies of the Watson controversy
by Julie Anne Sweet or Sarah B. Gober Temple and Kenneth Coleman: *Negotiating for Georgia*,
66–77; *Georgia Journeys*, (Athens, 1961), 82–9.

[109] *LES*, 101; [Thomas Stephens], *A Brief Account of the Causes that have Retarded the Progress
of the Colony of Georgia in America* (London, 1743), 54–7; JWD, 22 March 1736.

surrounding Watson's confinement under house arrest for the previous sixteen months—a controversy in which his predecessor, Samuel Quincy, had
been involved.[110] One rumour that was circulating was that the 'true Reason'
for his confinement was that 'on his first Arrivall [*sic*] in the Colony [Watson]
askt [*sic*] Mr. Oglethorpe what Laws he intended for the Colony, to Which Mr.
Oglethorpe as he believed very inadvertently answered. Such as the Trustees
thought proper, what business had Poor people to do with Law.' Therefore,
according to this story, Oglethorpe kept Watson imprisoned in order to prevent him from exposing these arbitrary designs. This gossip presented a con-
fusing addition to Causton's report that Wesley supported Watson because the
men who spread this rumour, Patrick MacKay and John Brownfield, 'believed
the Westley's [*sic*] were instructed by Mr. Oglethorpe to exercise the authority
he had pretended to sett [*sic*] up; The better to introduce a Slavish Obedience
among the People.'[111] This letter by Causton reveals the chaos and confusion
that engulfed Savannah at the time of the Williamson affair. If there was a
secret plan for the Wesleys to act as arbitrary rulers of Savannah, then surely
John Wesley would have had no interest in helping to free Watson, who could
have opposed his authority in the same way Watson was said to have contested
Oglethorpe's plans.

Wesley visited Watson again a few months after their first meeting and
penned the cryptic statement 'I know nothing!' Later in the same week Wesley
was present at his two-hour trial and heard Watson speak in his defence,
although he was remanded in custody. Two days afterward Watson sent for
Wesley and 'seemed much affected' by their religious conversation.[112] He continued to visit Watson periodically before Watson was brought into court
to be sentenced on 20 October 1737 by order of the Trustees. Wesley commented in his manuscript journal that Watson had never been sentenced but
was confined 'as a lunatic' and though he was not allowed to speak and was
remanded, 'oppression had not made him mad.'[113] The controversy that originally surrounded Watson's confinement resurfaced at the time of this court
date as forty-six men, including Wesley and several of his closest male friends,
signed a petition in his support protesting against what they saw as the illegal

[110] See Hammond, 300–6.
[111] Thomas Causton to Trustees (25 July 1738), *CRG*, 22.1:207–8. In the same letter, Causton
claimed that Wesley told him that he 'had Instructions, to Inforce [*sic*] some particular Designs
of the Trustees, which they the Trustees were apprehensive would be disagreeable to the People,
And that he was to represent them, All such who acted contrary or Opposed his measures. This
he expressed as if (in such a Situation) they who inform'd him of it imagin'd him to be a Tool.'
[112] JWD, 29 June, 3 and 5 July 1736.
[113] Part of the controversy surrounding Watson was whether he was found guilty of a crime by
the jury in 1734. The Trustees, who personally believed Watson was guilty of murder, thought he
was found guilty but given clemency by being declared a lunatic, while many colonists believed
he was found guilty of using 'unguarded expressions' but never formally sentenced: Ver Stegg
(ed.), *True and Historical Narrative*, 57; [Stephens], *Brief Account*, 54–9.

proceedings of the court.[114] Just over two weeks later he was released after having been confined for nearly three years and was admitted to communion by Wesley the following day.[115] It appears that from the beginning of his tenure in Georgia Wesley boldly opposed the magistrates' confinement of Watson whom, unlike Charles Wesley and William Stephens, he did not consider to be crazy.[116] Wesley carried the petition of protest to the Trustees, marking him as a malcontent according to Egmont, who bitterly remarked that he was an 'incendiary of the people against the magistracy.'[117] According to Egmont, a riot broke out in court on 20 October 1737 engineered by colonists such as Wesley, William Bradley, James Burnside, and John Coates, who publicly supported Watson.[118] It was apparently for this offence that Wesley was formally reprimanded by the court for being an 'enemy to and hinderer of the public peace.'[119]

Wesley's journals confirm that he had become disheartened with conditions in Georgia, which he thought he might help remedy 'by representing without fear or favour to the Trustees the real state the colony was in.' This desire, he claimed in his manuscript journal, was not for his own benefit 'but for the sake of the poor people.'[120] Towards this end Wesley wrote a fair but unflattering report 'concerning the real state of' Georgia's settlements and Indians, which he believed had been 'variously misrepresented.'[121] Ironically, portions of his account were republished by the authors of *A True and Historical Narrative*, who were otherwise obstinately antagonistic towards him.[122]

---

[114] [Stephens], *Brief Account*, 58.

[115] JWMSJ, 5 November 1737.

[116] Egmont, *Diary*, 8 December 1736, 2:313; Stephens, *Journal*, 11 November 1737, *CRG*, 4:23.

[117] Egmont, *Diary* and *Journal*, 26 April 1738, 2:481 and *Journal*, ed. McPherson, p. 350. Egmont also labelled Charles Delamotte as 'an implacable enemy to Mr. Causton our Magistrate, as much as he is a fast friend to all the malcontents in our Colony': *Diary*, 3 January 1739, 3:1; cf. Egmont, *Journal*, 20 December 1738, *CRG*, 5:84–5. Predictably, Wesley's successor, William Norris, was instructed by the bishop of London to 'not split on the Rock his Predecessor had done' and by the Trustees to 'promote a Spirit of Peace among the people' and give 'due Submission to the Magistracy': Egmont, *Journal*, 12 July 1738, *CRG*, 5:48 and *CRG*, 32:281. However, Norris also returned to England disillusioned with the governance of the colony: Reba Carolyn Strickland, *Religion and the State in Georgia in the Eighteenth Century* (New York, 1939), 65.

[118] *LES*, 7, 10. Thomas Christie was probably referring to this incident when five years later he accused Wesley of making 'an insurrection in the public court while sitting': *Progress of Methodism*, 59–60; JW to Captain Robert Williams (17 October 1742), *Works*, 26:89. It appears that popular excitement was not difficult to conger up, such as when a rumour that the public bell was rung for Wesley's trial caused an uproar: JWMSJ, 10 August 1737.

[119] JWMSJ, 22 November 1737. In a similar fashion Charles Wesley was accused by Oglethorpe of encouraging 'mutiny and sedition' in Frederica: CWJ, 25 March 1736, p. 10.

[120] JWJ and JWMSJ, 7 October 1737. George Whitefield later wrote to the Trustees citing his 'duty' to notify them of the 'declining state' of the colony: letter dated 7 April 1740 in Ver Stegg (ed.), *True and Historical Narrative*, xxii.

[121] JWJ, 2 December 1737; summarized in Egmont's *Journal*, ed. McPherson, 30 September 1737, pp. 306–9. Wesley may have had Oglethorpe's *New and Accurate Account* in mind, which he had probably read in May 1733.

[122] Tailfer, 67–71.

William Bradley arrived in Georgia in the same month as Wesley with a five-hundred-acre land grant, control over the Trustees' servants, and a commission to teach the inhabitants agricultural skills. He had minimal success in fulfilling his assignment, and the Trustees soon turned on him when he was accused of abusing his position by stealing and illegally killing their livestock.[123] Bradley became one of Wesley's closest friends in Georgia from May 1737, especially after Wesley counselled him following the death of his wife, Elizabeth, in June. Wesley was pleased with the way Bradley dealt with the death of his wife and regularly had religious conversations with him during his final few months in the colony. Bradley lost no time in sharing with Wesley his complaints about the injustice he believed he suffered under at the hands of Causton.[124] Forty-four jurors agreed with Bradley's Grievance that Causton intentionally gave him spoiled provisions from the town store when good ones were available.[125] The only direct reference to Bradley in Wesley's journals comes from this period in the form of a note that Bradley asked him to be a witness to the 'conclusion of a conference' that he had previously been present at between Bradley and Causton.[126] Read in the light of William Stephens's *Journal*, the extent of Wesley's advocacy for Bradley becomes clearer.

According to Stephens's account of his conversation with Causton and the magistrates of Savannah in November 1737, on several court dates (before he arrived in the colony in October 1737) that stemmed from affidavits sworn against Bradley for unlawfully killing the Trustees' cattle

> Mr. Wesley and he [William Bradley], and some others, who were closely link'd in opposing the Magistrates in the Execution of Justice, used to come into Court in a menacing Manner, crying out, Liberty, calling to the People to remember they were Englishmen, &c. and that Mr. Wesley was generally the principal speaker, to harangue the People though he had no Sort of Business, or any Call there.

The magistrates claimed that such incidents on several occasions made them 'apprehensive of being mobb'd and turned off the Bench' and divided the town into various opposing factions.[127] Stephens's assessment was that Wesley's conflict with the magistrates aided 'an angry Sett of people, against the Civil Magistrates', but that matters went much further than general support, since Wesley advised the discontented colonists at his parsonage and joined them in harassing the court, which 'plainly showed him the Head of that Party'.[128] From

---

[123] *LES*, 5.

[124] Causton, 'Journal', 9 June 1737, p. 250.

[125] 'Humble Representation of the Grand Jury', fo. 3.

[126] JWMSJ, 15 September 1737; Causton, 'Journal', 20 July 1737, pp. 274–7.

[127] Stephens, *Journal*, 8 November 1737, *CRG*, 4:18–19; cf. 4 December 1737, *CRG*, 4:42.

[128] Stephens to Trustees (20 December 1737), *CRG*, 22.1:35. Causton claimed that Wesley called their opposition to the magistrates 'the Inquisition at Savannah': Causton to Trustees (25 July 1738), *CRG*, 22.1:207.

Wesley's perspective, the magistrates were abusing their power and oppressing innocent colonists, while the magistrates were distressed that Wesley frequently used his formidable authority to oppose their proceedings.

On the Sunday following his admission of Watson to Holy Communion Stephens wrote an instructive account of Wesley's sermon on Mark 12:14: 'Is it lawful to give Tribute unto Caesar or not?' From this text Wesley

> discoursed largely on the duties of Magistrates in their several subordinate Ranks and Degrees, and the Obedience due from the People; setting forth how far it was, nevertheless consistent with Christian Liberty, for People to insist on their Rights, when they found themselves oppressed by inferior Magistrates exercising a discretionary Authority, which exceeded their Commission; as an Instance whereof, he laid down St. Paul's Behaviour, when the chief Captain had him before him, and how apprehensive the chief Captain was, of his having gone too far, as it is related in the twenty-second Chapter of the Acts; and on another Occasion, when St. Paul had been evil intreated [*sic*] of the Magistrates at Philippi, who the next Day ordered him to be set at Liberty, &c. he then put on a peculiar Spirit, in the thirty-seventh Verse of the Sixteenth of the Acts. This seeming to be urged with an uncommon Emphasis, some were of Opinion, that it pointed directly at Mr. Watson's Case, who was one of the Audience, and who has been advised by the Magistrates, upon his being newly discharged, to make haste out of the Province; and whom (it was said) Mr. Wesley was now very intimate with.

Wesley's chastisement reached few if any of the magistrates directly, since many of them had ceased attending public worship out of protest at Wesley's treatment of Sophia Williamson and in support of their fellow magistrate, Thomas Causton.[129]

Wesley's association with discontented settlers was sealed in the minds of some colonists at the time he fled via a circuitous route from Georgia to South Carolina with James Campbell, John Coates, and William Gough, Jr, the last two of which served on the Grand Jury that investigated Wesley's conduct. Stephens noted that 'This surprized most People (even many of those who wished him best) that he should take such Company with him; for there scarce could be found Men more obnoxious... I was now asked by divers, in a sneering Way, what my Sentiments were of him; which indeed puzzled me: *Noscitur ex Sociis* ['he is known by his companions'] was the common By-word'. Coates, along with Joseph Watson, had presented Stephens with a list of Grievances that they offered to make into an affidavit earlier in the week.[130] Stephens called Coates 'an Advocate and Pleader for any Delinquent' in court and Gough a seditious man determined to subvert civil authority. Stephens believed that

---

[129] Stephens, *Journal*, 13 November 1737, *CRG*, 4:24.
[130] Stephens, *Journal*, 30 November and 3 December 1737, *CRG* 4:39, 40–2. Coates did write an affidavit that Wesley took with him to England: JW to James Hutton (26 March 1738), *Works*, 25:535–6.

both Coates and Campbell escaped to South Carolina to elude their creditors.[131] On the day before they fled Gough carefully transcribed 'The Humble Representation of the Grand Jury for the Town and County of Savannah' containing a long list of Grievances against Thomas Causton by the Grand Jury that investigated Wesley's conduct. Wesley may have been embarrassed by his companions, since they are not named in his journals. Nonetheless, like them, he was disillusioned with the colony by this time.[132] And according to Johann Boltzius he was worried he might be killed or put under house arrest.[133] The end result of his hasty retreat from Georgia was that the gossip surrounding this event quickly turned into a scandal in the opinion of many colonists and Egmont.[134] A few days later, Stephens met with Causton and they agreed that the colony would be better off if Wesley had taken more of his malcontented supporters with him. Though Causton had effectively won his battle with Wesley, the representations of the Grand Jury probably had a role in the Trustees' decision to strip him of his authority in June 1738.[135]

Abundant evidence exists to show that Wesley continued to be a critic of the Georgia colony and Trustees. In his *Journal* published in 1740, Wesley included the critical statement that one of his goals upon his return to England was to inform the Trustees of the 'real state' of Georgia.[136] Speaking bluntly about the condition of the province seems to have been his chief concern in meeting with the Trustees on three consecutive Wednesdays in February 1738. He recorded that he gave 'an account, I fear, not a little differing from those which they had frequently received before, and for which I have reason to believe some of them have not forgiven me to this day'.[137] The Trustees had already received in December 1737 several documents critical of Wesley, including: Sophia Williamson's affidavit, the presentments of the Grand Jury, and several letters from William Williamson regarding the dispute at Savannah. Therefore, although Wesley delivered his own narrative of the Williamson controversy and three affidavits in his defence from Margaret and James Burnside and Charles Delamotte, some Trustees seem to have already turned against him.[138] Egmont recorded in his private journal that Wesley gave a 'bad State of the Colony', which he cites as one of several reasons why the

---

[131] Stephens, *Journal*, 3 December 1737, *CRG*, 4:41.

[132] See JWMSJ, 7 December 1737.

[133] Boltzius and Gronau to Heinrich Alard Butjenter (20 January 1738), in Boltzius, *Letters*, 1:225.

[134] See, for example, *Detailed Reports*, 15 December 1737, 4:218.

[135] *CRG*, 1:321–5; 2:247.

[136] JWJ, 7 October, 2 December 1737.

[137] JWJ, 8 February 1738; cf. 15 and 22 February 1738 and the comments for 8 and 22 February in Egmont's *Journal*, ed. McPherson, pp. 331, 333 and *Diary*, 2:466, 467.

[138] *CRG*, 7 December 1737 and 22 February 1738, 1:303, 308. However, Richard Bundy had defended Wesley from the beginning on the issues of trine immersion, and refusing burial and communion to parishioners: Egmont, 7 December 1737, *Diary*, 2:451 and *Journal*, ed.

'warm high Churchman' Richard Bundy and several other Trustees resigned in March 1738.[139] In the midst of these meetings, James Oglethorpe told Charles Wesley there was 'a very strong spirit raising against him [John Wesley]' and he was concerned about the rumours that Wesley had 'come over to do mischief to the colony.'[140]

Wesley continued his activities in support of Watson by carrying to England an affidavit and several papers in defence of Watson, which he passed on to Watson's wife. One of the documents Wesley transported was the petition he and forty-five other men signed to assist Watson that was later printed in Thomas Stephens's *A Brief Account of the Causes that have Retarded the Progress of the Colony of Georgia in America* (1743).[141] It is also likely that he presented the 'Humble Representation of the Grand Jury' to the Trustees. His sense of disillusionment was still fresh in September 1738 when, on his way back to England from Germany, he met some Swiss 'going "to make their fortunes in Georgia"' and 'plainly told them what manner of place it was'. This contented him with the thought that 'If they now leap into the fire with open eyes, their blood is on their own head'.[142] In February 1741, Wesley met with Thomas, the son of William Stephens, twice in London to discuss Georgia and may have given Stephens copies of some of the documents that he had already presented to the Trustees. Stephens had become the chief spokesman for a group that Milton Ready has dubbed the 'constitutional malcontents', who were primarily concerned to convince the Trustees to reform their system of governance.[143] There is no evidence regarding the content of their conversations, but the fact that Stephens sought him out and they met twice indicates that Wesley may have sympathized with Stephens's goals. Because of the unfavourable comments about him, to some extent, it is not surprising that when Wesley read William Stephens's two-volume *Journal* (1742) in 1750, he found it 'trifling and dull'.[144] One of the important features of Wesley's succinct criticism of Stephens's account lies in the fact that he rejected what the Trustees considered to be their official and unbiased account of the Georgia colony.

In conclusion, Wesley believed that the paradigm for serving the poor was found in Christ's ministry and the social ethics of the primitive church, which prioritized a disciplined habit of sharing one's material goods with the poor. This concern is reflected in Wesley's statement reproduced by Tailfer '*That he*

McPherson, pp. 322–3. For the Trustees' replies both to Wesley and Williamson, see Harman Verelst to Wesley and Verelst to Williamson (14 December 1737), *CRG*, 29:246–7, 252.

[139] *Journal*, 1 March 1738, pp. 334–5.
[140] CWJ, 16 February 1738, p. 96.
[141] JW to James Hutton (26 March 1738), *Works*, 25:535–6; [Stephens], *Brief Account*, 58.
[142] JWJ, 2 September 1738, 19:11.
[143] JWD, 13 and 16 February 1741, 19:451; Ready, 'The Georgia Trustees and the Malcontents: The Politics of Philanthropy', *GHQ* 60 (1976), 272–7.
[144] JWJ, 22 November 1750, 20:366.

never desir'd to see Georgia *a Rich, but a Religious Colony.*[145] Wesley's solution to the problem of poverty was to cultivate the Church's glebe land in order to share its produce with the poor, and it also appears that he wanted the Trustees to increase their charity to the poor if the accusations are true that Wesley helped procure goods from the Trustees' store for his impoverished follow-ers. Wesley returned to England with the intention to present the plight of poor Georgians to the Trustees. Because he believed the magistrates exceeded the authority annexed to their commission and publicly agitated against them, this placed him amongst the malcontents, according to Egmont. It appears that Wesley's opposition to the magistrates convinced him of deeper problems with the governance of Georgia, which he believed that only the Trustees could rec-tify. Thus, his opposition to the magistrates led to hostility toward the Trustees' policies, which caused some Trustees to label him as a troublemaking mal-content. Like the 'constitutional malcontents', Wesley's concern was with the Trustees' system of governance. However, because of his overriding concern with religion, it is not clear whether he developed a fully fledged critique of the Trustees or entirely identified himself with the constitutional malcontents. Wesley's concern for the poor and oppressed propelled him boldly to address problems in Georgia in a piecemeal manner, as he was confronted with them.

At first glance, it is difficult to believe that Wesley could have been at the same time Causton's 'Advocate for every Discontented person he mett [*sic*] with' and the malcontents' and jurors' ecclesiastical tyrant.[146] Indeed, Causton accused him of the seemingly contradictory role of being both an overzealous advocate for discontented colonists and a usurper of illegal priestly power. But although Wesley would have denied both charges, Causton's claims are not as contradic-tory as they seem. Wesley was an activist for colonists he believed were being oppressed and he held a high view of his clerical authority and the need to strictly wield ecclesiastical discipline, since he believed this power to lie fully within the bounds exercised by the primitive church and in keeping with his commission from the Trustees. As the Georgia Trustees' designated minister for Savannah, Wesley was placed in an important position, which pushed him towards the top of the social hierarchy; therefore, the way in which he conducted his ministry was bound to have a significant impact on Georgian society. His actions pro-vided plenty of ammunition for his enemies to attack him on multiple fronts.

We can learn a good deal about the social impact of Wesley's missionary work in Georgia by analysing the nature of the opposition to his ministry. The opposition to Wesley's High Churchmanship was caused by his insistence on implementing what he believed to be the practices of the primitive church. This manifested itself in polemical caricatures of Wesley as an enthusiast, Roman

---

[145] Tailfer, 41; cf. JW to James Vernon (11 September 1736), *Works*, 25:474.
[146] Causton to Trustees (25 July 1738), *CRG*, 22.1:205.

Catholic, and divisive clergyman. His dream of reviving the early church in the Georgia wilderness was an extension of his fascination with the primitive church at Oxford and was central to his self-understanding of his mission. This dream was so compelling for him that it was not dropped, even in the face of stiff opposition—in fact, opposition served to strengthen his resolve, since he expected to be persecuted as the ancient Christians were. Wesley's attitude in this respect was far from conducive to social stability. The utopia he envisioned involved persecution and hardship and would lead to spiritual harmony among pious Christians, rather than large-scale social harmony. His promotion of women to positions of spiritual authority was not an elaborate plan to relieve the oppression of women within the Church. It was rather a result of his past experience of relating to his mother and sisters on an equal spiritual plane. That women were spiritually equal to men was taken for granted and there is no indication that the opposition he faced in Georgia had any effect in altering this basic assumption. Wesley was interested in encouraging people whose lives gave evidence of integrated faith and practice regardless of their gender. His advocacy for the poor and oppressed was conceived of as a manner of acting in imitation of Christ and the primitive church in defence of the marginalized. In an unstable frontier environment it had the predictable result of causing public conflicts.

Conclusion

Scholars writing from within the tradition of evangelical Methodism, in particular, have tended to view Wesley's mission to Georgia as a glaring failure. They have commonly seen the Georgia period as a time of mounting spiritual crisis for Wesley. Their interpretation has tended to note that during his voyage back to England Wesley felt he lacked inner certainty of salvation. A number of additional 'failures' have often been cited: Wesley failed to find assurance of salvation through imitating the spiritual discipline and liturgical practices of the primitive church. He had become disillusioned with mystical quietism and rejected it as a possible means of assurance. His spiritual struggles were compounded by the stress he endured from the legal action taken against him. Perhaps worst of all, he failed in his primary goal of converting Indians to Christianity. By contrast, this study had found few signs of impending or inevitable spiritual crisis in primary documents relating to Wesley's Georgia mission. Nonetheless, Wesley himself gave some justification for negative evaluations if one literally interprets his very harsh assessment of the period in the Aldersgate narrative (published in 1740) as one in which he was relying on works-righteousness.[1] However, Wesley left little evidence for his own assessment of himself in his writings contemporary to the Georgia mission.[2]

Scholars who interpret Wesley's experience in Georgia with hindsight are generally drawn to view it in negative terms in comparison to his later evangelical successes. However, when his ministry is evaluated in context, a more balanced view emerges. For example, it is possible to argue that he both adapted and failed to adapt his ministry to the new colony. On the one hand, his statement 'that there is a possible case wherein a part of his [the clergyman's] time ought to be employed in what *less* directly conduces to the glory of God' shows his willingness to adjust to the realities of Georgia.[3] At the same time, in his zeal for implementing what he deemed to be the practices of the primitive Christians, it might be argued that he failed to heed John Burton's advice to 'distinguish between what is essential and what is merely circumstantial to Christianity, between what is indispensable and what is variable, between what is of divine and what is of

---

[1] JWJ, 24 May 1738, 246–7.
[2] Cf. Heitzenrater, 'Founding Brothers', 35. His comments in *A Plain Account of Christian Perfection* (1766) and recollection in *A Short History of the People Called Methodists* (1781) also strike a different tone than the 1738 *Journal* entry.
[3] JW to Archibald Hutcheson (23 July 1736), *Works*, 25:467.

human authority.'[4] Wesley can perhaps be charged with failing to abide by his own conviction 'that prudence, as well as zeal, is of the utmost importance in the Christian life.'[5] Nonetheless, not all parishioners remembered him as a legalistic High Churchman: some criticized him for narrow-minded austerity, while others praised him for consistent efforts to care for their physical and spiritual needs. Similarly, he received both praise and criticism from the Moravians and Lutheran ministers to the Salzburgers.

Although Wesley was evidently in a state of spiritual anxiety during his voyage to England, his ministry should not be judged to have been fruitless for this reason. One of his greatest accomplishments was his publication of the first hymnal that seems to have been intended in part for use in an Anglican congregation: *Collection of Psalms and Hymns*. Wesley rightly noted that his 'parish of above two hundred miles laughs at the labour of one man',[6] yet his sincerity and commitment to his parishioners was unquestionable, as illustrated by his almost daily habit of visiting them from house to house. His wide-ranging activities led him to gain a deep understanding of German religious language. He read prayers to French settlers and learned enough Italian to read prayers to Italian-speaking colonists.[7] He even went so far as to begin to learn Spanish in order to converse with some Spanish-speaking Jews in his parish.[8] Wesley showed a strong concern for the children of Savannah and taught them the catechism on Saturday and Sunday afternoons.[9] His diary contains evidence that his pastoral work bore fruit through rising attendance at Savannah's parish church. In 1737 average attendance at daily morning and evening prayer increased by an average of ten worshippers compared to 1736. Likewise, 1737 saw an average rise of over seventeen parishioners at the three Sunday services, with growth in attendance of nearly twenty-four at the second morning prayer accompanied by a sermon and the communion office.[10]

Wesley's occasional but steady praise of his parishioners indicates that his ministry should not be readily characterized as a failure consisting of a series of conflicts with the colonists. He believed there were some noteworthy signs of spiritual vitality in Savannah, as when he arrived in the colony and found that 'Many seem to be awakened' and more chose to attend prayers than a public ball scheduled at the same time. To the Earl of Egmont, Wesley stated his opinion that in Savannah 'there are more who desire and endeavour to be Christians than I ever found in any town of the same size in England.' He even

[4] Burton to JW (28 October 1735), *Works*, 25:436.
[5] JW to William Wogan (28 March 1737), *Works*, 25:500.
[6] JW to James Vernon [11 September 1736], *Works*, 25:474.
[7] JWJ, 29–30 October 1737.
[8] JWD, 28 June 1736 and JWMSJ, 4 April 1737.
[9] JW to Dr Bray's Associates (26 February 1737), *Works*, 25:494–5. Compare the description of his activities given earlier with *A Short History of the People Called Methodists*, in *Works*, 9:430.
[10] For details, see Hammond, appendix 11.

went so far as to declare to James Hutton that 'There is a strange *motus animorum* ['moving of spirits'], as it seems, continually increasing... Not only young men and maidens praise the name of the Lord, but children too (in years, though in seriousness and understanding, men) are not terrified from bearing the reproach of Christ.'[11] Wesley was in no doubt that the Spirit of God was at work amongst some of his parishioners.

A number of innovative clerical practices that became characteristic of the Evangelical Revival can readily be observed in examining the Georgia mission.[12] Ingham reported that on the *Simmonds* 'Wesley began to preach without notes, expounding a portion of Scripture extempore, according to the ancient usage.'[13] Charles Wesley's statement to the Trustees that his brother 'preaches by heart' indicates that John continued this practice in Georgia.[14] At the request of the Anglican clergyman, Thomas Thompson, Wesley prayed extemporaneously on account of the large number of Dissenters in the congregation when he conducted divine service at Ponpon Chapel, South Carolina.[15] In Georgia, he began a rough itinerant ministry making occasional rounds to the smaller settlements outside Savannah, where he read prayers either in private homes or in the open air.[16] Wesley's extensive use of lay leaders was perhaps his most innovative practice. Delamotte was employed as a teacher and catechist. In Wesley's absence, he took over the pastoral work of his parish and possibly led the religious societies in Savannah.[17] Robert Hows played a crucial role in initiating the Savannah society before Wesley's arrival in the colony and Wesley encouraged Hows in his work as a leader of a Saturday evening communion preparation class and other devotional gatherings. After Charles Wesley left Frederica, John Wesley relied on lay leaders to read prayers and

---

[11] JW to Charles Wesley (22 March 1736), *Works*, 25:452; JW to Susanna Wesley (18 March 1736), *Works*, 25:451; JW to Egmont [12 November 1736], *Works*, 25:486; JW to Hutton [16 June 1737], *Works*, 25:509–10; cf. JWMSJ, 30 April 1737. His generalized negative statements such as calling Americans indolent and lazy should not be ignored: JWMSJ, 15 April 1737.

[12] Frank Baker has shown that in Georgia Wesley instituted a number of practices that later became standard Methodist practices: *John Wesley*, 51–4.

[13] BIJ, 19 October 1735, p. 68; cf. JWJ and JWMSJ, 17 and 19 October and JWD, 19 October 1735.

[14] Egmont, *Diary*, 8 December 1736, 2:313–14.

[15] JWMSJ, 24 April 1737.

[16] Wesley gave evidence that he was thinking in terms of an itinerant ministry in his letter 'To George Whitefield and the Oxford Methodists' by referencing the work to be done in the 'smaller settlements' (10 September 1736), *Works*, 25:472; cf. JW to [Richard Morgan, Jr] [16 February 1737], *Works*, 25:491. Curnock (JWJ [Curnock], 1:274) saw Savannah, Frederica, Thunderbolt, Skidaway, Irene, and Yamacraw or (Cowpen) as on his itinerancy, along with the German parts of Savannah, New Ebenezer, and Darien. This type of roving ministry was encouraged by the SPG: *A Collection of Papers*, 25.

[17] JWJ and JWMSJ, 30 April 1737; cf. Delamotte to Wesley (23 February 1738), *Works*, 25:529–31. Ingham, a deacon, baptized children and supplied Wesley's place in Savannah on occasion: BIJ, 20 January 1736, pp. 73–4; BIJ, 14 April 1736, Lincoln Cathedral Library MS 299; JWJ, 12 October 1736.

lead religious societies there. Perhaps the most radical aspect of his Georgia ministry was his extensive use of women in lay leadership within his religious societies. There is no doubt that Wesley's religious societies were thriving from the autumn of 1736 until at least a year later when the Sophia Williamson controversy broke out and Wesley stopped keeping a daily diary record of his activities.

Wesley was by no means the only clergyman who faced difficult challenges in colonial Georgia; in fact, all Anglican missionaries, with the notable exception of the Swiss clergyman Bartholomew Zouberbuhler (served 1746–66), experienced similar trials and had short tenures in the colony. In his study of religion in colonial Georgia, Harold Davis has concluded that 'The overpowering testimony from [contemporary] lay people and ministers alike' was that colonial Georgians were an irreligious people.[18] Although Wesley's ministry was by no means smooth sailing, the available evidence shows that serious opposition to his work in Savannah did not arise until disputes erupted following his denial of communion to Sophia Williamson.[19] Even after this event, attendance at divine service and communion increased, although over time the weight of opposition and unlikelihood of the controversy being resolved made his position untenable. During the whole of the Georgia mission there were few signs of the spiritual doubts that plagued him on his voyage back to England. It seems that for the most part Wesley was happy in Georgia, although conditions there were never ideal and certain elements of frustration were always present (e.g. his inability to be a missionary to the Indians and his unstable relationship with Oglethorpe). His self-flagellating autobiography of 24 May 1738 in which he stated that in Georgia 'I sought to establish my own righteousness' should be read alongside other positive recollections made later in life.[20]

The aim of this study has been to demonstrate that for Wesley Georgia was conceived of as a laboratory to implement his views on primitive Christianity that had been intensely studied and practised during his last three years at

---

[18] Davis, *Fledgling Province*, 197; cf. Phinizy Spalding, 'Life in Georgia under the Trustees', in Kenneth Coleman (ed.), *A History of Georgia* (Athens, 1977), 39 and H. P. Thompson *Into All Lands: The History of the Society for the Propagation of the Gospel in Foreign Parts 1701–1950* (London, 1951), 55. In the larger context of southern history, John B. Boles has argued that unlike in the north, there was no 'great awakening' in the south until the nineteenth century, while Thomas J. Little has contended that southern evangelicalism originated in early eighteenth-century South Carolina revivalism. However, Little does not associate Georgia with early eighteenth-century evangelicalism: Boles, 'Evangelical Protestantism in the Old South: From Religious Dissent to Cultural Dominance', in Charles Regan Wilson (ed.), *Religion in the South* (Jackson, MS, 1985), 13–34; Little, 'The Origins of Southern Evangelicalism: Revivalism in South Carolina, 1700–1740', *Church History*, 75 (2006), 768–808.

[19] This is affirmed by William Stephens: Stephens to Trustees (27 May 1738), *CRG*, 22.1:167.

[20] For example, his *Journal* entry for 24 May 1738 might be compared to his sermon 'The Late Work of God in North America' (1778), in which he claimed he witnessed 'an awakening among the English, both at Savannah and Frederica': *Works*, 3:598–9. For further discussion of the 'success' or 'failure' debate, see Hammond, 'John Wesley in Georgia: Success or Failure?', 297–305.

Oxford. In a 1758 letter to Dr John Free, Wesley accurately remarked that the Oxford Methodists were not interested in any 'new-model'; in fact, 'during their whole stay at Oxford they were High Churchmen in the strongest sense—vehemently contending for every circumstance of Church order according to the *old model*. And in Georgia too we were rigorous observers of every *rubric* and *canon*, as well as (to the best of our knowledge) every tenet of the Church.'[21] He believed missionary work to the Indians presented an opportunity to restore the early church amongst a primitive (i.e. uncorrupted) people in a primitive environment. Although this aspiration proved unattainable, his interaction with the Moravians, Lutheran Pietists, and other colonists demonstrates that the restoration of the primitive church was the motivating ideal behind his ecclesiastical and devotional practice. Wesley did not dismiss the value of the Georgia mission later in life, as evidenced by his organization of the Methodist movement in *A Short History of the People called Methodists* (1781) into three stages taking place prior to 1739: Oxford, Savannah, and London.[22]

Until recently, the traditional prejudice of Wesley's Methodist biographers against his High Churchmanship and an inadequate use of primary sources from Wesley and other contemporary sources relating to his experience in Georgia have conspired to veil the centrality of his endeavour to restore the primitive church to his Georgia sojourn. Likewise, a lack of interest in and understanding of the influence wielded by the Essentialist Nonjurors on Wesley has often led to inadequate appraisals of the Georgia mission. Critical study of the primary sources shows that the restoration of primitive Christianity was at the forefront of Wesley's thinking and practice throughout his time in Georgia. In Wesley's own summary, he went to America in the 'spirit' of 'the Bible, the primitive church, and the Church of England' and returned from the New World in the same 'spirit'.[23]

PRIMITIVE CHRISTIANITY AFTER GEORGIA

Wesley had a long and eventful life after Georgia leading the Wesleyan Methodist movement. What became of his view of primitive Christianity? Luke Keefer, Jr and Ted Campbell have demonstrated that primitivism was a major factor throughout Wesley's life.[24] After Aldersgate, Keefer believed

---

[21] Letter dated (24 August 1758), *Works*, 9:325.
[22] *Works*, 9:430.
[23] 'Farther Thoughts on Separation from the Church', *Works*, 9:538.
[24] Keefer, 'John Wesley: Disciple of Early Christianity' (1982); Campbell; cf. Kelly D. Carter, 'The High Church Roots of John Wesley's Appeal to Primitive Christianity', *Restoration Quarterly*, 37 (1995) [online] <http://www.acu.edu/sponsored/restoration_quarterly/archives/1990s/vol_37_no_2_contents/carter.html>, accessed 12 July 2013 and in relation to Wesley's ecclesiology Gwang Seok Oh, *John Wesley's Ecclesiology: A Study in its Sources and Development*, Pietist

Wesley's primitivism did not diminish but that he placed more emphasis on soteriology alongside his ecclesiological concerns.[25] In her insightful study of Wesley's *Primitive Physic* (1747), a popular medical text aimed at ordinary people, Deborah Madden also affirmed Wesley's lifelong primitivism, arguing that 'Primitivism provided a holistic framework for Wesley's thinking and praxis, both generally and in *Primitive Physic*.' She argued that 'After Aldersgate, there was no significant change in Wesley's preoccupation with Primitive Christianity.'[26] Wesley did indeed maintain a strong concern for primitive Christianity, though the intensity of his focus on the early church peaked in the period from 1732–7. While he remained considerably 'preoccupied' with primitive Christianity, his conception of it—as discussed later—was modified in several ways.

Though Keefer and Madden have seen considerable consistency in Wesley's primitivism, many other studies have argued for substantial discontinuity in Wesley's life and theology pre and post-Georgia, particularly after his Aldersgate experience. It was particularly prevalent amongst nineteenth-century Methodist writers in the aftermath of the Oxford Movement to assert that Georgia marked the end of Wesley's High Church phase and its associated primitivism and the beginning of his true calling as an evangelist. In this line of thinking, Wesley's evangelical 'conversion' in May 1738 resulted in the transformation of his ministerial calling and theology. The argument for a sudden or rapid reformulation of his theology, when viewed from the perspective of Wesley's convictions about the primitive church, is inaccurate. An analysis of Wesley's theology post-Georgia reveals, as one might expect, areas of continuity, modification, and discontinuity in his understanding of the early church.

We have seen that although Wesley began to have some doubts about the authority of the *Apostolic Canons* while in Georgia, this did not lead to a rapid change in his theology or practice. Evidence from his January 1738 theological reflection en route to England shows that Wesley came to see Christian antiquity as subordinate to scripture. Whilst not repudiating the authority of the early church, Wesley began to take a more critical and nuanced view of it. Not long before penning his reflection, 'the great mercy of God' had brought

---

and Wesleyan Studies, 27 (Lanham, MD, 2008). Martin Schmidt strongly asserted lifelong continuity of Wesley's primitivism, though he did not extensively investigate the details of his claim: Schmidt, *John Wesley*, 222–3; *John Wesley: A Theological Biography*, volume II part II: John Wesley's Life Mission, trans. Denis Inman (London, 1973), 191–2.

[25] However, Keefer inaccurately argued that after Aldersgate Wesley's primitivism prioritized soteriology over ecclesiology. In fact, Wesley's goal continued to be the restoration of the form and spirit of primitive Christianity. Cf. Howard A. Snyder, 'Spirit and Form in Wesley's Theology: A Response to Keefer's "John Wesley: Disciple of Early Christianity", *Wesleyan Theological Journal* 19 (1984), 33–5.

[26] '*A Cheap, Safe and Natural Medicine*', 31, 46. This contrasts with Eamon Duffy's stark assertion that in 1738 Wesley abandoned the primitive ideal: 'Primitive Christianity Revived', 299–300. *Primitive Physic* went through twenty-three editions in Wesley's lifetime.

him to read the *Works* of St Cyprian causing him to exclaim 'Stand thou in the good old paths.'[27] Wesley's reaction suggests he probably identified to some degree with Cyprian's sacerdotal view of the church, which makes it hard to believe that 'Wesley's homeward voyage, in 1738, marks the conclusion of his High-Church period.'[28]

As A. B. Lawson has demonstrated, Wesley's Aldersgate experience did not mark a watershed in his view of the Christian ministry. There is little evidence of change in Wesley's churchmanship from 1738–45. In this period, he continued to believe in the threefold Anglican order of ministry, the necessity of episcopal ordination, and apostolic succession. However, his view on the relationship between the threefold orders changed (or eventually changed) with his reading of Lord Peter King's *An Enquiry into the Constitution, Discipline, Unity & Worship of the Primitive Church* (1691) in January 1746.[29] Wesley adopted King's conclusion 'that bishops and presbyters are (essentially) of one order', while he continued to believe in the scriptural and apostolic origins of the orders.[30] By July 1755 he had read Edward Stillingfleet's *Irenicum* (1659) leading him to accept Stillingfleet's view (and that of Richard Hooker and other early Anglican reformers) that episcopacy was scriptural and apostolic, though not 'prescribed in Scripture'.[31] (Wesley did not indicate whether he was aware of the fact that both men later altered their views.[32]) Leading on from this, Wesley later rejected both Roman Catholic and Anglican views of '*uninterrupted*' apostolic succession, while upholding a modified form of episcopal succession.[33]

What might Wesley's controversial 1784 ordinations for the American Methodists tell us about his churchmanship? Multiple interpretations are possible, but he was convinced that there was a primitive precedent for his actions. Wesley had come to believe that he was 'a scriptural ἐπίσκοπος as much as any man in England or Europe' and 'as real a Christian Bishop as the Archbishop

---

[27] JWJ, 9 January 1738.

[28] Wedgwood, *John Wesley*, 140.

[29] Lawson, *John Wesley*, chapters 2–3.

[30] JWJ, 20 January 1746, 20:112; *Minutes of Conference* (1747), *Works*, 10:202; Sermon 'Catholic Spirit' (1750), *Works*, 2:90; [Lord Peter King], *An Enquiry into the Constitution, Discipline, Unity & Worship of the Primitive Church* (1712), chapter 4.

[31] JW to Charles Wesley (16 July 1755), *Letters* (Telford), 3:136; JW to James Clark (3 July 1756), *Letters* (Telford), 3:182; cf. JW to the Earl of Dartmouth (10 April 1761), *Letters* (Telford), 4:150; JW to Charles Wesley (8 June 1780), *Letters* (Telford), 7:21.

[32] For this reason Outler rightly called them 'dubious authorities': 'Introduction', in *Works*, 1:86. But stronger authorities were available, such as Archbishop James Ussher: 'I have ever declared my opinion to be, That *Episcopus & Presbyter, gradu tantum differunt, non ordine* ['bishop and presbyter differ only in degree, not in order']; and consequently, that in places where Bishops cannot be had, the ordination by Presbyters standeth valid': *The Judgement of the late Archbishop of Armagh*, ed. N. Bernard (London, 1658), 112.

[33] JW to the Editor of the 'London Chronicle' (19 February 1761), *Letters* (Telford), 4:140; JW to Charles Wesley (19 August 1785), *Letters* (Telford), 7:284; Bowmer, 159. Cf. John Williams, *Popery Calmly Considered* (1779), ed. JW, *Works* (Jackson), 10:150, which seems to imply a succession in the apostolic ministry.

of Canterbury.' Extending the logic of Peter King's view 'that bishops and presbyters are of the same order', Wesley concluded that they 'consequently have the same right to ordain.' By extraordinary circumstances Wesley had become the superintendent of the Methodists, and due to 'a case of necessity' with the Methodists in America, drawing on the views of King and Stillingfleet, he was compelled to imitate the primitive practice that allowed for ordination by presbyters.[34] Even considering Wesley's irregular ordinations, he remained committed to his view that the Church of England was the most scriptural and primitive church in existence.[35] His view of Church polity remained similar to the statement of Jonathan Swift that 'A Church of England Man hath true veneration for the scheme established among us of ecclesiastic government; and though he will not determine whether Episcopacy be of divine right, he is sure it is most agreeable to primitive institution, [and] fittest of all others for preserving order and purity, and under its present regulations best calculated for our civil state.'[36]

After Georgia, Wesley returned to using the 1662 prayer book alone and valued it above any other liturgy, ancient or modern. His radical experimentation with altering the Book of Common Prayer and implementing Thomas Deacon's alternative liturgy ceased after the Georgia mission. In 1784, with awareness of previous unofficial revisions of the prayer book, he revised it for the American Methodists as *The Sunday Service of the Methodists in North America*.[37] What, then, does his revision reveal about his view of the primitive church and how it may have changed subsequent to the Georgia mission? In short, the evidence provided by *The Sunday Service* provides multiple areas of continuity and discontinuity in Wesley's conception of the primitive church. Though Wesley was bewildered that 'God has so strangely made them free' of the British State and Church of England, he was able to positively express

[34] JW to Charles Wesley (19 August 1785), *Letters* (Telford), 7:284; JW to Barnabus Thomas (25 March 1785), *Letters* (Telford), 7:262; JW to Our Brethren in America (10 September 1784), *Letters* (Telford), 7:238; Lawson, *John Wesley*, 52–3, 65; cf. A. Raymond George, 'Ordination', in Rupert E. Davies, A. Raymond George, and E. Gordon Rupp (eds), *A History of the Methodist Church in Great Britain* (London, 1978), 2:143–60. Samuel Drew claimed that Wesley told Thomas Coke that he 'admired' the practice of the primitive church in Alexandria of presbyters together ordaining a bishop from amongst their own ranks: *The Life of the Rev. Thomas Coke, LL.D.* (London, 1817), 64. For his argument that the ordinations were needed due to a 'case of necessity', Wesley could have drawn on the work of Richard Hooker: *Of the Laws of Ecclesiastical Polity*, VII.xiv.11, in *The Works of that Learned and Judicious Divine, Mr. Richard Hooker* (Oxford, 1850), 2:402–4.
[35] See chapter 1, note 8 and Jeremy Gregory, ' "In the Church I will live and die": John Wesley, the Church of England, and Methodism', in William Gibson and Robert G. Ingram (eds), *Religious Identities in Britain, 1660–1800* (Aldershot, 2005), 147–78.
[36] Quoted in Sykes, *Old Priest and New Presbyter*, 176.
[37] See the facsimile reprint: *John Wesley's Sunday Service of the Methodists in North America*, with an introduction by James F. White (Nashville, 1984). Wesley's was one of over fifty attempts to revise the prayer book between 1713 and 1854: see A. Elliott Peaston, *The Prayer Book Reform Movement in the XVIIIth Century* (Oxford, 1940), 34.

that 'They are now at full liberty simply to follow the Scriptures and the Primitive Church.'[38] Wesley clearly saw his revision as being faithful to the spirit of the Church of England and the primitive church.[39]

How does *The Sunday Service* compare to what we know of Wesley's liturgical views in Georgia? Continuity is most clearly seen in his treatment of the Lord's Supper. In both his Georgia ministry and *The Sunday Service*, Wesley accentuated the Eucharist as the centre of worship. *The Sunday Service* shifts from the prayer book focus on daily morning and evening prayer to a weekly Sunday service centring on the Eucharistic celebration. Wesley was deeply concerned about the lack of sacramental provision for the American Methodists. He made no major revisions to the prayer book liturgy on the Lord's Supper.

Some other areas of continuity can also be observed. Wesley included the litany to be read on the primitive fast days of Wednesday and Friday.[40] He also removed the prayer book rite for private baptism (suggesting that his opposition to it remained) and retained immersion (or dipping) of the child in the water. He also preserved the threefold order of ministry. At the same time, there is discontinuity in the baptismal service in allowance for sprinkling the child.[41] Wesley also differed from his practice in Georgia by removing saints' days and even major seasons in the Church calendar, such as Epiphany and Lent. Compared to Wesley's ministry in Georgia, *The Sunday Service* illustrates a more flexible view on liturgical matters, while aligning with his post-Georgia view that the Book of Common Prayer was the purest existing liturgical representation of 'solid, scriptural, rational Piety.'[42] In other words, he believed that the prayer book was a true expression of scripture and rational piety, which was best exemplified by the primitive church.

Soon after his return from Georgia, Wesley altered his view that communion was only for 'the faithful' who had adequately prepared for it. He came to believe that it could be 'a *means of conveying* to men either *preventing, justifying,* or *sanctifying grace*', and 'there is *no previous preparation* indispensably necessary.'[43] Concurrently, Wesley required communicants at Methodist gatherings to have class-tickets and railed against 'spectators' at the Lord's Supper.[44] Members

---

[38] JW to Our Brethren in America (10 September 1784), *Letters* (Telford), 7:239.

[39] Cf. Karen B. Westerfield Tucker, 'Form and Freedom: John Wesley's Legacy for Methodist Worship', in Karen B. Westerfield Tucker (ed.), *The Sunday Service of the Methodists: Twentieth-Century Worship in Worldwide Methodism. Studies in Honor of James F. White* (Nashville, 1996), 21.

[40] In *The Sunday Service* Wesley recommends fasting on Fridays. Cf. *An Earnest Appeal to Men of Reason and Religion* (1743), in *Works*, 11:79.

[41] Cf. Wesley, 'Treatise on Baptism', *Works* (Jackson), 10:188–90 and Wesley's comment on Colossians 2:12 in his *Explanatory Notes upon the New Testament* (1755).

[42] See Wesley's preface to *The Sunday Service*. Even after making *The Sunday Service* available for British Methodists, it appears that he preferred the BCP: see Baker, *John Wesley*, 255.

[43] JWJ, 27–8 June 1740, 19:158–9. See also note 135 in chapter 2. He innovated from Anglican practice by using hymns and extemporaneous prayer when the Eucharist was offered in Methodist settings: Dearing, *Wesleyan and Tractarian Worship*, 12–13.

[44] JWJ, 1 April 1759, 21:181.

of Band Societies were instructed to be at the Lord's Table at every opportunity.[45] Despite his adherence in Georgia to the strict separation of catechumens and communicants as found in the *Apostolic Constitutions*, Wesley's intention was to increase the number of communicants. He was therefore deeply gratified to regularly administer the sacrament to crowds running into the hundreds in the 1780s.[46]

Henry Rack has accurately stated that 'It is in the Wesleys' eucharistic doctrine and practice that the most lasting effects of Nonjuror influence can be seen.'[47] John and Charles Wesley's *Hymns on the Lord's Supper* (1745) show that nearly a decade after returning from Georgia the Wesleys had retained their High Church theology of the Eucharist and desired to pass it on to the Methodists. The hymns clearly refer to three of the usages of the Nonjurors: the mixture of water and wine (hymns 31, 37, 74, 75), oblation (hymns 116, 118, 121–6), and invocation (hymns 16, 72) and draw on the *Apostolic Constitutions*.[48] He also later defended prayers for the dead.[49] Wesley's note on I Corinthians 11:25 ('Do this in remembrance of me') also reflects High Church theology: 'The antient Sacrifices were in remembrance of Sin. This Sacrifice once offered is still represented in the remembrance of the Remission of Sins.'[50] Wesley bequeathed extracts from William Wall's *The History of Infant Baptism* to the Methodists in his *Thoughts on Infant-Baptism* (1751). In addition to publishing editions of works that advocated trine immersion as the ancient baptismal practice, there is also some inconclusive evidence that Wesley continued to rebaptize Dissenters.[51]

Though Wesley discovered that his life's mission was not that of a patristics scholar, his interest in the Church Fathers was no mere whim of his early years. Ted Campbell listed 201 references to the Church Fathers in Wesley's writings, most of which occur after 1738 in his apologetic works.[52] Extracts

[45] 'Directions given to the Band Societies' (1744), in *Works*, 9:79.

[46] Rattenbury, *Eucharistic Hymns*, 5–6.

[47] Rack, 'The Wesleys and Manchester', 19; cf. F. Ernest Stoeffler, 'Tradition and Renewal in the Ecclesiology of John Wesley', in Bernd Jaspert and Rudolph Mohr (eds), *Traditio—Krisis—Renovatio aus Theologischer Sicht: Festschrift Winfried Zeller zum 65. Geburtstag* (Marburg, 1976), 312. See Rack, 'The Wesleys and Manchester', 17–23 for other suggestions on the legacy of the Nonjurors on Wesley's post-1738 theology and churchmanship.

[48] For example, *Apostolic Constitutions* VIII.12.39 in hymn 16; Karen B. Westerfield Tucker, 'Wesley's Emphases on Worship and the Means of Grace', in Randy L. Maddox and Jason E. Vickers (eds), *The Cambridge Companion to John Wesley* (Cambridge, 2010), 230–1.

[49] See note 90 in chapter 2.

[50] *Explanatory Notes Upon the New Testament* (1755).

[51] Evidence from Wesley's *Journal* seems to indicate that he continued to rebaptize Dissenters: JWJ, 25 January 1739, 10 February 1767, 26 December 1785, 19:32, 22:70, 23:383; CWJ, 20 October 1738, p. 150. It is unclear whether the two women mentioned in the later cases had been baptised, although both had been raised Baptists; in the first case, Wesley mentions that the man baptised was '(late an Anabaptist)', indicating that he was probably already baptised. See also the conclusions by Holland, *Baptism in Early Methodism*, 8 and Brian J. N. Galliers's 'Baptism in the Writings of John Wesley', *PWHS* 32 (1960), 156.

[52] Campbell, 125–34.

from Clement of Rome, Polycarp, Ignatius, and Macarius (all of whom Wesley read in Georgia) received pride of place in the first volume of his *Christian Library* (1749). In his *Address to the Clergy* (1756) aimed at giving advice to sympathetic clergy, Wesley recommended gaining 'knowledge of the Fathers' whom he called 'the most authentic commentators on Scripture, as being both the nearest the fountain, and eminently endued with that Spirit by whom all Scripture was given.'[53] After Georgia, Wesley returned to the Anglican doctrine in Article VI that there can be no 'rule of faith' regarding any doctrine or practice that cannot be proven by scripture.[54] Together with this he considered the ante-Nicene Fathers authoritative 'next to' scripture, yet he believed that it was not difficult to find examples of the Fathers and councils contradicting one another.[55] On occasion Wesley listed his most admired Fathers, which typically included the Apostolic Fathers: Clement of Rome, Ignatius, and Polycarp; the ante-Nicene Fathers: Tertullian, Origen, Clement of Alexandria, and Cyprian; and the fourth-century ascetic monks Chrysostom, Basil, Macarius, and especially Ephraem Syrus.[56]

Wesley did not abandon his belief in the primitive church as a normative model for doctrine and practice.[57] He rhetorically asked his critics, 'Why, must not every man, whether clergyman or layman, be in some respects "like the apostles", or go to hell? Can any man be saved if he be not holy like the Apostles?'[58] He continued to highly idealize the early church, even going so far as to critique William Cave's *Primitive Christianity* for 'relating every weak thing they ever said or did'.[59] Despite his professed dislike for controversy, he could be roused to defend the Fathers in print by Dr Conyers Middleton's *A Free Inquiry into the Miraculous Powers of the Primitive Church* (1749) and

---

[53] *Works* (Jackson), 10:484.

[54] For example, *A Letter to the Reverend Dr. Conyers Middleton* (1749), *Works* (Jackson), 10:14. See also his works against Roman Catholic doctrine and practice cited in note 55.

[55] *A Letter to the Reverend Dr. Conyers Middleton*, *Works* (Jackson), 10:14; Wesley to Joseph Benson (22 February 1782), *Letters* (Telford), 7:106; *The Advantage of the Members of the Church of England, Over Those of the Church of Rome* (1753), *Works* (Jackson), 10:134. John Williams, *A Roman Catechism* (1756), ed. JW, *Works* (Jackson), 10:94, 128, asserts in opposition to the Roman Catholic Church that it was not they but the Apostles who were infallible. The treatise also advocates the Vincentian Canon as a guide for Christian doctrine and practice. The *Roman Catechism* is lightly abridged from Williams's *A Catechism Truly Representing the Doctrines and Practices of the Church of Rome, with an Answer Thereunto* (1686).

[56] See his lists in 'On Laying the Foundation of the New Chapel' (1777), *Works*, 3:586 and *Address to the Clergy, Works* (Jackson), 10:484. Irenaeus, Augustine, and Ambrose are occasionally found in Wesley's lists. On this subject, see Campbell, 'Wesley's Use of the Church Fathers'.

[57] *A Letter to the Reverend Dr. Conyers Middleton*, *Works* (Jackson), 10:79; cf. Bowmer, 235; Outler, 'Introduction', in *Works*, 1:59. Campbell has argued that Wesley's emphasis was on the spiritual and moral purity of the primitive Christians and his concern was primarily 'programmatic' in that he appealed to the primitive church in the hope of reforming the Church of England.

[58] *A Farther Appeal to Men of Reason and Religion* (1745), *Works*, 11:295.

[59] JWJ, 6 October 1750, 20:363.

against Roman Catholic doctrine in several treatises.[60] Wesley commented that Middleton's erroneous work was largely derived from Jean Daillé, who by then had been considered the chief enemy of Anglican patristic scholars for over a century.[61] In 1774, Wesley commented that 'During the twelve festival days [of Christmas] we had the Lord's Supper daily, a little emblem of the Primitive Church. May we be followers of them in all things as they were of Christ!'[62] This note underscores the continuity in Wesley's thought on the purity of the primitive church as a model for devotional practice, though he was also willing to omit some practices, such as 'prescribing hair-shirts and bodily austerities', which he would have seen in a more favourable light during his time in Georgia.[63] Nonetheless, Christian discipline—which Wesley believed the primitive church had dependably handed down—remained very important to him.[64] Wesley continued to have such a regard for apostolic doctrine that in the preface to his collected *Works* (1771–4) he declared all he had written subject to the judgement of 'Scripture, reason, and Christian antiquity'.[65] He remained committed to Christian antiquity as a sure guide for doctrine: 'But whatever doctrine is *new* must be *wrong*; for the *old* religion is the only *true* one; and no doctrine can be right unless it is the very same "which was from the beginning." '[66] In this regard, Wesley was following the common Anglican and ancient ideal of opposing innovation and echoing the Vincentian Canon.[67]

Wesley's position on apostolicity evolved to resemble the views of the early Anglican reformers and later Nonconformists that the church was apostolic not due to '*uninterrupted*' apostolic succession but because it held to the apostolic faith.[68] He continued to believe that primitive Christianity provided a normative model to be restored. Wesley had no doubt that the doctrine, discipline,

---

[60] *A Letter to the Reverend Dr. Conyers Middleton*, *Works* (Jackson), 10:1–79; JWJ, 2 January 1749, 20:262; *Roman Catechism* (1756), *Works* (Jackson), 10:86–128; *Advantage of the Members of the Church of England* (1753), *Works* (Jackson), 10:133–40; Williams, *Popery Calmly Considered* (1779), ed. JW, *Works* (Jackson), 10:140–58. *Popery Calmly Considered* is also derived from Williams's *Catechism*.

[61] JWJ, 28 January 1749, 20:262.

[62] JWJ, 25 December 1774, 22:441; cf. JWJ, 30 March 1777, 23:45–6.

[63] *A Plain Account of the Methodists* (1746), *Works*, 9:269.

[64] JW to James Hutton (27 November 1738), *Works*, 25:593. In Williams's *Roman Catechism*, both private and, when appropriate, public confession and public penance are advocated: *Works* (Jackson), 10:123–4, 125.

[65] *The Works of the Rev. John Wesley, M.A. Late Fellow of Lincoln-College, Oxford*, ed. JW (Bristol, 1771), 1:vii. Randy L. Maddox has argued that like the Anglican reformers and Church Fathers, most of Wesley's writings are works of practical theology: 'Introduction to Wesley's Doctrinal and Controversial Treatises', *Works*, 12:1–5.

[66] Sermon 'On Sin in Believers' (1763), *Works*, 1:324; I John 1:1.

[67] See note 35 in chapter 1. 'In religion I am for as few innovations as possible': JW to Walter Churchey (20 June 1789), *Letters* (Telford), 8:145; cf. Outler's notes in *Works*, 1:58–9, 550 n. 2. Henry Chadwick, 'The Early Church', in Richard Harries and Henry Mayr-Harting (eds), *Christianity: Two Thousand Years* (Oxford, 2001), 3.

[68] Cornwall, *Visible and Apostolic*, 29.

and practice of the primitive church was embodied by the Methodist movement. For Wesley, Methodism was the restoration of primitive Christianity. Though the people called Methodists were not without their faults, their basic pattern was that of the primitive church.[69] When Bishop Richard Smalbroke charged the Methodists with confounding 'the *extraordinary* with the *ordinary* operations of the Spirit', in opposition to the scriptural interpretation of Chrysostom, Jerome, Origen and Athanasius, Wesley rigorously defended the Methodists of the accusation by extensive quotation from the same Fathers.[70] The equation of Methodism and primitive Christianity was expressed in both prose and poetry. In the first edition of John and Charles Wesley's *Hymns and Sacred Poems* (1739), they included a poem based on Clement of Alexandria's 'Description of a Perfect Christian' inspired by the fourth book of his *Stromateis*. A few years later, Wesley again utilized this work as the basic source for his apologetic *The Character of a Methodist* (1742).[71] Wesley concluded his *An Earnest Appeal to Men of Reason and Religion* (2nd edn, 1743) with the poem 'Primitive Christianity', setting forth the holiness of the early Christians as the goal of all earnest Christians.[72]

However, by the time he published an abridged version of Johann Lorenz von Mosheim's *Institutionum Historiae Ecclesiasticae Antiquae et Recentioris* (1755) as *A Concise Ecclesiastical History* (1781), Wesley had come to the view that 'the mystery of iniquity'[73] had affected the church even in the apostolic age, a point repeatedly made in sermons he published in the 1780s.[74] When

---

[69] For an example of Wesley's willingness to criticize decline in Methodist vitality, see his sermon 'The Wisdom of God's Counsels' (1784), *Works*, 2:559–66.

[70] *A Farther Appeal to Men of Reason and Religion* (1745), in *Works*, 11:141–2, 154–63.

[71] To the Editor of Lloyd's Evening Post [26 March 1767], JWJ, 22:72; cf. JW to Miss March (30 November 1774), *Letters* (Telford), 6:129; Knox, in Southey, *Life of Wesley*, 2:300.

[72] *Works*, 11:90–4.

[73] 2 Thessalonians 2:7.

[74] *A Concise Ecclesiastical History, From the Birth of Christ, to the Beginning of the Present Century* (London, 1781), 1:viii; Sermons 'The Mystery of Iniquity (1783), *Works*, 2:452–70; 'The Wisdom of God's Counsels' (1784), *Works*, 2:552–66; 'Of Former Times' (1787), *Works*, 3:442–53; 'On Attending the Church Service' (1787), *Works*, 3:469–70; Darren Schmidt, 'The Pattern of Revival: John Wesley's Vision of "Iniquity" and "Godliness" in Church History', in Cooper and Gregory (eds), *Revival and Resurgence*, 142–53. Not surprisingly, in addition to scripture, Wesley made his argument by appealing to testimonies of decline from Church Fathers, namely, Tertullian and Cyprian: *Works*, 2:461–2; 3:450–1.

It is difficult to determine to what extent the *Concise Ecclesiastical History* represents Wesley's view on the early church. Significant portions of the work relating to the primitive church match his beliefs in Georgia (e.g. reverence for the Apostles, unity of doctrine, love feasts, community of goods, deaconesses, hymns, weekly Lord's Supper, baptism by immersion, fasting on Wednesdays and Fridays), and his modified opinions to the 1780s (e.g. scripture as the only rule of faith, the Apostles prescribed no precise form of church government, original equality of bishops and presbyters), as well as his late views (e.g. corruption of the church not long after Pentecost, mixed views of the Church Fathers). The book sets primitive simplicity and developing ritualism in opposition, has an anti-institutional streak, and criticizes the 'spurious' *Apostolic Constitutions* and *Canons* and their 'melancholy author' (p. 61). The overall tone of the work is

Constantine 'called himself a Christian', was seen by Wesley as the major event leading to the fall of the church, yet he declared that in no age was the church better than the present one apart from the short period immediately following Pentecost.[75] This suggests that Wesley's view altered somewhat from Anglican pre-Nicene primitivism in the direction of a Pietist conception of New Testament primitivism, yet he never ceased to believe that examples of pure Christianity could be identified up to and beyond the age of Constantine.[76]

Wesley saw Methodist worship and devotional and charitable practice as modelled on the imitation of the early church, much of which was mediated to him by High Churchmen and Nonjurors. He subsequently continued to value and justify by primitive precedent Methodist societies (including their singing and use of class tickets), deaconesses, frequent/constant communion, trine immersion, baptismal sponsors, visiting the sick, poorhouses for widows and others in need, love feasts, watchnights, weekly fasts, festivals, community of goods, and penitent bands.[77]

Wesley persistently argued that Methodism was in its purest sense simply 'the old religion, the religion of the Bible, the religion of the primitive church, the religion of the Church of England.'[78] This equation of Methodism and the primitive church was shared by Wesley's Methodist contemporaries, who memorialized on his tombstone their view that his mission was

> to *revive, enforce,* and *defend*
> The Pure, Apostolical Doctrines and Practices of
> The PRIMITIVE CHURCH.[79]

rather uninspiring and more critical of the primitive church than the bulk of Wesley's writings, with the possible exception of his sermons in the 1780s.

[75] Sermons 'The Mystery of Iniquity' (1783), *Works*, 2:463 and n. 71; 'Of Former Times' (1787), *Works*, 3:448; Thomas Buchan, 'John Wesley and the Constantinian Fall of the Church: Historiographical Indications of Pietist Influences', in Collins Winn et. al. (eds), *Pietist Impulse*, 146–60.

[76] Buchan, 'John Wesley', 157; cf. Ted A. Campbell, 'Christian Tradition, John Wesley, and Evangelicalism', *Anglican Theological Review*, 74 (1992), 60–1, 67; Rack, 'The Wesleys and Manchester', 23. Further study is needed to test Buchan's thesis that Pietist historiography tempered Wesley's High Church primitivism.

[77] Campbell, 86–9, 94–100, 107–8; Dearing, *Wesleyan and Tractarian Worship*, 31–2, 46, 49, 53–4; Madden, 'A Cheap, Safe and Natural Medicine', 272; John Walsh, 'John Wesley and the Community of Goods', in Keith Robbins (ed.), *Protestant Evangelicalism: Britain, Ireland, Germany and America c.1750–c.1950. Essays in Honour of W. R. Ward*, Studies in Church History Subsidia, 7 (Oxford: Blackwell, 1990), 25–50. Many of these examples can be found in Wesley's *A Plain Account of the Methodists* (1746), *Works*, 9:254–80.

[78] 'On Laying the Foundation of the New Chapel' (1777), *Works*, 3:585; cf. Sermon 'The Signs of the Times' (1787), *Works*, 2:527 and *The Character of a Methodist* (1742), *Works*, 9:30–46.

[79] Whitehead, *Life of the Rev. John Wesley*, 2:458.

Bibliography

Primary Sources

An Account of the Proceedings in the Convocation...(London, 1706).

An Account of the Sufferings of the Persecuted Protestants in the Archbishoprick of Saltzburg...(London: J. Downing, 1732).

The Apostolic Constitutions and *Apostolic Canons* in Whiston, William, *Primitive Christianity Reviv'd*. Vol. 2: *The Constitutions of the Holy Apostles, by Clement; in English and in Greek; with the Various Readings from all of the Manuscripts* (London: for the Author, 1711) and Roberts, Alexander, James Donaldson, and A. Cleveland Coxe (eds), *Ante-Nicene Fathers*, vol. 7 (Peabody, MA: Hendrickson, 1994).

The Athenian Oracle: Being an Entire Collection of all the Valuable Questions and Answers in the Old Athenian Mercuries. Intermix'd with Many Cases in Divinity, History, Philosophy, Mathematics, Love, Poetry, 2nd edn corrected, 4 vols (London: Andrew Bell, 1706).

[Atterbury, Francis], *Some Proceedings in the Convocation, A.D. 1705: Faithfully Represented* (London: Jonah Bowyer, 1708).

Berkeley, George, *Passive Obedience: or, the Christian Doctrine of not Resisting the Supreme Power, Proved and Vindicated upon the Principles of the Law of Nature* (Dublin: Francis Dickson, 1712).

Beveridge, William, *Synodikon, sive Pandectae Canonum SS. Apostolorum et Conciliorum Ecclesia Graeca Receptorum*...2 vols (Oxonii: E. Theatro Sheldoniano, 1672).

——, *Codex Canonum Ecclesiae Primitivae Vindicatus ac Illustratus* (Londoni: S. Roycroft, 1678).

——, *Private Thoughts upon Religion, Digested into Twelve Articles, with Practical Resolutions form'd Thereupon* (London: R. Smith, 1709).

[Birchley, William a pseudonym for John Austin], *Devotions in the Ancient Way of Offices. With Psalms, Hymns, and Prayers for Every Day of the Week, and Every Holiday in the Year. To which are added, Occasional Offices, and other Devotions in the same Ancient Way. Reform'd by a Person of Quality, and Publish'd by George Hickes*, D.D., 6th edn (London: D. Midwinter, 1730).

Boltzius, Johann, 'The Secret Diary of Pastor Johann Martin Boltzius', ed. George F. Jones, *GHQ* 53 (1969), 78–110.

——, *The Letters of Johann Martin Boltzius, Lutheran Pastor in Ebenezer, Georgia: German Pietism in Colonial America, 1733–1765*, ed. and trans. Russell C. Kleckley, 2 vols (Lewiston, NY: Edward Mellen Press, 2009).

Bray, Thomas, *Apostolick Charity, Its Nature and Excellence Consider'd in a Discourse Upon Dan. 12.3 Preached at St. Paul's, at the Ordination of some Protestant Missionaries to be sent into the Plantations* (London: E. Holt, 1700).

——, *Several Circular Letters to the Clergy of Mary-land: Subsequent to Their Late Visitation, to Enforce Such Resolutions as Were Taken Therein* (London: William Downing, 1701).

[——], *Missionalia: or, a Collection of Missionary Pieces Relating to the Conversion of the Heathen; both the African Negroes and American Indians* (London: W. Roberts, 1727).

Brett, Thomas, *A Collection of the Principal Liturgies, Used by the Christian Church in the Celebration of the Holy Eucharist: Particularly the Ancient, viz. the Clementine, as it stands in the Book call'd The Apostolical Constitutions; the Liturgies of S. James, S. Mark, S. Chrysostom, S. Basil, &c. Translated into English by several Hands. With a Dissertation upon Them, Shewing their Usefulness and Authority, and pointing out their several Corruptions and Interpolations* (London: Richard King, 1720).

Brevint, Dan[iel], *The Christian Sacrament and Sacrifice: by Way of Discourse, Meditation, & Prayer upon the Nature, Parts, and Blessings of the Holy Communion* (Oxford: At the Theater, 1673).

Bull, George, *A Companion for the Candidates of Holy Orders. Or, the Great Importance and Principal Duties of the Priestly Office* (London: George James for Richard Smith, 1714).

Burnet, Gilbert, *A Discourse of the Pastoral Care* (London: R. R. for Ric. Chiswell, 1692).

Canons and Constitutions Ecclesiastical (1604), in Gerald Bray (ed.), *The Anglican Canons, 1529–1947*, Church of England Record Society, 6 (Woodbridge: Boydell Press, 1998).

Cave, William, *Primitive Christianity: or, the Religion of the Antient Christians, in the First Ages of the Gospel*, 7th edn (London: Daniel Midwinter and Benjamin Cowse, 1714).

——, *Primitive Christianity*, ed. John Wesley, in *A Christian Library*, vol. 31 (Bristol: E. Farley, 1753), 151–298.

Causton, Thomas, 'Journal of Thomas Causton Esq. 1st Bailif [*sic*] of Savannah', 24 June 1737, ed. Trevor R. Reese, in *Our First Visit in America: Early Reports from the Colony of Georgia, 1732–1740* (Savannah: Beehive Press, 1974), 243–77.

Cheyne, George, *An Essay of Health and Long Life* (London: George Strahan, 1724).

Clayton, John, 'Catalogue of the Library of the Revd John Clayton M.A. Fellow of the Collegiate Church Manchester', Manchester Central Library, MS, BRG 109.2 CLI.

Cole, R. E. G. (ed.), 'Speculum Dioceseos Lincolniensis Sub Episcopis Gul: Wake Et Edm: Gibson A.D. 1705–1723', *Publications of the Lincoln Record Society*, 4 (1913).

Coke, Thomas, *The Substance of a Sermon Preached…On the Death of the Rev. John Wesley*, 2nd edn (London: G. Paramore, 1791).

—— and Henry Moore, *The Life of the Rev. John Wesley, A.M.* (London: G. Paramore, 1792).

A Collection of Papers Printed by Order of the Society for the Propagation of the Gospel in Foreign Parts (London: Joseph Downing, 1715).

A Collection of Psalms and Divine Hymns, Suited to the Great Festivals of the Church, for Morning and Evening and other Occasions: To which is added, A Table of Psalms on practical Subjects, which may be of Use to Parish-Clarks (London: J. Downing, 1727).

Collier, Jeremy, *Reasons for Restoring some Prayers and Directions: as they Stand in the Communion-Service of the First English Reform'd Liturgy, Complied by the Bishops in the 2d and 3d Years of the Reign of King Edward VI*, 2nd edn (London: John Morphew, 1717).

The Colonial Records of the State of Georgia, vols 1–19, 21–6, ed. Allen D. Chandler and Lucian L. Knight (Atlanta, 1904–16); vols 20, 27–9, ed. Kenneth Coleman and

Milton Ready (Athens: University of Georgia Press, 1982–5); vols 30–2, ed. Kenneth Coleman (Athens: University of Georgia Press, 1985–9).

Vol. 1, *Georgia Charter, Laws, and Minutes of Trustees, 1732–52.*

Vol. 2, *The Minutes of the Common Council of the Trustees for Establishing the Colony of Georgia in America.*

Vol. 4, *Stephens' Journal 1737–1740.*

Vol. 5, *Journal of the Earl of Egmont, First President of the Board of Trustees,* From 14 June 1738, to 25 May 1744.

Vol. 20, *Original Papers, Correspondence to the Trustees, James Oglethorpe, and Others 1732–1735.*

Vol. 21, *Original Papers, Correspondence, Trustees, General Oglethorpe and Others, 1735–1737.*

Vol. 22.1, *Original Papers, Correspondence, Trustees, General Oglethorpe and Others, 1737–1739.*

Vol. 22.2, *Original Papers, Correspondence, Trustees, General Oglethorpe and Others, 1737–1740.*

Vol. 29, *Trustees' Letter Book, 1732–1738.*

Vol. 32, *Entry Books of Commissions, Powers, Instructions, Leases, Grants of Land,* etc. by the Trustees, 1732–1738.

A Communion Office, Taken Partly from Primitive Liturgies, and Partly from the First English Reformed Common-Prayer-Book: Together with Offices for Confirmation, and the Visitation of the Sick (London: James Bettenham/London: J. Smith, 1718).

A Copy of the Circular Letter from the Society at London, for Promoting Christian Knowledge &c: to Their Residing and Corresponding Members for the Year, 1735 (Dublin: George Grierson, 1735).

Coulter, E. Merton and Albert B. Saye (eds), *A List of Early Settlers of Georgia* (Athens: University of Georgia Press, 1949).

'An Extract from *The Country Parson's Advice to his Parishioners',* ed. John Wesley, in *A Christian Library,* vol. 26 (London: J. Kershaw, 1826), 425–522.

Deacon, Thomas, *The Doctrine of the Church of Rome Concerning Purgatory: Proved to be Contrary to Catholick Tradition, and Inconsistent with the Necessary Duty of Praying for the Dead, as Practised in the Ancient Church* (London: Richard King, 1718).

——, *A Compleat Collection of Devotions both Publick and Private: Taken from the Apostolical Constitutions, the Ancient Liturgies, and the Common Prayer Book of the Church of England* (London: for the author, 1734).

——, *The Order of the Divine Offices of the Orthodox British Church: Containing the Holy Liturgy, The Morning and Evening Prayer, The Penitential Office, And the Form and Manner of Making, Ordaining, and Consecrating Bishops, Priests, Deacons, and Deaconesses: Together with other Occasional Offices as authorized by the Bishops of the said Church. To be used in the Publick Assemblies of the Faithful* (London, 1734).

——, *A Full, True and Comprehensive View of Christianity: Containing a short Historical Account of Religion from the Creation of the World to the Fourth Century after our Lord Jesus Christ: As also the Complete Duty of a Christian in relation to Faith, Practice, Worship, and Rituals…laid down in Two Catechisms, a Shorter and a Longer,…to* which is prefixed a Discourse upon the Design of these Catechisms...(London: S. Newton, 1747).

Delany, Mary, *The Autobiography and Correspondence of Mary Granville, Mrs. Delany: with Interesting Reminiscences of King George the Third and Queen Charlotte*, ed. Lady Llanover, 6 vols (London: Ricahrd Bentley, 1861–2).

[Delany, Patrick], *The Doctrine of the Abstinence from Blood Defended...*(London: C. Rivington, 1734).

Drew, Samuel, *The Life of the Rev. Thomas Coke, LL.D....*(London: T. Cordeux, 1817).

Echard, Laurence, *A General Ecclesiastical History from the Nativity of our Blessed Saviour to the First Establishment of Christianity by Humane Laws, under the Emperour Constantine the Great* (London: W. Bowyer, 1702).

Ephraim, the Syrian, *A Serious Exhortation to Repentance and Sorrow for Sin, and a Strict and Mortified Life* (London: William Boyer, 1731).

Fell, John, *The Life of the most Learned, Reverend and Pious Dr. H[enry] Hammond* (London: J. Flescher, 1661).

Fleury, Claude, *The Manners of the Antient Christians*, ed. John Wesley, 5th edn (London: G. Paramore, 1791).

Fulham Papers, Lambeth Palace Library, American Colonial Section, vol. IV, Massachusetts, 1698–1729.

Fulham Papers, Lambeth Palace Library, American Colonial Section, vol. IX, South Carolina, 1703–34.

Francke, Augustus Hermannus, *Nicodemus, or, a Treatise against the Fear of Man...*(London: Joseph Downing, 1706).

A Further Account of the Sufferings of the Persecuted Protestants in the Archbishoprick of Saltzburg: Taken from Authentick Papers (London: Jos. Downing, 1733).

Gibson, Edmund, *Two Letters of the Lord Bishop of London: the First, to the Masters and Mistresses of Families in the English Plantations abroad; Exhorting them to Encourage and Promote the Instruction of their Negroes in the Christian Faith. The Second, to the Missionaries there; Directing them to distribute the said Letter, and Exhorting them to give their Assistance towards the Instruction of the Negroes within their several Parishes* (London: Joseph Downing, 1727).

Godwyn, Morgan, *The Negro's & Indians Advocate, Suing for their Admission to the Church: or, A Persuasive to the Instructing and Baptizing of the Negro's and Indians in our Plantations...*(London: for the author, 1680).

Halyburton, Thomas, *An Abstract of the Life and Death of the Reverend Learned and Pious Mr. Tho. Halyburton, M.A. Professor of Divinity in the University of St. Andrews*, ed. John Wesley and George Whitefield (London: John Oswald, 1739).

Hampson, John, *Memoirs of the Late Rev. John Wesley, A.M. With a Review of His Life and Writings, and a History of Methodism...*3 vols (Sunderland: James Graham, 1791).

Herbert, George, *The Temple* (Cambridge: Thom. Buck, 1714).

Hickes, George, *Two Treatises: One of the Christian Priesthood, the other of the Dignity of the Episcopal Order*, 2 vols (London: W.B., 1707).

——, 'A Letter to the Author', in R[oger] Laurence, *Lay Baptism Invalid*, 2nd edn (London: J. Baker and A. Collins, 1709), no pagination.

Hooker, Richard, *The Works of that Learned and Judicious Divine, Mr. Richard Hooker: With an Account of His Life and Death, by Isaac Walton*, 2 vols (Oxford: At the University Press, 1850).

Horneck, Anthony, *The Happy Ascetick: Or, the Best Exercise: To which is added, A Letter to a Person of Quality, Concerning the Holy Lives of the Primitive Christians* ([London]: T. N. for Henry Mortlock, 1681).

——, *Questions and Answers Concerning the Two Religions: Viz. That of the Church of England, and the other, of the Church of Rome* (London: Joseph Downing, 1727).

——, 'Letter to a Person of Quality Concerning the Lives of the Primitive Christians', ed. John Wesley, in *A Christian Library*, vol. 29 (Bristol: E. Farley, 1753), 111–38.

'The Humble Representation of the Grand Jury for the Town and County of Savannah', MARC, MAW MS 260.

Humphreys, David, *An Historical Account of the Incorporated Society for the Propagation of the Gospel in Foreign Parts* (London: Joseph Downing, 1730).

Ingham, Benjamin, *Diary of an Oxford Methodist Benjamin Ingham, 1733–1734*, ed. Richard P. Heitzenrater (Durham: Duke University Press, 1985).

——, Journal in Luke Tyerman, *The Oxford Methodists* (London: Hodder and Stoughton, 1873), 63–80.

——, MS Journal, MARC Lamplough Collection, MS 657 and Lincoln Cathedral Library, MS 299.

Jewel, John, *The True Copies of the Letters betwene the reuerend father in God Iohn Bisshop of Sarum and D. Cole vpon occasion of a Sermon that the said Bishop preached before the Quenes Maiestie, and hir most honorable Counsel* (London: John Day, 1560).

——, *Apologia pro Ecclesia Anglicana* (1562).

Johnson, John, *The Unbloody Sacrifice, and Altar, Unvail'd and Supported. In which the nature of the Eucharist is Explain'd according to the Sentiments of the Christian Church of the four first Centuries. Proving, That the Eucharist is a proper Material Sacrifice, That it is both Eucharistick and Propitiatory, That it is to be offer'd by proper Officers, That the Oblation is to be made on a proper Altar, That it is to be properly consum'd by Manducation*...2 vols (London: Robert Knaplock, 1714, 1718). [Volume 2 subtitle: *Shewing, The Agreement and Disagreement of the Eucharist with the Sacrifices of the Antients, and the Excellency of the former. The great Moment of the Eucharist as both a Feast, and Sacrifice. The Necessity of frequent Communion. The Unity of the Eucharist. The Nature of Excommunication. And the Primitive Method of Preparation. With Devotions for the Altar.*]

——, *A Collection of Discourses, Dissertations, and Sermons*, 2 vols (London: Edw. Cave, 1728).

Jones, George Fenwick (ed.), *Detailed Reports of the Salzburger Emigrants Who Settled in America...Edited by Samuel Urlsperger*, vols. 3–5 (Athens: University of Georgia Press, 1972–80).

Kettlewell, John, *The Practical Believer: Or, the Articles of the Apostles Creed, Drawn Out to Form a True Christians Heart and Practice*, 3rd edn (London: J. Heptinstall, 1713).

[King, Lord Peter], *An Enquiry into the Constitution, Discipline, Unity & Worship of the Primitive Church, That Flourish'd within the first Three Hundred Years after Christ: Faithfully Collected out of the Extant Writings of those Ages* (1712).

The King's Pious Proclamation, for Encouragement of Piety and Vertue, and for the Supressing and Punishing of Vice, Profaneness and Immorality; With an Abbreviate of the Laws to that Purpose... (Edinburgh, 1727).

Knox, Alexander, 'Remarks on the Life and Character of John Wesley', in Robert Southey, *The Life of Wesley and the Rise and Progress of Methodism*, vol. 2 (London: Longman, Brown, Green, Longmans, and Roberts, 1858), 293–360.

Lactantius, *A Relation of the Death of the Primitive Persecutors*, ed. Gilbert Burnet (London: A. Baldwin, 1713).

Lane, Mills (ed.), *General Oglethorpe's Georgia: Colonial Letters 1733–1737*, vol. 1 (Savannah: Beehive Press, 1975).

Law, William, *A Practical Treatise upon Christian Perfection* (London: William and John Innys, 1726).

——, *A Serious Call to a Devout and Holy Life* (London: William Innys, 1729).

Le Jau, Francis, 'The Carolina Chronicle of Dr. Francis Le Jau 1706–1717', ed. Frank J. Klingberg, *University of California Publications in History*, 53 (1956).

Leslie, Charles, *A Discourse Proving the Divine Institution of Water Baptism: wherein the Quaker-Arguments against it are Collected and Refuted* (London: C. Brome, 1697).

'The Life and Conversation of that Holy Man Mr. *John Wesley*, during his Abode at *Georgia*', Bodleian Library, Oxford, Rawlinson MS J., fo. 5.

Laud, William, *A Summarie of Devotions* (Oxford: William Hall, 1667).

Losa, Francisco de, *The Life of Gregory Lopez*, ed. John Wesley, in *A Christian Library*, vol. 27 (London: J. Kershaw, 1826), 387–438.

[Marshall, Nathaniel], *The Penitential Discipline of the Primitive Church, for the First 400 Years after Christ: Together with its Declension from the Fifth Century, Downwards to its Present State, Impartially Represented. By a Presbyter of the Church of England* (London: W. Taylor, 1714).

[Mather, Cotton], *An Epistle to the Christian Indians, giving them a Short Account, of what the English Desire them to Know and to do, in order to their Happiness* (Boston: Bartholomew Green, 1700).

Methodist Magazine (1798–1821).

Moore, Francis, *A Voyage to Georgia...* (London: J. Robinson, 1744).

Mosheim, Johann Lorenz, *A Concise Ecclesiastical History, From the Birth of Christ, to the Beginning of the Present Century*, ed. John Wesley, 4 vols (London: J. Paramore, 1781).

Moore, Henry, *The Life of the Rev. John Wesley, A.M.*, 2 vols (London: J. Kershaw, 1824).

[Nelson, Robert], *The Great Duty of Frequenting the Christian Sacrifice, and the Nature of the Preparation Required: with Suitable Devotions. Partly Collected from the Ancient Liturgies* (London: W. Bowyer, 1706).

[——], *A Companion for the Festivals and Fasts of the Church of England: with Collects and Prayers for Each Solemnity*, 15th edn (London: J. Walthoe, 1732).

Newman, Henry, *Henry Newman's Salzburger Letterbooks*, ed. George Fenwick Jones (Athens: University of Georgia Press, 1966).

Newspapers: *The Daily Gazetteer, The Daily Journal, The Gentleman's Magazine, The London Evening-Post, Read's Weekly Journal, Or, British-Gazetteer, The Weekly History, The Weekly Miscellany*.

Oglethorpe, James Edward, *A New and Accurate Account of the Provinces of South-Carolina and Georgia* (1732), in Rodney M. Baine (ed.), *The Publications of James Edward Oglethorpe* (Athens: University of Georgia Press, 1994), 200–40.

——, 'Bringing Moravians to Georgia: Three Latin Letters from James Oglethorpe to Count Nicholas von Zinzendorf', ed. George Fenwick Jones, trans. David Noble, *GHQ* 80 (1996), 847–58.

Outler, Albert C. (ed.), *John Wesley* (Oxford: Oxford University Press, 1964).

Patrick, Simon, *The Christian Sacrifice. A Treatise Shewing the Necessity, End, and Manner of Receiving the Holy Communion: Together with Suitable Prayers and Meditations for every Month in the Year; and the Principal Festivals in Memory of our Blessed Saviour*, 16th edn. (London: T. Wood, 1732).

Perceval, John, first earl of Egmont, *Manuscripts of the Earl of Egmont. Diary of Viscount Percival afterwards First Earl of Egmont*, ed. R. A. Roberts, 3 vols, Historical Manuscripts Commission (London: His Majesty's Stationary Office, 1920–3).

——, *The Journal of the Earl of Egmont: Abstract of the Trustees Proceedings for Establishing the Colony of Georgia 1732–1738*, ed. Robert G. McPherson (Athens: University of Georgia Press, 1962).

Plato's Dialogue of the Immortality of the Soul, trans. Mr. Theobald (London: Bernard Lintott, 1713).

Poole, Matthew, *A Dialogue between a Popish Priest, and an English Protestant. Wherein the Principal Points and Arguments of both Religions, Are truly Proposed, and fully Examined* (London, 1735).

The Progress of Methodism in Bristol: Or, the Methodist Unmask'd. Wherein the Doctrines, Discipline, Policy, Divisions and Successes of that Novel Sect are Fully Detected, and Properly Display'd, in Hudibrastick Verse (Bristol: J. Watts, 1743).

Pulpit Elocution: Or Characters and Principles of the Most Popular Preachers, Of Each Denomination, in the Metropolis and its Environs (London: J. Wade, 1782).

Reck, Philipp, Georg Friedrich von and Johann Martin Boltzius, *An Extract of the Journals of Mr. Commissary von Reck, who Conducted the First transport of Saltzburgers to Georgia: and of the Reverend Mr. Bolzius, One of their Ministers. Giving an Account of their Voyage to, and Happy Settlement in that Province. Published by the Direction of The Society for Promoting Christian Knowledge* (London: M. Downing, 1734).

——, *Von Reck's Voyage: Drawings and Journal of Philip Georg Friedrich von Reck*, ed. Kristian Hvidt (Savannah: Beehive Press, 1980).

Reeves, William, *The Apologies of Justin Martyr, Tertullian, and Minutius Felix, in Defence of the Christian Religion, with the Commonitory of Vincentius Lirinensis, Concerning the Primitive Rule of Faith, Translated from their Originals: With Notes...and a Preliminary Discourse upon each Author. Together with a Prefatory Dissertation about the Right Use of the Fathers*, 2 vols (London: W. B. for A. and J. Churchill, 1709).

[Sharp, Thomas], *An Enquiry about the Lawfulness of Eating Blood...* (London: John Pemberton, 1733).

A Short Refutation of the Principal Errors of the Church of Rome. Whereby a Protestant of a mean and ordinary Capacity may be enabled to defend his Religion against the most subtle Papist (London: J. Downing, 1714).

Smalbroke, Richard, *The Pretended Authority of the Clementine Constitutions Confuted, by Their Inconsistency with the Inspired Writings of the Old and New Testament. In Answer to Mr. Whiston* (London: Timothy Childe, 1714).

Society for Promoting Christian Knowledge, Minutes of the SPCK, SPCK Archives, Cambridge University Library.

Society for the Propagation of the Gospel, Journal, SPG Archives, Rhodes House Library, Oxford.

Spangenberg, August Gottlieb, 'A Moravian's Report on John Wesley—1737', ed. Douglas L. Rights, *South Atlantic Quarterly*, 43 (1944), 406–9.

——, '"We Have Come to Georgia With Pure Intentions": Moravian Bishop August Gottlieb Spangenberg's Letters from Savannah, 1735', ed. and trans. George Fenwick Jones and Paul Martin Peucker, *GHQ* 82 (1998), 84–120.

Spinckes, Nathaniel (ed.), *The True Church of England-Man's Companion to the Closet: or, A Complete Manual of Private Devotions Fitted for Most Persons and Cases. Collected from the Writings of Archbishop Laud, Bishop Andrews, Bishop Kenn, Dr. Hickes, Mr. Kettlewell, Mr. Spinckes, And other eminent Divines of the Church of England. With a Preface from the Reverend Mr. Spinckes*, 6th edn (London: C. Rivington, 1731).

Stephens, Edward, *The Liturgy of the Ancients Represented, as Near as Well may be, in English Forms: With a Preface Concerning the Restitution of the most Solemn Part of Christian Worship in the Holy Eucharist, to its Integrity, and just Frequency of Celebration* (London: for the author, 1696).

[Stephens, Thomas], *A Brief Account of the Causes that have Retarded the Progress of the Colony of Georgia in America; Attested upon Oath. Being a Proper Contrast to A State of the Province of Georgia. Attested upon Oath; And some other Misrepresentations on the same Subject* (London, 1743).

Stephens, William, *A Journal of the Proceedings in Georgia, beginning 20 October 1737. To which is added, a State of that Province, as attested upon Oath in the Court of Savannah, 10 November 1740*, 2 vols (London: W. Meadows, 1742).

Tailfer, Pat[rick], Hugh Anderson, Da[vid] Douglas, and others, *A True and Historical Narrative of the Colony of Georgia in America, From the first Settlement thereof until this present Period*... (Charles-Town: P. Timothy, 1741).

——, *A True and Historical Narrative of the Colony of Georgia in America*, ed. Clarence L. Ver Stegg (Athens: University of Georgia Press, 1960).

Taylor, Jeremy, *The Worthy Communicant: Or, a Discourse of the Nature, Effects, and Blessings consequent to the Worthy Receiving of the Lords Supper; And of all the Duties required in order to a Worthy Preparation*...(London: Richard Wellington, 1701).

——, *The Rule and Exercises of Holy Living*...23rd edn (London: J. L., 1719).

Thicknesse, Philip, *Memoirs and Anecdotes of Philip Thicknesse*...(Dublin: Graisberry and Campbell, 1790).

Thomas à Kempis, *The Christian's Pattern*, ed. John Wesley (London: C. Rivington, 1735).

Tilly, William, *Sixteen Sermons, All (except One) Preach'd before the University of Oxford, at St. Mary's, upon Several Occasions* (London: Bernard Lintott, 1712).

Töltschig, Johann, 'Töltschigs Diarium', in 'Berichte und Diaria von dem Etablissement der Brüder in Georgia, 1734–1744', MS, R.14.A.6.d.5, 7, 12a, Unitätsarchiv der Evangelischen Brüder-Unität, Herrnhut, Germany, translated by Dr Achim Kopp, Mercer University, Georgia.

Trapp, Joseph, *The Nature, Folly, Sin, and Danger of Being Righteous Over-much; With a particular View to the Doctrines and Practices of certain Modern Enthusiasts*...(London: S. Austen, 1739).

Turner, Robert, *A Discourse of the Pretended Apostolical Constitutions; wherein all the Principal Evidence, both External and Internal, brought by Mr. Whiston, in His Essay*

on those Books, to Prove them Genuine, is Examin'd, and Confuted (London: M. J. for
W. Innys, 1715).

[Ussher, James], *The Judgement of the late Archbishop of Armagh…* ed. N. Bernard
(London: John Crook, 1658).

*A View of the Articles of the Protestant and Popish Faith. To which is added, an Address
to the Laity* (London: M. Downing, 1735).

Wake, William, *The Genuine Epistles of the Apostolical Fathers, S. Barnabas, S. Ignatius,
S. Clement, S. Polycarp, the Shepherd of Hermas, and the Martyrdoms of St. Ignatius
and St. Polycarp… with a Large Preliminary Discourse Relating to the Several Treaties
Here Put together* (London: Ric. Sare, 1693).

——, *Bishop Wake's Summary of Visitation Returns from the Diocese of Lincoln 1706–
1715*, ed. John Broad, Records of Social and Economic History, 49–50, 2 vols
(Oxford: Oxford University Press/British Academy, 2012).

Wall, W[illiam], *A Conference between Two Men that had Doubts about Infant Baptism*
(London: Joseph Downing, 1706).

——, *The History of Infant Baptism, In Two Parts. The First, Being an Impartial Collection
of all such Passages in the Writers of the four first Centuries as do make For, or Against
it. The Second, Containing several Things that do help to illustrate the said History*, 3rd
edn, 2 vols (London: R. Bonwicke, 1720).

——, *Thoughts upon Infant-Baptism: Extracted from a Late Writer*, ed. John Wesley
(Bristol: Felix Farley, 1751).

[Wesley, Charles], *Hymns for Our Lord's Resurrection* (London: W. Strahan, 1746).

——, *The Letters of Charles Wesley: A Critical Edition, with Introduction and Notes,
Volume I*, 1728–1756, ed. Kenneth G. C. Newport and Gareth Lloyd (Oxford: Oxford
University Press, 2013).

——, *The Manuscript Journal of Reverend Charles Wesley, M.A.*, ed. S T Kimbrough,
Jr and Kenneth G. C. Newport, 2 vols. (Nashville: Kingswood Books, 2007, 2008).

Wesley, John, Abridgement of Claude Fleury's, *An Historical Catechism* and *Les Moeurs
des Israelites et des Chretiens*, MARC, MS Colman Collection 15.

——, *Apostolic Constitutions* and *Canons*, Wesley's Chapel, City Road, London, MS,
LDWMM/1998/7129 and LDWMM/1994/2067.

——, Extract of Robert Nelson's *The Great Duty of Frequenting the Christian Sacrifice*,
MARC, MS Colman Collection 20.

Letters to John Wesley Box, MARC.

——, 'Prayers', MARC, MS Colman Collection 8.

——, Transcription of John Johnson's *The Primitive Communicant*, MARC, Colman MS
Collection 12.

——, 'Water Baptism is the Baptism of Christ', MS in 'Portraits and Letters of Presidents
of the Wesleyan Methodist Conference', MARC, vol. 1, fo. 14.

——, 'Of the Weekly Fasts of the Church', MARC, MS Colman Collection 12.

[——], *Collection of Psalms and Hymns* (Charles-Town: Lewis Timothy, 1737).

[——], *Collection of Psalms and Hymns* (London: William Bowyer, 1738).

——, *Collection of Psalms and Hymns* (London: W. Strahan, 1741).

——, *Instructions for Children* (Newcastle upon Tyne: John Gooding, 1746).

——, *A Second Letter to the Author of The Enthusiasm of Methodists and Papists
Compar'd* (London: H. Cock, 1751).

——, *A Collection of Forms of Prayer for Every Day in the Week*, 5th edn (Bristol: J. Palmer, 1755).

——, *Explanatory Notes upon the New Testament* (London: William Bowyer, 1755).

[——], *Queries Humbly Proposed to the Right Reverend and Right Honourable Count Zinzendorf* (London: J. Robinson, 1755).

——, *The Works of the Rev. John Wesley, M.A. Late Fellow of Lincoln-College, Oxford*, ed. John Wesley, 32 vols (Bristol: William Pine 1771–4).

——, *Thoughts upon Slavery* (London: R. Hawes, 1774).

——, *The Works of the Rev. John Wesley*, ed. Thomas Jackson, 3rd edn, 14 vols (London: Mason, 1829–31).

——, *The Letters of the Rev. John Wesley, A.M.*, ed. John Telford, 8 vols (London: Epworth Press, 1931).

——, *The Journal of the Rev. John Wesley, A.M.*, ed. Nehemiah Curnock, 8 vols (repr. London: Epworth Press, 1938).

——, *A Plain Account of Christian Perfection* (Kansas City: Beacon Hill Press, 1966 [1766]).

The Works of John Wesley (Bicentennial Edition), general ed. Frank Baker and Richard P. Heitzenrater (Oxford: Clarendon Press, 1975–83 and Nashville: Abingdon Press, 1984–).

Vols 1–4, *Sermons I–IV*, ed. Albert C. Outler (Nashville: Abingdon Press, 1984–7).

Vol. 7, *A Collection of Hymns for the Use of the People Called Methodists*, ed. Franz Hildebrant and Oliver A. Beckerlegge (Oxford: Clarendon Press, 1983).

Vol. 9, *The Methodist Societies: History, Nature, and Design*, ed. Rupert E. Davies (Nashville: Abingdon Press, 1989).

Vol. 10, *The Methodist Societies: The Minutes of Conference*, ed. Henry D. Rack (Nashville: Abingdon Press, 2011).

Vol. 11, *The Appeals to Men of Reason and Religion and Certain Related Open Letters*, ed. Gerald R. Gragg (Oxford: Clarendon Press, 1975).

Vol. 12, *Doctrinal and Controversial Treatises I*, ed. Randy L. Maddox (Nashville: Abingdon Press, 2012).

Vols 18–24, *Journal and Diaries*, ed. W. Reginald Ward and Richard P. Heitzenrater (Nashville: Abingdon Press, 1988–2003).

Vols 25–6, *Letters I–II*, ed. Frank Baker (Oxford: Clarendon Press, 1980, 1982).

——, *John Wesley's Sunday Service of the Methodists in North America*, with an introduction by James F. White (Nashville: United Methodist Publishing House, 1984).

—— and Charles Wesley, *A Collection of Psalms and Hymns for the Lord's Day* (London: Strahan, 1784).

——, *Hymns on the Lord's Supper: With a Preface Concerning the Christian Sacrament and Sacrifice. Extracted from Doctor Brevint* (Bristol: Felix Farley, 1745).

Wesley, Samuel, *Advice to a Young Clergyman* (London, [1735]). Reprinted in Thomas Jackson, *The Life of the Rev. Charles Wesley, M.A.*, 2 vols (London: John Mason, 1841), 2:500–34.

——, *The Pious Communicant Rightly Prepar'd: Or, A Discourse Concerning the Blessed Sacrament...* (London: Charles Harper, 1700).

Wesley, Samuel Jr, *Poems on Several Occasions* (London: E. Say, 1736).

Wheatly, Charles, *A Rational Illustration of the Book of Common Prayer of the Church of England, And Administration of the Sacraments, And Other Rites and Ceremonies of the Church, According to the Use of the Church of England...* 3rd edn (London: A. Bettesworth, 1720).

[Whiston, Daniel], *A Primitive Catechism; By Way of Question and Answer. In Two Parts. Useful for Charity Schools. With the Texts of Scripture Proper for the Proof of Several Answers* (London: J. Senex, 1718).

Whiston, William, *Primitive Christianity Reviv'd*, 5 vols (London: for the Author, 1711–12).

Vol. 2: *The Constitutions of the Holy Apostles, by Clement; in English and in Greek; with the Various Readings from all of the Manuscripts.*

Vol. 3: *An Essay on the Apostolical Constitutions.*

——, *The Liturgy of the Church of England, Reduc'd nearer to the Primitive Standard: Humbly propos'd to Publick Consideration* (London: for the author, 1713).

——, *Memoirs of the Life and Writings of Mr. William Whiston. Containing, memoirs of Several of his Friends also. Written by Himself*, 2nd edn, 2 vols (London: J. Whiston and B. White, 1753).

Whitefield, George, *George Whitefield's Journals* (Edinburgh: Banner of Truth Trust, 1960).

Whitehead, John, *The Life of the Rev. John Wesley, M.A.*, 2 vols (London: Stephen Couchman, 1796).

[Williams, John], *A Catechism Truly representing the Doctrines and Practices of the Church of Rome, with an Answer thereunto. By a Protestant of the Church of England* (London: Richard Chiswell, 1686).

Wilson, Thomas, *The Diaries of Thomas Wilson, D.D. 1731–37 and 1750*, ed. C. L. S. Linnell (London: SPCK, 1964).

Worthington, John, *The Great Duty of Self-Resignation to the Divine Will* (London: A. C., 1675).

Young, E[dward], *Sermons on Several Occasions*, 3rd edn, 2 vols (London: R. Knapock, 1720).

The Young Students Library: Containing Extracts and Abridgements of the Most Valuable Books Printed in England and in the Foreign Journals... (London: John Dunton, 1692).

Ziegenbalg, Bartholomaeus, *Propagation of the Gospel in the East: Being an Account of the Success of Two Danish Missionaries, Lately sent to the East-Indies, for the Conversion of the Heathens in Malabar...* (London: J. Browning, 1709).

Secondary Sources

Abelove, Henry, *The Evangelist of Desire: John Wesley and the Methodists* (Stanford, CA: Stanford University Press, 1990).

Allen, W. O. B. and Edmund McClure, *Two Hundred Years: The History of the Society for Promoting Christian Knowledge, 1698–1898* (London: SPCK, 1898).

Apetrei, Sarah, '"The Life of Angels": Celibacy and Asceticism in Anglicanism, 1660–c.1700', *Reformation & Renaissance Review*, 13 (2011), 247–74.

Atwood, Craig D., 'Spangenberg: A Radical Pietist in Colonial America', *Journal of Moravian History*, 4 (2008), 7–27.

Avis, Paul D. L., '"The True Church" in Reformation Theology', *Scottish Journal of Theology*, 30 (1977), 319–45.

Baine, Rodney M., 'Philip Thicknesse's Reminiscences of Early Georgia', *GHQ* 74 (1990), 672–98.

——, 'New Perspectives on Debtors in Colonial Georgia', *GHQ* 77 (1993), 1–19.

Baker, Frank, 'The Birth of John Wesley's Journal', *MH* 8 (1970), 25–32.

——, *John Wesley and the Church of England* (London: Epworth Press, 1970; repr. 2000).

——, *From Wesley to Asbury: Studies in Early American Methodism* (Durham: Duke University Press, 1976).

——, 'John Wesley and Bishop Joseph Butler', *PWHS* 42 (1980), 93–100.

——, *A Union Catalogue of the Publications of John and Charles Wesley*, 2nd edn (Stone Mountain, GA: G. Zimmermann, 1991).

—— and George Walton Williams (eds), *John Wesley's First Hymn-book* (Charleston and London: Dalcho Historical Society/Wesley Historical Society, 1964).

Barnard, Leslie W., 'The Use of the Patristic Tradition in the Late Seventeenth and Early Eighteenth Centuries', in Richard Bauckham and Benjamin Drewery (eds), *Scripture Tradition and Reason, A Study in the Criteria of Christian Doctrine: Essays in Honour of Richard P. C. Hanson* (Edinburgh: T & T Clark, 1988), 174–203.

Barnes, A. M., 'Americana. The South Carolina Gazette', *PWHS* 16 (1927), 58–62.

Beasley, Nicholas M., 'Domestic Rituals: Marriage and Baptism in the British Plantation Colonies, 1650–1780', *Anglican and Episcopal History*, 76 (2007), 327–57.

——, 'Ritual Time in British Plantation Colonies, 1650–1780', *Church History*, 76 (2007), 541–68.

Beckwith, R. T., 'The Anglican Eucharist: From the Reformation to the Restoration', in Cheslyn Jones et. al. (eds), *The Study of Liturgy*, rev. edn (London: SPCK, 1992), 309–18.

Bennett, Gareth Vaughan, 'Patristic Tradition in Anglican Thought, 1660–1900', in G. Gassmann and V. Vajta (eds), *Oecumenica: Jahrbuch für ökumenische Forschung 1971–72* (Güterslog, Germany, 1972), 63–87.

Bett, Henry, *The Spirit of Methodism* (London: Epworth Press, 1937).

Black, Jeremy, *A Subject for Taste: Culture in Eighteenth-Century England* (London: Hambledon and London, 2005).

Boles, John B., 'Evangelical Protestantism in the Old South: From Religious Dissent to Cultural Dominance', in Charles Regan Wilson (ed.), *Religion in the South* (Jackson: University Press of Mississippi, 1985), 13–34.

Borgen, Ole E., *John Wesley on the Sacraments: A Theological Study* (Nashville: Abingdon Press, 1972).

Bowden, Haygood S., *History of Savannah Methodism from John Wesley to Silas Johnson* (Macon, GA: J. W. Burke Company, 1929).

Bowmer, John C., *The Sacrament of the Lord's Supper in Early Methodism* (London: Dacre Press, 1951).

Broxap, Henry, *A Biography of Thomas Deacon: The Manchester Non-Juror* (Manchester: Manchester University Press, 1911).

Brunner, Daniel L., *Halle Pietists in England: Anthony William Boehm and the Society for Promoting Christian Knowledge*, in K. Aland, E. Peschke, and G. Schäfer (eds), Arbeiten zur Geschichte des Pietismus, 29 (Göttingen: Vandenhoeck & Ruprecht, 1993).

Buchan, Thomas, 'John Wesley and the Constantinian Fall of the Church: Historiographical Indications of Pietist Influences', in Christian T. Collins Winn et. al. (eds), *The Pietist Impulse in Christianity* (Eugene, OR: Pickwick Publications, 2011), 146–60.

Burdick, Oscar C., 'Wall, William (1647–1728)', *Oxford Dictionary of National Biography* (Oxford: Oxford University Press, 2004) [online edn].

Burnham, Paul, 'The "Nonjuror" Influence on the Eucharistic Hymns of Charles Wesley and its Relevance for Today', paper given at 'An Eighteenth-Century Evangelical for Today: A Tercentenary Celebration of the Life and Ministry of Charles Wesley', Liverpool Hope University, 2007.

Buxton, Richard F., *Eucharist and Institution Narrative: A Study in the Roman and Anglican Traditions of Consecration of the Eucharist from the Eighth to the Twentieth Centuries* (Great Wakering: Mayhew-McCrimmon, 1976).

Campbell, Ted. A., 'John Wesley's Conceptions and Uses of Christian Antiquity', Ph.D. diss. (Southern Methodist University, 1984).

——, *John Wesley and Christian Antiquity: Religious Vision and Cultural Change* (Nashville: Kingswood Books, 1991).

——, *The Religion of the Heart: A Study of European Religious Life in the Seventeenth and Eighteenth Centuries* (Columbia: University of South Carolina Press, 1991).

——, 'Christian Tradition, John Wesley, and Evangelicalism', *Anglican Theological Review*, 74 (1992), 54–67.

——, 'Wesley's Use of the Church Fathers', *Asbury Theological Journal*, 50:2–51:1 (1995–6), 57–70.

——, 'The Image of Christ in the Poor: On the Medieval Roots of the Wesleys' Ministry to the Poor', in Richard P. Heitzenrater (ed.), *The Poor and the People Called Methodists 1729–1999* (Nashville: Kingswood Books, 2002), 39–57.

Cannon, William, 'John Wesley's Years in Georgia', *MH* 1 (1963), 1–7.

Carrier, E. Theodore, 'Wesley's Views on Prayers for the Dead', *PWHS* 1 (1898), 123–5.

Carter, Kelly D., 'The High Church Roots of John Wesley's Appeal to Primitive Christianity', *Restoration Quarterly*, 37 (1995) [online] <http://www.acu.edu/sponsored/restoration_quarterly/archives/1990s/vol_37_no_2_contents/carter.html>, accessed 12 July 2013.

Cashin, Edward J., *Guardians of the Valley: Chickasaws in Colonial South Carolina and Georgia* (Columbia: University of South Carolina Press, 2009).

Chadwick, Henry, *The Early Church*, rev. edn (London: Penguin Books, 1993).

——, 'Tradition, Fathers and Councils', in Stephen Sykes, John Booty, and Jonathan Knight (eds), *The Study of Anglicanism*, rev. edn (London: SPCK, 1998), 100–15.

——, 'The Early Church', in Richard Harries and Henry Mayr-Harting (eds), *Christianity: Two Thousand Years* (Oxford: Oxford University Press, 2001), 1–20.

Church, Leslie F., *Oglethorpe: A Study in Philanthropy in England and Georgia* (London: Epworth Press, 1932).

Clark, J. C. D., *English Society 1660–1832: Religion, Ideology and Politics during the Ancien Regime*, 2nd edn (Cambridge: Cambridge University Press, 2000).

Clarke, Adam, *Memoirs of the Wesley Family; Collected Principally from Original Documents*, 4th edn, 2 vols (London: William Tegg, 1860).

Coe, Bufford W., *John Wesley and Marriage* (Bethlehem, PA: Leigh University Press, 1996).

Cornwall, Robert D., 'The Search for the Primitive Church: The Use of Early Church Fathers in the High Church Anglican Tradition, 1680–1745', *Anglican and Episcopal History*, 59 (1990), 303–29.

——, 'The Later Nonjurors and the Theological Basis of the Usages Controversy', *Anglican Theological Review*, 75 (1993), 166–86.

——, *Visible and Apostolic: The Constitution of the Church in High Church Anglican and Non-Juror Thought* (Newark, NJ: University of Delaware Press, 1993).

——, 'The Rite of Confirmation in Anglican Thought During the Eighteenth Century', *Church History*, 68 (1999), 359–72.

——, 'Deacon, Thomas (1697–1753)', *Oxford Dictionary of National Biography* (Oxford: Oxford University Press, 2004) [online edn].

——, 'Politics and the Lay Baptism Controversy in England, 1708–15', in William Gibson and Robert D. Cornwall (eds), *Religion, Politics and Dissent, 1660–1832: Essays in Honour of James E. Bradley* (Aldershot: Ashgate, 2010), 147–64.

——, 'The Theologies of the Nonjurors: A Historiographical Essay', in M. Caricchio and G. Tarantino (eds), *Cromohs Virtual Seminars. Recent Historiographical Trends of the British Studies (17th-18th Centuries)* [online journal], (2006–7), 1–7, <http://www.cromohs.unifi.it/seminari/cornwall_nonjuror.html>, accessed 16 August 2012.

Coulter, E. Merton, 'When John Wesley Preached in Georgia', *GHQ* 9 (1925), 317–51.

Cowie, Leonard W., *Henry Newman: An American in London 1708-43* (London: SPCK, 1956).

——, 'Beveridge, William (bap. 1637–1708)', *Oxford Dictionary of National Biography* (Oxford: Oxford University Press, 2004) [online edn].

Crockett, William, 'Holy Communion', in Stephen Sykes, John Booty, and Jonathan Knight (eds), *The Study of Anglicanism*, rev. edn (London: SPCK, 1998), 308–21.

Cross F. L. and E. A. Livingstone (eds), *The Oxford Dictionary of the Christian Church*, 3rd edn (Oxford: Oxford University Press, 1997).

Crowley, J. E., *This Sheba, Self: The Conceptualization of Economic Life in Eighteenth-Century America* (Baltimore: Johns Hopkins University Press, 1974).

Davis, Harold E., *The Fledgling Province: Social and Cultural Life in Colonial Georgia* (Chapel Hill, NC: University of North Carolina Press, 1976).

Dearing, Trevor, *Wesleyan and Tractarian Worship: An Ecumenical Study* (London: Epworth Press/SPCK, 1966).

Doll, Peter, *After the Primitive Christians: The Eighteenth-Century Anglican Eucharist in its Architectural Setting*, Joint Liturgical Studies, 37 (Cambridge: Grove Books, 1997).

——, ' "The Reverence of God's House": The Temple of Solomon and the Architectural Setting for the "Unbloody Sacrifice" ', in Peter Doll (ed.), *Anglicanism and Orthodoxy 300 Years After the 'Greek College' in Oxford* (Oxford: Peter Lang, 2006), 193–223.

——, 'The Architectural Expression of Primitive Christianity: William Beveridge and the Temple of Solomon', *Reformation & Renaissance Review*, 13 (2011), 275–306.

Drakeford, John W., *Take Her, Mr. Wesley* (Waco, TX: Word Books, 1973).

Duffy, Eamon, 'Primitive Christianity Revived; Religious Renewal in Augustan England', in Derek Baker (ed.), *Renaissance and Renewal in Christian History*, Studies in Church History, 14 (Oxford: Blackwell, 1977), 287–300.

Eller, David B., 'The Recovery of the Love Feast in German Pietism', in Fred van Lieburg (ed.), *Confessionalism and Pietism* (Mainz: Philipp von Zabern, 2006), 11–30.

English, John C., 'John Wesley and the Liturgical Ideals of Thomas Cranmer', *MH* 35 (1997), 222–32.

——, 'The Duration of the Primitive Church: An Issue for Seventeenth and Eighteenth Century Anglicans', *Anglican and Episcopal History*, 73 (2004), 35–52.

Ethridge, Willie Snow, *Strange Fires: The True Story of John Wesley's Love Affair in Georgia* (New York: Vanguard Press, 1971).

Fogleman, Aaron Spencer, 'Shadow Boxing in Georgia: The Beginnings of the Moravian-Lutheran Conflict in British North America', *GHQ* 83 (1999), 629–59.

——, *Jesus is Female: Moravians and the Challenge of Radical Religion in Early America* (Philadelphia: University of Pennsylvania Press, 2007).

Fries, Adelaide L., *The Moravians in Georgia 1735–1740* (Raleigh, NC: Edwards and Broughton, 1905).

Friesen, Abraham, 'The Impulse Toward Restitutionist Thought in Christian Humanism', *Journal of the American Academy of Religion*, 44 (1976), 29–45.

Galliers, Brian J. N., 'Baptism in the Writings of John Wesley', *PWHS* 32 (1960), 121–4, 153–7.

George, A. Raymond, 'Ordination', in Rupert E. Davies, George A. Raymond, and E. Gordon Rupp (eds), *A History of the Methodist Church in Great Britain*, 4 vols (London: Epworth Press, 1978), 2:143–60.

Green, Richard, *The Conversion of John Wesley* (London: Epworth Press, 1937).

Green, V. H. H., *The Young Mr. Wesley* (London: Edward Arnold, 1961).

——, *John Wesley* (London: Nelson, 1964).

Greenslade, Stanley L., 'The Authority of the Tradition of the Early Church in Early Anglican Thought', in G. Gassmann and V. Vajta (eds), *Oecumenica: Jahrbuch für ökumenische Forschung 1971–72* (Gütersleg, Germany, 1972), 9–33.

Gregory, Jeremy, 'Gender and the Clerical Profession in England, 1660–1850', in R. N. Swanson (ed.), *Gender and Christian Religion*, Studies in Church History, 34 (Woodbridge: Boydell and Brewer, 1998), 235–71.

——, '*Homo Religiosus*: Masculinity and Religion in the Long Eighteenth Century', in Tim Hitchcock and Michèle Cohen (eds), *English Masculinities 1660–1800* (London: Longman, 1999), 85–110.

——, ' "In the Church I will live and die": John Wesley, the Church of England, and Methodism', in William Gibson and Robert G. Ingram (eds), *Religious Identities in Britain, 1660–1800* (Aldershot: Ashgate, 2005), 147–78.

Grisbrooke, W. Jardine, *Anglican Liturgies of the Seventeenth and Eighteenth Centuries*, Alcuin Club Collections (London: SPCK, 1958).

—— (trans. and ed.), *The Liturgical Portions of the Apostolic Constitutions: A Text for Students*, Alcuin/GROW Liturgical Study, 13–14 (Bramcote: Grove Books, 1990).

Haaugaard, William P., 'Renaissance Patristic Scholarship and Theology in Sixteenth-Century England', *Sixteenth Century Journal*, 10 (1979), 37–60.

Hammond, Geordan, 'John Wesley in Georgia: Success or Failure?', *PWHS* 56 (2008), 297–305.

——, 'John Wesley's Mindset at the Commencement of the Georgia Sojourn: Suffering and the Introduction of Primitive Christianity to the Indians', *MH* 47 (2008), 16–25.

——, 'Restoring Primitive Christianity: John Wesley and Georgia, 1735–1737', Ph.D. thesis (University of Manchester, 2008).

——, 'The Revival of Practical Christianity: The Society for Promoting Christian Knowledge, Samuel Wesley, and the Clerical Society Movement', in Kate Cooper and Jeremy Gregory (eds), *Revival and Resurgence in Christian History*, Studies in Church History, 44 (Woodbridge: Boydell and Brewer, 2008), 116–27.

——, 'High Church Anglican Influences on John Wesley's Conception of Primitive Christianity, 1732–1735', *Anglican and Episcopal History*, 78 (2009), 174–207.

——, 'Versions of Primitive Christianity: John Wesley's Relations with the Moravians in Georgia, 1735–1737', *Journal of Moravian History*, 6 (2009), 31–60.

——, 'The Wesleys' Sacramental Theology and Practice in Georgia', *Proceedings of The Charles Wesley Society*, 13 (2009), 53–73.

——, 'John Wesley and "Imitating" Christ', *Wesleyan Theological Journal*, 45 (2010), 197–212.

——, 'John Wesley's Relations with the Lutheran Pietist Clergy in Georgia', in Christian T. Collins Winn et. al. (eds), *The Pietist Impulse in Christianity* (Eugene, OR: Pickwick Publications, 2011), 135–45.

Harper, Steve, 'The Devotional Life of John Wesley, 1703–1738', Ph.D. diss. (Duke University, 1981).

Hatchett, Marion J., *Commentary on the American Prayer Book* (New York: Seabury Press, 1980).

Haydon, Colin, *Anti-Catholicism in Eighteenth-Century England, c.1714–80: A Political and Social Study* (Manchester: Manchester University Press, 1993).

Hayes, Alan, 'John Wesley and Sophy Hopkey', in H. F. Thomas and R. S. Keller (eds), *Women in New Worlds: Historical Perspectives on the Wesleyan Tradition*, 2 vols (Nashville: Abingdon Press, 1981), 1:29–44.

Heitzenrater, Richard P., 'John Wesley and the Oxford Methodists', Ph.D. diss. (Duke University, 1972).

——, *Mirror and Memory: Reflections on Early Methodism* (Nashville: Kingswood Books, 1989).

——, 'John Wesley as Historian of Early Methodism', in Neil Semple (ed.), *Papers of the Canadian Methodist Historical Society*, 7 (Toronto, 1990), 37–53.

——, 'The *Imitatio Christi* and the Great Commandment: Virtue and Obligation in Wesley's Ministry with the Poor', in M. Douglas Meeks (ed.), *Good News to the Poor in the Wesleyan Tradition* (Nashville: Kingswood Books, 1995), 49–63.

——, *The Elusive Mr. Wesley*, 2nd edn (Nashville: Abingdon Press, 2003).

——, 'Wesley in America', *PWHS* 54 (2003), 85–114.

——, 'The Founding Brothers', in William J. Abraham and James E. Kirby (eds), *The Oxford Handbook of Methodist Studies* (Oxford: Oxford University Press, 2009), 30–50.

——, *Wesley and the People Called Methodists*, 2nd edn (Nashville: Abingdon Press, 2013).

[Heber, Reginald], 'The Life of Wesley; and the Rise and Progress of Methodism', *The Quarterly Review*, 24 (Oct. 1820), 1–55.

Hempton, David, *Methodism: Empire of the Spirit* (New Haven: Yale University Press, 2005).

Holland, Bernard G., *Baptism in Early Methodism* (London: Epworth Press, 1970).

Hunter, Frederick, 'The Manchester Nonjurors and Wesley's High Churchism', *London Quarterly and Holborn Review*, 172 (1947), 56–61.

——, *John Wesley and the Coming Comprehensive Church* (London: Epworth Press, 1968).

——, 'Wesley: Separatist or Searcher for Unity?' *PWHS* 38 (1972), 166–9.

Ingram, Robert G., *Religion, Reform and Modernity in the Eighteenth Century: Thomas Secker and the Church of England*, Studies in Modern British Religious History, 17 (Woodbridge: Boydell and Brewer, 2007).

Jackson, Thomas, *The Centenary of Wesleyan Methodism: A Brief Sketch of the Rise, Progress, and Present State of the Wesleyan-Methodist Societies Throughout the World* (London: John Mason, 1839).

Jones, Charles C., *The History of Georgia* (Boston: Houghton Mifflin, 1883).

Jones, George Fenwick, *The Salzburger Saga: Religious Exiles and Other Germans along the Savannah* (Athens: University of Georgia Press, 1984).

——, *The Georgia Dutch: From the Rhine and Danube to the Savannah, 1733–1783* (Athens: University of Georgia Press, 1992).

Källstad, Thorvald, *John Wesley and the Bible: A Psychological Study* (Stockholm: University of Uppsala, 1974).

Keefer, Luke L., Jr, 'John Wesley: Disciple of Early Christianity', Ph.D. diss. (Temple University, 1982).

——, 'John Wesley: Disciple of Early Christianity', *Wesleyan Theological Journal*, 19 (1984), 23–32.

Kisker, Scott Thomas, *Foundation for Revival: Anthony Horneck, the Religious Societies, and the Construction of an Anglican Pietism*, Pietist and Wesleyan Studies, 24 (Lanham, MD: Scarecrow Press, 2008).

Klingberg, Frank J., 'The Indian Frontier in South Carolina as Seen by the S.P.G. Missionary', *Journal of Southern History*, 5 (1939), 479–500.

Lannen, Andrew C., 'James Oglethorpe and the Civil-Military Contest for Authority in Colonial Georgia, 1732–1749', *GHQ* 95 (2011), 203–31.

Lawson, A. B., *John Wesley and the Christian Ministry: The Sources and Development of His Opinions and Practice* (London: SPCK, 1963).

Lee, Umphrey, *John Wesley and Modern Religion* (Nashville: Cokesbury Press, 1936).

Lelièvre, Matthew, *John Wesley: His Life and Work* (London: Wesleyan Methodist Conference Office, [1871]).

Little, Thomas J., 'The Origins of Southern Evangelicalism: Revivalism in South Carolina, 1700–1740', *Church History*, 75 (2006), 768–808.

Madden, Deborah, *'A Cheap, Safe and Natural Medicine': Religion, Medicine and Culture in John Wesley's Primitive Physic* (Amsterdam: Rodopi, 2007).

Maddox, Randy L. (ed.), *Aldersgate Reconsidered* (Nashville: Kingswood Books, 1990).

——, 'Reclaiming an Inheritance: Wesley as a Theologian in the History of Methodist Theology', in Randy L. Maddox (ed.), *Rethinking Wesley's Theology for Contemporary Methodism* (Nashville: Kingswood Books, 1998), 213–26.

—— (ed.), 'John Wesley's Poetry and Hymn Collections', *Duke Center for Studies in the Wesleyan Tradition*, <http://divinity.duke.edu/initiatives-centers/cswt/wesley-texts/poetry-hymn>, accessed 19 August 2012.

Manning, David, '"That is Best, Which Was First": Christian Primitivism and the Reformation Church of England, 1548–1722', *Reformation & Renaissance Review*, 13 (2011), 153–93.

Marsh, Ben, *Georgia's Frontier Women: Female Fortunes in a Southern Colony* (Athens: University of Georgia Press, 2007).

Maser, Frederick E., 'Preface to Victory: An Analysis of John Wesley's Mission to Georgia', *Religion in Life*, 25 (1956), 280–93.

Mather, F. C., 'Georgian Churchmanship Reconsidered: Some Variations in Anglican Public Worship 1714–1830', *Journal of Ecclesiastical History*, 36 (1985), 255–83.

Matthew, H. C. G. and Brian Harrison (eds), *Oxford Dictionary of National Biography*, 60 vols (Oxford: Oxford University Press, 2004) [online edn].

McAdoo, H. R., *The Spirit of Anglicanism: A Survey of Anglican Theological Method in the Seventeenth Century* (London: Adam & Charles Black, 1965).

McIntosh, Lawrence, 'The Nature and Design of Christianity in John Wesley's Early Theology', Ph.D. diss. (Drew University, 1966).

Meyers, Arthur C., 'John Wesley and the Church Fathers', Ph.D. diss. (St Louis University, 1985).

Mitchell, Leonel L., 'The Influence of the Rediscovery of the Liturgy of the Apostolic Constitutions on the Nonjurors', *Ecclesia Orans*, 13 (1996), 207–21.

Moore, Robert L., *John Wesley and Authority: A Psychological Perspective* (Missoula, MT: Scholars Press, 1979).

Morgan, David T., 'John Wesley's Sojourn in Georgia Revisited', *GHQ* 64 (1980), 253–62.

Müller-Bahlke, Thomas J. and Jürgen Gröschl (eds), *Salzburg—Halle—Nordamerika: Ein zweisprachiges Find- und Lesebuch zum Georgia-Archiv der Franckeschen Stiftungen* [*Salzburg—Halle—North America: A Bilingual Catalog with Summaries of the Georgia Manuscripts in the Francke Foundations*] (Tübingen: Publishing House of the Francke Foundations Halle in the Max Niemeyer Publishing Company, 1999).

Nelson, James, 'John Wesley and the Georgia Moravians', *Transactions of the Moravian Historical Society*, 23 (1984), 17–46.

Newton, John A., *Susanna Wesley and the Puritan Tradition in Methodism*, 2nd edn (London: Epworth Press, 2002).

Nockles, Peter, 'Church Parties in the Pre-Tractarian Church of England 1750–1833: The "Orthodox"—Some Problems of Definition and Identity', in John Walsh, Colin Haydon, and Stephen Taylor (eds), *The Church of England c. 1689–c. 1833: From Toleration to Tractarianism* (Cambridge: Cambridge University Press, 1993), 334–59.

Nottingham, Elizabeth Kristine, 'The Making of an Evangelist: A Study of John Wesley's Early Years', Ph.D. diss. (Columbia University, 1938).

Nuelsen, John L., *John Wesley and the German Hymn*, trans. Theo Parry, Sydney H. Moore, and Arthur Holbrook (Calverley: A. S. Holbrook, 1972 [1938]).

Oh, Gwang Seok, *John Wesley's Ecclesiology: A Study in its Sources and Development*, Pietist and Wesleyan Studies, 27 (Lanham, MD: Scarecrow Press, 2008).

Outler, Albert C., 'John Wesley as Theologian—Then and Now', 'A New Future for Wesley Studies: An Agenda for Phase III', 'The Place of Wesley in the Christian Tradition', 'Towards a Re-Appraisal of John Wesley as a Theologian', in Thomas C. Oden and Leicester R. Longden (eds), *The Wesleyan Theological Heritage: Essays of Albert C. Outler* (Grand Rapids: Zondervan, 1991).

Overton, John H., *John Wesley* (London: Methuen, 1891).

Parris, John R., *John Wesley's Doctrine of the Sacraments* (London: Epworth Press, 1963).

Peaston, A. Elliott, *The Prayer Book Reform Movement in the XVIIIth Century* (Oxford: Basil Blackwell, 1940).

Periodical Accounts Relating to the Missions of the Church of the United Brethren... vol. 12 (London: W. M'Dowall for the Brethren's Society for the Furtherance of the Gospel Among the Heathen, 1831).

Peucker, Paul, 'The Ideal of Primitive Christianity as a Source of Moravian Liturgical Practice', *Journal of Moravian History*, 6 (2009), 7–29.

Podmore, C. J., 'The Fetter Lane Society, 1738', *PWHS* 46 (1988), 125–53.

Podmore, Colin, 'Töltschig, Johann', in Donald M. Lewis (ed.), *The Blackwell Dictionary of Evangelical Biography 1730–1860*, 2 vols (Oxford: Blackwell, 1995).

——, *The Moravian Church in England, 1728–1760* (Oxford: Clarendon Press, 1998).

——, '"The Moravian Episcopate and the Episcopal Church": A Personal Response', *Anglican and Episcopal History*, 72 (2003), 351–84.

Pritchard, John, *Methodists and their Missionary Societies 1760–1900*, Ashgate Methodist Studies Series (Farnham: Ashgate, 2013).

Quantin, Jean-Louis, *The Church of England and Christian Antiquity: The Construction of a Confessional Identity in the Seventeenth Century* (Oxford: Oxford University Press, 2009).

Rack, Henry D., *Reasonable Enthusiast: John Wesley and the Rise of Methodism*, 3rd edn (London: Epworth Press, 2002).

——, 'The Wesleys and Manchester', *Proceedings of The Charles Wesley Society*, 8 (2002), 6–23.

——, 'Wesley, Samuel (bap. 1662, d. 1735)', *Oxford Dictionary of National Biography* (Oxford: Oxford University Press, 2004) [online edn].

——, 'Wesley Portrayed: Character and Criticism in Some Early Biographies', *MH* 43 (2005), 90–114.

Rainey, David, 'The Established Church and Evangelical Theology: John Wesley's Ecclesiology', *International Journal of Systematic Theology*, 12 (2010), 420–34.

Randolph, J. Ralph, 'John Wesley and the American Indian: A Study in Disillusionment', *MH* 10 (1972), 3–11.

Rattenbury, J. Ernest, *The Conversion of the Wesleys: A Critical Study* (London: Epworth Press, 1938).

——, *The Eucharistic Hymns of John and Charles Wesley* (London: Epworth Press, 1948).

Ready, Milton, 'The Georgia Trustees and the Malcontents: The Politics of Philanthropy', *GHQ* 60 (1976), 272–7.

Rigg, James H., *The Churchmanship of John Wesley: And the Relations of Wesleyan Methodism to the Church of England* (London: Wesleyan Conference Office, 1878).

Rogal, Samuel J., 'William Stephens and John Wesley: "I cannot pretend to judge"', *GHQ* 90 (2006), 260–80.

Rogers, Charles Allen, 'The Concept of Prevenient Grace in the Theology of John Wesley', Ph.D. diss. (Duke University, 1967).

Rowe, Kenneth E., 'Editor's Introduction: The Search for the Historical Wesley', in Kenneth E. Rowe (ed.), *The Place of Wesley in the Christian Tradition* (Metuchen, NJ: Scarecrow Press, 1976).

Rupp, E. Gordon, *Religion in England 1688–1791* (Oxford: Clarendon Press, 1986).

Sanders, Paul S., 'Wesley's Eucharistic Faith and Practice', *Anglican Theological Review*, 48 (1966), 157–74.

Schmidt, Darren, 'The Pattern of Revival: John Wesley's Vision of "Iniquity" and "Godliness" in Church History', in Kate Cooper and Jeremy Gregory (eds), *Revival and Resurgence in Christian History*, Studies in Church History, 44 (Woodbridge: Boydell and Brewer, 2008), 142–53.

Schmidt, Martin, *The Young Wesley, Missionary and Theologian of Missions*, trans. L. A. Fletcher (London: Epworth Press, 1958).

——, *John Wesley: A Theological Biography*, volume 1: From 17th June 1703 until 24th May 1738, trans. Norman P. Goldhawk (London: Epworth Press, 1962).

——, *John Wesley: A Theological Biography*, volume II part II: John Wesley's Life Mission, trans. Denis Inman (London: Epworth Press, 1973).

Scott, John Thomas, '"Next to Nothing?": Benjamin Ingham's Mission to Georgia', *GHQ* 92 (2008), 287–320.

Sharp, Richard, '100 Years of a Lost Cause: Nonjuring Principles in Newcastle from the Revolution to the Death of Prince Edward Stuart', *Archaeologia Aeliana*, 5th series, 8 (1980), 35–55.

——, 'New Perspectives on the High Church Tradition: Historical Background 1730–1780', in Geoffrey Rowell (ed.), *Tradition Renewed: The Oxford Movement Conference Papers* (London: Darton, Longman & Todd, 1986), 4–23.

Shine, Hill and Helen Chadwick Shine, *The Quarterly Review under Gifford: Identification of Contributors 1809–1824* (Chapel Hill, NC: University of North Carolina Press, 1949).

Simon, John S., *John Wesley and the Religious Societies* (London: Epworth Press, 1921).

——, *John Wesley and the Methodist Societies* (London: Epworth Press, 1923).

Smith, George, *History of Wesleyan Methodism*, 5th edn, 3 vols (London: Longman, Green, Reader, and Dyer, 1866).

Smith, James David, *The Eucharistic Doctrine of the Later Nonjurors: A Revisionist View of the Eighteenth-Century Usages Controversy*, Joint Liturgical Studies, 46 (Cambridge: Grove Books, 2000).

Smith, Warren Thomas, 'The Wesleys in Georgia: An Evaluation', *Journal of the Interdenominational Theological Center*, 7 (1979), 1–11.

Snow, M. Lawrence, 'Methodist Enthusiasm: Warburton Letters, 1738–1740', *MH* 10 (1972), 30–47.

Snyder, Howard A., 'Spirit and Form in Wesley's Theology: A Response to Keefer's "John Wesley: Disciple of Early Christianity"', *Wesleyan Theological Journal* 19 (1984), 33–5.

Southey, Robert, *The Life of Wesley and the Rise and Progress of Methodism*, 2 vols (London: Longman, Brown, Green, Longmans, and Roberts, 1858 [1820]).

Spaeth, Donald, *The Church in An Age of Danger: Parson and Parishioners, 1660–1740* (Cambridge: Cambridge University Press, 2000).

Spalding, Phinizy, 'Life in Georgia under the Trustees', in Kenneth Coleman (ed.), *A History of Georgia* (Athens: University of Georgia Press, 1977), 34–44.

——, *Oglethorpe in America* (Chicago: University of Chicago Press, 1977).

Spurgeon, C. H., *The Two Wesleys: A Lecture Delivered in the Metropolitan Tabernacle Lecture Hall, on 6th December 1861* (London: Passmore & Alabaster, 1894).

Spurr, John, *The Restoration Church of England, 1646–1689* (New Haven: Yale University Press, 1991).

——, '"A Special Kindness for Dead Bishops": The Church, History, and Testimony in Seventeenth-Century Protestantism', *Huntington Library Quarterly*, 68 (2005), 313–34.

Stevens, Laura M., *The Poor Indians: British Missionaries, Native Americans, and Colonial Sensibility* (Philadelphia: University of Pennsylvania Press, 2004).

Stevens, William Bacon, *A History of Georgia* (New York: D. Appleton & Co., 1847).

Stevenson J. and W. H. C. Frend (eds), *A New Eusebius: Documents Illustrating the History of the Church to AD 337*, 2nd edn (London: SPCK, 1987).

Stevenson, Kenneth W., ' "The Unbloody Sacrifice": The Origins and Development of a Description of the Eucharist', in Gerard Austin (ed.), *Fountain of Life: In Memory of Niels K. Rasmussen, O.P.* (Washington, D.C.: Pastoral Press, 1991), 103–30.

——, 'Brevint, Daniel (bap. 1616–95)', *Oxford Dictionary of National Biography* (Oxford: Oxford University Press, 2004) [online edn].

Stewart, M. A., 'Halyburton, Thomas (1674–1712)', *Oxford Dictionary of National Biography* (Oxford: Oxford University Press, 2004) [online edn].

Stoeffler, F. Ernest, 'Tradition and Renewal in the Ecclesiology of John Wesley', in Bernd Jaspert and Rudolf Mohr (eds), *Traditio—Krisis—Renovatio aus Theologischer Sicht: Festschrift Winfried Zeller zum 65. Geburtstag* (Marburg: N. G. Elwert, 1976), 298–316.

Strickland, Reba Carolyn, 'Building a Colonial Church', *GHQ* 17 (1933), 276–85.

——, *Religion and the State in Georgia in the Eighteenth Century* (New York: Columbia University Press, 1939).

Sweet, Julie Anne, *Negotiating for Georgia: British-Creek Relations in the Trustee Era 1733–1752* (Athens: University of Georgia Press, 2005).

Sykes, Norman, *Old Priest and New Presbyter: Episcopacy and Presbyterianism since the Reformation with Especial Relation to the Churches of England and Scotland* (Cambridge: Cambridge University Press, 1956).

——, *William Wake: Archbishop of Canterbury 1657–1737*, 2 vols (Cambridge: Cambridge University Press, 1957).

Telford, John, *The Life of John Wesley*, rev. edn (London: Epworth Press, 1924 [1886]).

Temple, Sarah B. Gober and Kenneth Coleman, *Georgia Journeys* (Athens: University of Georgia Press, 1961).

Thompson, H. P., *Into All Lands: The History of the Society for the Propagation of the Gospel in Foreign Parts 1701–1950* (London: SPCK, 1951).

Turner, John Munsey, 'John Wesley's Primitive Christianity', in John Vincent (ed.), *Primitive Christianity*, The Methodist Conference Colloquium (Blackpool, 2007), 21–8.

Tyerman, L[uke], *The Life and Times of the Rev. Samuel Wesley, M.A., Rector of Epworth, and Father of the Revs. John and Charles Wesley, the Founders of the Methodists* (London: Simpkin, Marshall & Co., 1866).

——, *The Life and Times of the Rev. John Wesley, M.A., Founder of the Methodists*, 3 vols (London: Hodder and Stoughton, 1870).

——, *The Oxford Methodists: Memoirs of the Rev. Messrs. Clayton, Ingham, Gambold, Hervey, and Broughton, with Biographical Notices of Others* (London: Hodder and Stoughton, 1873).

Urlin, R. Denny, *The Churchman's Life of Wesley* (London: SPCK, 1880).

Wainwright, Geoffrey, '"Our Elder Brethren Join": The Wesleys' *Hymns on the Lord's Supper* and the Patristic Revival in England', *Proceedings of The Charles Wesley Society*, 1 (1994), 5–31.

Wallace, Charles, 'Eating and Drinking with John Wesley: the Logic of his Practice', in Jeremy Gregory (ed.), *John Wesley: Tercentenary Essays, BJRL* 85.2–3 (2003), 137–55.

Walmsley, Robert, 'John Wesley's Parents: Quarrel and Reconciliation', *PWHS* 29 (1953), 50–7.

Walsh, John, 'John Wesley and the Community of Goods', in Keith Robbins (ed.), *Protestant Evangelicalism: Britain, Ireland, Germany and America c.1750–c.1950. Essays in Honour of W. R. Ward*, Studies in Church History Subsidia, 7 (Oxford: Blackwell, 1990), 25–50.

Ward, W. R., 'Power and Piety: The Origins of Religious Revival in the Early Eighteenth Century', *BJRL* 63 (1980), 231–52.

——, 'The Renewed Unity of the Brethren: Ancient Church, New Sect, or Interconfessional Movement?', *BJRL* 70 (1988), 77–92.

——, *The Protestant Evangelical Awakening* (Cambridge: Cambridge University Press, 1992).

Watson, Richard, *The Life of the Rev. John Wesley, A.M.* (New York: J. Emory and B. Waugh, 1831).

Wedgwood, Julia, *John Wesley and the Evangelical Reaction of the Eighteenth Century* (London: MacMillan and Co., 1870).

Westerfield Tucker, Karen B., 'Form and Freedom: John Wesley's Legacy for Methodist Worship', in Karen B. Westerfield Tucker (ed.), *The Sunday Service of the Methodists: Twentieth-Century Worship in Worldwide Methodism. Studies in Honor of James F. White* (Nashville: Kingswood Books, 1996).

——, 'Wesley's Emphases on Worship and the Means of Grace', in Randy L. Maddox and Jason E. Vickers (eds), *The Cambridge Companion to John Wesley* (Cambridge: Cambridge University Press, 2010), 225–41.

Williams, Glyndwr, 'Savages Noble and Ignoble: Concepts of the North American Indian', in P. J. Marshall and Glyndwr Williams (eds), *The Great Map of Mankind: British Perceptions of the World in the Age of Enlightenment* (London: Dent, 1982), 187–226.

Wood, A. Skevington, *The Burning Heart: John Wesley, Evangelist* (London: Paternoster Press, 1967).

Wood, Joseph Allen, 'Tensions Between Evangelical Theology and the Established Church: John Wesley's Ecclesiology', Ph.D. thesis (University of Manchester [Nazarene Theological College], 2012).

Young, Carlton R., *Music of the Heart: John & Charles Wesley on Music and Musicians: An Anthology* (Carol Stream, IL: Hope Publishing, 1995).

Young, John T., 'Worthington, John (*bap.* 1618, *d.* 1671)', *Oxford Dictionary of National Biography* (Oxford: Oxford University Press, 2004) [online edn].

Zehrer, Karl, 'The Relationship between Pietism in Halle and Early Methodism', trans. James A. Dwyer, *MH* 17 (1979), 211–7.

Zele, Adam Scott, 'John Wesley's America', Ph.D. diss. (Duke University, 2008).

Zeman, J. K., 'Restitution and Dissent in Late Medieval Renewal Movements: The Waldensians, the Hussites and the Bohemian Brethren', *Journal of the American Academy of Religion*, 44 (1976), 7–27.

Index